ARMSTRONG WHITWORTH AIRCRAFT
SINCE 1913

Siskin IIIA fighters carrying the black and white checks of No.43 Squadron, RAF. The squadron flew Siskin IIIAs from 1928 to 1931, and in 1930 gave the first public exhibition in Great Britain of tied-together aerobatics. (*Flight International*)

ARMSTRONG WHITWORTH AIRCRAFT SINCE 1913

OLIVER TAPPER

PUTNAM
LONDON

ISBN 0 370 10004 2
Filmset in Photon Times 11 pt. by
Richard Clay (The Chaucer Press), Ltd.,
Bungay, Suffolk
and printed in Great Britain by
Fletcher & Son, Ltd., Norwich
for
Putnam & Company Limited
9 Bow Street, London WC2E 7AL
First Published 1973

Contents

Foreword

The early history of Armstrong Whitworth conformed to a pattern common among the pioneer aircraft companies: after small beginnings and a sudden period of unprecedented expansion during the 1914–18 war, there came the abrupt cancellation of government contracts in 1919 and the closing of the company's aircraft department. As was the case with other elements of the industry, a new company arose from the remnants of the old, but, unlike most of its contemporaries, the new organization retained the essence of the well-established name but there was no continuity in the managerial or technical staff. In fact, the new company's true beginning stemmed more from the Siddeley Deasy company in Coventry than from it's namesake in the north. It was the Siddeley Deasy team, led by John Siddeley, later to become Lord Kenilworth, which formed the nucleus of the new company destined to assume a prominent position in the British aircraft industry. As will be evident from the narrative that follows, the story of Sir W. G. Armstrong Whitworth Aircraft Ltd, of Coventry, is inseparable from that of the two parent bodies from which it originated, and this is the justification, if one is needed, for including in this work, not only the aircraft built in Newcastle upon Tyne, but also the few, mainly experimental, aircraft built under the Siddeley Deasy name.

The archives of Armstrong Whitworth have suffered greater depredations than most; the closure of the Newcastle upon Tyne factory and the dispersal of its records, was followed, in due course, by the bombing of the Parkside factory in the Coventry 'blitzes' of 1940 and 1941 in which the company's records and photographs were decimated. Finally came the amalgamations of 1960 which led to the successive closing of virtually all the Armstrong Whitworth factories and the destruction of practically all the company's remaining records. It is easy to understand that those concerned with the closing of factories and offices may well have faced more pressing problems than providing for the preservation of historic material, but their failure to do so has resulted in much valuable information being lost for ever.

Doubts which still exist about certain historical facts, for example the continuing uncertainty about some early Armstrong Whitworth type numbers, are discussed in the appropriate chapters of the book, but here a word of warning must be given about the aircraft performance figures quoted:

these have been culled from a variety of sources which, broadly speaking, offer an almost equal number of alternative values. When comparing official records it has been found that the data on performance often vary significantly from one document to another, while the maker's figures, where they exist, invariably offer a quite different set of alternatives. The performance information given in this book represents what is thought to be the most realistic distillation of these confusing alternatives, but the figures are, nevertheless, open to argument and should therefore be treated with some reserve.

The author is particularly grateful to the many people who, directly or indirectly, have given valuable assistance in overcoming the problems of research. First and foremost, he would like to acknowledge the unstinted help given by John 'Jimmy' Lloyd, the chief designer of all the Coventry-built aircraft up to, and including, the Apollo; without his wholehearted co-operation much hitherto unpublished information would never have been recorded. Hardly less indispensable has been the help, in the form of reminiscences and log-book entries, provided by many of the company's test pilots, and especial thanks for their assistance go to Frank Courtney, Alan Campbell-Orde, Charles Turner-Hughes, Norman Macmillan and John Grierson. Invaluable, too, has been the work already done in the past by such eminent aviation historians as Jack Bruce, A. J. Jackson, Bruce Robertson, John Stroud, H. A. 'Tony' Taylor, Owen Thetford and others. Members of the Hawker Siddeley Group, many with an Armstrong Whitworth background, have made their contribution, including R. A. Courtman, James Corfield, Cyril Luckham, John Gray and Michael Farlam, while special mention must be made of Albert Whitehouse who has succeeded in preserving some valuable company records.

Needless to say, full use has been made of the unrivalled photographic collections of *Flight International* and the Imperial War Museum, and the author's thanks go to Ann Tilbury of the former and Ted Hine of the latter; photographic and other assistance was also received from the librarian of the Royal Aeronautical Society, Arnold Naylor, and his assistant Philip Jarrett, from Ernest Stott, of the Royal Aircraft Establishment, the Historical Branch of the Ministry of Defence (Air), from Philip Moyes, the editor of *Aircraft Illustrated*, and from Gordon Swanborough, the editor of *Air Enthusiast*. For the immaculate three-view drawings the credit goes to L. E. Bradford. Among others who have helped in various ways are Gordon Adams and James Allison, both of Newcastle upon Tyne; Keith Bishop, the Newcastle upon Tyne city archivist; Sir Alan Cobham; Michael Goodall; Captain Michael Hooper, general manager of BEA's cargo operations; Eric Morgan; J. Randle; Major K. G. Roberts of the Canadian Department of Defence; H. E. Scrope of Vickers Ltd; Selwyn Sharp of Rolls-Royce Ltd; Alastair Smith, curator of the Newcastle upon Tyne Museum of Science and Engineering; Alan Stratford; and Mrs R. Taylor, the keeper of the BOAC archives.

Armstrong Whitworth from the Beginning

The names of Armstrong and Whitworth have been, separately and together, synonymous with engineering since the early nineteenth century, but of the men themselves, each famous in his time, little is now remembered. Certainly they were never concerned with aviation and, indeed, they were both dead by the time the Wright brothers first flew in 1903. But Lord Armstrong and Sir Joseph Whitworth were both men of vision in the forefront of progress and, had they lived in a later age, they would doubtless have applied their inventive genius, with which they were well endowed, to the new science.

Both men achieved fame and owned well-established heavy-engineering businesses. In 1897, the companies, finding themselves in direct competition, wisely decided to amalgamate and they joined forces to found Sir W. G. Armstrong, Whitworth & Co Ltd of Newcastle upon Tyne.

William George Armstrong, born in 1810, first practised as a solicitor, an unlikely enough beginning for a man who was later to become a leading engineer. But clearly his heart was not in the law and all his spare time was spent in studying physics and in inventing mechanical devices. In 1845 he perfected a liquid power-transmission system, and his water-driven crane, installed on a Tyneside quay, was the forerunner of all subsequent hydraulic transmission devices. A year later the invention of a so-called 'steam-jet electric engine' won for him a fellowship of the Royal Society, and in 1847 he opened a small workshop at Elswick, in Newcastle, the first step towards the great factory and shipyard which later grew on the site.

But Armstrong was, perhaps, best known for his contribution to the craft of gun making. He invented the breech-loading mechanism and the rifled barrel firing a cylindrical shell instead of a ball; he also developed a method of shrinking strengthening coils of wrought iron around steel tubes to make extremely strong gun barrels. It was for his work in developing the gun that Armstrong was knighted in 1859. The engineering business that Armstrong established in Newcastle flourished and developed rapidly; in addition to the main works at Elswick there were two shipyards, one adjoining the Elswick works for building battleships, and another, for building merchant ships, at Walker-on-Tyne. In 1887 Armstrong was created a baron, and he died in 1900, much loved and respected, at the age of 90.

William George Armstrong (*left*): 1810–1900; born in Newcastle upon Tyne; knighted 1859; created Baron Armstrong 1887. Joseph Whitworth (*right*): 1803–1887; born in Stockport; elected to the Royal Society 1857; knighted 1869. (*Courtesy J. Allison*)

Joseph Whitworth, born in 1803, was in engineering from the start; after working with various machine-tool manufacturers, he set up in business on his own as a tool maker in Manchester in 1833. At an early stage he became almost fanatically dedicated to mechanical accuracy and meticulous workmanship, qualities seldom to be found at the time, and it was not long before his Manchester factory was turning out machine tools to far higher standards and of much better quality than any of his competitors. His products earned high commendation—and a good deal of useful publicity—at the Great Exhibition held in Hyde Park in 1851.

Whitworth had first come into prominence in 1841 as a result of a paper dealing with the value of standard threads and gauges, which he read before the Institution of Civil Engineers. Up to then the characteristics of screw threads had varied with almost every individual workshop, but the advantages of uniformity, as advocated by Whitworth, could not be resisted, and by 1860 his standard threads were in use throughout the country. Like Armstrong, Whitworth was a prolific inventor, devising, among other things, a knitting machine and a mechanical street sweeper. He, too, introduced a new method of gun making based on an improved method of tempering steel: he thus found himself competing in the same field as Armstrong in Newcastle. Sir Joseph Whitworth died in January 1887, but the rivalry between the two firms continued and it was this overlapping of interests which eventually led to the first of a series of amalgamations which were to feature so largely in the history of Armstrong Whitworth. In this first take-over it was the Whitworth works at Openshaw in Manchester which were purchased by Armstrong and, as already mentioned, a new joint company was formed in 1897.

The new company, with its emphasis on heavy engineering, guns and ships, was fortunate in having been formed at just the right moment and, as time went on, it became virtually a government-supported arsenal. Its activities reached a crescendo during the 1914–18 war; in addition to the aeroplanes and airships with which this book is concerned, Armstrong Whitworth had, up to 1919, built forty-seven warships, including HMS *Courageous* and HMS *Furious*, and twenty-two merchant ships. In addition, the company had produced 13,000 guns, 14½ million shells, 18 million fuses, 21 million cartridge cases, and had added armament to 583 vessels.

The company's first tentative essay into the aeroplane business took place towards the end of 1910 when it undertook the rebuilding of a Farman biplane and the repair of its Gnome engine after the aircraft had crashed on hitting a flagpole during a demonstration flight at Boldon racecourse near Newcastle. The racecourse was used as a flying ground by the Northumberland Aero Club, which had several Armstrong Whitworth people among its members, and the Farman was being flown at the time by a woman pilot who went by the name of 'Madame Franke', although she was, in fact, the wife of a British journalist named Hewetson. After the repair was completed early in 1911, the aircraft was sold to the Avro Flying School at Brooklands.

Early in 1912 a report on the possibilities of aeroplane manufacture was considered by the company's executive committee, but the proposal was turned down, as was another suggestion put forward in a letter received from H. Verdon Roe, A. V. Roe's brother and the business manager of the Avro company, inviting Armstrong Whitworth to undertake the manufacture of Avro aeroplanes; after due consideration the board decided that '. . . it is undesirable to accede to this proposition'. Had they but known it, they were merely deferring an arrangement that was to be implemented some forty years later. In October 1912 Sir George White, of the British and Colonial Aeroplane Co, asked whether Armstrong Whitworth's Italian company, based in Pozzuoli, would undertake the manufacture of thirty-five Bristol aeroplanes as ordered by the Italian Government. Although the Newcastle company was willing in principle, agreement could not be reached and the project fell through.

The year 1912 also saw Armstrong Whitworth's first venture into the aero-engine business when they began making A.B.C. engines to the design of Granville Bradshaw. The A.B.C. engine, a product of the All British Engine Co Ltd, first came into prominence in October 1912, when the 40 hp version was used by Harry Hawker in his Sopwith-Wright biplane to set up a British endurance record of 8 hr 23 min at Brooklands. Larger versions of the A.B.C. engine were to have been fitted to the Avro and the Flanders biplanes built for the Military Aeroplane Trials held in August 1912, and it is probable that these engines were being made by Armstrong Whitworth but, in the event, neither was ready for the competition.

In December 1912 Armstrong Whitworth signed an agreement with the A.B.C. company and undertook to build an engine to A.B.C. design for the Government engine competition due to be held early in 1914. The entry for the competition was made in the name of Armstrong Whitworth, but the two engines built for the trials had to be withdrawn in April 1914 because they had failed during preliminary tests. Concurrently, towards the end of 1912, a batch of 100 hp A.B.C. engines was put in hand at Elswick, and the first of these was installed in an Avro biplane purchased specially for the purpose by Armstrong Whitworth at a cost of £500.

This engine, which was tested at Brooklands in January or February 1914, also failed to come up to expectations, and the company decided that, unless Bradshaw was prepared to reside at Elswick during the design of future engines, they would end the agreement and change over to designs of their own. In June 1914 it was reported to the executive committee of Armstrong Whitworth that the reply from the A.B.C. company was not satisfactory and that in future Armstrong Whitworth would build engines without the assistance of Mr Bradshaw.

The break with Bradshaw brought to an end the early experiments with aero-engines, and it was not until later, in 1916 or 1917, that a new venture was started in collaboration with Harry Ricardo, who had prepared designs for a supercharged engine to develop about 300 hp. Several examples of this engine were made and tested at Elswick during the years 1917 to 1919, but by then the commercial prospects seemed slim and Armstrong Whitworth decided to go no further with the project. The licence and the engine assets were accordingly handed back to Ricardo, who subsequently set up his own company.

Writing in *The Aeroplane* in August 1913, C. G. Grey, the editor, stated that Armstrong Whitworth had been financing an experimental aeroplane for at least three years. If there is any substance in this report it may refer to experiments with tailless, automatically-stable aircraft started in 1907 by J. W. Dunne, and conducted in great secrecy at Blair Atholl in Scotland. In any case it is true that in 1913 negotiations were started with Dunne's company, the Blair Atholl Syndicate, which resulted in Armstrong Whitworth acquiring an interest in that concern in March 1914. In the following May the board of directors gave sanction for a Dunne biplane to be built at a cost not exceeding £500, and in July some semi-completed components, engines and other materials from Blair Atholl were delivered to Gosforth, but the outbreak of war put a stop to the project as the Dunne aeroplane was thought to have no military potential.

Another activity which engaged the company's attention during 1913 was concerned with the design and manufacture of hollow-steel-blade propellers of the type developed by Henry Leitner. The blades made in the Elswick factory were fabricated from thin high-tensile steel sheet and were welded along their edges. The finished blades were mounted in a steel hub and secured by locking rings and collars. This type of propeller was developed further after the war and marketed by The Metal Airscrew Co Ltd.

In March 1913, the Admiralty invited Armstrong Whitworth to tender for one large rigid airship, and one large and three small non-rigid airships. In the same period the War Office asked the company to undertake the construction of aeroplanes and engines to official design. As a result a new 'aerial department' was formed in June 1913 with a temporary manager. In the following month the board of directors came to the decisions:

1. That the manufacture of aeroplanes should be undertaken in the Newcastle factory.
2. That a factory for the manufacture of airships should be established at Selby in Yorkshire.
3. That Captain Fairbairn-Crawford, then assistant manager in the Elswick machine inspection department, should be appointed as superintendent of both the aeroplane and airship works, and that an assistant to manage the airship works should be engaged at a salary not exceeding £600 per annum.
4. That Mr Frederick Koolhoven be appointed as assistant to Captain Fairbairn-Crawford.

Captain I. F. Fairbairn-Crawford, who had served in the Royal Engineers, was an athlete of international repute and his first practical connection with aviation was the part he played in the formation of the Northumberland Aero Club; later he acted as an official at the Doncaster and Bournemouth meetings of 1910. Before opening the Armstrong Whitworth aircraft department he made a tour of the French aircraft industry in the Paris area to study factory layout and production methods. During the war, in 1915, he learned to fly and took his aviator's licence at Hendon. Fairbairn-Crawford continued to act as general manager of the company's aircraft department until it was closed in September 1919, after

Captain I. F. Fairbairn-Crawford (*left*), general manager of the 'aerial department' of Armstrong Whitworth in Newcastle upon Tyne, from July 1913 until the department was closed in 1919. (*Flight International*). Frederick Koolhoven (*right*), appointed as assistant to Fairbairn-Crawford in 1913, was responsible for the Armstrong Whitworth designs until he left the company in 1917. (*Royal Aeronautical Society*)

which he was put in charge of the company's car manufacture in the Gosforth factory until that venture, too, was abandoned in 1920.

Before going to Newcastle, Koolhoven had been chief engineer and works manager of the British Deperdussin Syndicate Ltd at their north London works at Highgate, where he had been concerned with monoplanes of French design built by that firm. Koolhoven was a highly imaginative and very able designer; he was capable of creating both strictly conventional and successful aircraft such as the F.K.3 and the F.K.8, as well as the distinctly unorthodox, and not so successful, triplanes and quadruplanes of 1916. In later years, after he had left Armstrong Whitworth, he was responsible for the series of B.A.T. aeroplanes, notably the F.K.23 Bantam and the F.K.26 passenger aircraft of 1919. Later still, back in his native Holland, he was the creator of a number of designs, most of which were highly individualistic in concept.

Following the decision in July 1913, the company started negotiations for the purchase of land for the airship factory. The site selected, which covered about 1,000 acres, was close to the village of Barlow, some three miles southeast of Selby on the estate of Lord Londesborough. For the manufacture of aeroplanes, it had been suggested originally that the company's sawmills at Elswick could be used but these premises proved to be unsuitable and temporary arrangements were made to use another of the company's buildings at Scotswood, and it was here that two B.E.2as, the first of a batch of eight ordered in 1913 by the War Office, were built. These two aircraft were erected and tested at Farnborough in April 1914 with the happy result that the company was complimented on the quality of

Armstrong Whitworth built B.E.2as in the converted skating rink at Gosforth. Just discernible, in the left-hand corner of the picture, behind the Armstrong Whitworth car, is the airship gondola built in 1914 to the order of the Admiralty for HMA No.2. (*Vickers Ltd*)

B.E.2c aircraft on the assembly line at Gosforth during the early months of 1915. On the left is the fuselage of the F.K.1 single-seat biplane. (*Vickers Ltd*)

its workmanship. In the meantime, an order had been received for twenty-five B.E.2bs and, in September 1913, the board of directors gave authority for the hire of a disused skating rink at Gosforth for use as an aeroplane factory at a rental of £300 a year. It was here that the remaining B.E.2as were completed and the B.E.2bs put into production. Following the outbreak of war, and the placing of large orders with the company for B.E.2c aircraft, the Gosforth factory, and the labour force, were rapidly expanded and the output rose quickly, eventually reaching six aircraft a week. Figures quoted in an Armstrong Whitworth brochure issued after the war claim that eight aeroplanes were built in 1914, 63 in 1915, 124 in 1916, 423 in 1917 and 429 in 1918. In addition, according to the brochure, there were fifteen 'experimental aircraft' which, it is believed, included the triplanes and quadruplanes of 1916 and various trial engine installations in the F.K.8.

The Gosforth factory was situated at the western end of Duke's Moor, part of Newcastle's Town Moor, and it was from here that the early Armstrong Whitworth aeroplanes were tested. For a few months after the beginning of the war, Duke's Moor was also used by a unit of the Royal Naval Air Service, but this moved elsewhere in 1915. In June 1916 Duke's Moor was condemned as unsafe by the authorities: this was not surprising for the field was only some 600 yards long by about 150 yards wide, and was surrounded by trees. A new aerodrome was accordingly set up in the northeast corner of the main Town Moor, with the company bearing half the cost amounting to £600. This aerodrome later became a Government acceptance park; but it was far from ideal, the surface was rough and when the time came to test the F.M.4 Armadillo fighter in 1918, the Royal Air Force aerodrome at Cramlington was used.

The first Armstrong Whitworth aeroplane to be designed by Koolhoven was a small single-seater. This aeroplane was known, probably correctly, as the F.K.1; the qualification arises because there is considerable uncertainty about the true sequence of the F.K. numbers. Koolhoven himself seems to have applied, in retrospect, F.K. numbers to all the designs with which he had been in any way concerned, and in one Dutch publication the F.K.1 appears as the F.K.14. The uncertainty about the F.K. numbers is made worse by the secrecy concerning its experimental types which Armstrong Whitworth maintained even after the war.

The completed F.K.1, also known as the Sissit, was originally designed as a monoplane. It was first flown by Koolhoven himself, probably in 1914. (*Courtesy J. M. Bruce*)

The F.K.1, originally planned as a monoplane, was altered in the design stage to a biplane. It was a simple, straightforward, single-seat aircraft with single-bay wings, no stagger and a large gap. The fuselage terminated in a horizontal knife-edge, and there were divided elevators but no fixed tailplane. When first flown, by Koolhoven himself, the F.K.1 proved to be seriously underpowered, having been fitted with a Gnome engine of 50 hp in place of the intended 80 hp version. Later, the aircraft was given larger ailerons and a fixed tailplane and in this form was flown by B. C. Hucks and some naval pilots; but there was clearly no future for the type and its development was abandoned.

In his position as chief engineer and works manager, Koolhoven had control of B.E.2c production, and it was not long before his active brain devised means by which the design could be improved, mainly from the viewpoint of simplifying production. His new design received government

F.K.8 biplanes under construction in the Newcastle factory of Angus Sanderson and Co. The site is now occupied by Durham University. (*Courtesy G. A. Adams*)

approval and, as a result, the F.K.3 was put in hand in August 1915. As Koolhoven had predicted, this aeroplane was a distinct improvement on the B.E.2c and was ordered in comparatively large numbers, but it was not allowed to compete seriously with the Government's own design. Much the same attitude was adopted by the authorities towards the next Armstrong Whitworth product, the F.K.8, which shared with the officially-designed R.E.8 unspectacular artillery-observation duties; although much more suitable for the task, the F.K.8 was never built in such numbers as the R.E.8, which it was not allowed to supplant. None of the other aeroplanes designed by Koolhoven, or those of his successor, F. M. Murphy, in Newcastle, went into large-scale production, and it is the stolid, trustworthy F.K.8 biplane that will always be remembered as the outstanding Armstrong Whitworth aeroplane of the 1914–18 war.

Armstrong Whitworth's airship department at Barlow opened in 1915. The factory, looked after by H. H. Golightly, under the general managership of Fairbairn-Crawford, was initially engaged in the design and production of cars for the S.S. and Coastal-type non-rigid airships which were so notably successful in protecting Allied shipping from submarine attack in coastal waters around the British Isles. Later there followed three rigid airships built for the Royal Navy and the RAF, the R 25, the R 29 and the R 33. Neither of the first two was particularly outstanding, but the R 33, and her sister ship the R 34 built by Beardmore, were perhaps the most successful rigid airships ever built in Great Britain, having been copied down to the smallest detail from a captured German Zeppelin.

The Armstrong Whitworth airship works at Barlow in 1917. On the left, nearing completion, is the R 25, with the first frames of the R 29 alongside. (*Imperial War Museum Q55548*)

In 1917 Frederick Koolhoven left Armstrong Whitworth to become chief designer for the British Aerial Transport Co (B.A.T.), and, as already mentioned, F. M. Murphy took his place as chief designer and works manager at the Gosforth factory under Fairbairn-Crawford. With the departure of Koolhoven, Armstrong Whitworth abandoned, for the time being, all efforts to produce new aircraft of their own design. For the next few months the company was content to concentrate on production of the F.K.8, which continued until the summer of 1918 when it was replaced on the production line by the Bristol Fighter, of which 250, with Sunbeam Arab engines, had been ordered earlier in the year. Production of this aeroplane was continued after the Armistice and kept the aircraft department in being until this contract, too, was cancelled in September 1919.

One of the last jobs undertaken by the aircraft department during 1919 was the fabrication of components, mostly metal joints and high-tensile steel struts, for the controversial Brennan helicopter which was built at Farnborough with government money but was abandoned in 1925 after it was damaged during a test hop.

Not much is known about Murphy, who eventually became the company's designer, except that he came from Bristol and had been with Armstrong Whitworth for a period before Koolhoven left. Towards the end of 1917 the company decided to take up original design work once again, and two new types, the Armadillo and the Ara, both single-seat fighters, were built to Murphy's design. The first of these bore the type number F.M.4, and was built mainly as an exercise to evaluate the capabilities of Murphy's design team. The Ara which followed was, perhaps, a more serious contender for a contract but, like a number of its contemporaries, was rendered ineffective by the failure of the A.B.C. Dragonfly engine.

The Ara was the last Armstrong Whitworth aircraft to be produced in Newcastle, and it marked the end of a considerable war effort which had produced three rigid airships and some 1,275 aeroplanes. But there were hard times ahead and, although the aircraft department remained occupied until September 1919, the coming of peace caused a shortage of work in the shipbuilding and armament departments. In reply to an enquiry by the editor of *The Aeroplane* in October 1919, Armstrong Whitworth stated:

'It is our intention to close down both our aeroplane and airship departments owing to the curtailment of the Government aircraft programme. The stoppage of aircraft contracts and the lack of policy as regards civil aviation has necessitated the discharge of our experienced staff and personnel. Enquiries both in England and abroad as to aircraft business to be obtained or contemplated show that it is so small as not to justify our going on with aircraft manufacture for some years to come.'

In spite of efforts to secure new business, the fortunes of the company continued to decline and, in 1928, Armstrong Whitworth's armament, shipbuilding and steel interests were taken over by the Vickers company under the title Vickers-Armstrongs Ltd, and, in 1937 the remaining assets of Armstrong Whitworth were sold and the company went into liquidation.

Two F.K.10 quadruplanes and an F.K.8 biplane, with a Lorraine-Dietrich engine, at Duke's Meadow aerodrome at Gosforth. (*Courtesy J. Allison*)

It now becomes necessary to go back in time and consider the other main branch of the family tree, a parallel development which brought forward a personality whose influence on the future of Armstrong Whitworth was to be crucial. In 1906, in the City of Coventry, a certain Captain H. P. Deasy formed a company known as The Deasy Motor Car Manufacturing Co with works at Parkside, about half-a-mile south of the City centre. The Deasy cars, although of advanced design, were not altogether successful, and acute differences of opinion on technical matters within the company led, in 1908, to the resignation of Captain Deasy from the board of directors: thus the man, but not the name, disappeared from the scene.

Following the reorganization that took place after Deasy's resignation, the fortunes of the company seem to have improved somewhat, but the next significant event, and, indeed, a turning point in the firm's history, came in 1909 with the appointment of John D. Siddeley as general manager. Within a matter of months he had transformed the company and in June the same year he was made managing director. So great was his influence on the company's progress and fortunes that three years later the name of the company was changed to The Siddeley Deasy Motor Car Co Ltd.

John Siddeley (third from left) seen with those who helped him make his lightweight racing bicycle on which he rode from Land's End to John o' Groats in 1892. (*Courtesy the Hon Ernest Siddeley*)

John Davenport Siddeley, later Sir John and later still Lord Kenilworth, was born in 1866. In his early days he won distinction as a racing cyclist and, at the age of 26, became the first man to cycle from Land's End to John o' Groats. His first engineering job was in the drawing office of the Humber Cycle Co, but by the end of the century his interest had become centred in the motorcar, and in 1900 he took part in the 1,000 Miles Motor Trial, driving his own 6-hp Daimler car. In the following years he developed a four-cylinder car of his own design, and in 1902 he formed the Siddeley Autocar Co to market it. The reputation which he gained from this successful enterprise led, in 1908, to his being invited to join the Wolseley Tool and Motor Car Co where he ultimately became the managing director and responsible for the range of Wolseley-Siddeley cars. It was during this period that Siddeley first became involved in the production of an aero-engine, an eight-cylinder vee water-cooled affair developing some

50 hp. This engine met with considerable success and was the forerunner of the Wolseley Viper engine of the First World War.

But Siddeley did not remain long with the Wolseley company. The general manager at that time was Herbert Austin, later to become Baron Austin of Longbridge, and it was perhaps inevitable that between two such headstrong personalities there should be differences of opinion. Matters came to a head early in 1909 and Siddeley resigned from Wolseleys and, as already recorded, moved over to the Deasy company. From then on, until he finally retired in 1936, 'JDS', as he was always known in the Coventry works, dominated the activities of the Siddeley Deasy company and its successor, the Armstrong Siddeley organization.

Throughout his career, Siddeley's main interest seems to have been centred on the motorcar, with aero-engines taking second place; his interest in aeroplanes clearly came third, and it has been said that he looked upon them only as a convenient outlet for his aero-engines. He was undoubtedly a great leader but also a staunch individualist with a strong personality which many found disconcertingly overpowering. His engineering knowledge was limited and was gathered mainly from his practical experience, admittedly extensive, with motorcars. With his high degree of intelligence he could, with proper training from the start, have well become a brilliant engineer; as it was, many of his mechanical hunches had, in the early days, real merit, but as time went on he was not able to follow, or even appreciate the necessity for, the more scientific approach, and particularly the need for research and development which later became so essential. As a consequence, he would often override the opinions of the more erudite members of his staff and fail to give adequate support to development programmes. This was to lead, particularly on the engine side, to the departure of good men and eventually to the loss of the company's leading position in the manufacture of high-power air-cooled piston engines. But for all his idiosyncrasies, Siddeley was a great man who left his mark on the engineering and industrial world. For his services he was created a CBE in 1918 and was knighted in 1932. In 1937, in King George VI's Coronation Honours, he was raised to the Peerage and chose the title Baron Kenilworth of Kenilworth. He died in 1953.

Under Siddeley's guidance the fortunes of the Siddeley Deasy Motor Car Co improved steadily and the name became synonymous with high-quality cars, but there were still some years to go before the company became involved in the aviation business—and then it was more by force of circumstances than by choice. On the outbreak of war in 1914 it was at first the intention to close down the Parkside works so that all able-bodied men should be free to fight; at that time the cavalry was still considered to be the spearhead of the army and the potentialities of mechanical transport, let alone tanks and attack vehicles, had not become apparent to the army chiefs.

The illusion that the Parkside factory was redundant in war time did not last for long: within a fortnight men were being recalled to fulfil an urgent order from Russia for one hundred lorries, and as might be expected this was followed by an increasing flood of Government orders for cars and other vehicles. In January 1915, the board of directors authorized John Siddeley, then the managing director, to place contracts for the extension of the works and to negotiate contracts with the War Office for the building of aeroplanes.

The first aviation contract received by Siddeley Deasy was, however, for engines, in the shape of the Royal Aircraft Factory's RAF 1A, an eight-cylinder vee air-cooled unit developing 90 hp. Later, production at Parkside was switched to the larger RAF 4A, a twelve-cylinder air-cooled vee engine of 150 hp which was used in the R.E.7, the R.E.8 and the B.E.12 aircraft. This latter order was for 300 engines, and a delivery rate of ten engines a week was called for.

John Davenport Siddeley (*left*): 1866–1953; created CBE 1918; knighted 1932; raised to Peerage, as Lord Kenilworth of Kenilworth, in 1937. (*Courtesy Audrey Siddeley*). John Lloyd (*right*) joined Siddeley in 1917 and became chief designer with Armstrong Whitworth until 1948. He retired as technical director in 1959.

In 1916 Siddeley was asked to undertake production of the new BHP engine, a design evolved by Major Frank Halford in collaboration with Beardmores and T. C. Pulinger. The first engines of the type, built by the Galloway Engine Co in Scotland, proved unsatisfactory and a major re-design was undertaken by Siddeley Deasy, involving new cylinder heads and water jackets of aluminium. The engine then emerged as the Puma, the first aero-engine to bear the Siddeley name. Numerous production problems still continued to beset the Puma and it never did succeed in producing the 300 hp for which the BHP had originally been designed; but eventually it became a very reliable unit and, by the end of the war, Siddeley Deasy were producing about 600 Pumas a month, and in all some 6,000 were completed.

For the large-scale production of the Puma, Siddeley employed a number of sub-contractors, the most significant being the Armstrong Whitworth company in Newcastle: it was this contract which formed the first link between the two companies. For the Puma, Armstrong

Ten days' output of Siddeley Puma engines in the Parkside factory of Siddeley Deasy in 1918.

Whitworth supplied cylinder heads, first as raw castings and later as machine-finished parts, and, possibly, also connecting rods. John Siddeley was much impressed by the fine quality of workmanship produced by Armstrong Whitworth, and this led to a continuation of the sub-contract arrangement after the war.

It was during 1917 that the first aeroplanes were built in the Parkside factory, the initial order being for 100 R.E.7s. The first two aircraft to be completed were erected and tested at Farnborough, but, subsequently, production machines were flown from the Radford aerodrome situated in what were then the northern outskirts of Coventry where the Daimler factory was later built. The next type to be put into production at Parkside was the R.E.8, of which a total of 1,024 was eventually completed, with production rate reaching about twenty aircraft a week. A contract for fifty D.H.10s followed, but it is doubtful whether any had been completed when the Armistice led to the order being cancelled.

In the meantime, in 1916, significant events were taking place. As a result of an outcry in Parliament against alleged inefficiency at the Royal Aircraft Factory, a committee of enquiry was set up under the chairmanship of Sir Richard Burbidge. The committee's report, issued in 1917, recommended that the design and construction of aircraft and engines should no longer be undertaken by the Factory. The recommendation was accepted by the Government with the consequence that many highly experienced engineers and scientists departed from Farnborough.

Whatever may be thought about the apparent wisdom of such a drastic move in the midst of a devastating war, it must be admitted that the results were, on the whole, beneficial: certainly they were for the Siddeley Deasy company, which recruited three notable personalities from the Royal Aircraft Factory staff. They were Major Frederick M. Green, who became the company's chief engineer, John Lloyd, who headed the aeroplane design team, and S. D. Heron, an engine designer.

R.E.8 fuselages in the Siddeley Deasy factory. In the alleyway on the right is the partially-completed fuselage of a D.H.10A.

Major Green had been engineer in charge of design at Farnborough from 1910 until his departure in 1917, and as such, carried overall responsibility for the Factory aircraft, notably the S.E.5. At Coventry he wielded a strong influence, particularly on engine matters, in the affairs of Siddeley Deasy and Armstrong Siddeley until he retired in 1933 to become a consulting engineer. John Lloyd, always known as 'Jimmy' Lloyd, was head of the stress department at Farnborough. He soon demonstrated his talents as a designer, and it was he who was responsible for all the Siddeley Deasy and Armstrong Whitworth aircraft designs up to and including the Apollo. In 1948 he relinquished the post of chief designer and was appointed technical director, a position he held until his retirement in 1959. S. D. Heron, another brilliant engineer who had done valuable work on piston-engine valve design at Farnborough, did not stay long in Coventry: he had serious differences of opinion with John Siddeley over the design of the Jaguar valve gear, and eventually left to work in the United States where, incidentally, he contributed significantly to the design of the Wright Whirlwind, the engine that carried Lindbergh across the Atlantic to Paris in 1927.

While still at Farnborough, Green and Heron had been working on the design of the projected RAF 8 engine, a two-row fourteen-cylinder air-cooled radial. When work on this design was stopped in 1917, Green was asked to take the project with him to Siddeley Deasy, but with the proviso that first priority must be given to bringing the BHP-Puma engine to a satisfactory state of development. For a time therefore, work on the radial engine was more or less in abeyance, and by the time it was re-started in earnest, Heron had left and the design work was then undertaken mainly by F. R. Smith, a colourful and popular personality, who was largely responsible for producing the Puma, and S. M. Viale, who had moved down from Armstrong Whitworth in Newcastle during 1919. By the middle of 1920, after some initial trouble and considerable redesign work, the radial engine was running well and developing about 300 hp: thus was created the famous Jaguar, the engine that for the next few years was without a rival among high-powered air-cooled powerplants.

In 1917, while Major Green and F. R. Smith were engaged in getting the Puma into large-scale production, John Lloyd was busy setting up a Siddeley Deasy aeroplane design office. His first product for the company was the Siddeley R.T.1, a modification of the R.E.8, with which Lloyd had been concerned at Farnborough and which was then in production in the Siddeley Deasy shops. The next, and most important, Siddeley Deasy aircraft was the S.R.2, named the Siskin; it was this aeroplane, one of the best of the contemporary fighter designs, which overlapped the link-up between Siddeley Deasy in Coventry and Armstrong Whitworth in Newcastle. Finally there was the Sinaia, an ambitious design for a bomber, which also overlapped the take-over period, having been designed and started under the Siddeley Deasy name and finished off, after the war, under that of Armstrong Whitworth.

With the end of the fighting in November 1918 both Siddeley Deasy and Armstrong Whitworth were faced, like many other concerns, with the formidable task of re-adjusting to peace-time conditions. As early as 1917 a Government committee, set up to advise industrial undertakings on possible post-war activities, had suggested to Armstrong Whitworth in Newcastle that they might consider embarking on the manufacture of motorcars, an activity in which they had been engaged in a small way before the war.

Some time later, probably during the autumn of 1918, Armstrong Whitworth had been approached by John Siddeley about the possibility of

The first Siskin, the S.R.2, designed by Lloyd and built in 1918 by the Siddeley Deasy company. The engine was a 320 hp A.B.C. Dragonfly.

a link-up between the two firms. As already mentioned, Siddeley had been much impressed by the engineering skills of the Newcastle firm, which had supplied castings and finished parts for his Puma production, and he wished to ensure continuity of this source of supply; he was also attracted by the prospect of being able to make use of Armstrong Whitworth's existing world-wide sales organization.

In December 1918 Armstrong Whitworth decided that negotiations should be started with the Siddeley Deasy concern, and by February 1919 the board of directors in Newcastle agreed that all the ordinary and preference shares of Siddeley Deasy should be acquired for the sum of £400,000, an amount '... which could be stretched to £419,750 or, if necessary, £450,000'. The proposal was to establish a subsidiary company with a nominal capital of £1 million preference shares and £1 million ordinary shares. These negotiations led to a satisfactory agreement and the deal was concluded at a figure of £419,750 to be paid in 6 per cent non-cumulative preference shares in the subsidiary company. This was registered in May 1919 as the Armstrong Whitworth Development Co Ltd, with Sir Glyn West, Mr Alfred Cochrane and Mr Brackenburg as directors. Strangely, John Siddeley was not nominated and he was not elected to the board until July 1926.

The Development Company started off with its own subsidiary entitled Armstrong Siddeley Motors Ltd, which was, in fact, the old Siddeley Deasy company: in April 1920 Armstrong Siddeley Motors submitted to the Newcastle board a proposal that the company should '... continue aircraft work on a limited scale by forming a subsidiary company ...' The board agreed, and shortly afterwards, on a date not specifically noted, there came into existence The Sir W. G. Armstrong Whitworth Aircraft Co Ltd.

At first, both engine and aircraft work were centred in the Parkside factory, but in 1920 the company purchased, for £5,000, the aerodrome at Whitley which had recently been vacated by the RAF. As far back as February 1918 the Siddeley Deasy board had decided in principle to negotiate for the purchase of the Whitley estate so that, in the words of the minutes, '... an aerodrome could be completed there for the testing of aeroplanes ... in view of the fact that it is the company's intention to continue in the aeronautical business after the war'.

The aerodrome had, in fact, been completed during 1917 and 1918, the buildings having been erected by German prisoners of war, and it had been used by the RAF as a stores depot. It was not a particularly good aerodrome, and Lloyd recalls advising against its purchase because he thought that, even for those days, it was too small and of a very awkward shape.

One of Siddeley's first actions on acquiring Whitley in 1920 was to form a flying school with Major Griffiths as chief instructor. Later, in 1923, the company received a contract from the Government to train pilots of the RAF Reserve; this was one of five such schools that were established throughout the country at that time, each one owned and operated by an aircraft manufacturer.

COVENTRY (WHITLEY ABBEY)

Classification :

COVENTRY
AERODROME
Willenhall
Baginton
Scale of ½ Inch to 1 Mile = 1:126.720
1 ½ 0 1 2 3 *Miles*
1 ½ 0 1 2 3 4 *Kilometres*

Telegrams :
" Armcraft
Coventry."

Telephone :
Coventry 2333.

Lat. 52° 23′ N. **Long.** 1° 29′ W.

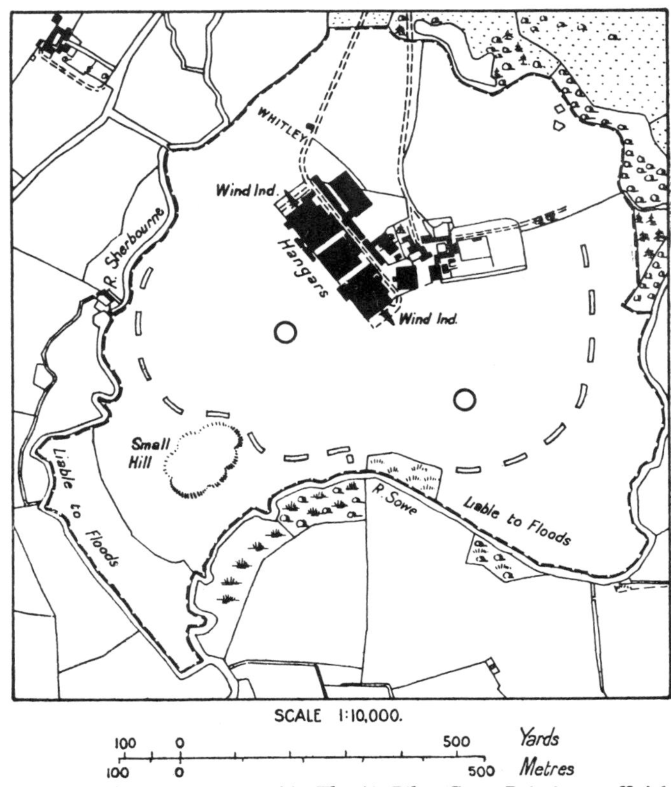

Whitley Abbey aerodrome as presented in *The Air Pilot: Great Britain*, an official publication compiled by the Air Ministry between the two wars.

The one-and-only Armstrong Whitworth Tadpole, a much-modified D.H.9A, built in 1920 as a reconnaissance aircraft for the Admiralty. (*Imperial War Museum MH3251*)

For a time, even after the purchase of Whitley, the Armstrong Whitworth design office and what little aircraft construction work there was, remained at Parkside; there was also a smaller shed, made largely of corrugated iron, situated not far away on the London Road in which the original Siddeley Siskin had been built in 1918. One of the first design tasks undertaken was the building of a carrier-borne fleet-reconnaissance aircraft for the Royal Navy. For economy reasons, the contract called for the aircraft to be based on a conversion of the D.H.9A, of which large numbers were available from wartime production. The result was the Armstrong Whitworth Tadpole, a singularly ugly machine which could hardly have given much satisfaction to its makers or its users. As far as is known, only one Tadpole, J6585, was built, the production contract being awarded to Westlands, who built a similar, but even uglier, aircraft known as the Walrus.

In 1923 the works were moved to Whitley, although the design staff under Lloyd remained at Parkside until 1930. Among the first aircraft to be flown from Whitley was the original Siskin, now fitted with the first of the Jaguar engines, and this was followed, in 1922, by the Siskin II and, in the summer of 1923, by the Awana troop transport. But it was not until the following year that the factory began to get reasonably busy; in addition to completing the first of the Wolf biplanes, the works were occupied with producing the first batch of Siskin III fighters that had been ordered for the RAF during the previous year. In 1924 the number of people employed by Armstrong Whitworth was 351, of whom 30 were women; by 1925 the total had risen to 444 and the output of Siskins reached 71. This was also the year that saw the first flight of the prototype Atlas.

Three stages in the development of the Whitley Abbey factory from the original buildings of the 1920s to its final form in 1960.

SIR W G ARMSTRONG
AIRCRAFT LD

It was during these early post-war years that the company took a leading part in the development of metal construction. Towards the end of the war there were ominous signs that the high-grade timber used for aircraft construction was becoming scarce and, with production running at some 3,000 aircraft a month, it was clear that there would be a serious crisis if the war were to continue for any length of time. Fortunately the Armistice came before the position became too critical, but the significance of this narrowly-avoided shortage was not lost on the Air Ministry and, as a matter of policy, it was decided that, from 1924 onwards, all aircraft ordered into production for the RAF should be of metal construction.

Of the two available metals, steel and aluminium alloys, the former was generally preferred in Great Britain, both by the authorities and by the majority of the manufacturers, partly because steel was an indigenous product and partly because of a lingering suspicion about the qualities of the 'new-fangled' light alloys, doubts which were not without some justification at that early stage in their development. Steel had, in fact, many attractive characteristics: it was stronger, weight for weight, than duralumin; it could be readily cast, forged, pressed, machined, ground, welded, brazed and soldered, and its temper could be varied from extreme softness and ductility to a diamond-like hardness. Furthermore, it was fairly easily made corrosion-resistant.

The main difficulty with steel was that, in order to achieve the necessary degree of lightness in an aircraft structure, the metal had to be so thin that it buckled under any form of load except pure tension. Sheet steel of this degree of thinness was quite unsuitable for any form of stressed-skin construction and this was one of the main reasons why steel eventually gave way to light-alloy sheet which, for the same weight, could be used in thicker, and therefore more stable, sections.

An example of steel construction by Armstrong Whitworth; the port upper wing of the Atlas II.

Thus, for Great Britain, turning over to metal construction in the 1920s meant, to most designers, a straight substitution of steel spars, ribs, longerons and struts for their wooden counterparts, the whole being covered with doped fabric as before. Considerable ingenuity was shown by Armstrong Whitworth and other British manufacturers in perfecting these steel structures and they were successful in as much as they were lighter and stronger than their wooden predecessors but, as can now be seen, in the long term it was a technical blind alley. British designers have been criticized for this conservative approach to the problem, and it may be conceded that both they and the authorities were somewhat high-handed in their deprecation of the rather more imaginative ideas of some continental constructors. But it is easy to be wise after the event, and the fact remains that for the best part of fifteen years British manufacturers were building high-quality steel aeroplanes that were as strong and as durable as any in the world.

In the development of the Armstrong Whitworth method of steel construction, Green and Lloyd were assisted by Major Hamilton Wylie, a consulting structural engineer, who, when serving with the Royal Naval Air Service during the war, had been engaged in research into the use of steel in aircraft. He had made considerable progress in developing wing spars made of thin steel strip stiffened by longitudinal corrugations, and later, at Armstrong Whitworth, he was responsible for evolving methods of drawing thin-steel sections. He also devised a novel form of heat treatment for fabricated steel spars and other components, in which the completed spar was held in tension between two electrodes and then heated to the desired temperature by the passing of an accurately-controlled alternating current. This form of heat treatment enabled built-up steel units to be tempered to a greater degree of hardness and toughness than had hitherto been practicable.

The development of metal construction led to the devising of many novel and interesting methods of fabrication. In an endeavour to produce the ideal strut, the possibilities of locked-joint tubes were investigated in 1932. In standard tubing there is liable to be a variation in wall thickness and, perhaps, an eccentricity between the inside and the outside diameters, both of which faults introduce design problems with thin-wall struts intended to take heavy loads. The locked-joint tubes were produced from high-tensile steel strip of uniform thickness with a seam having interlocking flanges inside the tube. During the rolling process a brass rod was introduced between the flanges, and the joint was finally brazed by heat generated electrically.

After much thought and many trials, Lloyd succeeded in devising a method of attaching wing ribs to spars without using rivets which, apart from presenting production problems, were also a potential cause of weakness in the spar unless the riveting operation was done with unvarying precision. The ribs designed by Lloyd incorporated a hand-operated clamp which gripped both sides of the spar with spring-steel abutments made to fit into the web corrugations. Not only did the spar benefit from the absence of rivet holes, but the clamps had the effect of stiffening the spar web. The ribs themselves were made of light-gauge open-seam tubes, and for these tubes, some of which were as small as $\frac{3}{8}$th of an inch in diameter, it was found necessary to make special drawing dies and to devise a tool for bending the tubes to the desired profile for the ribs.

The first Armstrong Whitworth aeroplanes to make considerable use of metal were the Siskin II, which emerged in 1922, and the Awana troop carrier of 1923 both of which had a steel-tube fuselage but conventional wooden wings. The Siskin III of 1924 was the first Armstrong Whitworth aeroplane to have an all-steel structure and it was also the first such aeroplane to go into production in Great Britain.

It is interesting to reflect that by 1940 the wheel had turned the full circle: a potential shortage of light alloys was one of the factors which helped to wring from the Ministry of Aircraft Production a reluctant agreement to the all-wood de Havilland Mosquito project, and which later resulted in the Armstrong Whitworth Albemarle, designed by Lloyd to use wood and steel as its basic structural materials.

Armstrong Whitworth's study of metal construction led to other developments; as early as 1921 the firm began experimenting with steel propellers, and a three-blade unit of welded construction was tested. This particular exercise went no further, but later, in 1930, experimental work on hollow-steel blade propellers was undertaken. The blades were shaped by means of formers and riveted and welded along the trailing edge; the hub provided for the adjustment of the blade angle on the ground. Propellers of this type were tested over a considerable period on Armstrong Siddeley engines, but no production order was forthcoming.

In 1931 experiments were undertaken with seaplane floats made of stainless steel with a view to producing an article having the same strength-

One of the few examples of an Atlas seaplane. This aircraft was used as a practice hack by the 1931 RAF Schneider Trophy team. (*Imperial War Museum MH2817*)

to-weight ratio as the normal duralumin float, but with superior anti-corrosion properties. The first pair of stainless-steel floats was fitted to an Atlas and subjected to prolonged tests at Calshot and at Felixstowe with very satisfactory results. Subsequently, three sets of floats were designed for the Hawker Osprey, one pair of which had flat top-decks and sides. These were tested in 1935, but the pilots reported that the flat-topped floats had an adverse effect on the handling of the aircraft in the air. Static tests by Short Brothers showed that the stainless-steel specimens were fully up to strength and comparable in weight to the duralumin floats.

A small but important item which stemmed from the development of metal construction was the invention by Armstrong Whitworth of the so-called 'pop rivet', designed for use in places where there is access to one side of the work only and where, consequently, the normal dolly cannot be used. The pop rivet, the subject of a company patent, was widely adopted and is still in general use to-day.

By 1925 the Armstrong Whitworth Development Co was prospering; the success of the Jaguar engine, which had passed its first official type tests in 1922, was by now assured, as was that of the Lynx engine which followed it. The Siskin III was in quantity production for the RAF and orders for the improved Siskin IIIA, and for the newly-flown Atlas two-seater, were imminent. On the other hand, for the parent company in Newcastle, the position was just the reverse: heavy engineering and ship-building had suffered badly in the immediate post-war years, and the company's fortunes were declining sharply.

As mentioned earlier, John Siddeley was elected to the Newcastle board in 1926, but already he was far from happy about the situation. As matters stood in 1925 and 1926, the successful subsidiary companies in Coventry were being used to support the failing parent, and this was naturally unacceptable to a man of Siddeley's temperament and ambition. The action he took is recorded in the minutes of a board meeting held in Newcastle in November 1926, when a discussion took place about '. . . Mr Siddeley's offer to buy the Armstrong Whitworth Development Co for £1,500,000'. The minute goes on to record that the board was '. . . wholly averse to the suggestion that Armstrong Whitworth (of Newcastle) should be debarred from making motorcars or aeroplanes'.

This seemingly audacious bid by John Siddeley was made possible by the promise of a loan by the Midland Bank, whose chairman, Reginald McKenna, was on friendly terms with Siddeley. John Siddeley's son, Ernest, relates that this loan was made without any formal written agreement and that the degree of trust in Siddeley's integrity which this action demonstrated gave him great satisfaction and constituted, in his own words, '. . . one of the proudest moments of my life'. The sale of the Development Company to Siddeley was concluded in December 1926; for a time he maintained his personal connection with the Newcastle company, but in March 1927 he gave up his post as senior managing director and a year later resigned from the board.

John Siddeley, now firmly in control of his own company, called an extraordinary general meeting in March 1927 for the purpose of changing the company's name from the Armstrong Whitworth Development Co to the Armstrong Siddeley Development Co, the assets of which, he noted, included Armstrong Siddeley Motors Ltd and Sir W. G. Armstrong Whitworth Aircraft Ltd. Followers of the more recent history of the Hawker Siddeley Group may be interested to note that Siddeley also disclosed that his company owned 250,000 shares in a Chelmsford firm of electrical manufacturers known as Crompton & Co Ltd.

The year 1927, following Siddeley's successful take-over, was one of continued progress. The Siskin IIIA had followed the Siskin III on to the production line and large orders for the Atlas had been placed. This year, too, saw the completion of the first three Argosies ordered by Imperial Airways. By the end of the year the work force had risen to more than 700, or about double the 1924 figure. On the engine side the Jaguar was still in demand (although gradually being overtaken in popularity by the Bristol Jupiter), while the lower-powered Lynx was still dominant in its class. During the previous five years these two engines had played a major part in building up the company's fortunes.

In 1928 John Siddeley acquired A. V. Roe & Co Ltd; for some time the fortunes of that company, a wholly-owned subsidiary of the Crossley Motors Group, had been declining, and the first suggestion that Avro might be willing to join forces with Armstrong Siddeley was made to Siddeley at a luncheon at which John Lord, Avro's managing director, and Roy Chadwick, their chief designer, were present. The idea had its attractions for Siddeley: at the time the Avro 504N, with its Siddeley Lynx engine, was in production for the RAF, and Siddeley was anxious that this lucrative business should continue uninterrupted. Furthermore, it was known that Crossley Motors would not be averse to ridding themselves of the Avro liability. The deal was concluded in May 1928 for a price said to

The Argosy served with Imperial Airways from 1926 until 1935. Khartoum aerodrome is the scene of this meeting between an Argosy I (*left*) and an Argosy II.

have been something less than £250,000; be that as it may, the transaction proved to be an extremely profitable one for John Siddeley.

The same year, 1928, saw the formation of another company which was to become a prominent subsidiary of the Development Company. High Duty Alloys Ltd was the child of Wallace Devereux, formerly works manager of Peter Hooker Ltd, an old-established firm well known during the war as the makers of Gnome rotary engines, and which had, more recently, been supplying aluminium pistons for Siddeley's engines. Hookers got into difficulties, and Devereux approached Siddeley for £10,000 to keep the firm going. The first £10,000 was soon absorbed and twice more Devereux came to Siddeley for help. Thus, in 1928, High Duty Alloys, with Devereux as chairman, came into being and, for an investment of £30,000, Siddeley became the owner of still another potentially prosperous company. The acquisition of these companies, a prime example of John Siddeley's business acumen, can be seen as the first positive steps in the formation of what was to become in later years the Hawker Siddeley Group.

When John Siddeley took over, the company's buildings in Coventry and at Whitley covered an area of some 36 acres and were well equipped for the production of cars, aero-engines and metal aeroplanes. A useful addition to the facilities at Whitley was the installation, in 1928, of a wind tunnel built to the design of William Farren (later Sir William). He had been on the technical staff of Siddeley Deasy and Armstrong Whitworth from 1917 until 1920. Like Green and Lloyd, he had come from the Royal Aircraft Factory at Farnborough, but when he designed the wind tunnel he was a lecturer in aircraft structures at the Imperial College of Science and Technology in South Kensington.

The tunnel at Whitley, which was powered by a 25 hp electric motor driving a 10-ft diameter four-blade fan, was of the open-ended type with a wind speed of 75 ft per second. The working section measured 5 ft by 4 ft, and the structure of the tunnel, which was 46 ft long, was of wood supported on a frame of steel girders. In spite of its limitations the Whitley tunnel certainly gave good value for money: in 1948, when it was already twenty years old, it was moved, lock, stock and barrel, to Baginton and then, in the spring of 1952 when the Whitley factory was re-activated for guided missile work, it was returned once more to its original home.

The Siskin production line virtually came to an end in 1929, but by then the Atlas production, which was eventually to outnumber that of the Siskin, was well under way with the added advantage that it served to maintain the demand for the Jaguar engine. Also completed in 1929 were the last four Argosies ordered by Imperial Airways. By the end of the year the work force was just short of 1,000.

It is not within the purpose of this book to deal in detail with the products of Armstrong Siddeley Motors, but the performance and the prospects of the Armstrong Whitworth aeroplanes were so closely bound up with the Siddeley engines that the subject cannot be entirely ignored.

The fact that John Siddeley's main interest was centred in his engines resulted in the invariable rule that Siddeley engines, and Siddeley engines only, could be fitted to Armstrong Whitworth aircraft. It was on this issue that, in November 1933, John Lloyd was dismissed for arguing that another type of engine should be used: fortunately saner opinions prevailed, and Lloyd was reinstated in January 1934.

John Siddeley's engine policy was of no particular disadvantage during the middle 1920s when the Jaguar was certainly the best, if not the only practicable high-powered air-cooled engine: it is also probably true that, in the period immediately after the war, when engine development was largely a matter of trial and error, Siddeley's habit of dictating engineering policy was not as harmful as it was later to become when more scientific methods of design and development became essential.

Much of the success of the Jaguar engine can be attributed to the work of F. R. Smith, to whom reference has already been made, and to Frank Baron, who was responsible for the test work carried out on the engine until his death in 1931. Subsequently, the high-power production engines that followed, namely the Panther (known at first as the Jaguar Major), the Leopard and the Tiger, all seem to have suffered from a lack of vigorous development and thus never succeeded in achieving the well-merited reputation of the Jaguar or of their contemporary rivals.

Following the eclipse of the Jaguar and the failure of its more powerful

The low-speed wind-tunnel first installed at Whitley in 1928. It was transferred to Baginton in 1948 and then returned to Whitley in 1952.

Atlas aircraft of No.13 Army Co-Operation Squadron, RAF, demonstrate supply dropping at the RAF Display in 1931. (*Flight International*)

successors to make the top grade, the continued prosperity of the engine company rested mainly on the success of the seven-cylinder Lynx engine, which was virtually half a Jaguar and which benefited from the development of that engine and inherited its good qualities. The Lynx engine was in quantity production for the Avro 504N, and it was the possible threat to this business that helped to persuade John Siddeley to purchase the Avro company. This deal paid off handsomely, in as much as the Avro Tutor, which followed the Avro 504N as the RAF's elementary trainer, was also powered by the Lynx engine. A further variation on the theme was the still smaller Mongoose, a single-row engine with five Jaguar cylinders which developed 150 hp. Although technically satisfactory, the Mongoose enjoyed only a moderate success commercially, and it was followed by the Double Mongoose, later renamed the Serval, which was a ten-cylinder two-row affair, and was, in effect, a Jaguar with two cylinders omitted from each row. This engine, which developed 340 hp, was used to power the Atalanta monoplane in which it initially gave some trouble due to high-frequency vibration.

Even more successful than the Lynx was the Lynx Major, soon to be renamed the Cheetah. This engine, which appeared in 1932, was selected

An interior view of the Whitley factory in wartime; the detail shop in 1944. (*Courtesy P. Jarrett*)

A batch of experimental twenty-one cylinder Deerhound engines being assembled in the Parkside factory of Armstrong Siddeley Motors. Development of the Deerhound ceased in March 1940. (*Courtesy J. Rait*)

for both the Avro Anson and the Airspeed Oxford, so its commercial success was assured and, indeed, it proved to be a thoroughly reliable and satisfactory power unit. By the end of the war in 1945, the number of Cheetah engines produced had exceeded 35,000, and the power output of the engine had risen from 375 to 475 hp.

At the lower end of the scale, the smallest engines were the 80 hp five-cylinder Genet, and the Genet Major of 100 hp with five larger cylinders; there was also, rather confusingly, another Genet Major with seven cylinders which developed 140 hp. The permutations of cylinder size and number of cylinders was seemingly endless, and the overall picture was still further complicated, in the range of high-power engines, by the alternatives of geared or ungeared and of supercharged or unsupercharged variants, according to choice.

Two engines which were test flown but never put into production were the Hyena and the Deerhound. Both were three-row air-cooled radials, the Hyena with fifteen cylinders, disposed in three rows of five, and the Deerhound with twenty-one cylinders in three rows of seven. Not much is known about the Hyena which was test flown in the A.W.XVI, G-ABKF, by Charles Turner-Hughes, then the company's chief test pilot, who recalls that, although rather heavy and prone to overheat, it was basically a good design. Development of the Deerhound went further and eventually achieved an output of 1,500 hp. Several examples were built and it was flight-tested in a Whitley, which first flew with these engines in January 1939. As recounted elsewhere, development ceased when the Whitley was destroyed in a crash.

Armstrong Siddeley Motors was early in the field in gas-turbine development, but its activities in this respect are not so closely related to Armstrong Whitworth aircraft—except in one instance—as were the earlier piston engines. The first production Armstrong Siddeley gas-turbine was the Python, a powerful propeller-turbine unit which found an outlet in the Westland Wyvern. Next came the Mamba, a smaller propeller-turbine used to power the Armstrong Whitworth Apollo airliner and which, because of its undeveloped state, was largely responsible for the failure of that aircraft to catch the market. The Mamba was further developed and, with two engines linked together, Siamese-twin fashion, with each driving separate contra-rotating propellers, it became the Double Mamba, the powerplant of the Fairey Gannet. But Armstrong Siddeley's most successful turbine engines were the Sapphire and the Viper, both pure-jets. The former was used extensively both in bombers and fighters for the RAF, while the latter found a satisfactory market in trainers and business jets. In 1959 the Hawker Siddeley Group and Bristol Aero-Engines Ltd formed a joint company to take over the engine-building interests of the two concerns; from then on, therefore, Armstrong Siddeley Motors Ltd ceased to exist but became part of Bristol Siddeley Engines Ltd, which itself was amalgamated with Rolls-Royce Ltd in 1968.

By 1930 the flying school at Whitley had become an important part of the company's business. With a fleet of Avros, D.H.9s and the three Armstrong Whitworth Wolves, the school had become one of the training centres for the Reserve of Air Force Officers, and the experience gained led Siddeley to the conclusion that there was a real demand for an 'air university' where civilians could obtain comprehensive flying training of a standard equal to that established by the RAF's Central Flying School. In pursuit of this idea a new company known as Air Service Training Ltd was formed in February 1931 with a capital of £25,000 vested in Armstrong Whitworth Development Co Ltd. The chairman of the new company was Air Marshal Sir John Higgins (who at the time was also chairman of Armstrong Whitworth Aircraft). The first commandant of the school was Grp Capt Robert Barton and the chief instructor was Flt Lieut Harold Jenkins, an ex-CFS instructor. Barton subsequently became managing director from 1950 to 1952 when he was succeeded by Air Marshal Sir Hugh Walmsley.

The Armstrong Whitworth flying school, established at Whitley in 1920, became Air Service Training Ltd in 1931 and moved to Hamble aerodrome. (*Flight International 12302*)

Air Service Training began operating from its new premises at Hamble aerodrome in April 1931, but it was not until the following June that the school was officially opened by HRH Prince Henry, Duke of Gloucester. At that time the fleet consisted of Avro Avians, Avro Tutors, Atlases, two-seat Siskins and D.H.9Js, the three veteran Wolf aircraft having been retired from flying duties. The school's syllabus included an *ab initio* course for overseas Service pilots, a commercial pilots' course, a seaplane course for Service or civil pilots and a special course for private pilots, consisting of ground and air instruction occupying three weeks and estimated to cost £87.

Air Service Training flourished and continued to be a profitable member of Armstrong Siddeley Development until 1940, when it became a separate company with control passing to the Hawker Siddeley Group. In 1960 the Hawker Siddeley Group itself relinquished control, and the school at Hamble was taken over by a company sponsored by the Ministry of Aviation and the two state airlines and called The College of Air Training.

A Starling, an Atlas and a Siskin on exhibition at the Aero Show, held at Olympia in 1929. (*Flight International*)

The end of the decade saw Armstrong Whitworth busy and prosperous; the Siskin contracts had been completed in 1929, but Atlas production was in full swing, the output averaging nearly eleven aircraft each month in 1930 and more than thirteen a month in 1931, by which time the work force had risen to 1,240. During 1930 Imperial Airways had put out a specification for a new airliner to serve on its African routes, then in the planning stage, and the subsequent order was placed with Armstrong Whitworth. In February 1931 details of the aircraft, the Atalanta, were released; it was Armstrong Whitworth's first monoplane and their first four-engined aircraft.

After the delivery of the last of the eight Atalantas and the end of the Atlas contracts in 1933, work in the factory fell off sharply, and by the end of the year the number of employees was down to 819, a figure which suffered a further reduction of about sixty in the following year. In 1933, for the first time since the Newcastle days, Armstrong Whitworth started sub-contract work, an activity that was to become a predominating feature

The A.W.XV Atalanta was used initially on the African routes of Imperial Airways and then on the Indian section of the Far East route. *Aurora* (*left*) and *Astraea* were based, as seen here, at Calcutta.

of the future. The first of a large number of Hawker Harts was built in 1933, with production starting in earnest during 1934, a year which also marked the emergence of the A.W.19 general-purpose aircraft and of the A.W.35 Scimitar, an excellent single-seat fighter which, with its radial engine, was at a disadvantage compared with its sleeker Kestrel-powered rivals (it was Handley Page who once remarked that if a starfish could fly, it wouldn't fly on its side).

Although the volume of work at Whitley was still at a comparatively low ebb during 1935, significant events were taking shape. In September 1934 Armstrong Whitworth had received an order from Imperial Airways for the A.W.27 Ensign airliner, the biggest civil aircraft so far undertaken by the British aircraft industry. In June 1935 the one and only A.W.23 bomber-transport made its first flight at a time when the prototype of its more famous successor, the Whitley, was already under construction. During this period the factory was mainly occupied by the production line of the Hawker Harts, of which about seventy were built during 1935.

In the summer of 1935 Sir John Siddeley, as he had become, sold out his interest in the Armstrong Siddeley Development Co. This deal, which came as a surprise even to the senior management at Coventry, was completed in July 1935, when a new company known as the Hawker Siddeley Aircraft Co was formed to acquire the whole of the share capital, 419,751 ordinary shares of £1, of Armstrong Siddeley Development Co Ltd,* and fifty per cent of the ordinary share capital of Hawker Aircraft Ltd. The board of directors of the new company were T. O. M. Sopwith, F. Sigrist, F. S. Spriggs and P. Hill; Siddeley was not included, but his name remained in the company title and he agreed to remain chairman of the Armstrong Siddeley Development Co, and he continued to hold this appointment until he finally retired in June 1936.

The advent of the large twin-engined A.W.23 served to emphasize the obvious fact that Whitley aerodrome was too small for future needs and this, coupled with the receipt in August 1935 of an order for eighty A.W.38 Whitley bombers, led to a decision to expand capacity by building a new factory at the recently established municipal aerodrome at Baginton, about a mile and a half southeast of Whitley and some three and a quarter miles from the centre of Coventry.

The building of the first two large sheds at Baginton fell behind schedule, but in 1936 the first Whitley jigs were moved into the unfinished buildings. The site of the new factory had previously been a farm, some of whose buildings were still occupied, and the first fitters in the factory worked on an earthen floor with farm livestock wandering in and out among the growing forest of jigs.

* At the time of the sale, Armstrong Siddeley Development Co Ltd controlled the following companies: Sir W. G. Armstrong Whitworth Aircraft Ltd; A. V. Roe & Co Ltd; Armstrong Siddeley Motors Ltd; Stoneleigh Motors Ltd; Burlington Carriage Co Ltd; and Air Service Training Ltd. It also had a substantial interest in the Self Changing Gear Trading Co Ltd and in High Duty Alloys Ltd.

The Atalanta featured prominently in a Shell poster of the 1930s.

The first Armstrong Whitworth aircraft to fly from Baginton was a Scimitar which took-off on 26 May, 1936. It was flown by Alan Campbell-Orde, who can probably be regarded as the company's first regular test pilot. Before him there had been a number of part-time test pilots, one of

The Armstrong Whitworth factory at Baginton as it appeared in the early 1950s.

the first being Frank Courtney, the well-known test pilot, who had test-flown the Siddeley Siskin in 1919 and who, as a freelance, worked for the firm on and off until 1926. Subsequently the chief instructors of the Armstrong Whitworth flying school, starting with Major Griffiths, were called upon to do test flying as and when necessary. Griffiths, who was killed flying a Siskin III, was followed by James Bennett-Baggs, acting in the same dual capacity until he left to fly for the Avro company. Douglas Hughes, who succeeded Bennett-Baggs, was also killed during a demonstration flight.

Campbell-Orde, who was appointed chief test pilot after Hughes, had been one of the pilots of the pioneer continental air services operated by Aircraft Transport & Travel in 1919. After a spell instructing in China, he joined Armstrong Whitworth in 1924 as an instructor at the flying school, and he became chief test pilot in 1930. He left the company towards the end of 1936 to join British Airways. Campbell-Orde was followed by

Test pilot, 1930 style; Alan Campbell-Orde poses for his photograph.

Frank Courtney (*left*), who tested many of the early Armstrong Whitworth aeroplanes up to the middle 1920s. Alan Campbell-Orde (*right*) joined the company in 1924 and was chief test pilot until 1936. (*Courtesy A. Campbell-Orde*)

Charles Turner-Hughes, who had made a name for himself as an aerobatic pilot with Sir Alan Cobham's Air Displays in Africa flying the A.W.XVI single-seat fighter. He gave a notable demonstration of this aircraft at the SBAC Exhibition held at Hendon Aerodrome in June 1933 and was subsequently offered the post of test pilot by S. W. Hisscocks, the general manager; he retired from test flying in 1946.

Two Armstrong Whitworth test pilots; *left*: E. S. Greenwood, assistant test pilot 1937–1941, and *right*: C. Turner-Hughes, who joined the company in 1933 and retired as chief test pilot in 1946.

The year 1936 saw a substantial rise in the number of workers, the total reaching 2,345, and the virtual doubling of the factory floor area. The output of Hawker Hart biplanes reached a peak of 258 and the prototype Whitley flew from Whitley aerodrome piloted by Campbell-Orde in March 1936. Another aircraft that made its maiden flight late in the year was the A.W.29 single-engined day bomber, a type that suffered a quick demise, partly because the one and only prototype made a wheels-up landing early on in its career, and partly because the project was pushed aside in the company's preoccupation with the Whitley.

A feature which the rejected A.W.29 shared with the A.W.23 bomber-transport was the cupola gun turret designed by Lloyd. The turret was manually operated, being rotated by the gunner's feet; to control the gun in elevation, the gunner merely leant forward or backward in his saddle-type seat. The weight of the single gun was balanced against the weight of the gunner, and a special link motion connecting the gun mounting and the seat ensured that the gunner's line of sight remained in the same relation to the gun sights throughout the range of elevation. The Armstrong Whitworth turret was adopted as standard for the early Avro Ansons and

In 1937 the A.W.23 was handed over to Flight Refuelling Ltd for use in air-to-air refuelling experiments.

The A.W.27 airliner G-ADSS *Egeria* at Croydon Airport in 1938.

for the nose and tail positions on the first Whitleys. The turret was both ingenious and comparatively light, but it was inevitably soon outmoded when war broke out and the need for greater defensive fire-power led to the introduction of power-operated turrets armed with two or four machine-guns apiece.

With the completion of the large three-bay hangar at Baginton, production of the Whitley went ahead quickly under the pressure of the RAF expansion programme. In 1937, twenty-one of these twin-engined bombers were completed and in the following year, by which time the heat was really on, the output rose to fifty-nine and the work force had increased to almost 5,000. To make room for the expanding Whitley production the Ensign jigs and components were transferred to the Air Service Training workshops at Hamble, and the unfortunate airliner became a very poor second in the company's priorities. It was also badly delayed by the vacillation of Imperial Airways, and it eventually flew in 1938, some two years behind schedule. On the other hand Whitley production seems to have been efficient and well organized from the start, and credit for this, and for the lasting reputation which the firm established for reliable delivery and good workmanship, goes largely to two men, Herbert Woodhams and Walter Lockwood.

Both had joined the Coventry organization in its early days; Lockwood being the first to arrive in 1919, having been recruited by Lloyd, who was then engaged in building up his design team. Lockwood had studied at the University of Bristol, after active service in France during which he was badly gassed. In 1921 he left the design team to become assistant works

Whitley bombers under construction in the Baginton factory in 1941. (*Flight International*)

manager. Woodhams joined the company in 1923 as chief inspector, having already established a reputation as a first-class engineer. He had worked throughout the war with Peter Hooker, building Gnome rotary engines; afterwards he was employed by the pioneer airline, Aircraft Transport & Travel Ltd and then by de Havilland at Stag Lane. In 1919 Woodhams gained the distinction of becoming the possessor of the first Air Ministry ground engineer's licence for aero-engines.

At the time the Whitley first went into production, Woodhams was

The Whitley wing shop.

works manager, but in 1937 he was promoted to general manager under Christopher Oliver, who had filled the post of managing director since the retirement of Sir John Siddeley. His position as works manager was taken over by Percy Crabbe, who later became managing director of the Gloster Aircraft Co, and he, in turn, was succeeded by Lockwood in 1940. Under the guidance of Woodhams the heavy programme of Whitley production was kept well up to schedule; by the end of 1939 some 200 Whitleys had been completed and the output rose to a peak in 1942, in which year 596 were built. During the period of Whitley production numerous other factories were brought into the Armstrong Whitworth orbit, including plants at Leicester, Nuneaton, Northampton and some hangars at Sywell Aerodrome and at Bitteswell, which latter became a dispersed final-assembly plant and test-flight station. By the end of 1940 the number of employees had risen to more than 8,000.

When the last Whitley came off the production line in July 1943, a total of 1,814 had been built, but by then the factory had already started production of Avro Lancasters. The change-over, which occurred during 1942 and 1943, took about twelve months to complete, and involved the

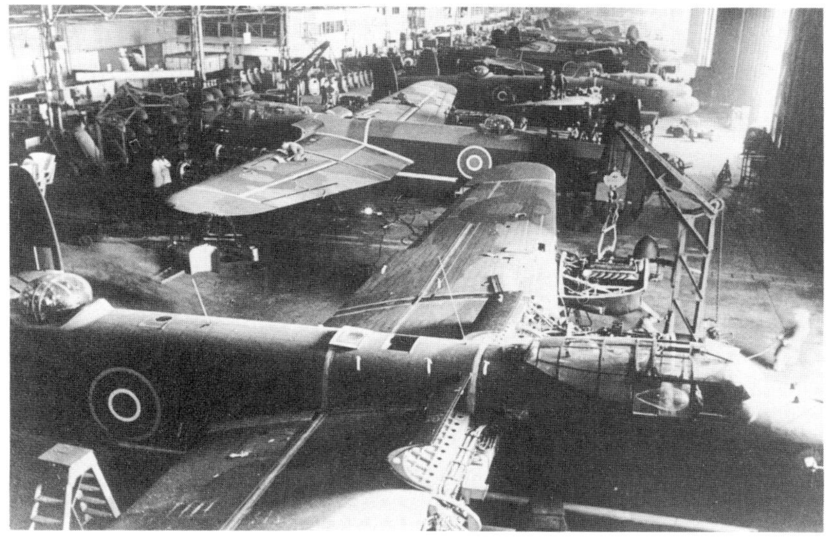

Avro Lancaster bombers began to replace the Whitleys on the Baginton assembly line in 1942.

installation of new jigs and tools and the removal of the redundant equipment according to a rigid pre-set timetable. The whole operation was conducted with considerable smoothness, as is shown by the fact that during 1943 the factory completed 277 Whitleys and 96 Lancasters. In all, 1,328 Lancasters were built by Armstrong Whitworth, but before the end of the war an order was placed for the line to be changed over to Lincoln production, and work on this aircraft continued well into the years of peace, with 281 aircraft having been completed when production was finally tapered off in 1951.

In addition to the wartime production at the main Armstrong Whitworth plants, and because of the excellent record achieved both before and during the war, the company was asked by Sir Stafford Cripps, then Minister of Aircraft Production, to take charge of Short Brothers' factory at Swindon where Stirling bombers were being built. Soon afterwards the company also became responsible for the production of Fairey Barracudas at the Boulton Paul factory at Wolverhampton.

Armstrong Whitworth's other contribution to the war was the A.W.41 Albemarle, a twin-engined reconnaissance bomber, designed by Lloyd at the Government's request, making use of wood and steel as an insurance against a possible shortage of light alloy. The first Albemarle was flown from Hamble in March 1940 by Turner-Hughes. It was not put into production by Armstrong Whitworth but was widely sub-contracted under the overall supervision of A. W. Hawksley Ltd, of Brockworth, a subsidiary company of the Hawker Siddeley Group.

With the build up of Whitley production, Turner-Hughes, the company's chief test pilot, was joined in 1937 by Eric Greenwood, and it was these two who were mainly responsible for the testing of the many hundreds of Whitleys and Lancasters that emerged from Baginton. They were assisted at one period by John Grierson, who was working primarily for Armstrong Siddeley Motors, and also, from time to time, by RAF pilots who had completed their tour of operations. Greenwood left Coventry in 1941 to go to Hamble and then, in 1944, he went as chief test pilot to Glosters. John Grierson, who also went on to Glosters, had had a varied career, including making a record flight from India to England in 1931, and a flight from England to Ottawa in 1934 in a de Havilland Fox Moth seaplane. After three years' jet-development flying at Glosters, he operated a Walrus flying-boat on a whaling expedition in the Antarctic in 1946.

Turner-Hughes was forced to give up flying after receiving head injuries when a large bird crashed through the windscreen of a Lancaster. His place as chief test pilot was taken for a short period by his deputy R. Midgley, and he was followed, in 1948, by Eric Franklin, who retained the post until Armstrong Whitworth was disbanded, after which he moved to Hawker Siddeley Aviation at Manchester. Franklin was originally an apprentice with Armstrong Whitworth in 1937, and he learnt to fly before the war with the Leamington Aero Club. After serving throughout the war in the RAF, he did a course at the Empire Test Pilots' School in 1944 and returned to Armstrong Whitworth a year later. One of his team at Coventry was J. O. Lancaster, who holds the distinction of being the first pilot to use the Martin-Baker ejection seat in an emergency. This event occurred on 30 May, 1949, when he had to abandon the A.W.52 flying-wing aircraft.

Armstrong Whitworth, and Lloyd in particular, were among the first in Great Britain to take practical steps to investigate the potentialities of

In front of the A.W.52G glider RG324 is R. Midgley, chief test pilot in 1946; in the cockpit is E. G. Franklin.

laminar flow and the control of the boundary layer. Following discussions with J. L. Nayler, who was then at the National Physical Laboratory, Lloyd was asked to consider designing and making a laminar-flow wing. To maintain laminar flow, the surface of the wing had to be absolutely smooth, with surface irregularities limited to $\pm$ one thousandth of an inch. To achieve this Lloyd built his wing—which was designed to fit a Hurricane fuselage—in two halves from the outside inwards; in other words, the outer skin was accurately shaped and held in a jig after which the internal structure was built on to it. Lloyd relates that the wing was tested by the RAE at Farnborough and performed quite well, but only for a limited time because dirt and flies soon accumulated on the surface and broke down the laminar flow. The next development was the A.W.52G glider, a three-fifths scale model of the A.W.52 jet-propelled flying-wing aircraft which followed it. On both these aircraft the boundary layer was sucked in to the wing to prevent tip stalling. Following tests, Lloyd came to the conclusion that laminar flow could not be satisfactorily maintained on a swept wing.

With the coming of peace in 1945, and the wholesale cancellation of contracts, a large-scale redundancy programme was drawn up; by the end of the year some 2,500 people had left the company, followed by more than 7,000 in 1946, bringing the total work force down to a mere 3,066 by the year's end. By then all the dispersal factories had been vacated and production had ceased at the Whitley factory, all the workshop equipment and office people having been moved to Baginton, which had been entirely re-planned. At first the factory at Whitley was used as a clearing house for redundant material and jigs and later as a bonded store for raw materials.

In these immediate post-war years the main tasks in hand consisted of Lancaster and Lincoln production, at a much reduced tempo, and a certain amount of conversion work on both types, work which included anti-corrosion treatment, adaptation for maritime patrol duties and for photographic-reconnaissance and survey work, and the fitting of H2S radar equipment. In 1947 the work force, at 2,794, had touched its lowest point since 1936, but already the company had embarked on a programme of basic research into the guided weapon field, and this led, in 1946, to the receipt of a Government contract for the manufacture of liquid-propellant motors and other components for a research rocket, the RTV 1, then being developed by the RAE at Farnborough. Later, in 1947, Armstrong Whitworth built a number of experimental rockets designed jointly by the company and the Guided Projectiles Establishment (later renamed the Rocket Propulsion Establishment) at Westcott. This experimental vehicle was the forerunner of a proposed ship-to-air guided missile, and was dimensionally similar to the Sea Slug which was evolved from it.

The growing volume of missile work soon became too much for Baginton to handle and in 1948 the factory at Whitley was reactivated. Under the direction of Lockwood, now works director, the Whitley factory was enlarged and re-equipped at a cost of more than £1 million, and it soon became one of the finest independent research centres in the country. Lockwood was also responsible for opening, in 1952, an Australian division, based in Salisbury in South Australia, which controlled the flight-trial facilities at the Woomera rocket range.

The supersonic wind-tunnel installed at Whitley in 1955. With an operating speed of M:3, it was used principally for missile development. (*Flight International 18391*)

In the years that followed, the equipment at Whitley was expanded to include five wind tunnels,* structural and metallurgical laboratories, telemetry apparatus, and airborne television equipment for recording and transmit-

* These wind tunnels comprised: the original low-speed tunnel built in 1928, already described; a six-inch diameter low-speed tunnel designed for flow study; a turbulence tunnel measuring seven feet by four feet having a wind speed of 165 mph; a ten-inch by eight-inch intermittent trans-sonic tunnel with speeds up to M:1·5 and a running time of 15 to 20 seconds every 15 minutes; and a supersonic tunnel driven by a 7,700 hp electric motor giving speeds up to about M:3.

A Sea Slug Mk.I being fired during successful trials from HMS *Girdle Ness*. Subsequently, the Admiralty claimed that Sea Slug was the best ship-borne, surface-to-air missile in the Western World.

ting data both from aircraft and missiles. In fact, during this period, Whitley fully retained its importance as the design and development centre for aircraft and missiles as well as for a variety of other techniques which sprang from the company's growing experience in the field of electronics.

Following the early rocket research, a contract was awarded by the Government early in 1949 for 'Project 502', the code name for the Sea Slug weapon system, which included not only the missile itself, but the whole of the handling, refuelling, radar, fire control, and launching equipment. The development of Sea Slug involved many trials and tribulations before final success was achieved. Trouble occurred early on during firing trials with special test vehicles, most of which broke-up in the air from unknown causes. The solution to this problem was eventually found by Charles Bayly, then the chief project engineer of the company's armament division, who was recruited by Lockwood in 1955 after they had met and discussed rocket problems by the side of a camp fire at the Woomera range.

Bayly's success in tracking down the complex phenomena which were causing the missiles to disintegrate, and his skill in overcoming the trouble, opened up the way for the ultimate success of the Sea Slug, which later went into full-scale production for the Royal Navy. Subsequently, in 1960, Bayly became a director and general manager of Armstrong Whitworth Aircraft and then general manager of Hawker Siddeley Aviation's Avro Whitworth Division at Manchester until he left the Group in 1965.

The excellent record for production established by Armstrong Whitworth, during and immediately after the war, led to the placing of still further large contracts for the building of aircraft designed by other members of the Hawker Siddeley Group. The first order to follow the Lancaster and Lincoln contracts was received in 1949 and was for forty-five Gloster Meteor Mk.4 aircraft; this order, which was completed in April 1950, was followed by a further contract for the Mk.8 version of which a total of 430 had been completed by the time the line came to an end in 1953.

While the Meteor Mk.8 was still on the production line, the company embarked on the redesign and development of the Meteor as a night fighter. The production of this version, the NF.11, involved a major redesign task which was undertaken under direct contract with the Ministry of Supply, rather than as a sub-contract from Glosters. Small variations of the theme resulted in the NF.12, the NF.13 and the NF.14, some of which went to the air forces of Denmark, France and Syria as well as to the Royal Air Force. In all, 592 Meteor night fighters were built by Armstrong Whitworth between 1951 and 1954. In later years, between 1957 and 1965, twenty-four Meteor NF.11s were converted by the company into TT.20 high-speed target-towing aircraft.

Gloster Javelin all-weather fighters in the final assembly shop at Bitteswell aerodrome.

The next large production order received in Coventry was for the Hawker Sea Hawk. This aeroplane, Hawker's first jet aircraft, was initially put into production at Hawker's Kingston factory but, towards the end of 1952, the Government introduced their 'super-priority' system which meant that Hawkers could not meet the target date for both the Sea Hawk

Part of the Bitteswell complex, the only one-time Armstrong Whitworth factory to remain active with Hawker Siddeley Aviation into the 1970s.

and the Hunter. As a result the entire development and production programme of the Sea Hawk was transferred to Armstrong Whitworth, and the first of these aircraft for the Royal Navy made its first flight at Baginton in December 1962. Altogether 400 Sea Hawks (Marks 1, 2, 3, 4 and 6) were built at Baginton for the Royal Navy, with a further 90 which were supplied to Holland, Germany and India.

While the Sea Hawk production was still under way, the company was given another order, for Hawker Hunters and Gloster Javelins. Hunter production, which included the Mk.2, the Mk.5 and the Mk.6, totalled 278 aircraft; in the case of the Javelin, the first of which came off the line in 1956, there were, in all, 133 aircraft comprising Mks.4, 5, 7 and 9.

In addition to its preoccupation with quantity production, Armstrong Whitworth also earned for itself a reputation for efficient overhaul and conversion work, a reputation which, in fact, survived in the Bitteswell organization long after the company was finally absorbed into the Hawker Siddeley complex. One of the earliest tasks of this nature was the modification, in 1944, of a DC-4 Skymaster for the use of Winston Churchill, then Prime Minister. The general layout of the interior and the colour schemes were decided by Churchill and his wife, while Armstrong Whitworth designed and manufactured the furnishings. Most of the woodwork was finished in walnut veneer, and grey-blue leather was used for the upholstery. A conference table to seat twelve people was installed and there was sleeping accommodation for six. Other furniture included a sofa and a special easy chair for Churchill. As the DC-4 was unpressurized, an iron lung was installed to protect the Prime Minister from the effects of high altitude, but it is said that he refused to use it.

The modifications to the aircraft, which bore the Service number EW999, were completed in October 1944, and on 6 November it was flown from Baginton to Northolt where it was inspected by the Prime

Minister. The test flying, undertaken by Turner-Hughes, included a proving flight to Montreal and back during November and December 1944.

Much later, in 1948 and 1949, when the hot war with Germany had given place to the cold war with Russia, Armstrong Whitworth undertook a massive programme of overhaul work on the aircraft used to overcome the Soviet blockade of Berlin. During the twelve months of the Berlin airlift, some eighty-six aircraft were overhauled at Baginton and returned to service. At the peak of the operation, Avro Yorks were being turned round in under three days. Most of the aircraft, which flew into Baginton direct from Germany, were in poor shape and extremely dirty, especially those which had been carrying coal. At Baginton a team of some forty men was engaged in the work of stripping, cleaning, disinfecting and servicing the aircraft and their equipment and, if necessary, changing the engines.

Soon after the company began building high-speed jet aircraft it became apparent that the Baginton airfield, lacking a runway, was no longer suitable for test flying. As a consequence, arrangements were made with the Ministry of Supply to rent two large hangars at the Bitteswell airfield near Lutterworth and some twelve miles northeast of Baginton. From 1952 onwards all aircraft built at Baginton were assembled and flight-tested at Bitteswell and in 1956 the company purchased the airfield outright, little realizing that by the end of 1965, this would be the only unit of the Armstrong Whitworth Aircraft Coventry complex to survive with Hawker Siddeley Aviation.

Between the years 1943, when the Whitley bomber was phased out of production, and 1960, which saw the last of the Sea Hawks leave the factory, Armstrong Whitworth built more than 3,600 aircraft to other companies' designs, and there can be no doubt that their success with this lucrative business served to some extent to deflect the company from adopting the traditional, but more risky, policy of producing aircraft to its own design. In the first few years after the war the imaginative A.W.52 flying-wing aircraft was built and an effort was made, initially, to break into the civil airline market with the Apollo. However, by the time the first Apollo flew in 1949, the first order for Meteors had been received, and this may well have taken some of the urgency out of the drive to perfect the airliner. However that may be, the fact remains that although a number of projects were sketched out, no further original Armstrong Whitworth designs appeared for another decade, until the emergence of the Argosy freighter in January 1959.

The Apollo was the last aircraft to be designed by John Lloyd who, in 1948, gave up his post as the company's chief designer to become technical director; from 1950 until he retired in 1959 he was in overall charge of Sea Slug development. Lloyd was succeeded as chief designer by H. M. Watson, and he in turn was followed by Edward Keen who took up the post in 1955. Keen had joined Armstrong Whitworth in 1928 as a technical assistant in the structural-test laboratory. In 1939 he became research engineer and deputy chief technician and in 1949 was appointed

The A.W.650 Argosy fuselage about to enter the structural-test water-tank at Bitteswell.

assistant chief designer to Watson. In his capacity of chief designer, Keen was the man responsible for the design of the Argosy freighter.

On the management side, Herbert Woodhams, the company's general manager from 1937, was elected to the board in 1941. In 1944 he was awarded a CBE for his war services and in 1950 was appointed chairman and managing director of the company, a post which he held until his retirement in 1960. He died at the age of 74 in January 1965. Walter Lockwood finished the war as works manager and was elected to the board as works director in 1950, having, in the meantime, been awarded an OBE for his war services. In 1955 he became general manager and five years later was promoted to managing director. He subsequently became managing director of the Whitworth Gloster company and finally retired in 1964 as a director of Hawker Siddeley Aviation.

The last Armstrong Whitworth aeroplane, the Argosy, emerged in January 1959. First proposals had been for a military transport, but no orders for this were forthcoming; the firm then decided, after an intensive

The Argosy G-APVH, furnished as a freighter-coach, on display at the Farnborough Air Show in 1959.

review of freighting prospects world wide, to go ahead with a civil version out of their own resources, and design work was started in September 1956. The Argosy had the distinction, rare for a British transport, of being ordered by an American operator before any had been sold to a home airline. The type was eventually purchased by British European Airways, but several further promising prospects from abroad never came to fruition and the aircraft did not achieve the success in the civil market that it would seem to have deserved. In 1959 an order for a military version, entailing extensive redesign work, was received and the first of 56 Argosies for the RAF flew in March 1961. Unfortunately, it has to be recorded that the company made a substantial loss on this military business, a fact that should be borne in mind when, as so frequently happens, the aircraft industry comes under criticism for its seemingly high profit margins.

The crew which took the first Argosy, G-AOZZ, into the air on 8 January, 1959; *left to right*: E. G. Franklin, captain; W. Else, second pilot; K. Oldfield and H. R. Hadley, flight observers.

In 1961, following the Conservative Government's White Paper on the aircraft industry, the Sir W. G. Armstrong Whitworth Aircraft Co Ltd was merged with the Gloster Aircraft Co Ltd, to form a new concern within the Hawker Siddeley Group known as Whitworth Gloster Aircraft Ltd, with, as already stated, Walter Lockwood as managing director. A further consolidation took place in 1963 which resulted in an even closer link with the one-time Avro establishment in Manchester, the formation of the Avro Whitworth Division of Hawker Siddeley Aviation.

During this period the last of the Armstrong Whitworth projects, the A.W.681, a military V/STOL transport, was under study: by the time a contract was received in September 1963, the aircraft had become a Hawker Siddeley project and its designation had changed to the HS.681.

A model of the A.W.681, later known as the H.S.681, a V/STOL military transport started in 1963 and cancelled in 1965.

But the Government had not yet finished its depredation of the aircraft industry and, in 1965, this promising design was cancelled. This action brought about the closure of the Baginton factory in July 1965, leaving the overhaul and repair department at Bitteswell as the sole survivor of the Coventry organization.

The final move in the consolidation of Hawker Siddeley's aircraft interests was taken in 1963 when it was decided to do away with the divisional organization and suppress the names of the pioneer companies on which its success had been built: the Avro Whitworth Division thus lost its identity within the compass of Hawker Siddeley Aviation, and the last remnants of the name Armstrong Whitworth, along with other famous names, disappeared forever from the aviation scene.

One of the first seven F.K.3 aircraft, a batch ordered in April 1915. In this early version the pilot occupied the rear cockpit. (*Imperial War Museum Q66206*).

The Wartime Veterans

When Frederick Koolhoven joined Armstrong Whitworth in 1914 the works at Gosforth were being prepared for B.E.2c production and he concluded, after studying the official design, that it was unnecessarily difficult to build. He therefore straightway offered to design an aircraft which, without sacrifice of performance, would be easier to produce. Rather surprisingly, in view of their unshakable faith in the B.E.2c, the authorities agreed and, in August 1915, Koolhoven went ahead with the construction of the Armstrong Whitworth version, the F.K.3.

F.K.3

The F.K.3 bore an obvious resemblance to the B.E.2c, and it is evident that Koolhoven's ideas about improving the design were concerned mainly with the structural features; indeed, his aim was, among other things, to eliminate welding and intricate metal fittings. The F.K.3, like the B.E.2c, had a slender fuselage, high aspect ratio wings, and two-bay bracing; unlike the B.E. it had more dihedral on the top plane than on the bottom. The prototype, which was test-flown by Norman Spratt, was fitted with a 70 hp Renault engine, but production aircraft were powered by the RAF 1a of 90 hp. One F.K.3, No.5519, was tested in June 1916 with the more powerful RAF 1b engine, but the tests with this aircraft were plagued by constant engine failures due to faulty pistons.

Seating arrangements in the F.K.3 prototype followed the B.E.2c precedent of placing the observer in the front in a separate cockpit underneath the top wing, but this was later changed so that both crew members were accommodated in one large cockpit, with the observer at the back where he could use his Lewis gun with much greater effect. The rear portion of the long cockpit opening was shielded by side screens extending forward to the rearmost centre-section struts, giving from the side the appearance of two separate cockpits. All the earlier production aircraft with the observer's seat in front, of which there were twelve, were afterwards modified to reverse the crew positions. The undercarriage was of unusual design in that it employed oleo shock-absorbers mounted vertically on the sides of the fuselage from which struts extended down to the ends of a divided axle. A central skid extended forward from the axle to protect the propeller in the event of a tail-high landing.

The F.K.3 was notable for its elaborate oleo undercarriage; on the right, an ingenious, but not altogether successful, attempt to provide a forward-firing gun. (*Courtesy P. Jarrett*)

No provision was made for a forward-firing gun, but the observer was provided with a Lewis gun mounted on a pillar behind his seat. As was the case with the B.E. aeroplanes, pilots used considerable ingenuity in attempts to equip themselves with some form of gun mounted to fire past the propeller, but none of the methods adopted was noticeably successful. External bomb racks fitted under the lower mainplane were capable of carrying bombs up to the weight of 112 lb but, because of weight limitations, it was usual to fly without the observer when bombs were carried.

An F.K.3, No.5552, with a 90 hp RAF 1a engine, was tested alongside a B.E.2c at the Central Flying School at Upavon in May 1916. The tests showed that the F.K.3 had a slightly better all-round performance and that it was lighter on the controls and more pleasant to handle. The report commented favourably on the crew positions, the roomy rear cockpit, and

The crew positions were reversed in the second F.K.3 production batch so that the observer could use his gun to better effect. (*Royal Aeronautical Society*)

the ease of communication between the pilot and observer even without the use of a speaking tube; it criticized the positioning of control column and rudder bar and mentioned a draught in the cockpit coming from the fuselage openings at the junction of the undercarriage struts. In general the aircraft was considered to be well designed and easy to manufacture; it was simple to control and the oleo undercarriage was adjudged to be very good, although the long shock-absorber travel allowed the wingtips to touch the ground.

Early in the F.K.3 production run the RAF 1a engine became temporarily unobtainable and, at one time, according to a contemporary

The standard F.K.3 was similar in appearance to the B.E.2c but had a rather better performance. This picture was taken at Doncaster in 1916. (*Courtesy C. A. Pike*)

account, there were about a hundred complete aircraft awaiting engines. This may have been something of an exaggeration, but there is no doubt that a crisis had arisen and, in an endeavour to overcome it, some 120 hp Beardmore engines were sent to Newcastle in the hope that they might provide a satisfactory substitute.

The fitting of this engine into the F.K.3 presented many problems: the six-cylinder inline water-cooled Beardmore engine was some twenty inches longer than the RAF 1a and, even without the radiator, it was at least 90 lb heavier. To make room for the bigger engine, the fuel tank was removed from the fuselage and a larger, streamlined tank was located under the top centre section, together with a small header tank for the radiator. When installed, the engine sat high on its bearers and virtually blocked the forward view. The all-up weight of the aircraft was increased by about 400

One of a small number of F.K.3 aircraft that were fitted temporarily with the 120 hp Beardmore engine. (*Courtesy G. Quick*)

lb, of which about 100 lb was accounted for by the additional fuel. To compensate for this extra load, the wing span of the aircraft was increased by two feet.

The first two Beardmore-powered F.K.3s (one of which was numbered 5528) were tested at Upavon in March 1916, and a report issued in May indicated that, although the climb performance was better than that of the RAF 1a version, the speed showed only a marginal improvement. That the Beardmore installation was not considered satisfactory is evident from the fact that all of the twelve aircraft so adapted were re-converted to standard as soon as RAF 1a engines again became available.

Precise production figures for the F.K.3 are difficult to ascertain because most of the official records of the time refer indiscriminately to Armstrong Whitworth biplanes without making any distinction between

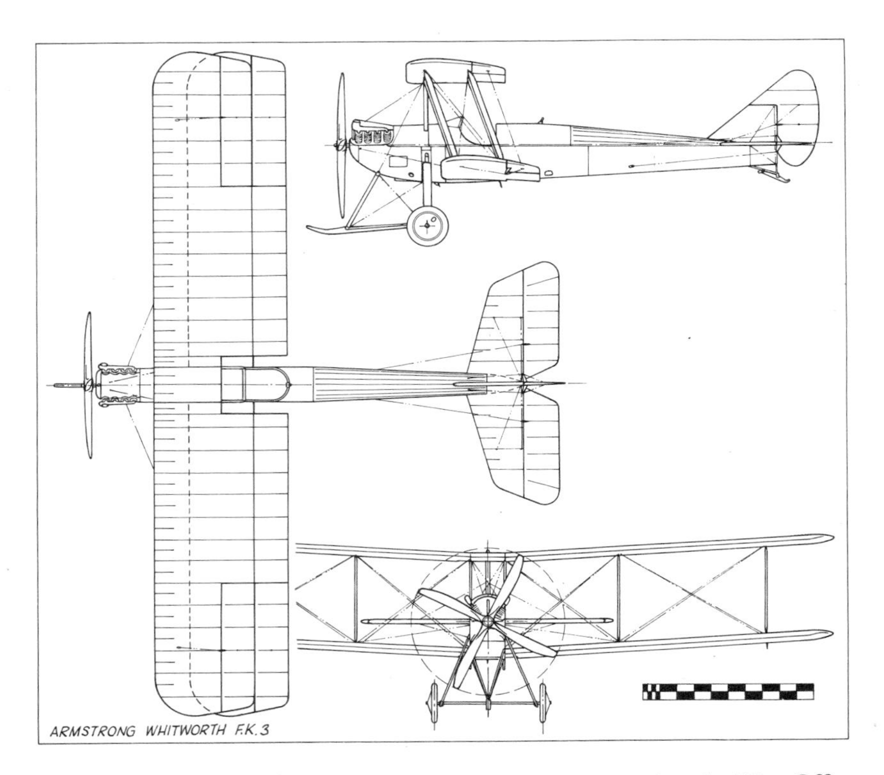

the F.K.3 and the F.K.8 which followed it. It is known that the War Office ordered one hundred and fifty F.K.3s from Armstrong Whitworth in 1915 and that the production rate is said to have reached 35 to 45 aircraft a month. In addition, orders for three hundred and fifty F.K.3s were placed with Hewlett & Blondeau of Luton, in Bedfordshire, a firm formed before the war by Gustav Blondeau, an early French aviator, and Mrs Maurice Hewlett, the wife of the author and herself the first British woman pilot.

In spite of the fact that the F.K.3 was clearly a better proposition than the B.E.2c, if only because it could defend itself more adequately if attacked from the rear, it seems that the type saw no active service on the Western Front, and the only operational unit that used it was No. 47 Squadron which served in Salonika from September 1916 until the end of the war. In that theatre the F.K.3s gave excellent service, performing a variety of duties including ground straffing, artillery spotting and bombing.

At home, the F.K.3 was used extensively for training, for which rôle its ease of handling and its ability to perform aerobatics made it eminently suitable, and it was probably the best of the British trainers until the arrival of the Avro 504. It was also used for observer training at the observer and air gunnery schools at Dymchurch, Hythe, Stirling and Turnberry. An

One of the first batch of fifty F.K.3s built by Hewlett and Blondeau Ltd. (*Royal Aeronautical Society*)

F.K.3 was used as a personal transport by Major-General Sir Sefton Brancker, later to become the first Director General of Civil Aviation. He was a brave and resourceful man but a notoriously poor pilot, and his choice of the F.K.3 was a tribute to its ease of handling.

At the end of the war, in November 1918, there were sixty-two F.K.3s

Instructor, in front, with a pupil in an F.K.3 training aircraft. (*Courtesy C. A. Pike*)

An F.K.3 with an interesting example of dazzle painting; or was it just a light-hearted decorative scheme? (*Courtesy J. M. Bruce*)

still serving with the RAF, fifty-three at home, mostly based at flying schools, and nine in the Middle East. After the war only four found their way on to the civil register: G-EABY (ex B9629) and G-EABZ (ex B9518) which operated from Porthcawl, in South Wales, flown by E. D. C. Herne. Another, G-EAEU (ex B9612), was owned by the Kingsbury Aviation Co Ltd, but was crashed after a few months of civilian life. Finally, there was G-EALK (ex B9603) which was registered in the name of L. G. Lowe and held a certificate of airworthiness until September 1920.

A noticeable feature of the F.K.3 was an engine cowling panel carrying the initials 'AW'. These were not merely painted on but heavily embossed into the metal. As a result, perhaps not surprisingly, the aircraft soon became known, in the vernacular of the day, as the 'Ack-W' and, when its successor, the F.K.8, appeared with similar embellishment, it inevitably became another 'Ack-W': from then on the two aircraft were invariably referred to as the 'Little Ack' and the 'Big Ack'.

This aircraft was one of the second batch of three hundred F.K.3s built by Hewlett and Blondeau. (*Vickers Ltd*)

F.K.8

It was presumably a coincidence that two types of aircraft designed in 1916 for corps-reconnaissance duties should both bear the number 8 as their type designation; certainly, in all other respects they could not have been more dissimilar. The Armstrong Whitworth F.K.8 and the R.E.8, designed by the Royal Aircraft Factory, were both intended as B.E.2c replacements, and it was unfortunate for the long-suffering reconnaissance pilots of the RFC that it was the inferior R.E.8 that was chosen for massive production at the expense of the more popular F.K.8. Nevertheless, the F.K.8 was produced in considerable numbers and played a significant, if unspectacular, part in the war from the beginning of 1917 until the Armistice, including actions which led to the award of two Victoria Crosses.

One of the first production F.K.8 aircraft with its characteristic oleo undercarriage, angular cowling and clumsy radiators. (*Imperial War Museum Q69244*)

Although designed for the same duties as its predecessor, the F.K.8 represented a considerable advance over the F.K.3; it was planned from the start to accommodate internally all the various trappings of army co-operation, such as cameras, which, in previous types had been hung on outside with a noticeable effect on the aircraft's performance. The result, in the F.K.8, was a fuselage of ample proportions with comfortable separate cockpits for pilot and observer.

In construction the F.K.8 was a conventional biplane with two-bay wings of equal span and greater dihedral on the top plane than on the bottom. The upper wing was built in two portions which met on the centre line at the apex of two inverted-V centre-section struts. The controls were conventional; ailerons were fitted to all four wings and the incidence of the tailplane was adjustable by means of a handwheel in the pilot's cockpit. The observer was provided with a rudimentary method of control in the

Another view of an early production F.K.8. (*Imperial War Museum Q67522*)

shape of a side-mounted stick to operate the elevators, and hand grips on the rudder control cables where they passed through the observer's cockpit. There was no means of operating the ailerons from this position but, as was shown several times in practice, it was quite possible to fly the aircraft satisfactorily without the aid of the ailerons and there were a number of occasions on which the aircraft was brought back safely by the observer after the pilot had been incapacitated.

The undercarriage was of similar design to that of the F.K.3, with oleo shock-absorbers mounted on the fuselage sides and with a central skid which, in the case of the F.K.8, was truncated at the forward supporting struts. In April 1917 the RFC headquarters in France reported that the F.K.8's undercarriage was unsatisfactory and suggested that it should be replaced by a plain V-type specimen from a Bristol Fighter. This modification proved a big improvement and No.1 Aircraft Depot proceeded to convert a number of aircraft until, in the following July, the supply of Bristol Fighter undercarriages dried up and B.E.2c undercarriages had to be used instead. The gauge of tube used and the angle of the V was the same in both types, but the rear legs of the B.E. landing gear were shorter. This seems to have been of no great significance. Later, a modified type of undercarriage with a wider V appeared, and this may have been the production version fitted by the makers. The simpler type of landing gear improved the climb performance and raised the top speed by about 5 mph.

There is a widely-held opinion that the first production F.K.8s were powered by the 120 hp Beardmore engine, but in the light of recent research this belief is now thought to have been due to a misunderstanding. As already mentioned, both Armstrong Whitworth and the Service authorities were unusually lax in differentiating between the F.K.3 and the F.K.8, and this seems to have led to some confusion over the powerplants as well as over production figures. The mistake probably arose in the first place because the small batch of F.K.3s fitted with the 120 hp Beardmore engine, as described earlier, were loosely referred to as 'Armstrong Whitworth 120 hp biplanes' and, because this variant was little known, it was naturally assumed that this description applied to the F.K.8. Apart from a statement in *Jane's All the World's Aircraft* for 1918 which was repeated in the following year and which may well have been the original source of the misunderstanding, there is a marked absence of direct evidence in favour of the 120 hp engine, and all the indications are that the F.K.8 was powered by the 160 hp Beardmore from the start.

During the course of production, other engines were tried out experimentally in the F.K.8. Two aircraft, B214 and B215, were fitted with variants of the twelve-cylinder air-cooled RAF 4 engine, the type which had, by its early unreliability, added to the unpopularity of the R.E.8. Another aircraft, A2696, was fitted with a Lorraine-Dietrich engine of 150 hp, but none of these engines bestowed any significant improvement on the F.K.8's performance and there was no move to adopt them as standard.

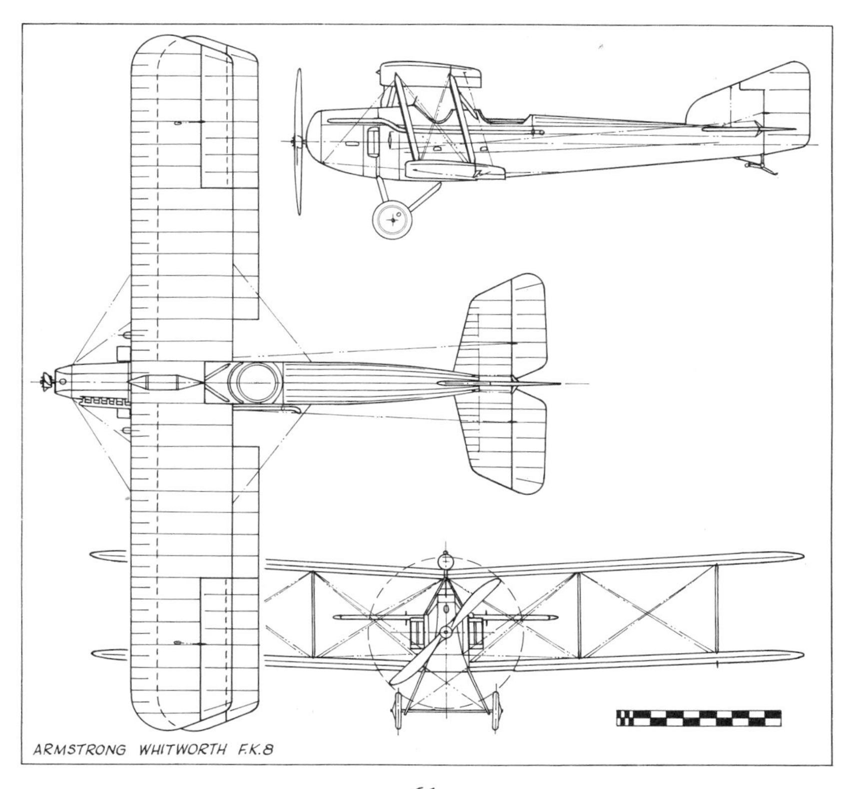

An F.K.8, A2696, fitted experimentally with a 150 hp Lorraine-Dietrich engine. (*Royal Aeronautical Society*)

As first produced, the F.K.8 had a somewhat angular form of engine cowling, which gave the aircraft a vaguely Germanic appearance, and a crude form of radiator consisting of honeycomb blocks mounted on the sides of the fuselage and extending upwards and inwards to meet at a point in front of the top wing. This radiator proved to be inefficient in service and, as a result of a flood of complaints from the Western Front, a new type was adopted. This new radiator, which consisted of two elements mounted one each side of the fuselage, proved more effective as a radiator as well as improving the view from the cockpit. With the new compact type of radiator, a more rounded form of cowling was introduced, changes which resulted in a marked improvement in the appearance of the machine.

Another complaint voiced by Service pilots concerned the distortion of the view caused by the mirage effect of the fumes from the stub exhaust

Another experimental installation, an F.K.8 with a 150 hp RAF 4a engine. (*Imperial War Museum MH3218*)

pipes. To overcome this, some enterprising officers of No.10 Squadron in France devised and constructed a stack-type exhaust pipe which carried the fumes over the top wing. Permission was granted by RFC HQ in France for tests to be made with this exhaust system, but a warning was given that the large side area of the stack might affect the directional stability of the aircraft, and the advice was added that '. . . pilot ought to be warned not to do any short turns near the ground with it'. In fact, tests showed that there was no deterioration in directional stability, and the pilots of No.10 Squadron were favourably impressed with the improvement in visibility and the fact that the after part of the aircraft was no longer smothered in oil: it was, however, noted that the design would have to be strengthened to withstand vibration. In the end this design was not adopted, but a modified system, consisting of a long exhaust pipe extending to a position aft of the observer's seat, was introduced.

An F.K.8 with the improved type of engine cowling, and, on the right, an experimental exhaust system devised by No.10 Squadron, RFC, in France to eliminate the distorting mirage effect from the open exhaust pipes.

The first flight of the F.K.8 took place in May 1916, and in the middle of the following month an F.K.8 numbered A411, which was almost certainly the prototype, was flown by a Service pilot from Newcastle to the Central Flying School at Upavon for official tests. The journey took two days, 16 and 17 June, and the pilot reported favourably on the aircraft's handling qualities. The tests by the CFS pilots were carried out on 18 and 19 June, and the top speed of the aircraft, the average of six runs over a measured course, was recorded as 98·4 mph. In the official report the

F.K.8's performance was compared with that called for in the specification; it achieved 93 mph at 8,000 ft, as against the 100 mph called for, and it climbed to that height in 20 min, 4 min longer than the specified time. A criticism was made that the tailskid was not strong enough; later this fault was the cause of numerous complaints from the Western Front and, in 1917, the rudder shape was modified to avoid damage to its base when the skid broke. The test pilot also noted that when the aircraft was trimmed to fly level at 70 mph, it glided fast at 90 mph when the throttle was closed and that it would be an advantage if this tendency could be corrected. To this rather naïve comment was added the remark that the aircraft would be good for reconnaissance but poor for bombing. Later, a cut-out between the spars at the root of the lower wing was provided to improve the pilot's view directly downwards. After tests at Upavon the F.K.8, A411, was returned to the makers for experimental work.

The F.K.8 in its final form, with a revised cowling, a V-type undercarriage and more compact radiators. (*Vickers Ltd*)

For reasons already stated when dealing with the F.K.3, production figures for the F.K.8 are not now readily obtainable. The first production order for the F.K.8 was apparently that placed at the beginning of August 1916 with Armstrong Whitworth under contract 87/A/508, and such records as are available indicate that this, and two other contracts placed with Armstrong Whitworth, covered a total of 701 aircraft, not including the prototype. The F.K.8 was also built in large numbers by Angus Sanderson & Co, another Newcastle firm which had previously co-operated with Armstrong Whitworth by building bodies for their motor-cars. Orders for some 950 F.K.8s were placed with this firm, which brings the total number of F.K.8s ordered to at least 1,652. By the end of 1917 between eighty and one hundred F.K.8s a month were coming off the Armstrong Whitworth line at Gosforth, and the type continued in production there until July 1918, by which time arrangements had been made for Angus Sanderson to continue with F.K.8 production while Armstrong Whitworth turned their attention to building the Bristol Fighter.

The first production F.K.8s were emerging from the Armstrong Whitworth factory at Gosforth at the end of 1916, and there are reports of individual aircraft being with the RFC in France before the year ended. However, the first squadron to be fully equipped with the type was No.35, which received its F.K.8s before proceeding to France in January 1917. Then came a gap until June, when No.2 Squadron, already in France, had its B.E.s replaced by F.K.8s, which continued to be the squadron's equipment until the Armistice. Other squadrons in France which used the F.K.8 through to 1918 were Nos. 8, 10 and 82, while in the Near East the type, among others, was used by No.17 Squadron in Salonika and by No.142 in Palestine. The F.K.8 also formed part of the mixed equipment used in 1916 and 1917 for home defence by Nos. 36, 47 and 50 Squadrons. It was an F.K.8 of No.50 Squadron, flown by 2nd Lieut F. A. D. Grace and 2nd Lieut G. Murray, that scored one of the few victories against a raiding Gotha, shot down in the North Sea on 7 July, 1917. The F.K.8 was also used quite extensively for training at home, particularly in the specialized arts of army co-operation, photography, map reading and reconnaissance.

In France the F.K.8 undertook a multitude of duties including night and day bombing, reconnaissance, artillery spotting, photography, trench straffing and even the dropping of supplies to forward troops. It was, like the B.E.s before it, a maid of all work, but, unlike them, it was capable of putting up a fair degree of resistance when attacked, and had relatively good performance. The observer, with a Scarff mounting for his Lewis gun, had a good field of fire, while the pilot could operate a forward-firing, synchronized Vickers machine-gun. This defensive armament was used to good effect on 29 November, 1917, when Lieuts Pattern and Leicester, after a prolonged fight with five enemy fighters, succeeded in shooting down the German 'Ace' Erwin Böhme.

The battle-worthiness of the F.K.8 was demonstrated on two other occasions which, as already mentioned, resulted in the award of the Victoria Cross to two pilots. On 27 March, 1918, 2nd Lieut A. A. McLeod of No.2 Squadron with Lieut A. W. Hammond as his observer, flying in B5773, were attacked by eight Fokker Triplanes. In spite of being repeatedly wounded, between them the British pair accounted for four of the enemy before their aircraft, already severely damaged, caught fire. Lieut McLeod was forced by the flames to climb out of his cockpit but while standing on the wing managed to control the aircraft by manipulating the control column with one hand, side-slipping away from the flames and directing it towards the Allied lines; meanwhile Hammond, who had been wounded no less than six times, continued to hold the enemy at bay with his machine-gun. In spite of his wounds and the flames, McLeod succeeded in bringing his aircraft to a comparatively soft crash landing in no-man's land from which both officers were rescued, still under heavy fire, by the infantry. The second F.K.8 pilot to be awarded the Victoria Cross was Captain (later Air Commodore) F. M. F. West of No.8 Squadron who,

The prototype F.K.8, A411, undergoes a test to destruction at the Royal Aircraft Factory, Farnborough. The load was applied with loose sand heaped on the underside of the mainplanes. (*Courtesy P. Moyes*)

with his observer Lieut J. A. G. Haslam, was returning from a low-level bombing attack on German gun positions when his aircraft was attacked by six fighters. Although severely wounded in the legs, West managed to fly back to the Allied side of the lines and then refused to allow himself to be taken to hospital until he was able to pass on some important information about enemy troop concentrations.

The sturdy F.K.8 continued to serve on the Western Front until the war ended. At that time there were 182 of them in France, with 320 aircraft in reserve or under repair at home. Outside Europe there were fifty-six F.K.8s in Egypt and Palestine, forty-four in Salonika and two in the North

West Province of India. In Great Britain there were sixty-nine aircraft on home airfields, mostly with training units.

After the war's end, the F.K.8 quickly faded from the scene in the RAF, and only eight found their way on to the British civil register; of these, three were sold abroad while the others were all crashed or otherwise written off before the end of 1920. The F.K.8's sole claim to fame in civil aviation is that of flying the first regular airmail service to be operated by a small Australian company, Queensland and Northern Territory Aerial Services Ltd, later to become better known as QANTAS. Formed in 1920 by two ex Australian Flying Corps pilots, W. Hudson Fysh and P. J. M. McGinnis, the company had been operating a successful hire service from their base at Longreach using a mixed fleet consisting of an Avro 504K with a Sunbeam Dyak engine, a D.H.4, an Avro Triplane, and two F.K.8s bearing the registrations G-AUCF and G-AUDE.

In 1922 the company was given a contract to operate a mail service between Charleville and Cloncurry with principal stops at Blackall, Longreach and Winton, railheads all connecting with the coast railway but not directly with each other. The route distance of 577 miles was scheduled to be flown in two days, with a night stop about half way at Longreach. The first service, which left Charleville at 5.30 a.m. on 2 November, 1922, was flown by McGinnis in the F.K.8 G-AUDE and carried a mail package containing 106 letters; it arrived at Longreach at 10.15 a.m., having averaged 82 mph excluding stops. The Longreach–Cloncurry sector was scheduled to be flown on the following day by Hudson Fysh using the other F.K.8, G-AUCF, but, due to a slight drop in engine revolutions, this aircraft failed to take-off in the high temperature and G-AUDE was pressed into service again. This time the take-off was successful and the aircraft was soon on its way carrying the mail and one passenger, an 87-year-old settler named Alexander Kennedy.

The F.K.8 used by Queensland and Northern Territory Aerial Services Ltd, later Qantas Empire Airways Ltd, to fly Australia's first air mail service. The flight took place on 2 and 3 November, 1922, between Charleville and Cloncurry. (*Qantas*)

The F.K.8, G-AUDE, arrives with the mail at Winton on 3 November, 1922. The pilot was Wilmot Hudson Fysh, later Sir Wilmot. The date on the photograph is wrong. (*Qantas*)

The F.K.8s gave good service to QANTAS despite the fact that the rate of climb seldom exceeded 500 feet a minute and was often considerably less in the full heat of the day. At first some trouble was experienced with engines overheating, but this was cured by the fitting of larger radiators and a header tank which served to condense the steam if the radiator water did boil.

Thus, both in war and in peace, the F.K.8 carved for itself a positive niche in history for which it has received scant recognition, either in the annals of the time or since: perhaps it was its very qualities of stolid strength and reliability and its consistent but unspectacular performance which made everyone accept it and then forget about it.

F.K.3

Dimensions: Span 40 ft (12·19 m); length 29 ft. (8·84 m); height 11 ft 11 in (3·63 m); wing area 457 sq ft (42·46 sq m).

	90 hp RAF 1A	*120 hp Beardmore*
Max weight:	2,056 lb (933 kg)	2,447 lb (1,110 kg)
Empty weight:	1,386 lb (629 kg)	1,682 lb (763 kg)
Max speed		
Sea level:	89 mph (143 km/hr)	91 mph (146 km/hr)
6,500 ft (1,981 m)	81 mph (130 km/hr)	84 mph (135 km/hr)
Stalling speed:	48 mph (77 km/hr)	56 mph (90 km/hr)
Climb		
to 6,500 ft (1,981 m):	26·5 min	19 min
to 10,000 ft (3,048 m):	48·9 min	35 min
Service ceiling:	12,000 ft (3,658 m)	12,000 ft (3,658 m)
Endurance:	3 hr	3 hr

F.K.8

Dimensions: Span 43 ft 6 in (13·26 m); length 31 ft 5 in (9·58 m); height 10 ft 11 in (3·33 m); wing area 540 sq ft (50·17 sq m).

	160 hp Beardmore	*150 hp Lorraine Dietrich*	*150 hp RAF 4A*
Max weight:	2,811 lb (1,275 kg)	2,816 lb (1,277 kg)	2,827 lb (1,282 kg)
Empty weight:	1,916 lb (869 kg)	1,936 lb (878 kg)	1,980 lb (898 kg)
Max speed			
Sea level:	95 mph (153 km/hr)	—	—
6,500 ft (1,981 m):	—	89 mph (143 km/hr)	94 mph (151 km/hr)
8,000 ft (2,438 m):	88 mph (142 km/hr)	—	—
10,000 ft (3,048 m):	—	83 mph (134 km/hr)	89 mph (143 km/hr)
Climb to			
6,500 ft (1,981 m):	15·4 min	16·5 min	16·4 min
8,000 ft (2,438 m):	20 min	—	—
10,000 ft (3,048 m):	27·8 min	33·2 min	32 min
Service ceiling:	13,000 ft (3,962 m)	11,000 ft (3,353 m)	12,000 ft (3,658 m)
Fuel capacity:	50 Imp gal (227 lt)	50 Imp gal (227 lt)	50 Imp gal (227 lt)
Endurance:	3 hr	4 hr	3 hr

The first version of the Armstrong Whitworth triplane, probably known as the F.K.5. It is believed that this aircraft never flew. (*Courtesy J. M. Bruce*)

The Koolhoven Multiplanes

In the early stages of the 1914–18 war, before the pattern of aerial warfare had developed, there was a school of thought in Great Britain which argued the merits of the 'flying battleship' or 'aerial destroyer'. This concept, which envisaged a large aeroplane with a multiplicity of guns having a wide field of fire, arose perhaps from the nation's deep-seated naval traditions. The proponents of the theory gave little regard to the virtues of speed or manoeuvrability, the idea apparently being that the aircraft would proceed in a dignified fashion, possibly in line ahead, firing broadsides at the enemy, who, it might be supposed, would adopt similar tactics. This may be extending the analogy too far, but the fact remains that considerable effort was expended in devising large fighter aeroplanes in which performance took second place to armament. Needless to say, the concept proved unsound, and it was the more adaptable fixed-gun fighter which dominated the scene where the battles were actually fought.

The large multi-seat-fighter notion certainly produced some odd-looking aircraft, with both Sopwith and Vickers trying their hand at the idea, but perhaps the strangest of all were the two Armstrong Whitworth triplanes produced to the designs of Frederick Koolhoven. The first of these featured two machine-gun nacelles mounted on the top surface of the middle wing, which was considerably longer than the other two. In order to provide the best possible field of fire for the two gunners, the nacelles projected well forward of the tractor propeller, which was situated but a few inches ahead of the wing leading edge. The pilot was placed behind the wings where his view in any direction, except upwards and backwards, must have been minimal. The engine was the new 250 hp Rolls-Royce twelve-cylinder unit which later became known as the Eagle. The undercarriage, which, like the rest of the aircraft, was highly unconventional, consisted of a single centrally placed shock-absorber strut terminating in two closely-spaced wheels, lateral stability being provided by a small single wheel under each wingtip. The tail was supported by a skid carried on long struts emanating from the underside of the fuselage at a point just aft of the wings. The whole aircraft seemed ill-balanced and gave the impression of frailty, and it is, perhaps, not surprising that Fairbairn-Crawford, the works manager, is on record as saying that he refused permission for it to be flown.

The rebuilt triplane, probably the F.K.6, was designed as an escort fighter and Zeppelin destroyer. (*Vickers Ltd*)

Subsequently, the design was re-vamped to conform to a requirement initiated by the War Office for a multi-seat escort fighter and Zeppelin destroyer. Using the same type of Rolls-Royce engine, the new triplane was larger than its predecessor and the span of all three wings was greater than before, with the overhang of the centre wing being less pronounced. A second bay was added to the wing structure, and the bracing appeared to be more substantial. The engine and propeller projected ahead of the wing in the conventional tractor position, and the pilot, again seated behind the wings, had a marginally better view but still not one calculated to arouse much enthusiasm. The undercarriage was short and carried a cross-axle with two pairs of wheels; the track was narrow and ground clearance for the lower wing was small. The two gun nacelles, this time attached to the underside of the middle wing, may have been designed to take the Davis gun. In April 1916 Armstrong Whitworth were supplied with two wooden mock-ups of the 6-pounder and the 2-pounder models for fitment to '. . . a large aeroplane now under construction for the War Office', which can only have been the triplane. Four prototypes of the second triplane had been ordered in March 1916, but only No.7838 was built, it having by then become obvious that the large, ponderous fighting aeroplane was a mistake. Little is known about the test flights carried out by Peter Legh,

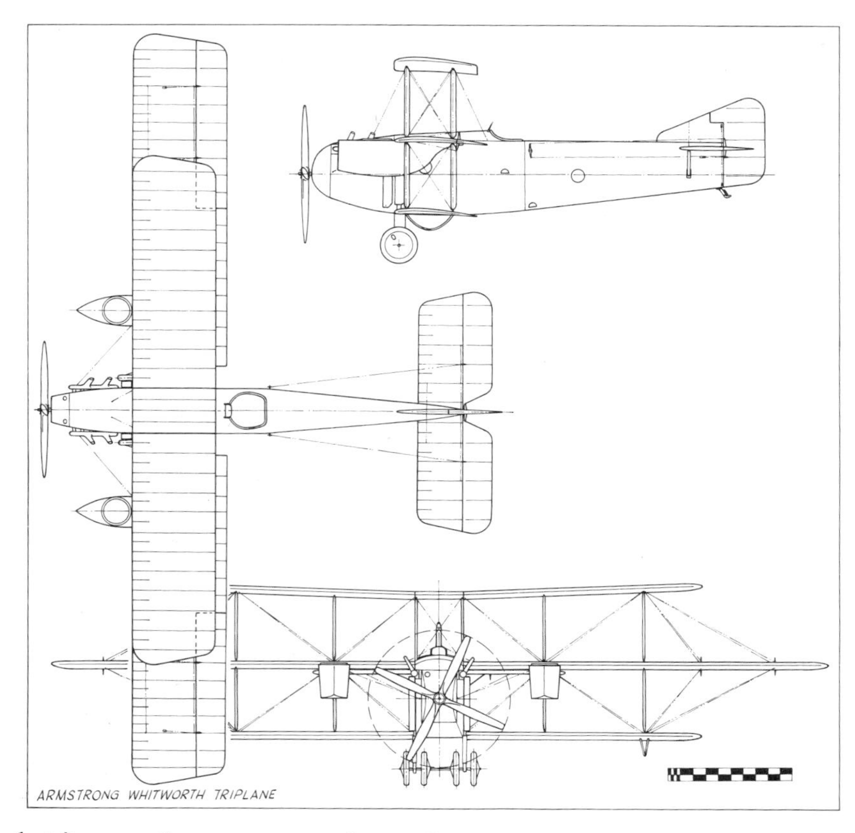

but it seems they were somewhat perfunctory, with the performance failing to come up to expectations; in any case, interest in the project had already evaporated and the type was soon abandoned.

The place occupied by the triplanes in the F.K. series remains a mystery: both have been referred to as the F.K.12, but all the evidence points to the conclusion that this number is wrong. The comparative immaturity of the triplane designs would seem to indicate that they pre-

Another view of the one and only F.K.6 triplane No.7838. (*Vickers Ltd*)

dated the more workmanlike and more modern looking F.K.8 biplane and the subsequent quadruplanes which, for all their eccentricity, were more in accord with the designs of the later war years. More conclusive, perhaps, is the fact that both triplanes were designed before the adoption of the machine-gun interrupter gear, whereas the quadruplanes were clearly laid out with this type of armament in view. The true sequence of the F.K. numbers may never now be discovered, but the best guess is that the airship car, previously mentioned, which was an adaptation of the F.K.3 fuselage, was the F.K.4, with the two versions of the triplane following as the F.K.5 and the F.K.6.

The prototype F.K.9 quadruplane after being modified. (*Royal Aeronautical Society*)

F.K.9 and F.K.10

The quadruplane which followed the F.K.8 was built in two forms, a prototype, which underwent considerable modification, and a production version of which, however, only a handful were actually built. The production model was certainly designated the F.K.10, and it is more than likely that the earlier version was called the F.K.9, although this nomenclature lacks positive confirmation. The quadruplane, which was probably built as a private venture, was designed to meet a requirement referred to in an official report as 'Spec. No.2c', for a two-seater fighter. At the time of its design the Sopwith Triplane was enjoying a considerable success; with its excellent manoeuvrability and high rate of climb, it had established a formidable reputation as a fighter, especially among enemy pilots. The prowess credited to the Sopwith, and to its equally successful antagonist, the Fokker Triplane, resulted in the production of a crop of triplanes, both friend and foe, most of which were, incidentally, without distinction. Koolhoven, perhaps, hoped to go one better on the principle that you cannot have too much of a good thing, and his new aircraft materialized with four heavily-staggered wings ranging from well below the fuselage to high above the pilot's head. The fuselage was comparatively slender, with pilot's seat situated immediately behind the rotary engine, from where his view, except rearwards and upwards, was virtually unobstructed. The observer's cockpit was placed immediately behind the third wing from the bottom, which itself was positioned just above the fuselage. This wing had no centre section and the leading edges protruded forward on either side of, and slightly above, the pilot's head. The wing structure was supported by plank-type centre-section and interplane struts with wire bracing, while the tailplane was adjustable and carried unbalanced elevators. There was a small fixed fin below the fuselage but none above, and the rudder was balanced. The undercarriage looked rather frail and consisted of two single wire-braced struts with a cross-axle and rubber-cord shock-absorbers. The wings of the F.K.9, as it first emerged, had no dihedral and the ailerons were set well in from the tapered wingtips. After flight trials the aircraft was modified with new wings whose ailerons extended to the wingtips and were rounded with no taper.

The final version of the quadruplane, the F.K.10. (*Vickers Ltd*)

The modified quadruplane, powered by a 110 hp Clerget engine, was tested at Upavon aerodrome, then the home of the Central Flying School, and was reported as being light to handle and easy to manoeuvre, but with a cockpit so cramped that the full movement of the control column, particularly from side to side, was not possible; in addition, the wheel for adjusting the tailplane trim was said to be inaccessible. The stability of the aircraft in all three senses was stated to be good, but the pilot complained of being smothered with oil and, not unnaturally, suggested that the cowling should be redesigned. During the trials it was found necessary to true-up the fuselage and undercarriage after every landing, however gentle, because of, in the words of the report, '. . . the absence of forward undercarriage struts . . . so that on landing the full weight comes on the two side bracing wires of the nacelle'. The test figures showed that the top speed at ground level was just short of 100 mph, and that at 6,700 ft it had fallen off to 94 mph. It took 12½ min to climb to 6,000 ft and the ceiling was about 13,000 ft, while the endurance was quoted as barely three hours. The report concluded that the performance was far below that called for in the specification.

In spite of the disappointing performance of the first aircraft, a second, much modified, version was built. This was, indisputably, designated the F.K. 10 and it had a more powerful Clerget engine rated at 130 hp. It had a similar wing arrangement but with the span increased by six inches, and, in order to give more room for the crew, the fuselage was both deeper and wider. The tail surfaces were also modified; instead of the fixed tailplane and no upper vertical fin, the second aeroplane had balanced elevators without fixed surfaces and vertical fins above and below the fuselage supporting a conventional, if rather small, rudder. In an attempt to overcome the undercarriage weakness of the previous aircraft, the longerons, from the undercarriage struts forward, were strengthened with plywood, but the structure was still not strong enough and it was reported that the diagonal struts within the fuselage, designed to take the compression loads from the undercarriage, were bent when the aircraft was delivered for official trials.

These trials were undertaken in March 1917, and the performance

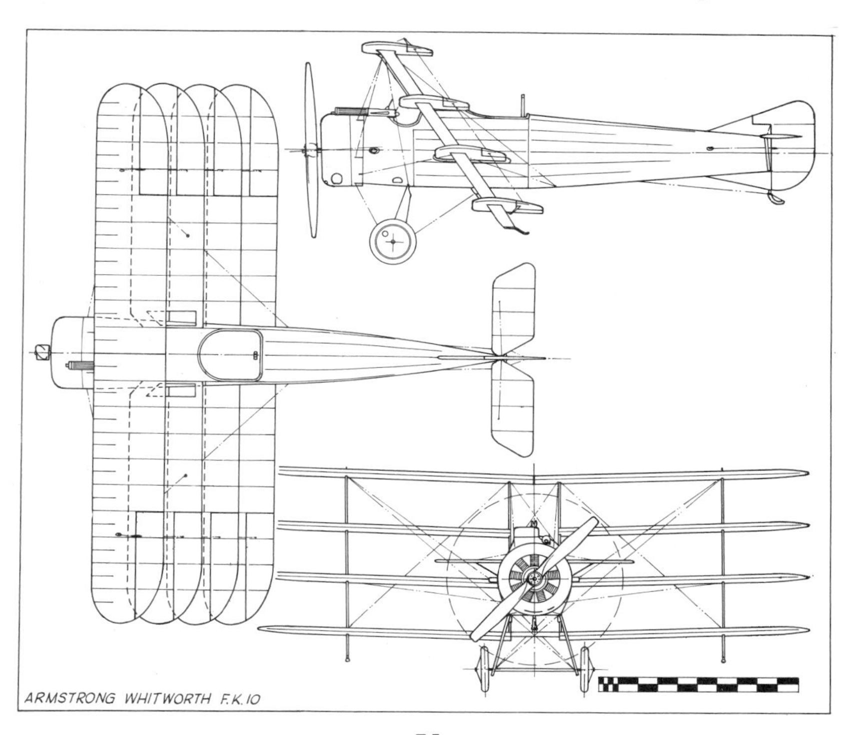
ARMSTRONG WHITWORTH F.K.10

Another view of the F.K.10 quadruplane. (*Vickers Ltd*)

seems to have been slightly inferior to that of the lower-powered version. This may have been due to the fatter fuselage, but it is equally possible that the difference between the two aircraft arose because of variations in piloting skill and because of the somewhat imprecise methods of performance measurement then in use. The test pilot reported that the machine handled well, with good controllability and with very little tendency to spin. The take-off and landing distance was measured as 80 yards. As might be expected with an all-moving tailplane, the aircraft was somewhat unstable longitudinally, and the pilot noted that the controls could not, therefore, be left alone. In other respects the aircraft was considered easy to fly. Minor criticisms were that the windscreen was inefficient and that it was necessary to remove the engine cowling in order to replenish the oil tank. Like its predecessor, the second aircraft was reported as having a performance below that specified.

In view of the poor performance, an order for fifty F.K.10s which had been placed with Angus Sanderson and Co was cancelled in March 1917, and the serial numbers A8950 to A8999 set aside for this batch were reallocated. However, small batches of the F.K.10 were produced by Armstrong Whitworth, Angus Sanderson and the Phoenix Dynamo Manufacturing Co. Most of the production aircraft had the 130 hp Clerget engine, but at least one of those built by Armstrong Whitworth was powered by a Le Rhône engine of 110 hp. There is some uncertainty about the numbers of quadruplanes actually built: two, with the serial numbers A5212 and A5213, were ordered from Armstrong Whitworth, one of which may have been the original F.K.9, and a further five, numbered B3996 to B4000, were ordered from Angus Sanderson, but it is not known whether all were delivered. Three more, N511, N512 and N514, were built for the Royal Naval Air Service, the first two by Phoenix Dynamo and the third by Armstrong Whitworth. The missing number, N513, was originally allotted to an Angus Sanderson F.K.10 which was cancelled, and there is some evidence that this number was subsequently re-allocated to an Armstrong Whitworth biplane, presumably an F.K.8, with a Sunbeam engine: this aircraft is said to have force-landed near Beverley on 7 April, 1917, while *en route* from Newcastle to Martlesham Heath.

In spite of the official test reports, which indicated that the aircraft at least handled reasonably well, pilots seem to have been suspicious of the F.K.10 from the start. It certainly had a rather daunting appearance, and no doubt this, coupled with the maintenance problems, seems to have resulted in the few available aircraft being little used. The two RNAS machines, N511 and N514, were reported to be at Manston aerodrome in April and May 1917, but they were apparently considered to be unsafe and by the late summer had been grounded. The RFC aircraft may have lasted rather longer, but they, too, were never taken seriously and eventually, in July 1917, were handed over to the technical department for use as ground targets. Thus, the F.K.10 faded from the scene with, apparently, few regrets.

An F.K.10 built by the Phoenix Dynamo Manufacturing Co of Bradford. (*Imperial War Museum HU1825*)

That Koolhoven's interest in the multiplane arrangement was not altogether damped by the failure of his three- and four-winged prodigies is evident from drawings that exist showing a design, known perhaps as the F.K.11, which had no less than fifteen narrow wings, each about 18-inches wide, attached to an F.K.10 fuselage. This project was never built, but the 'Venetian blind' arrangement of aerofoils had been tried before. One of the first to toy with the idea was Horatio Phillips, who tried out an apparatus with forty slats (if contemporary drawings are to be believed) on a circular track at Harrow in 1893. After the 1914–18 war the idea was revived by H. G. Leigh who, in collaboration with Bert Hinkler of the Avro company, fitted a modified form of the slatted-wing arrangement to the fuselage of an Avro Baby.

Armstrong Whitworth Triplane (Revised)
Dimensons: Span 62 ft (18·90 m); length 37 ft (11·8 m); height 17 ft (5·18 m).

F.K.9
Dimensions: Span 27 ft 9 in (8·46 m); length 25 ft 10 in (7·87 m); height 11 ft 4 in (3·45 m); wing area 355 sq ft (32·98 sq m).

F.K.10
Dimensions: Span 28 ft 3 in (8·61 m); length 25 ft 6 in (7·77 m); height 11 ft 6 in (3·50 m); wing area 361 sq ft (33·54 sq m).

	F.K.9 *110 hp Clerget*	**F.K.10** *130 hp Clerget*
Max weight:	2,038 lb (924 kg)	2,019 lb (916 kg)
Empty weight:	1,226 lb (556 kg)	1,236 lb (561 kg)
Max speed		
Sea level:	100 mph (161 km/hr)	—
3,000 ft (914 m):	—	95 mph (153 km/hr)
6,500 ft (1,981 m):	94 mph (151 km/hr)	84 mph (135 km/hr)
10,000 ft (3,048 m):	87 mph (140 km/hr)	74 mph (119 km/hr)
Climb to		
6,000 ft (1,829 m):	12·5 min	—
6,500 ft (1,981 m):	—	15·8 min
10,000 ft (3,048 m):	25 min	37·2 min
Service ceiling:	13,000 ft (3,962 m)	10,000 ft (3,048 m)
Endurance:	3 hr	2½ hr

The F.M.4 Armadillo, of which only one was built, was designed to the A1(a) fighter specification. (*Vickers Ltd*)

The Murphy Fighters

F.M.4 Armadillo

After Koolhoven left Armstrong Whitworth in 1917 to go to the British Aerial Transport Co, the design duties at Gosforth were undertaken by Frank Murphy, who had been the manager of the aeroplane department under Fairbairn-Crawford. The first aircraft to be built to Murphy's design was the F.M.4, the Armadillo, a single-seat fighter, powered by a Bentley B.R.2 rotary engine and fashioned to meet the requirements of the Air Board specification A1(a). The Armadillo was not ordered by the Government although in January 1918 the Air Board gave Armstrong Whitworth a licence '... to build two machines at their own risk and expense'. This was done because Armstrong Whitworth had expressed a wish to check the capabilities of the design staff with a view to taking up original design work once more. Thus, although the F.M.4 was nominally a contender for the fighter contract, it was, in fact, never seriously considered for this either by the company or by the Air Board. Indeed, officials of the Board were less than enthusiastic about the F.M.4, and an internal memorandum dated 26 February, 1918, stated that '... this machine is hardly likely to come into competition with other B.R.2 scouts'. In the event, the Sopwith Snipe had been ordered into production by the time the Armadillo appeared.

Although the licence specified two aircraft, only one, X19, was completed: the second aircraft, X20, being abandoned after it had reached a fairly advanced stage of construction. The first aircraft was designed to have three sets of interchangeable wings, two of which were designated 'AW No.1 Camber' and 'AW No.2 Camber', while the third set was of RAF 14 section and was of reduced span with a shorter overhang at the tips. The second F.M.4, besides other minor alterations, was to have had two sets of wings of RAF 14 and RAF 15 section. In appearance the Armadillo was a squat, two-bay biplane with a fuselage filling the rather narrow gap. The wings were of equal span, but the bottom wing, which alone had a slight dihedral angle, was narrower than the top. The 230 hp B.R.2 rotary engine was housed in a bulbous cowling set low on the fuselage with a top fairing housing two Vickers synchronized machine-guns. This also served to fair off the joint between the low-set cowling and the top line of the fuselage. Provision was also made for a hand-operated Lewis gun which could be elevated to fire forwards and upwards over the propeller. The pilot was seated just ahead of the trailing edge of the wing with his eyes slightly above the level of the wing; both upper and lower wings had a trailing-edge cut-out to improve the downward view. For the same reason the sides of the cockpit were also cut away quite deeply on either side, and this led to a discontinuity in the top longerons; to compensate for this the sides of the fuselage around the cockpit were covered with three-ply wood. For additional strength, the forward portion of the fuselage was reinforced with two channel-section duralumin girders which also supported the fuel tanks and the pilot's seat. The V-struts of the Armadillo's undercarriage were of rather light section and were later replaced by somewhat stronger members.

The design of the F.M.4 was completed in the autumn of 1917, and an officer from the Air Board inspected the mock-up in December 1917. At that time the bottom wing was carried on struts some ten inches below the bottom longerons. The inspector suggested that the fuselage should be made deeper to fill the gap between the wings; he also suggested a re-arrangement of the guns, moving the Lewis gun from the centreline so as not to interfere with the fitting of a windscreen and a gun sight. The licence for the two aircraft was issued on 7 January, 1918, and construction of the first aircraft went ahead quickly; by the middle of the month Armstrong Whitworth were pressing the Board for an early delivery of the B.R.2 engine.

During January 1918 the airframe of X19 was inspected by Commander Ogilvie of the Air Board and sometime in February he criticized the structural design, stating that in his opinion '. . . the machine is somewhat weak all over'. He added that the compression ribs were weak, the attachment of the tailplane front spar was unsatisfactory and the spindling of the wing spars had been continued too far towards the points of support. Correspondence on these matters went to and fro between the Air Board and the company during February and March 1918 (one letter from the Board referred to the aircraft as the 'armoured Dillo') until, at the beginning of March, the company wrote stating that the spars and

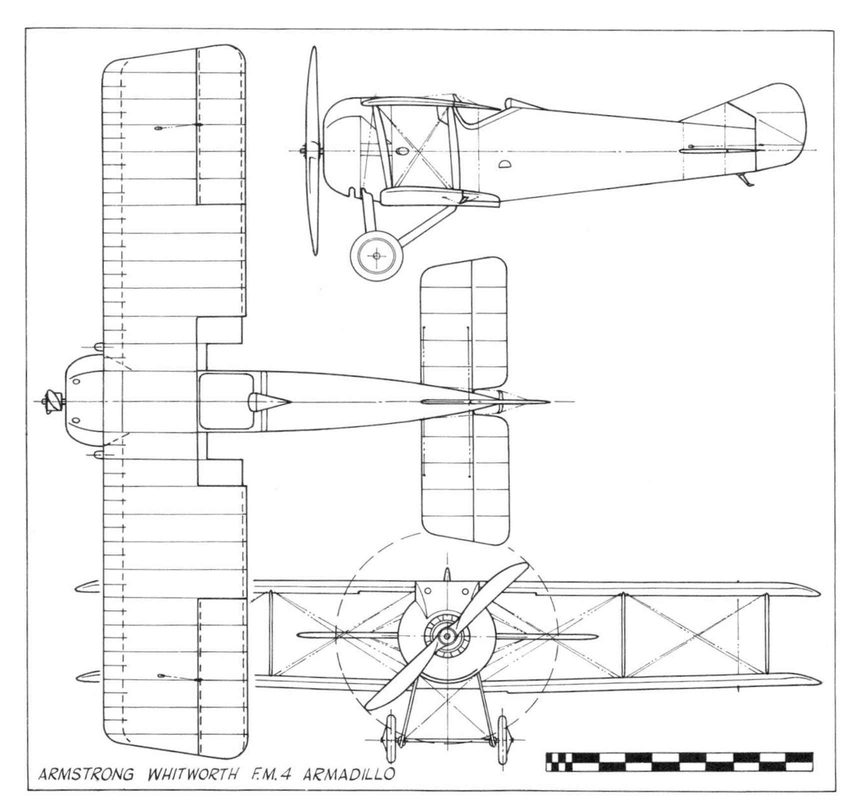

internal bracing of the mainplanes had been strengthened, the bracing of the fuselage modified and the interplane struts and front outer lift wires increased in section. Other modifications included an alteration to the tailplane bracing and the fitting of a stronger main tube in the rudder.

Following these modifications and a further inspection by Ogilvie, Armstrong Whitworth were informed towards the end of March 1918, that the aircraft was now up to strength everywhere and that it was passed for experimental flying. Whether the previous criticisms were in fact justified will never be known, but the fact remains that from a structural point of view the Armadillo seems to have had some merit. This is evident from the fact that in April the Air Ministry's stress expert, Professor A. J. Sutton Pippard, noted that the structure weight of the aircraft, which worked out at 26 per cent of the total, was unusually low. Following this assessment, Armstrong Whitworth were asked to supply a detailed break-down of the Armadillo's weight. This analysis, arrived at by weighing each component, gave a weight of 1,730 lb; after a further study of the design, Pippard stated that he could find no trace of weakness in the structure and

The Armadillo with a strengthened undercarriage and other modifications made in the spring of 1918. (*Imperial War Museum HU1830*)

suggested that the low weight could be due to the small gap, the light interplane struts and the absence of a centre section.

As was so often the case with new aircraft at this time, the first flight was delayed pending delivery of an engine; this was eventually received in March 1918 and on the 18th of the month Armstrong Whitworth wrote to the Air Ministry announcing the arrival of the engine and seeking permission to use Cramlington aerodrome for the Armadillo's first flight, stating that the Town Moor field was not suitable because of the surrounding obstructions and the rough surface. The company added that they had engaged a well-known test pilot to carry out the initial tests before the machine was handed over to the Air Ministry; this was probably Clifford Prodger, who did some further testing of the Armadillo at a later date. Permission to use Cramlington (then controlled by Headquarters, Training Division, RFC) was granted, and on 3 April Armstrong Whitworth telegraphed the Air Ministry reporting that the Armadillo would fly on the following Saturday, 6 April. Whether it did so or not is uncertain, but it undoubtedly flew before 1 May, on which day, a report states, '. . . it flew again'. On Wednesday, 8 May, the aircraft was tried out by an RAF pilot who reported back to the Air Ministry that he found it most unsatisfactory. According to this pilot the Armadillo was very tail heavy and flew left-wing low at full power; the aileron control was very heavy and it was difficult to move the stick laterally at high speed. He also complained that the control column was placed too far forward and that it fouled the instrument panel if the hand was placed on top of the stick. Another criticism was that the tailskid was too short so that the rudder was damaged during taxi-ing. All these faults could no doubt have been put right relatively easily: more serious was the fact that the pilot's view when landing was very bad, a defect that would have been difficult to rectify without considerable redesign. As a result of this report, the Assistant Controller, Design, at the Air Ministry wrote to the company on 18 May, 1918, saying that in view of the bad outlook from the cockpit during landing, the aircraft would not be sent to Martlesham and it would not be flown again by Service pilots. The Ministry's concern for the well-being of the RAF test pilots did not, apparently, extend to their civilian counterparts, for the letter went on to suggest that Armstrong Whitworth should conduct their own trials so as to obtain as much data as possible.

After some further modification, which included the fitting of the more robust undercarriage, Clifford Prodger made some tests on 7 June, 1918, and the figures that he recorded, although almost certainly optimistic, seemed to indicate that the aircraft had quite a respectable performance. The climb to 10,000 ft was said to have been accomplished in about 6½ min and the speed at that height was given as 112 mph; at an altitude of 4,000 ft the aircraft reached 120 mph with the engine turning over at 1,300 rpm. There is little on record regarding subsequent activities: the company stated its intention of trying out different propellers, one with four blades and another with a finer pitch but, in view of the discouraging attitude of the Air Ministry, no further serious development work was undertaken, Murphy having already turned his attention to the Armadillo's successor.

Ara

In 1917 a new engine had emerged which promised to give decisive air superiority to future British fighters: this was the A.B.C. Dragonfly radial engine which was supposed to give 320 hp for a weight of only 600 lb. Murphy, like many other designers, was quick to appreciate what might be accomplished with a powerplant of this calibre, and early in April 1918 Armstrong Whitworth asked the Air Ministry for blue prints of the Dragonfly; in reply, the Assistant Controller, Design, suggested that the company should not embark on a new design until the Armadillo had been tested, and that it would be advisable to have discussions with the Assistant Controller about which type of aircraft should next be undertaken. But Armstrong Whitworth had their own ideas on the subject and, in spite of the official advice, Murphy went ahead with the design of a Dragonfly-engined fighter. At some stage in the proceedings the official policy must have changed, for three examples of the new fighter, later to be named the Ara, were ordered. The Ara should logically have borne an F.M. number, presumably F.M.5, but it never seems to have carried this designation.

This second Armstrong Whitworth single-seat fighter retained the two-bay type of wing structure and the same type of slab-sided fuselage which characterized the Armadillo, but this time the top wing was raised a short distance above the fuselage, although the gap was still somewhat narrow.

The second Murphy-designed fighter, the Ara, first flew after the Armistice in 1918. Its A.B.C. Dragonfly engine was a failure. (*Vickers Ltd*)

The wings were of equal span, but the chord of the lower wing was less than that of the top wing. The tailplane was conventional, with the fin and rudder, like those of the Armadillo, rather on the small side. The Dragonfly engine was neatly installed in a cowling that faired smoothly into a pointed spinner on the propeller boss. Comparative figures, if they are to be believed, show that the Ara, like the Armadillo, had an unusually low structure weight; both aircraft were of roughly the same size, but the Dragonfly engine weighed some 150 lb more than the B.R.2 rotary; nevertheless, the Ara was only about 70 lb heavier than the Armadillo and both had approximately the same useful load.

Like its numerous contemporaries, the Ara had no chance of survival because the Dragonfly engine failed completely to fulfil its initial promise. It had been designed by Granville Bradshaw whose object was to produce a light, high-powered radial which would be easy to build on a large scale. Unfortunately, the authorities were too easily persuaded by Bradshaw's optimism, and the engine was put into production before adequate testing

Another view of the first Ara fighter, F4971. (*Vickers Ltd*)

had taken place. In the event, the Dragonfly, on which the nation's biggest production effort was to be concentrated, not only failed to develop the power expected, but suffered, among other troubles, from a species of high-frequency vibration which led to the wrecking of the engine after a few hours' running. At that time there was no known cure for this trouble and the whole engine production programme had eventually to be abandoned. Fortunately the war ended before the full impact of this debacle could have its effect.

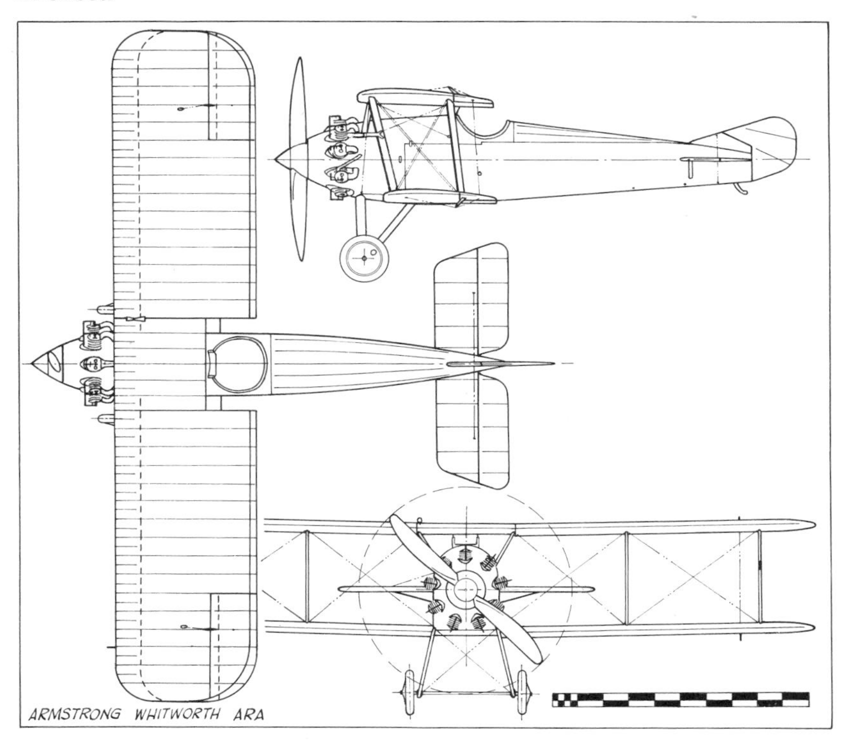

The first Ara, F4971, was completed during the summer of 1918, but no engine was immediately available. By the time the first engine was delivered to Armstrong Whitworth in December, it had already been decided that the Ara would not be put into production; the war was over, and by now the Dragonfly's troubles were beginning to become apparent. Nevertheless, two of the three aircraft ordered were completed, the second aircraft, F4972, having a larger gap with the lower wing running below the fuselage. Work on the third airframe was discontinued at a late stage of construction. Because of engine unreliability, no systematic trials were carried out with the Ara, but such figures as are available indicate that, when the engine worked, the aircraft had a good performance, with a top speed of about 150 mph at sea level, and the ability to climb to 10,000 ft in

The second Ara, F4972, differed from the first in having an increased gap between the wings. (*Imperial War Museum Q66207*)

4½ min. The ultimate fate of the two aircraft is not known, but doubtless they soon found their way on to the scrap heap. The Ara was the last of the Armstrong Whitworth designs to be built at Gosforth and, as recorded elsewhere, the company's aeroplane department was closed down at the end of 1919.

F.M.4 Armadillo
Dimensions: Span 27 ft 9 in (8·46 m); length 18 ft 10 in (5·74 m); height 8 ft 7 in (2·62 m); wing area 232 sq ft (21·56 sq m).

Ara
Dimensions: Span 27 ft 5 in (8·36 m); length 20 ft 3 in (6·17 m); height 7 ft 10 in (2·39 m); wing area 257 sq ft (23·88 sq m).

	F.M.4 Armadillo	**Ara**
	230 hp Bentley B.R.2	*320 hp A.B.C. Dragonfly*
Max weight:	1,860 lb (844 kg)	1,930 lb (875 kg)
Empty weight:	1,250 lb (557 kg)	1,320 lb (599 kg)
Max speed		
Sea level:	125 mph (201 km/hr)	150 mph (241 km/hr)
10,000 ft (3,048 m):	112 mph (182 km/hr)	145 mph (233 km/hr)
Climb		
to 10,000 ft (3,048 m)	6·5 min	4·5 min
Service ceiling:	24,000 ft (7,315 m)	28,000 ft (8,534 m)
Endurance:	2¾ hr	3¼ hr

The Airships

Armstrong Whitworth's first entry into the airship business occurred in the spring of 1913 and was the result of a letter from the Admiralty inviting the firm to tender for one large rigid, one large non-rigid and three small non-rigid airships. Official interest in the rigid airship had slumped after the fiasco of the Admiralty's Rigid Airship No. 1, the *Mayfly*, which, in 1911, had broken her back in a squall without ever becoming airborne. This lamentable affair might well have been the end of airship development in Great Britain but for a rumour that arose in 1912 to the effect that a German Zeppelin had been heard cruising over Sheerness Dockyard in the darkness of an October night. The report was in fact false, but the nation-wide outcry that followed caused the authorities to think again.

As a result of these new deliberations, the above-mentioned invitation to tender was sent to Armstrong Whitworth, and in response the company engaged, in May 1913, a certain Mr Liwentaal to design a rigid airship,

The non-rigid airship car was a development of the F.K.3 aircraft fuselage. The airship is the S.S.41 and the photograph was taken at Kingsnorth airship station in August 1918. (*Royal Aeronautical Society*)

Another view of the Armstrong Whitworth airship car. The engine was a 100 hp Green. (*Royal Aeronautical Society*)

agreeing to pay him £300 for a full set of drawings. Four months later, towards the end of September 1913, this design was submitted to the Admiralty together with a quotation of £100,000. No details have been found of the Liwentaal design, but the Admiralty tender on which it was based was turned down by the First Lord of the Admiralty, Winston Churchill, and Vickers were given an order to go ahead with their design, which eventually emerged as Airship No.9.

That Armstrong Whitworth had faith in their ability to build airships is shown by the fact that despite not having received the order, the board of directors gave authority for work to start on the establishment of an airship factory. The site chosen was adjacent to the village of Barlow, some three miles southeast of Selby in Yorkshire, on the estate of Lord Londesborough. There were, however, long delays and protracted negotiations with the Admiralty before work on the factory was actually started in January 1916, but by the middle of the same year the buildings were sufficiently advanced for work to start within them.

The main feature of the airship factory was the hangar which measured 700 ft in length and was built of steel girders covered with corrugated iron sheet. The door openings were 100 ft high and 150 ft wide, and the four doors which closed each end weighed, together, 175 tons. This shed was dismantled in the middle of the 1920s, but a smaller building measuring 260 ft by 100 ft and situated alongside the hangar, and used for fabricating the gasbags and other components, was still in existence in 1970, forming part of an army ordnance depot which then occupied the site.

Concurrently with the preparation of the Liwentaal design, Armstrong Whitworth, in July 1913, opened negotiations with a view to securing agency and licence rights for the semi-rigid airships then being built in Italy to the designs of Signor Forlanini. As a result of Armstrong Whitworth persuasion, Captain Murray Sueter (who was virtually the creator of the Royal Naval Air Service and who retired an Admiral) was sent to Italy for a trial ride in a Forlanini ship and, having been favourably impressed, he urged the Admiralty to adopt the type. In January 1914 Armstrong Whitworth concluded an agreement with Forlanini, and in the following May Captain Sueter told the company that they would shortly receive an order from the Admiralty for three ships of this design. It is not known when the order was actually placed but, to the disappointment of everyone concerned, it was cancelled in December 1914 and that was the end of the Forlanini exercise, except for a prolonged period of wrangling between the three parties concerned, which resulted in Armstrong Whitworth finishing up with a considerable loss.

In fact, Armstrong Whitworth's first practical airship work occurred in

The S.S.-type airship with the Armstrong Whitworth car had a top speed of about 50 mph and an endurance of twelve hours.

1914 and consisted of making a new car for the naval non-rigid airship HMA No.2, the Willows IV airship which had been purchased by the Admiralty in 1912. This ship, like all the small British airships of the time, experienced many adventures and underwent numerous modifications involving major changes in both the envelope and the car. Towards the end of 1914, at the naval air station at Farnborough, HMA No.2 was once more rebuilt and was fitted with the Armstrong Whitworth car which had been designed at Farnborough but built at Gosforth. The new car, which had a triangular framework and a Renault engine driving two swivelling propellers, accommodated a crew of three. The airship, in its new guise but still known as HMA No.2, made its first flight on 26 January, 1915, but the car cannot have found favour for it was not developed further. Instead, in March 1915, HMA No. 2 was tried out experimentally with still another car consisting of the fuselage of a B.E.2c aircraft. This proved highly successful and, with the B.E.2c then in quantity production, the problem of obtaining quick delivery was solved. Thus, HMA No.2 became S.S.1, the first of a fleet of 'blimps' which were to accomplish such valuable work during the First World War.

S.S.27

In March 1915 the Admiralty placed an order for an S.S. (Submarine Scout) ship with Armstrong Whitworth. For this airship the company purchased a complete envelope from the French firm of Clément Bayard, and to this was rigged the fuselage of an Armstrong Whitworth F.K.3 aircraft, which was similar in many respects to that of the B.E.2c. Apart from the use of a new type of fuselage, there were other innovations in the Armstrong Whitworth ship. An extra fuel tank, situated behind the pilot, gave an endurance of some ten to twelve hours, a considerable improvement compared with existing ships, and the blower used to cool the Renault engine also supplied air to the ship's compensating ballonets. Fixed fins, designed to have extra strength but without the normal king-post bracing were found, on test, to be lacking in stiffness. The first tests with this ship, which was numbered S.S.27, took place at the beginning of July 1915, at Kingsnorth, near Ashford in Kent, which since March 1915 had become the trials centre for naval non-rigid airships. On the first flight the rudder controls were found to be too heavy, and foot steering was substituted; during later flights some jamming of the controls was caused by the lack of stiffness in the new fins and they were consequently replaced by the standard pattern. After further tests on July 13, the ship was considered satisfactory and, on 15 and 16 July, she made cross-country flights to Polegate in Sussex and to Dover.

S.S.40—S.S.49

Following the success of S.S.27, the Admiralty ordered ten more S.S. ships from Armstrong Whitworth. These airships, numbered S.S.40 to S.S.49, were fitted with cars which, while still similar in appearance to the F.K.3 fuselage, were powered by the 100 hp Green water-cooled engine in place of the Renault engine of the S.S.27. The radiator for the engine was placed on top of the fuselage immediately behind the engine and directly in front of the observer, who occupied the front seat. The landing gear was similar to that of the F.K.3, with a central skid, a divided-axle, and long struts terminating in shock-absorbers housed in the sides of the car. Also within the car were an oil tank of 11 gal capacity and a ballast tank holding 30 gal of water. Two long cylindrical petrol tanks, each containing some 50 gal, were slung in the rigging above and on either side of the car. Each tank had feed pipes from either end to guard against fuel starvation when the ship climbed or dived, a precaution which was negated by the fact that when the ship was inclined nose up in a climb, the front bearing of the engine was apt to be starved of oil, with even more disastrous results.

Largely because of its water-cooled engine, the Armstrong Whitworth car, which weighed some 1,300 lb, was a good deal heavier than the B.E.2c fuselage, with its air-cooled Renault or RAF engine used by the majority of the S.S.-type airships. For this reason it was decreed that the Armstrong Whitworth car should be used only with the larger-capacity envelopes, that is, those with a volume of 70,000 cu ft, as compared with the more normal size of 60,000 cu ft. Some of the complexities of airship operation are highlighted by the instructions contained in the official handbook which laid down that, in the case of the 70,000 cu-ft ship, 1,709 lb was available for crew, fuel, ballast and armament '. . . with a gas purity of 87 per cent at 60°F and 30 inches of pressure'.

The normal armament consisted of eight 16-lb bombs carried in a standard bomb rack suspended below the floor of the car, but mounted sideways so that the noses of the bombs pointed to the right. The position of the actuating lever varied but was usually located inside the pilot's cockpit on the right-hand side. Defensive armament was not normally carried because these small S.S. ships usually operated fairly close inshore where, in the First World War, they were safe from attack by enemy aircraft. The observer's seat was equipped with radio, and the engine could be started from this cockpit, a distinct improvement on the B.E.-type car in which the observer had to stand on the landing skids to swing the propeller if for any reason the engine stopped in the air.

The S.S. airship with the Armstrong Whitworth car and the 100 hp Green engine had a top speed of just over 50 mph and an endurance, at that speed, of about twelve hours. Its rate of climb was some 500 ft/min (if the gas purity, ambient temperature and pressure were all as they should be), and it could complete a full 360 deg turn in just over 40 seconds. All the Armstrong Whitworth blimps were of 70,000 cu ft capacity except for S.S.40 which had an enlarged envelope having a capacity of 85,000 cu ft. This airship was detailed for special duties with the British Expeditionary Force in France and was doped black for night operations over the enemy lines. In the autumn of 1916 trial flights at night over the front line proved that the scheme had little value and the airship was sent back to England. During the course of tests, this ship once reached a height of 10,500 ft, which is thought to be a record for a blimp-type airship.

Not a great deal is known about the war work of the airships with Armstrong Whitworth cars. They appeared rather late on the scene, at a time when the S.S. ships were shortly to be superseded by the improved Coastal type. Four of the Armstrong Whitworth ships, S.S.44, S.S.45, S.S.46 and S.S.47, were delivered to the Italian government, while S.S.48 and S.S.49 were handed over to the French. Two others, S.S.40 and S.S.43, served in the eastern Mediterranean, based at Kassandra in Salonika, S.S.43 subsequently returning home to operate from the airship station at Caldale in the Orkney Islands. After being damaged in 1916, S.S.42 was rebuilt as S.S.42a, but in 1917 came down in the sea off the coast of Wales with the loss of the crew.

HMA No.25

On 13 October, 1915, Armstrong Whitworth received an order from the Admiralty for one rigid airship. This was to be one of the four ships of the 23 class, two of which were to be built by Vickers and one each by Armstrong Whitworth and Beardmore. The first of the class, No.23 itself, was designed by Vickers and was an improved version of their previous ship No.9, the first British rigid airship to fly. The Armstrong Whitworth ship, No.25, was built to the Vickers design and, in fact, incorporated a number of fittings, forgings, stampings, valves, controls and other mechanical gear supplied by the designers.

His Majesty's Airship No.25 had a total gas capacity of 942,000 cu ft; she was 535 ft long and 53 ft in diameter. The hull was built up of longitudinal duralumin lattice girders divided by transverse frames into eighteen gas-bag compartments. A noticeable characteristic of the 23-class ships was the V-section external keel running from just aft of the bow along the ship's belly to merge with the lower vertical fin at the stern. This keel, which added only slightly to the strength of the ship, served to carry the fuel and water-ballast tanks and to provide a walk-way between the three suspended cars. About half-way between the forward car and the midships car the keel widened out to form a cabin some 45 ft in length. This was divided into compartments comprising a bomb room, a wireless cabin, and quarters for the crew; right aft was a lavatory. A proposal to furnish the crew quarters with bunks, hammocks and folding tables was abandoned in an effort to save weight. Just forward of the front car a climbing shaft and a ladder 57 ft long led from the keel, between the gas-bags, to a gun platform situated on the top of the ship. From this platform an open walk-way—or perhaps crawl-way would be a more apt description—extended aft to the rudder-hinge line.

The first rigid airship built at Barlow was No.25, launched on 14 October, 1917. In December 1917 she became HMA R 25 by Admiralty order. (*Imperial War Museum Q69346*)

As originally built, the forward and aft cars each contained a single Rolls-Royce engine which drove a pair of four-blade, swivelling propellers. Subsequently, in an effort to improve the payload performance, which was minimal, the after car was removed and replaced by a lighter power-car housing a single engine with direct drive to the non-swivelling two-blade propeller. The midships car contained two engines each driving, through gears, a non-swivelling propeller situated one on either side of the car. The main control position of the airship was located in the front compartment of the forward car. The Rolls-Royce engines used in this airship were a modified form of the Eagle aeroplane engine, an adaptation which Rolls-Royce undertook with reluctance because of their preoccupation with normal production.

Early in 1917, while No.25 was under construction, the Barlow establishment was commissioned by the Admiralty as a sub-station of Barrow, and during the first days of October a party of 132 naval ratings were drafted to the base to form a handling party for the new airship. The official trim trials of No.25 were done inside the shed at Barlow, on 1 October, 1917, when the disposable lift was found to be 5·78 tons. In a last-minute effort to improve upon this disappointing figure, a dynamo and a searchlight were removed, as was the wheel on the lower fin and what little remained of the cabin furniture. After these changes, she was ready for launching on 6 October, but no suitable opportunity occurred for the first trial until the 14th of the month. On that day, before emerging from the shed, the ship was balanced up with 19 men on board, together with 385 gal of petrol, 32 gal of oil and 3,160 lb of water ballast. After emerging from the shed, the ship warmed up and, as a consequence, it was found necessary to add another man and three 50-lb bags of sand to the aftermost car. HMA No.25 took-off at eight minutes past four in the afternoon and, after circling Barlow and Selby, set off towards her operational base at Howden, some eight miles away, where she landed without incident 45 minutes later. During the journey she reached a height of 750 ft, used 40 gal of petrol and no less than 880 lb of water ballast.

On her first flight No.25 was found to be slightly less stable laterally than her sister ship No.23, but in elevation more stable and more easily controlled; it was only on later flights that she was found to be difficult to handle because her eighteen gas-bags were apt to surge fore and aft causing abrupt and unpredictable changes in trim. Some minor snags became apparent during the first short flight. The engine-room telegraphs and the intercom telephone proved unsatisfactory, and the engines in the centre car tended to overspeed, indicating a need for propellers of coarser pitch. The engineers in the centre car complained that their quarters became flooded when water ballast was discharged from No.4 tank, which was situated just ahead of the car. It was also observed that water from No.5 ballast tank drifted back in a mist as far as the after car, indicating that similar arrangements for jettisoning petrol must be in urgent need of revision.

Following various modifications the new airship underwent her official acceptance trials on 23 December, 1917: by that time she was known as R 25 in accordance with an Admiralty order issued earlier in the month. The acceptance flight lasted for 2 hr 35 min, a considerable portion of which was taken up making a difficult landing at Howden in thick mist. An attempt to measure the speed of the ship over a triangular course was also partially defeated by the mist and also by a slipping clutch in the forward engine car. It also became necessary to shut down one of the centre engines because of the breakage of one of the engine-mounting struts. After making allowances for these factors, and for the wind, which was blowing at 26 mph from the west-northwest, the mean speed was estimated to be slightly more than 48 mph. At the conclusion of the flight the ship was formally handed over to the commanding officer of the Howden base.

The 23-class ships were not a great success, but if they lacked something in performance, they did at least serve to demonstrate to all concerned some of the hard facts about the design, construction and operation of rigid airships. The R 25 was considered to be unsuitable for aircrew training because of the gas-bag surging already mentioned; nevertheless, she put in some 220 hours in the air before she finished her flying career in November 1918; she was finally 'deleted' in September 1919.

R 29

The second rigid airship to be built at Barlow was the R 29, ordered in 1915, one of the so-called '23X Class'. This was an Admiralty design and was a considerable improvement on the original 23 class. Indeed, R 29 has been described as the first really useful British rigid airship, having rather more than $8\frac{1}{2}$ tons disposable lift. Only two of the 23X class were built, the other, R 27, having been constructed by Beardmores. The most obvious difference between the R 25 and the R 29 was that the latter had no external keel, the structure having been so designed that the petrol, oil and water-ballast tanks, formerly housed in the keel, were now suspended from the radial bracing wires which served to maintain the ship's polygonal shape. The R 29 was slightly larger than her predecessor, having a capacity of 990,600 cu ft and a length of 539 ft; the maximum diameter was the

Described as the first really useful British rigid airship, the R 29 was launched at Barlow at the end of May 1918. (*Imperial War Museum Q48022*)

The R 29 had no external keel; in its place a non-structural walkway was accommodated within the hull. (*Imperial War Museum Q48021*)

same. The elimination of the external keel brought about a significant saving in weight and a reduction in drag. In place of the external keel, an internal walk-way was provided along the belly of the ship giving access to the cars and to the internal rigging and the gas-bags. With her increased disposable lift, R 29 was able to carry some armament in the shape of eight 120-lb bombs and numerous machine-guns, one of which was situated on top of the envelope and was reached, as in the case of the R 25, via a ladder in a tube between the gas-bags. As originally built, the R 29 was powered by four Rolls-Royce engines, each of 250 hp. The fore and aft cars had two swivelling propellers driven by a single engine, whilst the centre car had two engines, each driving its own fixed propeller through gearing. Later, both the R 29 and her sister ship the R 27 had the centre car replaced by two wing cars carried abreast, each with one engine driving a single propeller. Also, as was the case with the R 25, the rear car of the R 29 was modified, with one propeller at the rear replacing the two swivelling propellers originally fitted.

The R 29 emerged from the shed at Barlow at the end of May 1918 and, after successful preliminary trials, was commissioned on 20 June. She quickly showed herself to be superior in many ways to the 23-class ships. Because of the absence of an external keel, she could turn more quickly—her 'turning-radius coefficient' was 9·8 as against 11·2 for the R 25. One of the R 29's more serious defects, which came to light later, was the liability of the cotton fabric outer cover to absorb rain water; during a prolonged rain storm it was possible for a ton or more to be added to the weight of the ship.

After commissioning in June 1918, R 29 was soon engaged in operational flying and, in fact, gained the distinction of being the only British rigid airship to go into action against the enemy; this event occurred on 29 September, 1918, off the coast of Northumberland and led to the presumed destruction of the German submarine *UB-115*. Accounts of the action differ, but reports that the submarine was first damaged by a bomb from the R 29 are not substantiated in the official report which simply states that the R 29 was the first to sight the submarine's oil slick. The airship dropped bombs on the spot to indicate the position to nearby naval ships which then attacked with depth charges. During her short career, the R 29 flew a total of 438 hours, mostly before the end of 1918, and on one occasion, during 3–4 July, she remained airborne for 32 hr 20 min. In January 1919 she was damaged while entering her shed at East Fortune airship station, but was flying again on a wireless test by the spring. In June 1919 she accompanied the R 34 on two local flights and subsequently was flown to Cranwell where she ended her career undergoing ground experiments before being struck off strength on 24 October, 1919.

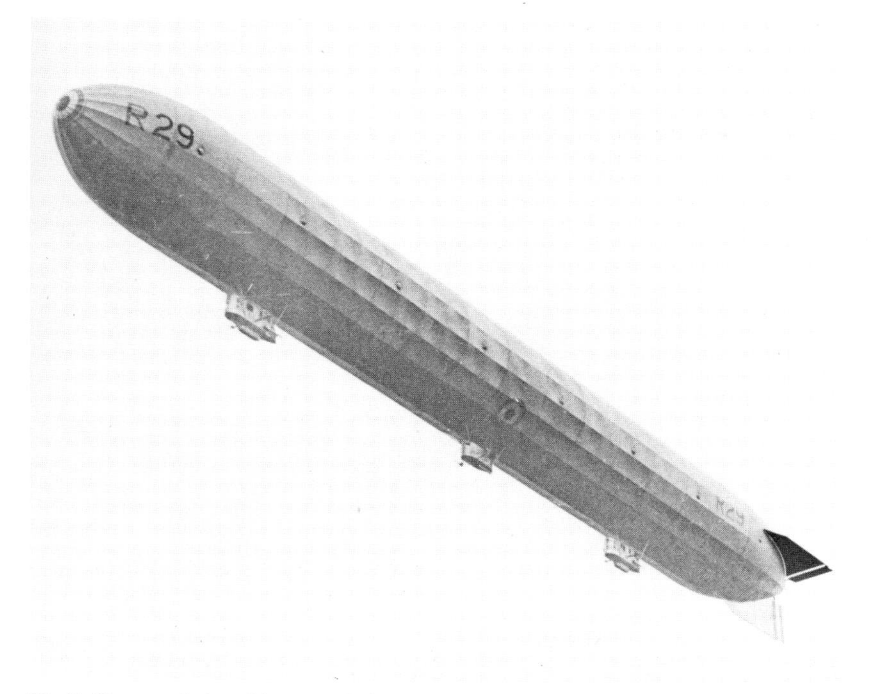

The R 29, commissioned in June 1918, took part in the presumed destruction of a German submarine in September 1918. (*Royal Aeronautical Society*)

Originally it had been intended that there should be four ships of the 23X-class, and R 30 had been ordered from Armstrong Whitworth, but an important event in the autumn of 1916 led to a drastic change of plan and the cancellation of the R 30 after some £11,500 had been spent on girder construction. During a raid on England on the night of 23–24 September, the Zeppelin L 33 was damaged by gunfire; she headed home across the North Sea but her captain, quick to realize that her leaking gas-bags would

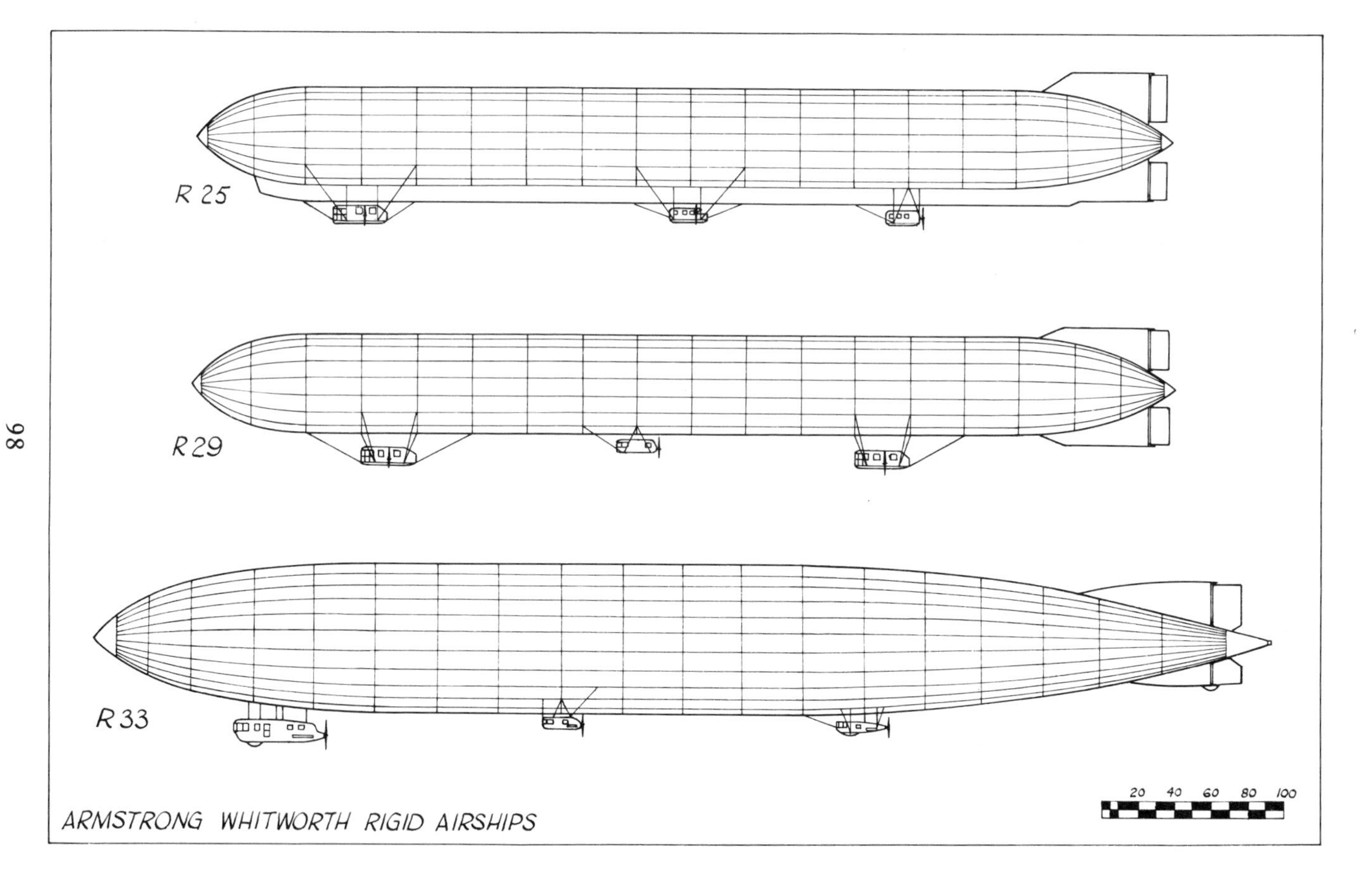
R 25
R 29
R 33
20 40 60 80 100
ARMSTRONG WHITWORTH RIGID AIRSHIPS

prevent her reaching the distant coast, prudently turned back and eventually grounded his ship on the coast of Essex near Mersea. An attempt by the crew to destroy the ship did not succeed because so little gas was left that she failed to burn properly and only the fabric covering was consumed. This splendid opportunity to glean the secrets of a modern Zeppelin was not to be missed, and a team of Admiralty airship designers set up a tented camp alongside the stranded airship and proceeded to measure and sketch her details down to the last wire. From this profitable exercise grew the next two British rigid airships: the fact that they were copies of the captured L 33 was acknowledged by the fact that the ships were known as the 33-class and the first of them was the R 33.

The launch of the R 33 on 6 March, 1919. Her design was based on the captured German Zeppelin L 33. (*Museum of Science and Engineering, Newcastle*)

R 33

The two new airships, the R 33 and the R 34, were ordered by the Admiralty in November 1916. The R 33 was built at Barlow by Armstrong Whitworth and was launched on 6 March, 1919, eight days ahead of her sister ship, the R 34, built by Beardmores at Inchinnan, near Glasgow. On her first flight on that day, the R 33 remained airborne for three hours before returning to her shed, somewhat prematurely, because of worsening weather. With a capacity of 1,950,000 cu ft, the R 33 was a good deal larger than previous British rigid airships and, with her good streamlined shape, she marked the first breakaway from the tubular hull with parallel sides and pointed ends which had characterized her forerunners.

The R 33 nearing completion in the Barlow hangar. (*Royal Aeronautical Society*)

In outline the R 33 resembled the Zeppelin L 33, the only significant outward difference being in the design and arrangement of her cars and propulsion arrangements. The forward car, although apparently all of a piece, was, in fact, built in two units separated by a small gap. The front section formed the control car and contained the radio cabin, while the after section housed one of the five Sunbeam Maori engines driving a 16-ft diameter two-blade propeller. Two more Maori engines were carried in wing cars slung alongside each other somewhat forward of the midship point. These two engines were equipped with reversing gearboxes for checking the airship's forward way when landing or coming up to the mast. The aftermost car contained two more Maori engines coupled by gears to a single 19-ft propeller. The Sunbeam Maori engine, specially designed for airship work, was a twelve-cylinder vee water-cooled unit rated at 275 hp at 2,100 rpm and weighing 890 lb dry. Each engine was fitted with a clutch and gears so that the engines could be tested in the hangar without turning the propellers. The framework of the ship consisted of twenty circumferential frames and thirteen main longitudinal girders with lighter intermediate girders, giving the outer envelope the shape of a 25-sided polygon. There was an internal keel which provided a walk-way between the cars and gave access to the mooring position in the extreme nose and to the gun position in the tail abaft the tail surfaces. The nineteen gas-bags were so shaped that they overlapped the internal gangway, which also served as a support for the fuel and water-ballast tanks.

The R 33 had a disposable lift of some 26 tons, of which about 15½ tons was taken up by fuel and water ballast. The normal crew complement was 22. The maximum speed was about 53 kt, but the normal cruising speed was between 40 and 45 kt. For extreme range the ship could be cruised at 40 kt on three engines, in which case the consumption worked out at about one mile per gallon. The ship was very manoeuvrable and, with the midships engines going astern and the slipstream from the rearmost propeller working on the rudder, she could be turned in her own length.

The R 33 and her sister ship the R 34 were, perhaps, the most successful British rigid airships ever built, before or since, and the R 33 did more flying than any other, achieving a total of more than 735 hours before she was finally dismantled in 1928. Soon after being commissioned in 1919 she made an extended tour of the north of England, going westwards as far as the Irish coast and landing back at her Pulham base after being airborne for 31 hours. In September 1919 she made another long flight of some 20 hours, this time to demonstrate to a party of business men the feasibility of airship travel. Specially equipped with bunks and carrying a chef and accompanied for some of the voyage by the R 32, she cruised up the coast of Belgium and Holland, doubled back to Antwerp and Brussels, returning to England after touring the Flanders battlefields. During the flight, which lasted from 9 p.m. on 12 September until 6.20 p.m. on the following day, meals, including a five-course lunch, were served and a ship's newspaper published.

The years 1920 and 1921 were the R 33's busiest period. In May 1920 she was used for an experiment to test a new fire-proof aeroplane petrol tank, and for this purpose a Sopwith Camel was carried aloft and released without a pilot but with the engine running. As it happened, the Camel did not catch fire in the ensuing crash, but nobody ventured to claim that the fire problem had been solved. At the end of 1920 all airship activity was transferred from the Admiralty to the Air Ministry, and R 33 joined

The forward control car of the R 33 under construction in the Armstrong Whitworth factory in October 1918. (*Vickers Ltd*)

The R 33, with some 735 hours to her credit, spent more time in the air than any other British rigid airship. (*Imperial War Museum Q48027*)

the RAF; but on 14 January, 1921, she acquired the civil registration G-FAAG, although throughout the remainder of her life she continued to be known simply as R 33.

In February 1921, after having her nose strengthened, the R 33 was flown to Pulham for a programme of tests with a newly-erected mooring mast. Soon afterwards, an unusual accident occurred which served to

A rare photograph of the R 33 at the Croydon Airport (Plough Lane site) mooring mast erected in the summer of 1921. After being used twice by the R 33 it was dismantled. (*Courtesy F. Brazier*)

demonstrate the value of the two emergency ballast tanks installed, one in the bow and the other in the stern of the airship. Each tank contained a ton of water which could be released directly from the control car. During a local flight, a rigger, while inspecting the internal bracing, lost his foothold and fell through the ship, ripping one of the rearmost gas-bags as he passed. Apart from a slight gassing, he was unharmed, but the airship tilted up sharply by the bows and was only brought under control after crew members crowded into the bow and the emergency ballast in the stern had been released. The ship subsequently landed safely at Pulham. The emergency ballast tanks were to be used once again in an even more hazardous situation, as will be related later. After repairs the R 33 continued the mooring tests during which she spent 96 days, between February and June 1921, tethered by the nose to the Pulham mast, during which time she encountered severe snow and rain squalls and rode out winds of up to 55 mph.

In January 1921 the R 33 was registered as a civil aircraft, but she continued to be known as R 33.

Early in 1921 the R 33 made several night flights between Croydon Airport and the Channel coast to evaluate the recently-installed lighting system on the Continental air route. In June 1921 she was used, with some success, to assist in the control of the Derby-day traffic near Epsom and for this purpose she was in wireless communication with a police post set up in the Epsom grandstand. In the following month she performed similar duties on the occasion of the RAF Pageant held at Hendon aerodrome on 2 July. But by then, it seemed, her fate had been sealed: on 28 June, 1921, it was announced in the House of Commons that, in the interests of economy, all Government airship activities would be discontinued, and that the existing ships (R 33, R 36, R 37, R 80 and the surrendered German Zeppelins L 64 and L 70) would be offered free to a suitable operator. The statement added that if this offer had not been taken up by 1 August, 1921, the airships would be handed over to the Disposal Board. No such offer was forthcoming and all activity ceased, but interest had been aroused and all sorts of proposals were being discussed; as a result the airships were not actually scrapped but kept in storage just in case something turned up.

The R 33 at the mooring mast at Pulham airship station in 1921. (*Flight International*)

The protracted discussions with the Dominions about possible Empire services by airship, the airship scheme proposed by Commander Burney, and the eventual decision by the Government to place orders for two large airships, the R 100 and the R 101, have no part in this narrative except in so far as they affected the R 33. Nearly three years were to elapse before the Government announced, in May 1924, the initiation of a comprehensive programme of research in connection with the new airships. For this purpose the airship stations at Cardington and Pulham were to be reactivated and the R 36 and R 33 were to be refitted, the latter being equipped with apparatus for measuring the air pressure and stresses at various points on the hull.

The overhauled R 33 emerged from the shed at Cardington on 2 April, 1925, and was flown direct to Pulham and secured to the mast. She made one experimental flight on 6 April, when the recording apparatus failed to work. Ten days later, on 16 April, she started out, quite inadvertently, on the most famous voyage of her career. While riding out a gale at Pulham she was struck by a series of severe gusts which caused her to break away from the mast with her nose structure badly damaged and the front gas-bag deflated. It was 9.50 a.m., and on board at the time was the duty watch consisting of an RAF flight sergeant and eighteen civilians under the command of Flt Lieut R. E. Booth. Rapidly sizing up the situation, Booth ordered the release of two tons of water ballast, thus enabling the ship to rise sufficiently quickly to pass safely over the station's gas holder and its 140-ft radio mast. Within two minutes of breaking away, one engine was running, followed by a second within another two minutes. From then on, the ship was under control and being steered into the wind, albeit drifting backwards at about 20 kt. Twelve minutes after the breakaway, the airship's radio operator was in touch with Pulham. Booth and some of the crew then proceeded to the top of the ship where they secured the flapping fabric and lashed the deflated gas-bag to No.2 frame to form a protective bulkhead. It was, undoubtedly, this skilful initiative that prevented the damage spreading further.

After leaving the coast at Lowestoft, the R 33 continued to be blown backwards throughout the day until by 6.30 p.m. she was off the coast of Holland near Ijmuiden. Meanwhile, the Dutch authorities had assembled 300 men at the aerodrome of Den Helder in case Booth decided to land, while, on the other side of the North Sea, the fishery-protection gunboat *Godetia* had put to sea from Lowestoft soon after the airship crossed the English coast in the hope of being able to render assistance. As the gale slowly abated, it was found possible to hold the airship stationary and, at 10.45 p.m., Booth signalled to Pulham that he would attempt to return to England. During the early hours of 17 April the wind continued to moderate and the R 33 began to make slow progress westwards, accompanied by the *Godetia* which was standing by, prepared, if necessary, to take the airship in tow. By 9 a.m., with the wind speed decreasing quickly, the R 33 was making good a speed of about 15 kt towards home and, without further incident, she crossed the Norfolk coast at lunch time and landed safely back at Pulham at 3.20 p.m. She had spent $29\frac{1}{2}$ hours in the air and her fight for survival had been followed with apprehension, not to say despair, from the ground: from the crew's point of view the story can best be summed up in the words of Flt Lieut Booth as quoted in the London *Times*: 'Throughout the whole time the ship behaved splendidly, and, apart from a few anxious moments, no one on board experienced the excitement of those who had to remain behind. We had plenty of food, hot drinks and tinned fruit, so there was no hardship . . .'

The enquiry which followed the breakaway concluded that the cause was a violent lateral gust which imposed a side load of at least three tons on the nose of the airship, and that the first failure occurred in the nose girders; this was followed by a fracture in the mooring head of the mast, part of which remained embedded in the wreckage of the airship's nose; there was no evidence of the airship having hit the mast during the breakaway.

The rebuilding of the airship, involving an extensive redesign of the nose portion, was put in hand at once, but it was not until 5 October, 1925, that

The R 33 back to a safe landing at Pulham in April 1925 after breaking away and riding out a gale for nearly thirty hours. (*The Times*)

The R 33, in the Pulham airship shed, being fitted with a new nose after her breakaway in 1925. (*Royal Aeronautical Society*)

she emerged from the hangar at Pulham and took the air again; her first flight on that day lasted 19½ hours and was concerned with the tests for which she had previously been prepared, the plotting of the pressure pattern on the envelope during various manoeuvres. On this flight, and on another test on 9 October, the design team of the R 101 was on board making observations. The pressure-plotting trials were quickly concluded, and the R 33 then underwent trials as an aeroplane carrier. On the first occasion, on 15 October, 1925, a D.H.53 light monoplane, suspended below the airship on a special trapeze, was released and later re-attached, although not without some damage to the aeroplane's propeller, which fouled a wire. The experiment was repeated again, with further slight damage to the aeroplane, on 28 October, and again, this time with complete success, on 4 December, 1925.

Then, once again, the Treasury stepped in, and early in 1926 it was announced that the R 33's experimental programme had been completed and that the airship and the station at Pulham were to be placed on a care and maintenance basis; this caused *Flight* magazine to comment '. . . really, it is difficult to know whether to laugh or cry'. But that was still not the end: in October 1926 the ageing R 33 was re-commissioned at Pulham with the dual object of testing the new mooring mast recently erected at Cardington for the R 100 and R 101, and with making further experiments to check the behaviour of the ship when relatively heavy aeroplanes were

In October 1925 a D.H.53 light aircraft (Service number J7325 but with the rudder of J7326) was launched from R 33 and subsequently re-attached.

released. When the R 33 was walked out of her hangar on 21 October, she had two Gloster Grebe fighters, each of which weighed more than a ton, slung underneath her hull. In fact, the releasing of these aeroplanes had a barely noticeable effect on the airship's trim because, at the launching speed of about 25 kt, the aircraft were already supporting a large proportion of their weight on their own wings. On arrival at Cardington after the Grebes had been safely launched, the R 33 made a somewhat heavy landing, bumping both forward and after cars and doing some slight damage to the supporting struts. The R 33 made two more flights, the last being on 23 November, 1926, during which she again launched her Grebes and dropped some parachutes before returning once more to the shelter of the Cardington hangar. She never flew again, and remained undisturbed in the shed until, in May 1928, she was finally dismantled to make way for the

In October 1926 experiments were conducted with two Gloster Grebe fighters which were successfully released on two separate occasions. (*Flight International 4240*)

erection of the R 101: thus ended, somewhat tamely, the eventful career of Britain's longest-lived and most successful airship.

The rest of the Armstrong Whitworth airship story can be briefly told: as the R 33 was nearing completion at Barlow, the company received orders for two more rigid airships, the R 35 during 1918, and the R 39 in January 1919. The former was to have been 672 ft long with a capacity of 2,100,000 cu ft, while the latter, similar to the R 38, was even larger, with a designed length of 695 ft and a capacity of some 3,000,000 cu ft. Both ships were cancelled at an early stage of construction, work on the R 39 coming to a halt in August 1919. Armstrong Whitworth had built up a first-class reputation for their work on rigid airships and, in an Admiralty report, it was stated that, of the firms engaged in building airships, Armstrong Whitworth were the best equipped and turned out the best work. The report added that the firms involved did not have much faith in the future of the airship. Nevertheless, in October 1919 Armstrong Whitworth did consider taking part in a co-operative scheme, in collaboration with the Beardmore and Cunard companies, for the operation of commercial airships, but made it a condition that they should be guaranteed against loss. Nothing came of the idea and, at the end of the month, the company announced their intention of closing down the Barlow factory: this marked the end of Armstrong Whitworth's work on lighter-than-air vessels.

	R 25 *Four 250 hp Rolls-Royce engines*	R 29 *Four 250 hp Rolls-Royce engines*	R 33 *Five 275 hp Sunbeam Maori engines*
Length:	535 ft (163·07 m)	539 ft (164·29 m)	644 ft (196·29 m)
Diameter:	53 ft (16·15 m)	53 ft (16·15 m)	79 ft (24·08 m)
Capacity:	942,000 cu ft (26,674 cu m)	990,600 cu ft (28,051 cu m)	1,950,000 cu ft (55,218 cu m)
Max speed:	52 mph (84 kph)	55 mph (89 kph)	61 mph (98 kph)
First cost:	£153,680	£142,000	£350,000

The Siddeley R.T.1 was a redesign of the R.E.8. This aircraft, B6626, had a 150 hp RAF 4A engine. (*Imperial War Museum Q67553*)

The Siddeley Deasy Designs

After F. M. Green and John Lloyd joined the Siddeley Deasy company in 1917, they were responsible for designing three types of aircraft which were put in hand before the take-over by Armstrong Whitworth in 1919. One of these, the S.R.2 Siskin, although designed and built originally as a Siddeley Deasy aeroplane, grew to maturity and became famous under the Armstrong Whitworth title and, as such, it merits a chapter of its own. The other two, dealt with here, achieved no fame, but one of them, like the Siskin, was also carried over into the Armstrong Whitworth hierarchy.

R.T.1

At the time of Green's and Lloyd's move to Coventry, the factory was occupied with large-scale production of the R.E.8, one of the aircraft which Lloyd had worked on while still at Farnborough: it was appropriate, therefore, that this was the aeroplane that formed the basis for the design that was the first to carry the Siddeley Deasy name. Known as the R.T.1, this aeroplane was an attempt to improve on the R.E.8 which, in the RFC, had earned a reputation, not altogether justified, for shedding its overhanging top wing in a dive; it was also reputed to have a dangerous tendency to spin. It was probably more in an endeavour to eliminate these characteristics, rather than to improve the performance, that was the purpose behind the R.T.1 design.

The fuselage of the R.T.1 was essentially the same as that of the R.E.8, but the wings were of entirely new design, being of equal span with two-bay bracing and with the top wing having a greater chord than that of the bottom. Modifications to the fuselage consisted only of raising the observer's gun-ring by a few inches and providing a deeper fuselage top fairing to match. The horizontal tailplane was similar to that of the R.E.8, but the fin and rudder were both of greater area and with a more rounded shape. The small ventral fin of the R.E.8 was retained.

Only three R.T.1s were built, each one growing from a fuselage taken from a batch of 150 R.E.8s then on the Siddeley Deasy production line. The first R.T.1 was powered by a 200 hp Hispano-Suiza engine and fitted with a nose radiator similar in appearance to that of the S.E.5; it bore the serial number B6625. The second aeroplane, B6626, had the same engine as the R.E.8, an RAF 4A, developing 150 hp, in a standard R.E.8 mounting, whilst the third aircraft, the final version, reverted to the 200 hp Hispano-Suiza engine, this time enclosed in a neatly rounded cowling with an underslung radiator. In this version, as with the RAF-powered aircraft, the engine exhaust gases were discharged over the top wing by means of twin stacks. The third aircraft also had modified wingtips and horn-balanced ailerons with rounded tips.

The cockpits of the R.T.1. This was John Lloyd's first design for The Siddeley Deasy Motor Car Co. (*Imperial War Museum Q67314*)

Another version of the R.T.1, with horn-balanced ailerons and a 200 hp Hispano engine. (*Imperial War Museum Q68184*)

The first flight of the R.T.1 was made from Radford aerodrome by J. H. James, later to become well known for his exploits with the Gloster 'Bamel' racer. He had with him as passenger the designer John Lloyd, who vividly recalls that a prolonged spin made this first flight more memorable than most. The date of the first flight is uncertain, but it is known that the second aircraft, the one with the RAF engine, was undergoing official tests by December 1917.

As compared with the R.E.8, the wing area of the R.T.1 was increased by some 12 per cent, with a wing loading of 6 lb/sq ft, as against nearly 7 lb/sq ft in the case of the R.E.8. In spite of this, the R.T.1 with the same engine was as fast as the R.E.8, clocking 101 mph at 6,500 ft, but, as might be expected, the climb performance was better, the R.T.1 reaching an altitude of 10,000 ft in 19·2 min, while the service ceiling was 16,000 ft, some 2,500 ft higher than that of the R.E.8. The view forward and downward from the pilot's seat of the R.T.1 had been criticized and to improve it a gap was cut in the lower wing root; this had the effect of reducing the speed by about 2 mph at 15,000 ft and increasing the time taken to reach 10,000 ft by about $3\frac{1}{2}$ min. The R.T.1 with the 200 hp Hispano-Suiza engine, and in its final form with the rounded nose, was tested in March 1919 and proved to be some 10 mph faster than the earlier version and to have a service ceiling higher by some 2,000 ft. The aircraft was reported to handle well and one of them underwent Service trials on the Western Front, whilst the other two went to training units; however, it must have been fairly clear from the start that there was little prospect of the R.T.1 going into production, and it seems probable that the design was undertaken more as an exercise for the newly established Siddeley Deasy design team than as a serious attempt to find a replacement for the R.E.8.

Sinaia

The design of the third Siddeley Deasy aircraft, the Sinaia bomber, was started early in 1918 but, when the war ended in November, the lack of urgency brought about a slowing down of the construction work and the aircraft was not, in fact, completed until the summer of 1921. By this time Siddeley Deasy had been absorbed by Armstrong Whitworth, but it would nevertheless seem proper that this aircraft should be considered as a Siddeley Deasy design.

The Siddeley Sinaia, for which the improbable type number 103 has been quoted, was built to meet an Air Ministry requirement for a large bomber suitable for daylight operation. A prerequisite for this type of work was an effective system of defensive armament which, in the Sinaia, took the form of two rear gunners situated behind the wings in rearward extensions of the two engine nacelles. Apart from the weight penalty of such an arrangement, it would appear to have had the advantage that in addition to providing rearward cover, it enabled both flanks to be defended simultaneously. Admittedly, both gunners would be working in the full slipstream of the propellers, but in this respect they would have been no worse off than the rear gunner of a normal single-engined two-seat aircraft. The forward-firing armament was probably intended to be a standard machine-gun but, during the building of the aircraft, a trial installation was made for the fitting of the Coventry Ordnance Works quick-firing cannon.

In most other respects the Sinaia was a fairly conventional, equal-span twin-engined biplane with the bottom wing having slightly less chord than

The Siddeley Sinaia bomber, J6858. The engines were 500 hp liquid-cooled Siddeley Tigers.

the top; horn-balanced ailerons were fitted to both top and bottom wings, which were designed to fold. The tailplane was in biplane form with a small triangular fin and three balanced rudders. A balanced elevator was fitted to the upper tailplane, but what appeared to be an elevator on the bottom tailplane was, in fact, a trimming surface. There were two separate V-type undercarriages located under the engine nacelles which themselves sat directly on the top surface of the lower wing. The engines were Siddeley Tigers, a new type of powerplant which had appeared towards the end of the war. Unlike the later Armstrong Siddeley radial engine of the same name, this first Tiger was a water-cooled engine with twelve cylinders arranged in vee form. It was directly descended from the six-cylinder Puma inline engine and was, in fact, two slightly enlarged and improved Puma cylinder blocks set on a common crankcase. With a nominal output of 500 hp, the Tiger engine was in an early stage of its development, and it is believed that it had not previously been flight-tested before being fitted to the Sinaia: it naturally gave considerable trouble during the Sinaia test flying and was not developed further. It had been intended that other engines, the Beardmore Atlantic, the Rolls-Royce Condor or the Napier Lion, should be fitted to the subsequent aircraft, but of the four Sinaia prototypes ordered, only the first, J6858, was built.

The Sinaia was assembled at Farnborough, where, during the design stage, wind-tunnel tests had been conducted to determine the rudder power needed to ensure that the aircraft could be flown safely on one engine. These tests showed that the most suitable combination was three rudders, the centre one of $35\frac{1}{2}$ sq ft and two side rudders each of 25 sq ft in area. With this arrangement, it was calculated that the Sinaia would be capable of asymmetric flight at speeds down to 67 mph. The aircraft first flew on 25 June, 1921, with Frank Courtney at the controls. He recalls that by

The Sinaia, at Farnborough, being prepared for its first flight which took place on 25 June, 1921.

1921 there was a marked lack of interest in either the aircraft or its engines, as by then it had become obvious that neither had any future; all that anybody cared about was the completion of the contract, including the maker's tests, with the minimum of expense. Courtney made a number of test flights at Farnborough, most of which were cut short by engine trouble. At the conclusion of one of these tests, he reported noticing an increasing amount of slackness in the elevator controls. The reason for this is revealed in two Farnborough reports issued in October and November 1921; these record that, as the Sinaia was being wheeled out of the hangar with the wings folded, it was noticed that the fuselage was showing signs of buckling behind the rear spar of the bottom wing. An inspection showed that the tubular rivets carrying the bracing-wire shackles had failed, and

Another view of the Sinaia; the airframe and the engines proved troublesome and both were soon abandoned.

the report tells how bolts had to be fitted in place of the rivets so that the aircraft could be taken back into the hangar. A detailed examination of the aircraft's structure showed that there was some splitting of the vertical struts in the fuselage and some of the splices and butt joints in the bottom longerons showed signs of opening up. In addition, the struts between the fuselage and the top plane were bowed with their fittings buckled; there were also signs of failure in the folding-wing hinges and considerable damage throughout due to wood shrinkage. The report concluded that the way the aircraft had been flown would not account for the failure, which would not have occurred if the parts had been up to the normal stress requirements. Needless to say, Farnborough's recommendations, that the design should be re-stressed and the aircraft rebuilt, were not implemented, and the Sinaia ended its days back in the same hangar at Farnborough where it had started life.

R.T.1

Dimensions: Span 41 ft 9 in (12·73 m); length 27 ft 8 in (8·43 m); height 11 ft 7 in (3·53 m); wing area 433 sq ft (40·23 sq m).

	150 hp RAF 4A	*200 hp Hispano-Suiza*
Max weight:	2,590 lb (1,175 kg)	2,707 lb (1,228 kg)
Empty weight:	1,773 lb (804 kg)	1,803 lb (818 kg)
Max speed		
6,500 ft (1,981 m):	101 mph (163 km/hr)	—
10,000 ft (3,048 m):	98 mph (158 km/hr)	108 mph (174 km/hr)
15,000 ft (4,572 m):	91 mph (147 km/hr)	100 mph (161 km/hr)
Climb		
to 6,500 ft (1,981 m):	10·5 min	10·6 min
to 10,000 ft (3,048 m):	19·2 min	18·5 min
to 15,000 ft (4,572 m):	41·5 min	36·4 min
Service ceiling:	16,000 ft (4,877 m)	18,000 ft (5,486 m)

Sinaia

Dimensions: Span 86 ft 10 in (26·47 m); wing area 1,823 sq ft (169·37 sq m).
Max weight: 16,000 lb (7,257 kg).

The Siddeley Siskin S.R.2 fighter completed in Coventry in 1919.

The Siskins

The most significant aircraft to be designed and built by the Siddeley Deasy company was the S.R.2, a single-seat fighter which, in its developed form, was to become famous in the RAF. Originally it had been intended that the S.R.2 should be powered by the proposed 300 hp fourteen-cylinder two-row radial engine which, as the RAF 8, was being designed under Major Green at Farnborough but was passed over to Siddeley Deasy when Green joined the company in 1917. In the event, the development of the radial engine was deferred so that priority could be given to bringing the Puma engine up to production standard. Thus it was that the Siddeley S.R.2, afterwards to be named the Siskin, was first flown with the ill-fated A.B.C. Dragonfly nine-cylinder radial engine.

It was natural that a fighter designed by John Lloyd under the direction of Green should bear a resemblance to the S.E. series built under Green's leadership at Farnborough and, in fact, the Siskin's S.E. parentage was clearly evident. It has been suggested that the design which emerged as the Siskin had already been roughed out by Green before he left Farnborough, but both he and Lloyd have denied that this was so: nevertheless, it seems likely that, but for the change in Government policy towards Farnborough, the aeroplane that became the Siskin might very well have been the S.E.7.

Whatever may be the truth of its origin, the Siskin was a very good aeroplane and, together with the engine which later became the Jaguar, it was responsible for the initial success of the Armstrong Whitworth company—although it was still some way into the future when the first

Siskin made its maiden flight from Coventry's Radford aerodrome in the spring of 1919. It was an elegant biplane with wings of unequal span and chord and a spidery-looking undercarriage with long-stroke oleo shock-absorbers, a feature that became familiar on all subsequent Siskin variants. The Dragonfly engine was neatly installed in a well-streamlined cowling with individual cooling channels for each cylinder and blending into a spinner on the propeller boss.

On test in the summer of 1919, the Siskin was found to have excellent handling and stability characteristics. Its performance, too, was generally superior to most of its Dragonfly-powered contemporaries. An Air Ministry test report records that the S.R.2 attained a speed of 145 mph at 6,500 ft and climbed to 10,000 ft in just under eight minutes.

The Siskin was considered to be among the best of the fighters fitted with the A.B.C. Dragonfly engine. (*Imperial War Museum Q69245*)

The original order for the Siddeley Deasy fighter was placed sometime early in 1918 and was for six aircraft, but later in the year the order was cut to three, by which time the first of the S.R.2 airframes was partially completed. By this time, too, it had become clear that the 300 hp radial would not be forthcoming in time and, as explained above, it was decided to substitute the A.B.C. Dragonfly engine. Even then, a shortage of Dragonfly engines held up the completion of the three aircraft—which bore the serial numbers C4541, C4542 and C4543—and although the first airframe was probably completed some time in the latter half of 1918, the first flight does not appear to have taken place until early in 1919. With the failure of the Dragonfly engine in 1919, the Siskin passed into eclipse and, apart from a brief appearance at the RAF Pageant at Hendon in June 1920, little was heard of it until C4541 reappeared in March 1921, now fitted with the new Armstrong Siddeley Jaguar radial engine and bearing the family name of Armstrong Whitworth in place of Siddeley Deasy.

The unusual undercarriage design of the S.R.2 was to be a characteristic feature of all subsequent Siskin variants.

The Air Ministry, impressed by the outstanding qualities of the Siskin now that it had an engine worthy of the name, encouraged Armstrong Whitworth to develop the type, but indicated that, as a matter of policy, future orders for the RAF would be given only for all-metal aeroplanes.

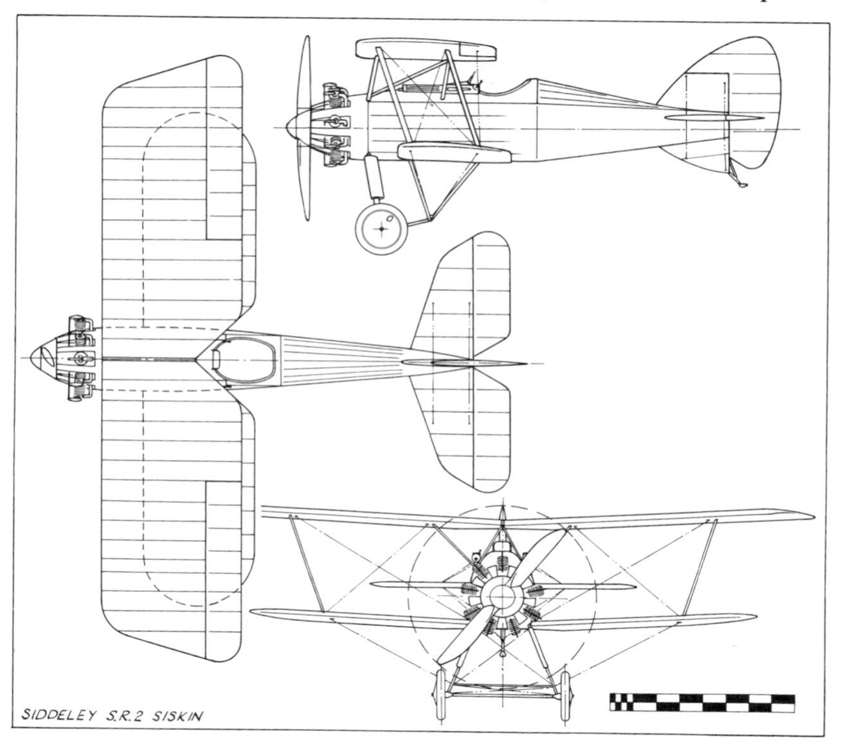

With the Dragonfly engine, the S.R.2 had a top speed of more than 145 mph.

The S.R.2, together with many of its contemporaries, was rendered ineffective by the failure of the Dragonfly engine.

In 1921 the S.R.2, C4541, now known as the Armstrong Whitworth Siskin, reappeared with an early example of the Jaguar engine. (*Courtesy J. M. Bruce*)

The Siskin II, of mixed wood and metal construction, flew as a two-seater in the 1922 King's Cup race. (*Flight International 2105B*)

The first new variant of the Siskin, built in 1922, therefore, went half-way to that end, having a wire-braced steel-tube fuselage with wings of conventional wood construction. The first Siskin II was a two-seater, but in other respects it bore a marked resemblance to the S.R.2. It had parallel interplane struts, a sharply tapered fuselage and a large fin and rudder extending well below the fuselage. The undercarriage was similar to that of the S.R.2, but the nose, with its uncowled Jaguar engine, was distinctly less elegant.

The two-seat Siskin was registered as a civil aircraft and, as G-EBEU, was flown by Frank Courtney in the 1922 King's Cup air race but was

Refuelling the Siskin II at Croydon Airport before the start of the King's Cup race in 1922. (*Flight International 2079*)

In the 1923 King's Cup race the Siskin II, G-EBEU, this time as a single-seater, won the race at 148·7 mph flown by Frank Courtney. (*Flight International*)

compelled to retire, after flying some 575 miles, because of a broken centre-section fitting. The same aircraft, now converted to a single seater, was more successful in the following year: entered by John Siddeley and again flown by Courtney, it won the King's Cup in July, covering the course of 809 statute miles at an average speed of 148·7 mph. Within a week of the King's Cup race a Siskin II was on show at the Gothenburg International Aero Exhibition; this was probably G-EBEU (it appeared at the show without markings) and later this aircraft was present at the Third Czechoslovak International Aero Exhibition held in Prague in June 1924. A second Siskin II, G-EBHY, was subsequently exported to Sweden where it was flown experimentally with a ski undercarriage.

The second Siskin II, G-EBHY, on test in Sweden with an experimental ski undercarriage. (*Royal Aeronautical Society*)

The first Siskin with an all-metal frame was J6583, ordered by the Air Ministry in 1920. This aircraft, the prototype Siskin III, was test flown by Frank Courtney on 7 May, 1923. During the course of its trials in the summer of 1923, it was flown with bench-type balances on the ailerons. During a dive, one of these balances collapsed and jammed the aileron; subsequently, at Courtney's suggestion, the ailerons were tapered at the tips, this modification being first tested in August 1923 and later adopted as standard. The first production order for the Siskin III, under contract No.342619/22, was for three aircraft, and the first of these, J6981, made its maiden flight on 24 March, 1924.

The Siskin III was the first aeroplane with an all-metal frame to be built in quantity for the RAF, but the transition to metal did nothing to improve the appearance of the aircraft, which emerged with a somewhat angular outline with, seemingly, little regard paid to cutting down air resistance.

The fourth production Siskin III, J6998, completed in the spring of 1924. (*Royal Aeronautical Society*)

Characteristic features of the design were the narrow single-spar lower wing contrasting sharply with the broad overhanging top wing, the outward-splayed V-shaped interplane struts, and the large balanced rudder extending well below the fuselage with a small ventral fin. The wing structure was so designed that if a bracing wire should break or be shot away, the load on it could be taken by two other wires; furthermore, the method of bracing was such that an interplane strut could be shot away without causing the wings to collapse.

The pilot sat just behind the top wing with his eyes roughly level with the trailing edge; his view upward and forward was, therefore, good. The view forward and downward was also reasonably good because of the narrow lower wings. The long-travel undercarriage had telescopic legs consisting of concentric steel tubes forming an oil dashpot which served to

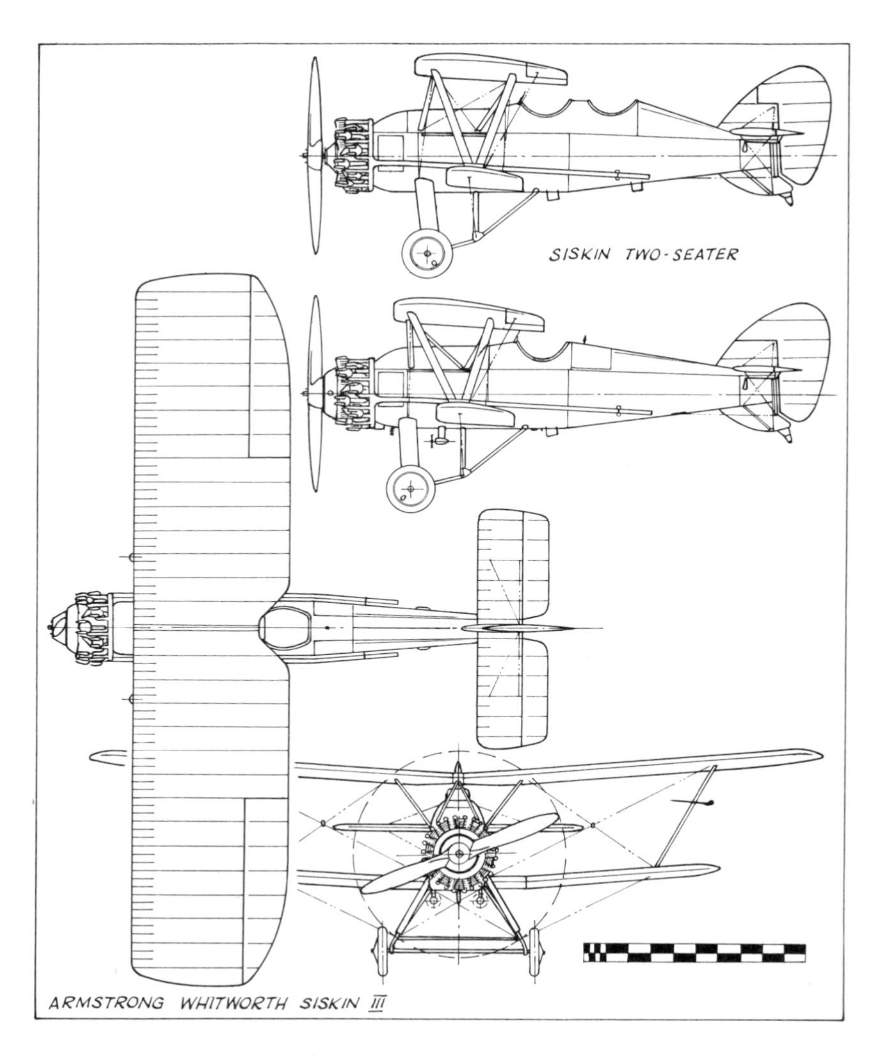

damp the action of the rubber shock-absorber cords. The oleo legs were stayed and braced to a structure similar in configuration to the normal V-type undercarriage. In a lecture delivered in 1920, Major Green claimed that the Siskin landing gear had the same weight and resistance as the S.E.5 undercarriage but was capable of absorbing twice the amount of energy.

When the first production Siskin III flew in March 1924, the line at Whitley was well established and two of the completed aircraft, with works numbers 66 and 67, were registered as civil aircraft carrying the marks G-EBJQ and G-EBJS respectively. Both were entered for the King's Cup race held in August 1924, G-EBJS by John Siddeley, and G-EBJQ by Sir

Two civil Siskin IIIs, with extra fuel tanks, flew in the 1924 King's Cup race. G-EBJQ came in fourth.

Glynn West, then chairman of the parent company in Newcastle. G-EBJS, flown by Courtney, was forced to land at Brough with a broken spinner, whilst G-EBJQ, piloted by Flt Lieut H. W. G. Jones, was only able to achieve fourth place out of five finishers. It nevertheless put up the fastest

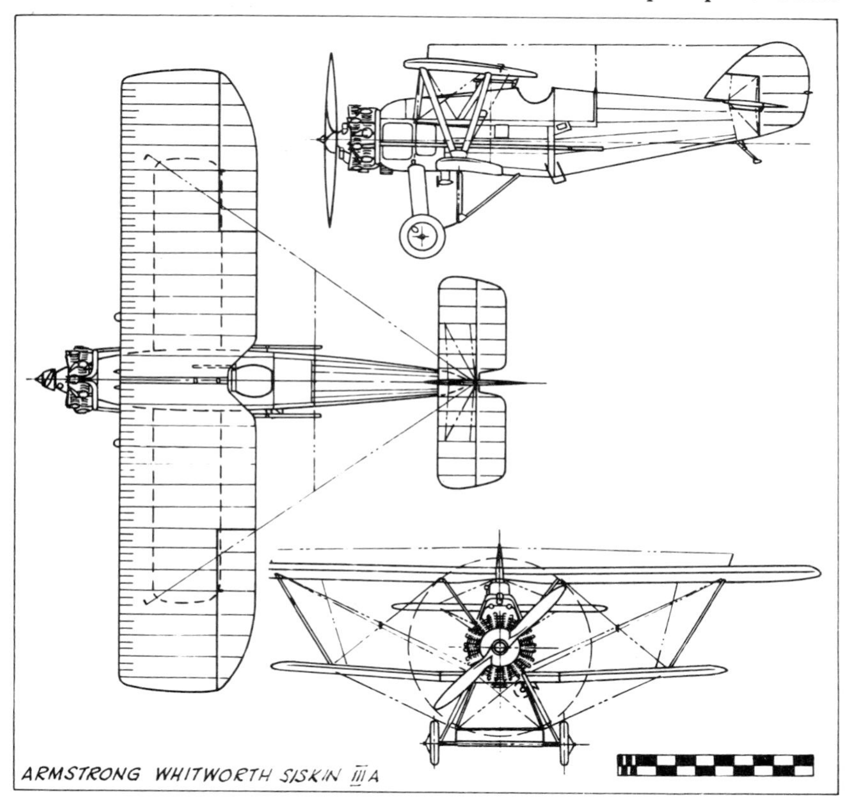

time over the course of 950 statute miles with an average speed of just on 126 mph. For the race both aircraft were provided with large extra fuel tanks beneath the top wing.

The fifth aircraft on the Siskin III production line, J7001, was set aside for conversion to Mk.IIIA configuration, but before this version was put into production, two other Siskin variants were built. The first of these, in order of production, was the Siskin V, which appeared in 1924 and represented a reversion to the two-spar lower wing with parallel interplane struts as on the Siskin II, to which it was similar in many other aspects, including a structure of mixed metal and wood.

The two Siskin Vs, registered G-EBLN and G-EBLQ, together with the one and only Siskin IV, G-EBLL, which was a Siskin V with wings of shorter span, all competed in the King's Cup race flown in July 1925. This race was over a course of 1,608 statute miles made up of two circuits of England and Scotland flown in opposite directions on two succeeding days. Fog caused havoc among the fourteen starters and only four completed the circuit on the first day, two of them being G-EBLQ, flown by F. L. Barnard, and the Siskin IV flown by H. W. G. Jones, now a Squadron Leader. The other Siskin V, flown by J. L. N. Bennett-Baggs, was damaged (as was also the Armstrong Whitworth Ajax flown by Courtney) by running into an unmarked ditch at the Newcastle landing ground situated on the Town Moor, the scene of the wartime activities of Armstrong Whitworth. The eventual winner of the race was Barnard who, in better weather, averaged 151·43 mph over the course on the second day, with Jones coming in second, 1 hr 23 min later.

The Siskin V, G-EBLQ. This aircraft, flown by F. L. Barnard, won the King's Cup race in 1925.

Another view of the Siskin V, G-EBLQ, outside the hangars at Whitley Abbey aerodrome. (*Courtesy A. Campbell-Orde*)

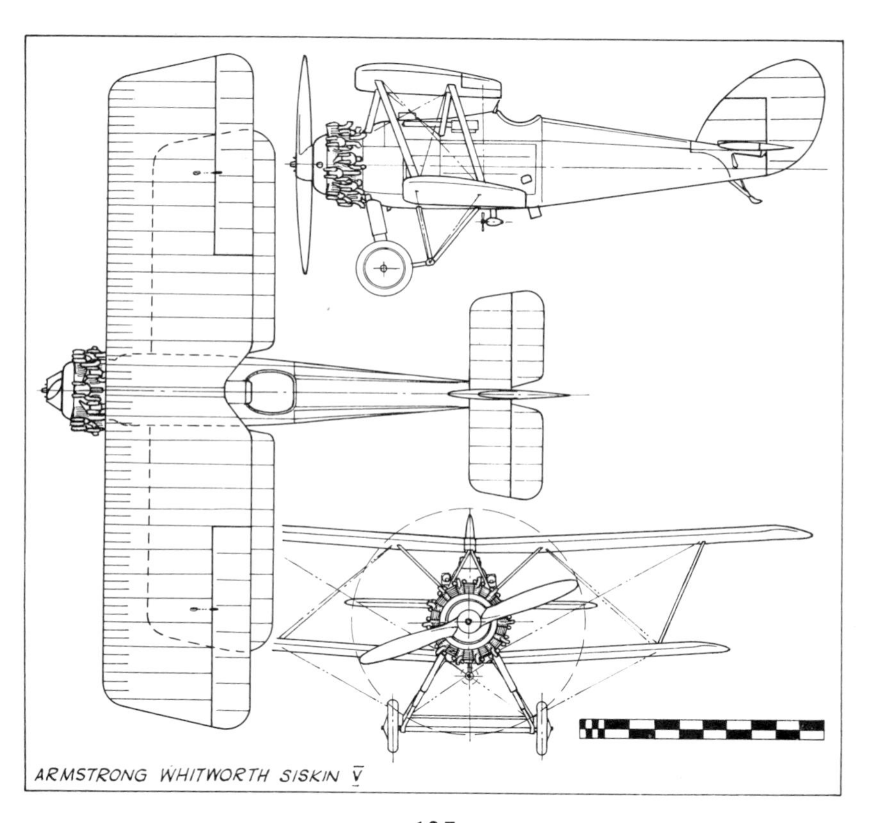

During the period 1922 to 1924 strenuous efforts were made to sell the Siskin overseas, and Frank Courtney gave demonstrations in Belgium, France, Holland, Roumania, Spain and Sweden. The only substantial result of this sales campaign was an order from Roumania. The contract was negotiated during 1925, and the story goes that the order was obtained largely through the efforts of the British Ambassador, who was friendly with the Roumanian King, but that the subsequent cancellation of the contract

A Siskin V built for the Roumanian Government; the order was subsequently cancelled.

was engineered by the minister in charge of purchasing aircraft, who was under heavy pressure from the French. The decision to cancel may also have been due, in some part, to the fact that a well-known Roumanian pilot, Major Sanatescu, was killed while flying one of the Roumanian Siskin Vs, No.29, in 1925. The Roumanian order was for sixty-five aircraft, and a sequence of works numbers, 68 to 132, was allotted in the Armstrong Whitworth production schedule. Records show that Siskin V No.1, the first of the Roumanian batch, was being test flown in October 1924. At least six more, Nos.2, 4, 10, 13, 14 and 15 were tested before the end of the year, and Nos.28, 29 and 33 were flown during the first half of 1925. How many others were actually completed before the order was cancelled is not known, but all of them, together with a number of components for others, were subsequently reduced to scrap at Whitley. Although the company was compelled to forego a valuable aircraft order, all was not lost because the Roumanian government took delivery of some Jaguar engines which were later said to have been installed in Roumanian-built aircraft.

In the latter part of 1924, a Siskin V airframe had undergone static load tests at Farnborough and, in a report dated 8 November, 1924, it was recorded that, with slight modifications, the structure satisfactorily withstood proof loads that were higher than those demanded by British regulations for high-speed fighters. Nevertheless, the accident to the Roumanian pilot had resulted from the aircraft breaking-up in the air. At the time, it was thought that the pilot had over-stressed the aircraft during a particularly exuberant display of aerobatics, but some suspicion that there may have been a weakness in the Siskin V's wing design was aroused when G-EBLQ crashed in 1927, resulting in the death of the company's pilot, Douglas Hughes: in this case it appeared that the leading edge of one of the wings had collapsed during a roll.

After the first Siskin III came off the production line towards the end of March 1924, it was not long before the new fighter joined the RAF: this occurred in the following May, when No.41 Squadron at Northolt aerodrome began to re-equip with the aircraft. In 1925 the squadron's Siskins made a public appearance at the RAF Display at Hendon in June, when they performed a converging bombing attack on a stranded tank. In 1926 No.41 Squadron again took part in the RAF annual show, this time in a fly-past of fighter squadrons in which fifty-four aircraft took part. The

A production Siskin III aircraft delivered to the RAF in the summer of 1924.

second unit to receive the Siskin III was No.111 Squadron, based at Duxford aerodrome, which received the aircraft in June 1924 in place of its Sopwith Snipes. In the summer of 1925 this squadron returned one of its Siskin IIIs (J7161) to Coventry so that it could be fitted with a Jaguar IV supercharged engine in place of the normally-aspirated Jaguar III previously fitted. The aircraft was returned to the squadron four months later, and other squadron aircraft were soon converted, so that by the beginning of 1926 No.111 Squadron became the first high-altitude fighter squadron in the RAF. A further development in tactics occurred towards the end of 1926 when the squadron started training for night fighting.

Altogether, a total of one hundred and eighteen Siskin IIIs were built, including a batch of forty-nine two-seat Siskin IIIDCs, two single-seaters lent to the Royal Canadian Air Force (and later purchased by them), two

The two-seat trainer version of the Siskin, known as the Siskin IIIDC. (*Ministry of Defence*)

A Siskin IIIDC of the first production batch. (*Ministry of Defence*)

One of two civil Siskin IIIDC aircraft used by Air Service Training at Hamble aerodrome.

two-seaters for Esthonia, and two other two-seaters for the Armstrong Whitworth flying school. These last, G-ABHT and G-ABHU, were completed in the spring of 1931. In addition to the batch of forty-seven two-seaters built as such for the RAF, at least another thirty-one single-seaters were later converted to two-seaters.

The Siskin III, J7001, which, as already mentioned, was converted to the prototype Siskin IIIA, first flew on 21 October, 1925, piloted by Frank Courtney, and an initial batch of thirteen was ordered in the same year under contract No. 625304/25. The most obvious differences between the two marks was a modification to the rear fuselage, which had the effect of raising the tailplane, and the abolition of the ventral fin. As was the case with the Siskin III, some aircraft were fitted with the unsupercharged Jaguar III engine, but most had the 385 hp supercharged Jaguar IV. The Siskin IIIA was armed with two forward-firing Vickers guns and carried

The first production Siskin IIIA for the RAF.

1,200 rounds of ·303-in ammunition; racks were fitted to carry four 20-lb high-explosive bombs. Wireless equipment, providing for two-way short-wave telephonic communication, was housed within the fuselage fairing immediately behind the cockpit; the wireless aerial ran from short masts on the upper surface of the top wing to the top of the rudder. The maximum speed of the Siskin IIIA with the supercharged engine was 153 mph at 10,000 ft, and its service ceiling was 27,100 ft, a considerable improvement on that of the Siskin III.

The first unit to receive the new aircraft was No.111 Squadron which collected its first Siskin IIIA from Coventry on 6 September, 1926. In the following year three more squadrons were equipped with the Siskin IIIA, No.41 in March, No.1 between August and November, and No.56 in September. This last mentioned squadron retained its Siskins longer than any other, finally changing them for Bristol Bulldogs in August 1932. Five more squadrons, Nos.29, 19, 32, 43 and 17, in that order, were re-equipped with the Siskin IIIA between March and September 1928. The

A production Siskin IIIA. (*Courtesy A. Campbell-Orde*)

last squadron to receive the aircraft was No.25, which completed its re-equipment in July 1929.

In spite of its somewhat ungainly appearance, the Siskin was very manoeuvrable and many were the aerobatic performances put on by Siskin squadrons. Outstanding among them was No.43 Squadron's exhibition of formation aerobatics with the three aircraft of each flight linked together by cords attached to the interplane struts. This act was first performed publicly at the RAF Display at Hendon in 1930 when the squadron went through a series of manoeuvres, including a squadron loop, without breaking the cords until the end of the performance when the links were sundered as the aircraft of each flight broke formation with a 'Prince of Wales Feathers' manoeuvre.

Another view of a production Siskin IIIA, of which a total of 340 were built for the RAF. (*Courtesy A. Campbell-Orde*)

Two flights of No.43 Squadron, RAF, performing tied-together aerobatics, first seen in public at the RAF Display in 1930. (*Ministry of Defence*)

Each Siskin fighter squadron had on its strength one two-seat Siskin IIIDC, and for a short period between the middle of January and the end of April 1930, No.54 Squadron, based at Hornchurch aerodrome, was equipped with a flight of Siskin IIIDCs as a stop-gap pending the delivery of their promised Bulldogs. A number of other RAF units were also equipped with Siskins; the Home Communications Flight at Hendon had two Siskin IIIs, and two other IIIAs were operating in the Middle East theatre in 1931. Some units were provided with both the Siskin IIIA and the Siskin IIIDC: among these were Nos.3 and 5 Flying Training Schools, the Central Flying School, then based at Wittering, and the establishments at Cranwell and Halton. In addition, the Armament and Gunnery School at Leuchars had three dual-control Siskins on their strength.

By 1931 the Siskins in squadron service were beginning to show their age, and by the middle of the year officials in the Air Ministry were considering whether to embark on a programme of re-conditioning, or whether to order some Siskin IIIBs as replacements. Another alternative discussed was to speed up the re-equipping of the fighter squadrons with the Bristol Bulldog. In June 1931 there was a total of 179 Siskins in service and in immediate reserve; of these 142 were Siskin IIIAs (serving with Nos.1, 19, 25, 29, 41 and 56 Squadrons) and 37 were Siskin IIIDCs.

The Siskin IIIB then being considered had the same dimensions as the IIIA but was some 230 lb heavier. The main differences between the two aircraft were the fitting of slotted ailerons and larger fuel tanks and the replacement of the Jaguar IVC engine by the geared and supercharged Jaguar VIII. This powerplant was able to develop more power to altitude because the reduction gear permitted the use of higher engine rpm. The performance figures quoted by the Air Ministry in correspondence concerning re-equipment showed that the Siskin IIIB (fitted with a Townend ring) reached 15,000 ft in $11\frac{1}{2}$ min (two minutes better than the Siskin IIIA) and its speed at that height was 164 mph (20 mph better than the IIIA). Martlesham Heath pilots were critical of the aircraft's handling

The Siskins of No.43 Squadron in echelon formation. (*Flight International 9407*)

The Siskin IIIB prototype, an improved and more powerful version that did not go into production. (*Courtesy P. Jarrett*)

characteristics and the fact that it had less than one hour's endurance at full throttle at 15,000 ft after allowing for the usual 30 min for take-off, climb and return to base. In the event, the Siskin IIIB was not ordered, and only two more squadrons, Nos.19 and 41, were re-equipped (with Bulldogs) during the remaining months of 1931, while the remaining four Siskin squadrons, Nos.1, 25, 29 and 56 received their new equipment in 1932.

Towards the end of 1925 two RAF Siskin IIIs were sent to Canada for winter trials by the Royal Canadian Air Force. The trials took place at Camp Borden between January and April 1926, and the RCAF were much impressed by the cold-weather performance of the aircraft and particularly with the ease with which the Jaguar engine could be started if it was well doped during sucking-in (it was noted with satisfaction that the US Army's method of spraying ether on a hot brick supported in front of the engine air intake was not necessary). Tested with skis in place of the wheels, which increased the weight by 84 lb, the aircraft's top speed was 142 mph, only one mph less than when fitted with wheels.

The satisfactory tests, during which one of the Siskins was destroyed in an accident, led to the purchase of the two aircraft and the placing of orders for more from England, some of which were sent direct from Coventry while others were delivered from RAF stocks. In all twelve Siskins were delivered to the RCAF, two being taken on strength in 1926, two in 1927, two in 1928, five in 1929 and one in 1931. The first two, as mentioned above, were Siskin IIIs, two of those supplied in 1929 were Siskin IIIDCs, and the remainder were Siskin IIIAs.

The Siskin quickly became popular with RCAF pilots and two of them performed with distinction at the US National Air Races held at Cleveland in September 1929. Subsequently, a Siskin aerobatic team, formed at Camp Borden, gave a number of demonstrations at various Canadian cities during the latter half of 1930 and, in 1931, the team, led by Sqdn Ldr

Hewson, gave numerous demonstrations at places in Canada and the United States as part of the Trans-Canada Pageant. The tour included another visit to the US National Air Races at Cleveland, where the team put up a spectacular performance including a finale of three successive loops finishing only a few feet off the ground. On the following day the organizers cut their programme time by half but, as one of the pilots later remarked, 'We had had our day and stole the headlines.' When the tour ended back in Montreal in September 1931, the team had flown 11,000 miles and visited twenty-six places since setting out from Hamilton two-and-a-half months earlier.

One of the two Siskin III aircraft sent to Canada for test and evaluation and subsequently purchased by the RCAF. (*Canadian Forces No.PL117076*)

During their service with the RCAF the Siskins formed the fighter Flight at Trenton and Camp Borden until 1937 when the flight became No.1 (Fighter) Squadron. In 1938 this squadron, still with five Siskins on its strength, moved to Calgary, and it was not until June 1939 that the Siskins finally gave place to Hurricanes. There is no record of the Siskins having flown again after they were put into storage at High River in 1939, but several presumably remained in existence until the last was finally struck off strength in August 1947, almost twenty years after its arrival in Canada. In the early 1960s the authorities in Canada made a thorough search for a Siskin to add to the Canadian National Aircraft Collection but were eventually forced to conclude that none had survived.

During its long career, many modifications and experiments were carried out on the Siskin. In 1925 Green experimented with a cowling on a

An RCAF Siskin IIIA on skis; note the camera gun mounted on the centre section. (*Canadian Forces No.RE16621*)

Another view of the RCAF Siskin No.22 in its summer guise with wheels. (*Canadian Forces No.RE642646*)

This Siskin IIIA, No.20, of the RCAF was later renumbered 302. Originally it had been allotted the RAF Service number J8632. (*Canadian Forces No.HC2093*)

The RCAF Siskin aerobatic team formed in May 1930. (*Canadian Forces No.RE18689*)

Siskin III which entirely enclosed the Jaguar engine except for a series of circular air inlets opposite each cylinder. Tests, which began on 6 January, 1925, showed that the top speed of the aircraft was increased by about four to five miles an hour, corresponding to a reduction in fuselage resistance of approximately thirty per cent. On the other hand, cooling efficiency was reduced and the weight was increased; additionally, the cowling made the engine less accessible, a disadvantage which, at that time, weighed more heavily with the authorities than a mere loss of performance.

A major modification introduced in 1930 was a new lower wing set at an increased angle of incidence of 4 deg and fitted with heavier-gauge anti-drag bracing. This new design was, apparently, not an unqualified success,

Any landing you can walk away from is a good one: one of the two Siskin IIIDC trainers supplied to the RCAF. (*Canadian Forces No.RD20704-2*)

An experimental cowling for the Jaguar engine of the Siskin, tested in 1925. It added about 5 mph to the top speed. (*Courtesy A. Campbell-Orde*)

and a further strengthening was found necessary after the leading edge of one of the new wings buckled as Siskin J9884 pulled out of a dive. Other airframe modifications introduced from time to time included improved longeron fittings in the engine bay, stiffening of the top plane wingtips, a new fireproof bulkhead, and an improved type of tail-operating jack.

At the request of the Aeronautical Research Committee some spinning trials were undertaken at Farnborough in November 1927 with Siskin IIIA J8428, to determine how the aircraft behaved in a prolonged spin. The tests, which were conducted by three pilots, involved spins of up to thirteen turns made between 14,000 and 8,000 ft. It was found that the Siskin was reluctant to spin, especially with the tail-trim forward, but that

Another view of the Siskin III J7148 with its enclosed Jaguar engine; cooling proved to be inadequate. (*Courtesy A. Campbell-Orde*)

when well established, the spin was somewhat slow for a single-seater and was rather jerky; the height loss was about 3,000 ft for seven turns. Even with the centre of gravity behind the normal full military load position, a spin in either direction always stopped quickly when the controls were centred.

Another series of trials was made at Farnborough in May 1929 with Siskin J8850 to investigate behaviour at the stall with various methods of lateral control. It is probable that these experiments were concerned more with basic research than with an attempt to improve the Siskin's control characteristics. In all, four different systems of lateral control were tried; a) interlinked slot and aileron; b) plain auto-slot; c) spoiled auto-slot, *i.e.*, slot practically closed when the aileron was raised; and d) interceptor auto-slot, *i.e.*, a blanking plate behind the slot which rose when the aileron was raised. The tests showed that, during normal flight, none of these systems differed appreciably from the standard arrangement, but that with b, c or d the aircraft would not spin. At the stall the interceptor auto-slot was distinctly superior and the wing could be raised against the rudder, but the ability to sideslip was diminished. The plain auto-slot gave stability at the stall without control, a characteristic that was considered undesirable in a fighter. As might be expected, no modifications were introduced as a result of these experiments and the Siskin's lateral control remained positive but somewhat heavy to the end.

Altogether, some 485 Siskins of all marks, including the S.R.2, were built, and of these about 348 were Siskin IIIAs. In fact, the great majority

This Siskin IIIA, J8390, was used experimentally aboard the battle cruiser HMS *Repulse* during fleet operations in the summer of 1929. (*Courtesy P. Moyes*)

A Siskin III, with skis, operating in the Canadian winter. (*Canadian Forces No.HC5990*)

of Siskin IIIAs, amounting to about 252, were built under contracts placed with Blackburn, Bristol, Gloster and Vickers; this was because Armstrong Whitworth were, by then, already engaged in large-scale production of the Atlas. Unfortunately no exact figure can be given for the number of Siskins built because of the doubt about the number of Siskin Vs and because some reconditioned aircraft may have been included in the totals claimed by some of the contracting firms.

The Siskin represented a landmark in the history of the RAF in that it was the first aircraft with all-metal structure to serve in quantity with that Service: it was also notable for the fact that it formed a link between the light, wooden fighters of the 1914–18 war, and the heavier, less manoeuvrable but more heavily armed metal aircraft of subsequent generations. The Siskin also pioneered the use of shortwave telephony, a significant step forward in fighter tactics.

The particular character of the Siskin has been admirably summed up in the writings of that well-known test pilot, writer and Farnborough Air Show commentator Oliver Stewart, who was one of the select few who tested the original S.R.2. Let him, therefore, have the last word on the Siskin fighter: '. . . the aeroplane was extremely easy to fly, and it is probable that it was, at the time it first appeared, the easiest single-seater fighter ever introduced into the flying service. In the past, single-seater fighters had been quick, snappy, short-tempered and sometimes vicious. But the Siskin was gentle, easy-going, calm, good-tempered—a marked contrast to previous machines. In the air the Siskin was amenable to discipline and would do loops, rolls . . . spins graciously, if not quickly. The outlook was markedly good and the cockpit arrangements comfortable. . . . It was an awkward-looking machine—a great uncouth brute of a thing, but with a heart of gold . . . it was certainly a safe machine . . .'

Siddeley S.R.2 Siskin
Dimensions: Span 27 ft 6 in (8·38 m); length 21 ft 3 in (6·48 m); height 9 ft 9 in (2·97 m); wing area 247 sq ft (22·95 sq m).

A.W. Siskin III
Dimensions: Span 33 ft 1 in (10·08 m); length 23 ft (7·01 m); height 9 ft 9 in (2·97 m); wing area 293 sq ft (27·22 sq m).

A.W. Siskin IIIA
Dimensions: Span 33 ft 2 in (10·11 m); length 25 ft 4 in (7·72 m); height 9 ft 8 in (2·95 m); wing area 293 sq ft (27·22 sq m).

A.W. Siskin V
Dimensions: Span 28 ft 4 in (8·64 m); length 21 ft 4 in (6·50 m); height 9 ft 4 in (2·85 m); wing area 256 sq ft (23·78 sq m).

	Siskin S.R.2 320 hp A.B.C. Dragonfly	Siskin III 325 hp Jaguar III	Siskin IIIA 385 hp Jaguar IVs	Siskin V 385 hp Jaguar
Max weight:	2,181 lb (989 kg)	2,735 lb (1,241 kg)	3,012 lb (1,366 kg)	2,440 lb (1,107 kg)
Empty weight:	1,463 lb (664 kg)	1,830 lb (830 kg)	2,061 lb (935 kg)	—
Speed				
Sea level:	—	—	143 mph (230 km/hr)	155 mph (249 km/hr)
6,500 ft (1,981 m):	145 mph (233 km/hr)	134 mph (216 km/hr)	—	—
10,000 ft (3,048 m):	143 mph (230 km/hr)	—	153 mph (246 km/hr)	147 mph (237 km/hr)
15,000 ft (4,572 m):	139 mph (224 km/hr)	128 mph (206 km/hr)	149 mph (240 km/hr)	140 mph (225 km/hr)
Climb				
to 6,500 ft (1,981 m):	4·5 min	5 min	—	—
to 10,000 ft (3,048 m):	7·8 min	8·5 min	6·35 min	6·2 min
to 15,000 ft (4,572 m):	13·8 min	16·5 min	10·6 min	11·5 min
to 20,000 ft (6,096 m):	—	—	16·9 min	20·2 min
Service Ceiling:	23,800 ft (7,254 m)	20,500 ft (6,248 m)	27,100 ft (8,260 m)	25,000 ft (7,620 m)
Endurance:	—	3 hr	1·2 hr (full throttle)	2½ hr

The Ugly Sisters

In any contest to select the ugliest aeroplane, the Wolf and the Ape would surely vie with each other for pride of place: both were seemingly designed to purely utilitarian standards, with little concession to aerodynamic refinement and even less to considerations of grace or elegance.

Wolf

The Wolf came first. It was designed, probably to Air Ministry specification D of R Type 3A, as a two-seat corps-reconnaissance aircraft, and three, numbered J6921, J6922 and J6923, were built for the Air Ministry under contract No.195547/21. Apart from its ungainly appearance, the Wolf was a more-or-less conventional biplane with slight sweepback and

The military version of the Wolf. (*Imperial War Museum H877*)

with the fuselage located about midway between the wings. The fuselage was built of steel tubing whilst the wings were of normal wooden construction. The engine was a Jaguar III of 350 hp, and the armament consisted of a forward-firing Vickers gun for the pilot, and a Scarff ring with a Lewis gun for the observer who was situated immediately behind and close to the pilot. An unusual feature was the method employed for providing aerodynamic balance for the ailerons. Small vertical fins, located above and

The Wolf in its original form as a two-seat reconnaissance aircraft. (*Courtesy P. Jarrett*)

below the lower wing, were carried on forward-pointing levers mounted on a common pivot placed near the rear spar; the levers were coupled to the controls in such a way that they moved in sympathy with the ailerons, thereby causing the slipstream to exert on the vertical surfaces a balancing force in the opposite sense to that exerted on the ailerons. The advantage of the system was that the degree of balance could be easily and quickly adjusted by altering the effective length of the lever arm.

The Wolf first flew on 19 January, 1923. The type was not adopted by the RAF and little is known about the subsequent history of the three Service aircraft. Existing RAE reports indicate that J6922 was used for general test and experimental work at Farnborough during 1924, and that tests with automatic controls were undertaken with J6923 at Farnborough in the winter of 1927–28.

Three other Wolves were built by the company for use as advanced trainers with the RAF Reserve Flying School which they operated at Whitley. The first of these, G-EBHI, first flew on 16 February, 1923, and the second, G-EBHJ, six months later on 16 August, while a third Wolf,

One of the three Wolves built as advanced trainers for the Armstrong Whitworth flying school at Whitley Abbey. (*Courtesy A. Campbell-Orde*)

'... in spite of occasional damage ... they continued to operate until 1931'. (*Courtesy A. Campbell-Orde*)

G-AAIY, was added to the fleet in 1929. These three aircraft became well known in the air around Whitley aerodrome from 1923 onwards and they were looked upon with much affection by many pilots of the Reserve of Air Force Officers; they were, perhaps, not quite so popular with the ground engineers who found the undercarriage difficult to maintain and the rigging something of a nightmare. Nevertheless, they must, in fact, have been unusually robust and reliable because, in spite of hard work and occasional damage, they continued to operate from Whitley until they were finally retired from active service when the school moved away from Coventry in 1931. Even then, the youngest of the three, G-AAIY, continued to play a useful rôle as an instructional airframe at the newly-established Air Service Training School at Hamble.

Another view of the Wolf trainer at Whitley Abbey. (*Courtesy A. Campbell-Orde*)

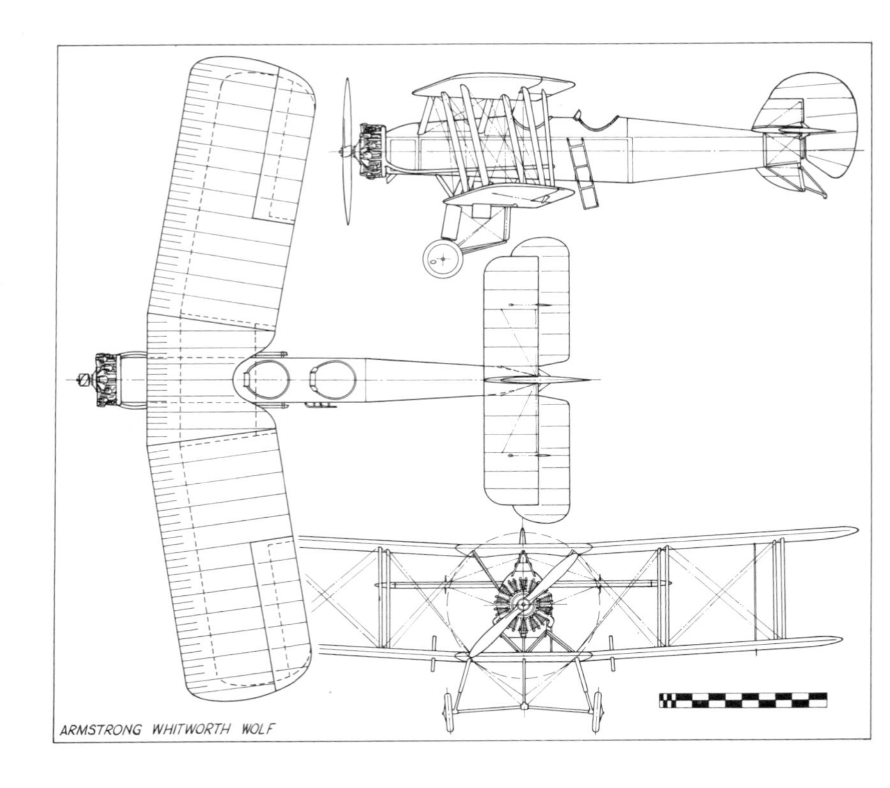

Ape

Although built by Armstrong Whitworth, the Ape, which appeared in 1926, was clearly the brain-child of the aerodynamic scientists at the RAE, who evidently thought that an infinitely adjustable aeroplane would provide them with all the answers. The design, somewhat reluctantly undertaken by Lloyd, was fashioned strictly according to Air Ministry specification 48/22 and, had the phrase been invented, it would quite rightly have been described as having 'variable geometry'.

The Ape's box-shaped fuselage was untapered in profile throughout its length, with a short fairing over the cockpits to give some protection to the crew. It was also parallel-sided in plan view except for a sharp taper over the rear four feet. With the basic fuselage, which was built of steel tubing, were supplied four additional sections; two of these, each 2 ft 9 in long, were for insertion, singly or together, in the rear fuselage, which could be split vertically at a point immediately aft of the rear cockpit. Two other sections, one measuring 21 inches long and the other 24 inches long, were available for altering the position of the Lynx III engine so that the position of the centre of gravity could be adjusted. This was necessary because not

The Ape experimental 'variable geometry' aircraft built to the requirements of the scientists at the RAE.

only could the length of the rear fuselage be varied but three alternative sizes of tailplane and rudder could be fitted according to requirements. In addition to being able to vary the position and the size of the horizontal tailplane, its angle of incidence could also be varied through a wide range, as will be evident from the accompanying photograph of J7754.

The mechanism for altering the tailplane incidence, which could be operated in the air by the pilot, was supported on an extension of the fuselage structure which surrounded the tapered rear portion of the fuselage. This 'scaffolding' of steel tubes carried the hinge on the front spar of

The second Ape biplane, showing the extent to which the tailplane incidence could be adjusted from the pilot's seat.

the tailplane and also the three-pronged operating levers, one on each side, which were operated by wires from the pilot's seat. The two-bay biplane wings, built of wood and of RAF 15 section, were also adaptable to a number of configurations: by varying the length and rake of the upper and lower centre-section struts the position of the wings in the fore and aft sense could be varied, as could the degree of stagger (from zero to 30 deg), the gap (from 4 ft to 9½ ft) and the dihedral (from zero to 7 deg). Surprisingly, no provision was made for incorporating sweepback and it was not possible, incidentally, to change the Ape from a biplane to a monoplane. Visually, one of the most outstanding features of the Ape was its truly imposing undercarriage which, together with a complicated tailskid structure built up under the rear fuselage, was designed to absorb the shocks of very heavy, fully-stalled landings. The spindly framework of steel tubes and the long-travel oleo legs of the undercarriage gave the appearance of a ferocious insect poised to leap, an impression which was far from being borne out by the aircraft's take-off and climb performance.

The 200 hp Lynx engine and the robust undercarriage of the first Ape aircraft.

Three Apes were built: J7753 was airborne for the first time on 5 January, 1926, but it was not until the following September or October that it was delivered to Farnborough. It may be presumed that the intervening months were occupied by the firm's test pilot evaluating the almost endless combinations and permutations offered by the multiform airframe. The second Ape, J7754, arrived at Farnborough from Coventry on 9 November, 1926, and the third was delivered soon afterwards, probably before the end of the year.

After a period of general testing at Farnborough, the Ape J7753 was used for a series of trials to study control at low speeds, but the performance of the aircraft was so disappointing that in July 1927 performance

The Ape J7753, with an extra bay inserted in the fuselage. (*Courtesy M. Goodall*)

tests were made '... to ascertain whether the low performance realised could have been foreseen'. The measured figures showed that the rate of climb at sea level was limited to 350 ft/min, falling off to 230 ft/min at 3,100 ft, and that the cruising speed at that height was 75 mph. These tests were made with one extra bay inserted in both the front and the rear fuselage, the smallest rudder and the middle-sized tailplane. In this configuration the Ape, as flown, weighed 2,875 lb and, with all its built-in head

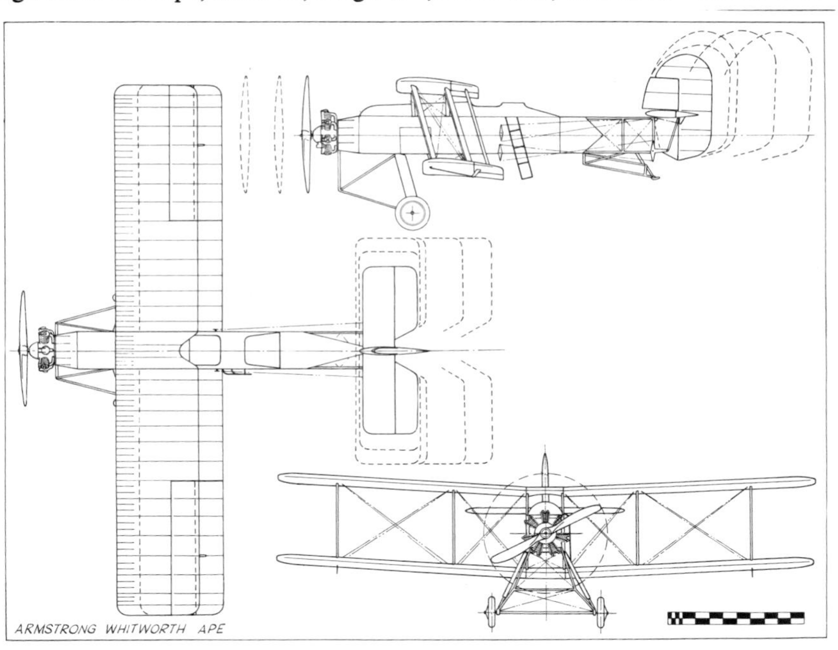

resistance and a Lynx engine developing only 180 hp at normal revolutions, the performance could hardly have been anything but poor. In the circumstances it seems strange that this should have come as a surprise to anybody, let alone the scientists at the RAE. The report on the tests suggested that the performance could be improved by fitting a supercharged Lynx engine of 230 hp which, it was estimated, would improve the rate of climb by some 80 ft/min, and by fairing the tubular struts of the undercarriage, which would add another 100 ft/min to the rate of climb at sea level. In fact, J7753 was later re-engined with a Jaguar and, as recommended, the undercarriage struts were fitted with streamlined fairings, but not before the aircraft had been damaged in a take-off accident on 8 May, 1928.

The second aircraft, J7754, was also powered by an unsupercharged Lynx engine at the time of its delivery to Farnborough in November 1926, but by August 1928 it had been fitted with the supercharged version and was engaged in testing a system of pilot planes fitted in front of the wings. By this time the weight of the aircraft had risen to 3,250 lb, an increase which may well have nullified the advantage of the extra power. The pilot planes, small aerofoils with a chord of about 7¼ inches, were mounted in front of, and somewhat below, the leading edge of both upper and lower wings. They were free to rotate about a hinge situated slightly in front of the pilot-plane leading edge, the amount of angular movement being limited by an adjustable stop. In normal flight the pilot planes trailed freely, but as the angle of incidence became large, the pilot planes moved up against the stops forming fixed slots in front of the mainplanes. The object of the tests was to determine the best maximum angle for the pilot planes. The scheme was somewhat complicated and impracticable, but it may have served to show the way to the automatic slot. The report on the tests stated that they

Another view of the second Ape, J7754. The Lynx-engined examples proved to be seriously underpowered.

The Wolf trainer G-EBHJ outside the hangars at Whitley Abbey.

were somewhat protracted by the poor performance of the aeroplane and that the tests began in August 1928 and were completed in May 1929. What the report does not say is that the trials were terminated abruptly when it crash-landed at Cove, near Farnborough, on 23 May, 1929.

The third Ape, J7755, was also delivered with a Lynx III engine, but it is not known whether this was later changed, as no test reports for this aircraft have come to light. The probability is that the people at the RAE had become somewhat disenchanted with the Ape and that the third aircraft was not much used. Between January and July 1927 it made a few flights classified as 'general tests' and, at one stage, it was used to evaluate a rate-of-descent meter.

The crash of J7754 in May 1929 seems to have been the end of the Ape story but, of the ultimate fate of the other two aircraft there is no record.

Wolf

Dimensions: Span 39 ft 10 in (12·14 m); length 31 ft (9·45 m); height 13 ft (3·96 m); wing area 488 sq ft (45·34 sq m).

Ape

Dimensions: Span 40 ft (12·19 m); length 28 ft 3 in to 38 ft 3 in (8·61 to 11·66 m); height 13 ft to 15 ft (3·96 m to 4·57 m); wing area 473 sq ft (43·93 sq m).

	Wolf *350 hp Jaguar III*	**Ape** *180 hp Lynx III*
Max weight:	4,090 lb (1,855 kg)	2,700–3,250 lb (1,225–1,474 kg)
Empty weight:	2,690 lb (1,220 kg)	2,020–2,570 lb (916–1,166 kg)
Max speed		
3,000 ft (914 m):	—	90 mph (145 km/hr)
10,000 ft (3,048 m):	110 mph (177 km/hr)	—
Climb		
to 1,000 ft (305 m):	1·3 min	3 min
to 3,000 ft (914 m):	—	11 min
to 5,000 ft (1,524 m):	6·5 min	—
to 10,000 ft (3,048 m):	19 min	—
Service ceiling:	15,150 ft (4,618 m)	6,400 ft (1,951 m)
Endurance:	$3\frac{3}{4}$ hr	—

The prototype Atlas, with the civil registration G-EBLK, as it appeared at the RAF Display in 1926. (*Courtesy A. Campbell-Orde*)

Atlas, Ajax and Aries

The Atlas, a conventional two-seat biplane designed for army co-operation work, followed the Siskin on the production line at Whitley and eventually surpassed it in total output. Altogether 478 Atlases were built and the type remained in production from 1927 until 1933, reaching a peak output in 1931, in which year 160 aircraft were built. The Atlas Mk.I and the trainer version served with the RAF for eight years until 1935.

The Atlas first appeared in public at the RAF Display held at Hendon on 3 July, 1926, but before that a very similar aeroplane called the Ajax had competed in the King's Cup air race flown from Croydon in July 1925. In this race the Ajax was flown by Frank Courtney who, after being delayed at the start by a reluctant engine, withdrew at the Newcastle control. The Atlas and the Ajax were so alike that one could be forgiven for concluding that the Ajax may have been the prototype of the Atlas and that for some reason the name was later changed, but this was apparently not so. The company's list of production numbers shows that the Atlas came first by a short head and there is no doubt that the two types existed alongside one another for a considerable time.

After the passage of time, it is difficult to determine the company's reason for making a distinction between the two types, unless it was that the Ajax was considered to be the 'general purpose' or 'fighter' version of the Atlas; in fact, the two aircraft were so similar, in outward appearance at any rate, as to be practically indistinguishable. The published dimensions and the contemporary works drawings show only minor variations, the most obvious being the absence of a gun ring around the rear cockpit of the Ajax. Both the Ajax and the prototype Atlas had wings of RAF 15 section and were built of wood, until those of the latter were altered, as recounted later.

Both the Atlas and the Ajax prototypes were initially registered as civil aircraft, but various sources which quote the constructor's numbers are contradictory: according to the company's list the first Atlas was given the constructor's number 139 and was registered G-EBLK, and this was followed by two Ajax, constructor's numbers 141 and 142, carrying the marks G-EBLM and G-EBNI respectively, although there is contrary evidence that the latter was registered as an Atlas. The prototype Atlas is believed to have made its first flight on 10 May, 1925; the date of the first flight of Ajax G-EBLM is not known, but it must have been before July 1925 and it seems likely that, in fact, all three aircraft, G-EBLK, G-EBLM and G-EBNI, were completed and flown in that order and within a comparatively short space of time.

The Ajax, G-EBLM, in its original form with RAF 15 wings and horn-balanced ailerons.

The prototype Atlas G-EBLK, first built as a private venture, was, according to company records, 'converted to standard' with a new constructor's number, 278, and the serial number J8675. The two aircraft, G-EBLM and G-EBNI, were similarly given serial numbers J9128 and J9129, respectively. Before this, however, G-EBLM had appeared as the only complete British aircraft at the Paris Aero Show held in December 1926, after which it was shipped to South America for a demonstration tour.

Two further Ajax aircraft appear in the company's list with constructor's numbers 273 and 274 and with RAF serials J8802 and J8803. There is a baffling note on the company's production list to the effect that these two were 'Day bombers from G-EBLM and G-EBNI', so, whether these were entirely new aircraft or merely conversions, remains in doubt, with the probability that they were in fact new machines.

The Atlas was selected in competition with the de Havilland Hyena, the Bristol Boarhound and the Vickers Vespa, all intended to meet specification 33/26. The Ajax, on the other hand, is said to have been designed to specification 20/25, as was also the Aries, the A.W.17, which, incidentally, was the only one of the three types with a traceable A.W. number.

The A.W.17 Aries, J9037, with a geared Jaguar IV engine; only one of the type was built.

The Aries, which is recorded as having made its first flight on 3 May, 1930, was an attempt to improve upon the Atlas, by then well established in service with the RAF. With the emphasis on ease of maintenance, the Aries had a wing structure of the Warren-truss type with few bracing wires. Also, the sides of the fuselage, back as far as the pilot's cockpit, were fitted with large, quickly-detachable metal panels for easy access to the internal equipment. There was no follow-up order, and only one Aries was built; it bore the serial number J9037 and the constructor's number 454.

Another view of the Aries, which was designed for ease of maintenance. (*Courtesy P. Jarrett*)

When the prototype Atlas, still carrying its civil registration G-EBLK, went to Martlesham Heath for official trials in November 1925, it still had its original wooden wings of RAF 15 section. The report (M437 of November 1925) which followed the trials stated that the aircraft was easy to fly, was neutrally stable fore and aft and handled well, with both longitudinal and lateral control '. . . very good and light at all speeds'; the rudder was, however, judged to be rather heavy. The only other note of criticism was that the aircraft could not be sideslipped at a steep angle. The report concluded that the Atlas was '. . . admirably suited to army co-operation duties'.

In an attempt to improve the sideslipping capability, the rudder of the prototype was given a greater range of movement; at the same time the incidence, sweepback and dihedral angles of the wings were increased by varying amounts. Tested again at Martlesham Heath in June 1926, the aircraft was found to have suffered a deterioration in flying qualities, with a sudden stall and a wing drop. The minimum gliding speed was increased, and, although the sideslip was improved, it was still not possible to sideslip steeply.

The Ajax G-EBLM after being fitted with Frise ailerons and wingtip slots in 1927. (*Courtesy A. Campbell-Orde*)

Some time in 1927 the prototype returned to Whitley to have a new set of wings, this time of metal with a modified RAF 28 section. This work was done under a separate contract, and the aircraft emerged with the serial J8675 and with the new constructor's number 278. In this form it underwent further tests at Martlesham Heath in November 1927 with, apparently, rather disappointing results. The stall was described as sudden, with an incipient wing drop. There was also a tendency for the aircraft to over-bank in turns combined with a risk of spinning unless the speed was maintained. During landing, the speed had to be kept high in order to retain enough control to flatten out properly and to prevent a wing drop. At high speed the aircraft showed instability and a tendency to hunt. The

The prototype Ajax, with a geared Jaguar engine and enlarged cockpit openings, after its transfer to the RAF as J9128. (*Imperial War Museum MH3300*)

report concluded '. . . in general the control characteristics are not considered to be up to modern standards'.

In February 1928 the aircraft was tested again at Martlesham Heath, this time with an increase in the dihedral angle and in the washout at the wingtips. The tests showed that the greater dihedral had decreased the tendency to over-bank in turns, but that the washout was ineffective in preventing a wing drop. The aircraft was then adjudged to be easy to take-off and land provided it was brought in and landed above the stalling speed. As a result of these trials, it was concluded that the Atlas needed automatic wingtip slots. After these had been fitted, the aircraft was again at Martlesham Heath in May 1928, when a great improvement in the aircraft's stalling characteristics was noted. The wing drop was eliminated, and the stall was followed by a gentle nose drop. However, it was again

The Atlas and the Ajax were virtually indistinguishable; according to the company records this was an Ajax.

stated that the control characteristics were still considered unsatisfactory. In a summing up of the test, it was concluded that the tendency to drop a wing near the stall was first observed after the dihedral and sweepback modifications and that it appeared to have no connection with the change of wing section. Regrettably, no records have been found to indicate what modifications were finally incorporated at this stage, but it is known that slots became a standard fitting, that the RAF 28 wing section was retained and that the sweepback of the wings was further increased to 6 deg.

It is probable that the lateral control near the stall remained somewhat unsatisfactory, as is evident from still other tests made in 1928 with a system of linked ailerons and slots, and in 1932 with Frise ailerons on the lower wing. The former arrangement gave some improvement at the stall, but at normal flying speeds the controls were adversely affected and the system was not adopted. With ailerons on the lower wing, the aircraft was said to handle more pleasantly than the standard Atlas, but the lateral control was considered to be still below the standards of the day. The additional ailerons were not adopted for the RAF aircraft, but the new Atlas aircraft supplied to the Royal Canadian Air Force were fitted with lower-wing ailerons.

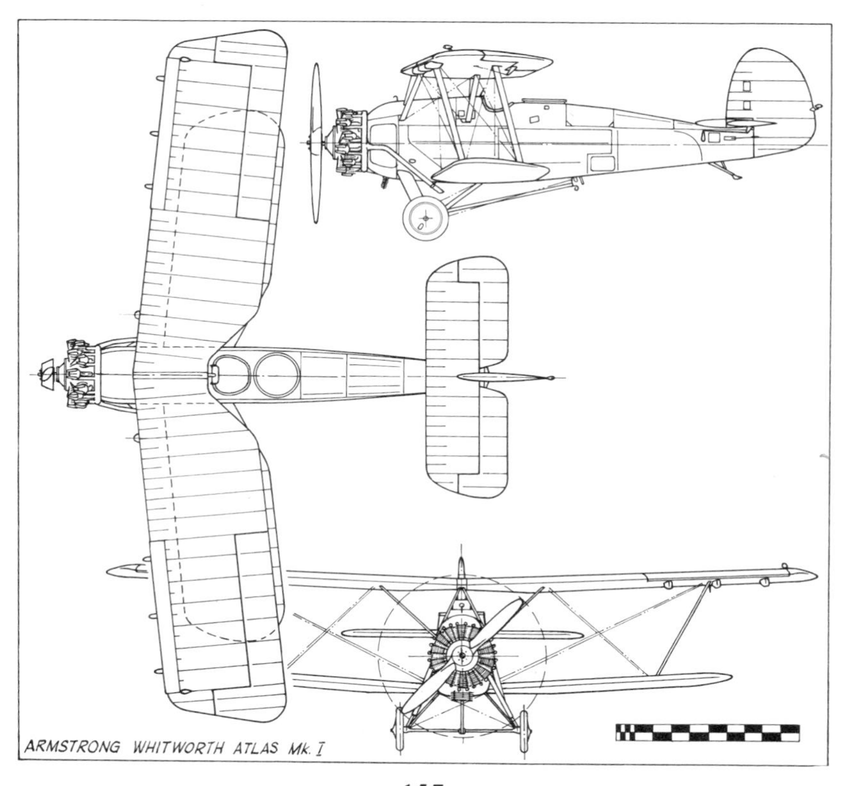

The Atlas was a solid, chunky-looking biplane with little grace but ample girth to accommodate the many pieces of equipment demanded by its army co-operation rôle. The standard powerplant was the Armstrong Siddeley Jaguar IVC, the direct-drive version of the engine, which developed 400 hp at 1,700 rpm. In the RAF the engine was normally uncowled, but the aircraft was offered with a Townend ring which, according to the maker's figures, gave a small increase in performance.

Provision was made for fitting of three alternative types of radio equipment, two for two-way working and the third for transmission only. The aircraft was also provided with a hook on a long pole which was hinged to the undercarriage axle and could be lowered to pick up a message attached to a cord strung between two posts stuck into the ground. The picking up of messages by Atlas biplanes in formation was a popular party trick at the

The first production contract for the Atlas was for thirty-seven aircraft; J8783 was the seventh off the line. (*Courtesy A. Campbell-Orde*)

pre-war RAF Displays at Hendon. For photographic-reconnaissance work, cameras of either the F8 or F24 type were located behind the observer's cockpit, with a remote control to the pilot's seat for use when no observer was carried. Armament consisted of two guns, a fixed Vickers gun firing through the propeller arc and a Lewis gun on a Scarff mounting for the rear cockpit. Four 120-lb bombs could be carried on two racks, one under each lower plane.

The production Atlas, like the Siskin, had an all-steel structure covered with fabric, except for the front portion of the fuselage which had detachable duralumin panels. The fuselage structure was mainly of steel tubing, wire-braced, and with ball and socket joints between the longerons and the strut ends. The sides and bottom of the front fuselage were faired by formers and stringers, while the top decking consisted of a wooden fairing around the cockpits with fabric-covered stringers further aft. The wing structure consisted of two spars built up of corrugated steel strip with light ribs, fabricated from top-hat-section strip and clipped in place on the spars. The top plane was divided into two sections meeting on the centreline of the aircraft and supported on a cabane of steel tubes in the form of a W as

The Atlas J9544. Six RAF Army Co-operation squadrons were equipped with Atlas I aircraft. (*Courtesy E. Morgan*)

seen from the front. Except in the case of the RCAF aircraft already mentioned, ailerons were fitted to the top wings only and all controls were balanced. Originally the aircraft had a normal fin and balanced rudder, but this was later replaced by a shapely balanced rudder with no fin. The tail surfaces were of cantilever construction without bracing wires.

With a loaded weight of 4,020 lb, the Atlas had a maximum speed of 142 mph at sea level, falling to 124 mph at 15,000 ft. It could climb to 5,000 ft in 5½ min and 15,000 ft in 28 min. The fuel capacity was 75 Imperial gallons, giving an endurance of 3¼ hours.

In addition to its army co-operation rôle the Atlas was also used as an advanced trainer and, incidentally, as a station communication aircraft. Externally the main difference was the altered rear cockpit and the omis-

An early production Atlas being demonstrated at Whitley Abbey aerodrome.

The RCAF Atlas aircraft differed from those of the RAF in having ailerons on the lower wings. (*Canadian Forces No.HC8365B*)

The message pick-up hook and the camera gun on the lower wing are evident in this photograph of Atlas J9537.

The prototype Atlas dual-control trainer, J8792. (*Ministry of Defence*)

sion of the Scarff gun-ring, the message hook and the forward Vickers gun. The major internal alterations were those necessary for the installation of a full set of dual controls and instruments in the rear cockpit. During instruction the pupil occupied the front seat.

Four Atlas trainers, G-ABHV, G-ABHW, G-ABHX and G-ABOO, were built in 1931 and allotted to the Armstrong Whitworth flying school, which that year moved from Whitley to Hamble and became Air Service Training Ltd. These aircraft remained in service with the school until 1939. Another variant, a rare one, was the Atlas seaplane; at least two RAF Atlas were so fitted and one of them was equipped with stainless-steel floats made by Armstrong Whitworth. Another, J9998, with the more normal type of duralumin float, was used as a practice aircraft by the RAF High Speed Flight when training for the 1931 Schneider Trophy race. The RCAF also experimented with an Atlas as a seaplane.

The Atlas J8799, one of the first production batch, under test as a seaplane. (*Imperial War Museum MH2957*)

The first of the Atlas biplanes to serve with the RAF were sent to No.13 Squadron at Andover for Service trials in the spring or early summer of 1927, but it was not until October of that year that the first squadron, No.26, then at Catterick, was fully equipped with the type. Subsequently, between 1927 and 1930, four other RAF squadrons, Nos.2, 4, 16 and 208, and No.13 itself received the type. Altogether 446 Atlas were supplied to the RAF, of which 271 were for army co-operation duties, and 175, with dual control, for training and communications. The last RAF army co-operation squadron to use the Atlas was No.208, which retained the type in the Middle East until 1934 but, as mentioned earlier, the advanced-trainer version was kept in service until 1935.

Some Atlas were exported: six went direct from the makers to Canada for the RCAF between December 1927 and October 1929, and a further

Two Atlas aircraft of No.208 Army Co-operation Squadron, RAF, on patrol in the Middle East. (*Ministry of Defence*)

ten were purchased from the RAF and added to the strength in November 1934. Other Atlas exports were two aircraft to Greece, one to Japan, one to Egypt (from the RAF), and fourteen to China, the latter being Atlas IIs.

The Canadian aircraft had a very long life; at the outbreak of the war in 1939 no less than thirteen of the original sixteen were still on the strength of the RCAF. These formed the equipment of No.2 (Army Co-operation) Squadron, based at Trenton. After the war started this squadron, with its Atlas, moved to Saint John, New Brunswick, and flew reconnaissance patrols over the Bay of Fundy. At the end of October 1939 the Atlas were transferred to No.118 (Combat Alert Centre) Squadron which had one flight detached to Halifax. The Atlas in the RCAF were soon afterwards replaced by Lysanders, but three of them survived until 1941 and one (No. 402, ex-17, which had been delivered in December 1927) until May 1942.

An RCAF Atlas being tested as a seaplane. (*Canadian Forces*)

A total of sixteen Atlas aircraft served with the RCAF, one of which remained on strength until 1942. (*Canadian Forces HC7283*)

The RCAF Atlas No.409 was originally allotted the RAF Service number K1531. (*Canadian Forces HC7279*)

Another view of the RCAF Atlas seaplane

The first step towards the Atlas Mk.II was G-EBYF, which had a Mk.I fuselage fitted with Mk.II wings.

The Atlas II, as supplied to China, was offered as a two-seat fighter, day bomber or army co-operation aircraft. The first 'half-way-stage' towards the Atlas II was a much-modified Atlas I, G-EBYF (c/n 346), which had originally been built in 1928. This aircraft re-appeared early in 1931 with its original Mk.I fuselage and the early type of fin and rudder, but with a new set of wings and a Jaguar Major, the engine that was later to be renamed the Panther. The new wings were of Clark YH section with auto-slots and square tips (as opposed to the raked tips of the Atlas I). Frise-balanced ailerons were fitted to both top and bottom wings. In 1931 G-EBYF was one of three British aircraft shipped to Argentina for the Buenos Aires exhibition (the others were an Avro Avian and an Avro 626 military trainer—the latter being the only one to secure an order). The Atlas was damaged in a collision on the ground and was subsequently shipped home for repair. According to the company records, this aircraft was rebuilt to full Mk.II standard, re-registered G-ACAI and given the new constructor's number 830.

The first Atlas to be built to full Mk.II standard. It was fitted with a Panther IIIA engine.

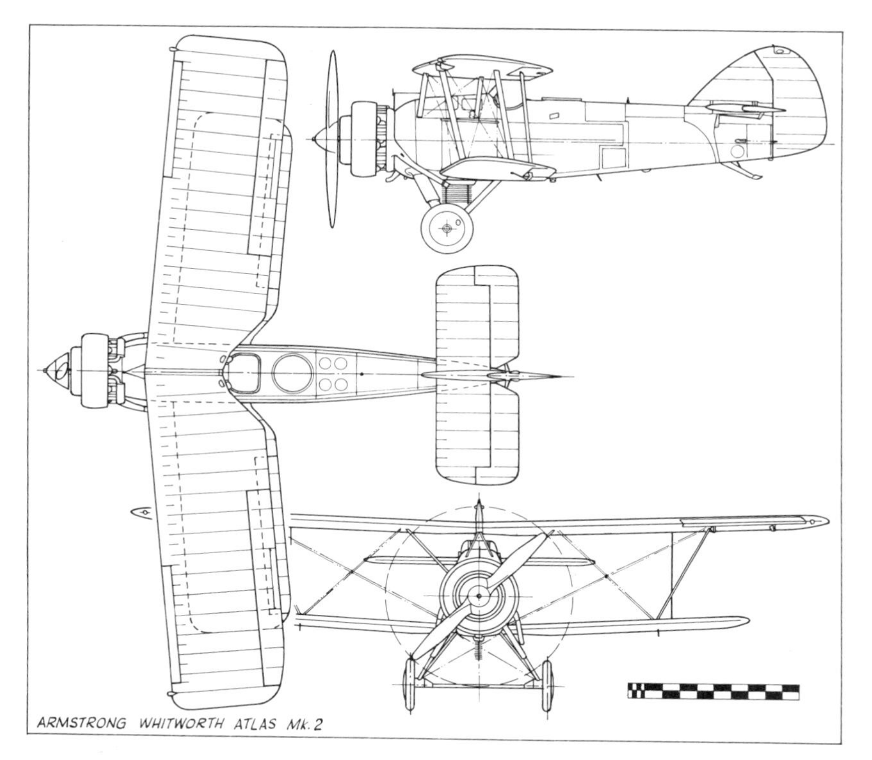

ARMSTRONG WHITWORTH ATLAS Mk. 2

The fourteen Atlas for China were all to full Mk.II standard, having a redesigned fuselage with a horizontal top decking and, in consequence, a much deeper stern post. The fixed fin was considerably larger than that of the original Atlas. Other detailed improvements included fairing the interplane and undercarriage strut ends, sinking the navigation lights into the wingtips and cleaning up the aircraft generally. The engine, by now designated the Panther IIIA, was cowled with a double Townend ring. Constructionally, the Atlas II was basically similar to the Mk.I. In 1933, drawings were prepared for a three-seat version with an additional cockpit behind the normal two; as far as is known this variant was not built.

The all-up weight of the Atlas II was 4,950 lb and it had a military load of 1,000 lb. Its speed was 153 mph at 5,000 ft, an altitude that was reached in 4 min. At 15,000 ft, reached in $19\frac{1}{2}$ min, the speed was 135 mph. The service ceiling was 18,200 ft. The aircraft was said to be an improvement on the Mk.I as regards its handling qualities, and its slow-flying ability was reported as being outstanding.

In an Atlas II brochure issued in the early 1930s, Armstrong Whitworth explained why they believed the biplane was superior to the monoplane, examples of which were beginning to appear in other countries. Among the reasons given for this preference were compactness and

The second Atlas Mk.II, G-ABKE, was used for the 100-hour test of the Panther engine.

better manoeuvrability, more effective lateral control with four ailerons instead of two, and the fact that the top wing of a biplane stalled earlier than the bottom wing, leaving the lower ailerons still effective. Finally, the brochure stated that the effect of slots on a biplane had been thoroughly investigated, whereas little was known about the behaviour of the slotted monoplane wing.

The first 'semi-Mk.II', G-EBYF, was demonstrated before Members of Parliament at Hanworth aerodrome in June 1931, and the fully-modified version was included in the parade of new and experimental types at the RAF Display on 25 June, 1932. But the Atlas II was not adopted by the RAF; instead, the company made determined efforts to sell the aircraft overseas. During October, November and December 1931, G-ABIV, flown by Campbell-Orde, toured Scandinavia giving demonstrations in Denmark, Sweden, Finland, Latvia, Lithuania and Esthonia. During the 4,000-mile journey the aircraft encountered continuous bad weather, including gales, snow, fog, rain and extreme cold. In spite of an impressive performance by both man and machine, no sales resulted, and the only export success for the Atlas II was the Chinese order. At a later date the Atlas II, G-ABIV, was used as a test vehicle for the Armstrong Siddeley Tiger engine.

The Atlas was notable as one of the RAF's first generation of post-war aircraft in that it replaced, somewhat belatedly, the wartime Bristol Fighter in the rôle of army co-operation. In spite of the early criticisms voiced by the test pilots at Martlesham and Farnborough, the Atlas proved in practice to be a safe and satisfactory aeroplane which gave excellent service to the RAF and the RCAF during many years of reliable, if unspectacular, operation.

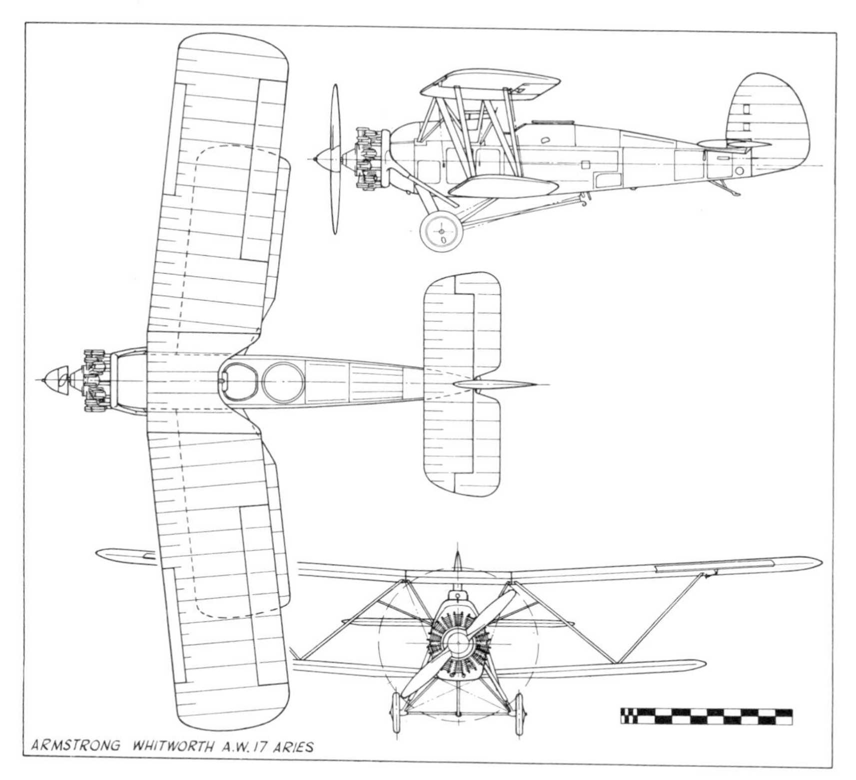

Atlas Mk.I

Dimensions: Span 39 ft 7 in (12·07 m); length 28 ft 7 in (8·71 m); height 10 ft 6 in (3·20 m); wing area 391 sq ft (36·3 sq m).

Atlas Mk.II

Dimensions: Span 40 ft 2 in (12·24 m); length 29 ft (8·64 m); height 10 ft 9 in (3·27 m); wing area 393 sq ft (36·50 sq m).

Ajax

Dimensions: Span 39 ft 6 in (12·04 m); length 28 ft 3 in (8·61 m); wing area 392 sq ft (36·42 sq m).

Aries

Dimensions: Span 42 ft (12·80 m); length 28 ft 4 in (8·64 m); height 10 ft 11 in (3·33 m); wing area 399·4 sq ft (37·12 sq m).

	Atlas Mk.I *400 hp Jaguar IVC*	**Atlas Mk.II** *535 hp Panther IIA*	**Ajax** *385 hp Jaguar*
Max weight:	4,020 lb (1,824 kg)	4,950 lb (2,245 kg)	3,700 lb (1,678 kg)
Empty weight:	2,550 lb (1,157 kg)	3,129 lb (1,419 kg)	2,240 lb (1,016 kg)
Max speed			
Sea level:	142 mph (229 km/hr)	152 mph (245 km/hr)	140 mph (225 km/hr)
5,000 ft (1,524 m):	139 mph (224 km/hr)	155 mph (250 km/hr)*	—
10,000 ft (3,048 m):	134 mph (216 km/hr)	147 mph (236 km/hr)	—
15,000 ft (4,572 m):	124 mph (200 km/hr)	135 mph (217 km/hr)	—
Climb to			
5,000 ft (1,524 m):	5·5 min.	4 min.	7 min.
15,000 ft (4,572 m):	28 min	19·5 min	21·5 min
Service ceiling:	16,800 ft (5,120 m)	18,200 ft (5,547 m)	19,700 ft (6,005 m)
Fuel capacity:	75 Imp gal (341 lt)	75 Imp gal (341 lt)	—
Endurance:	3¼ hr	3¼ hr	3¼ hr

* At 3,000 ft (914 m)

The first A.W.XIV Starling with its original wings of bi-convex section.

The Siskin Successors

The first Coventry-built Armstrong Whitworth aircraft to bear an identifiable type number emerged in 1927: it was also known as the Starling and it was the first of a series of fighters which were designed in the hope of repeating the success achieved by the Siskin. The start of type numbering was a laudable, if somewhat belated, innovation but unfortunately, at the outset, it seems to have been applied in a rather haphazard fashion. The first two fighters of the series, which differed in almost every important respect, were both named Starling and both carried the type number A.W.XIV. On the other hand, the next two fighters of the series, the A.W.XVI, which incidentally looked much more like the Starling Mk.I than the Starling Mk.II ever did, and the A.W.35 Scimitar, were given widely separated numbers although they were, in essence, the same aircraft.

A.W.XIV Starling

The earliest evidence of the A.W.XIV is given on an undated general arrangement drawing in which the type is shown as yet another variation of the Siskin theme, consisting of a Siskin V fuselage with a new wing arrangement having a larger gap, parallel interplane struts, and dihedral on the bottom wing only. The first A.W.XIV Starling, which made its first flight on 12 May, 1927, looked quite different; it had the appearance of being a cross between the RAF Siskin and the Atlas, and was characterized by a somewhat portly, humpbacked fuselage, and a plank-like upper wing with no dihedral and with square wingtips. It was designed as a day-and-night fighter to specification 28/24 and the prototype, J8027, was powered by a Jaguar VII engine developing 385 hp. The standard equipment included navigation lights, mountings for Holt flares, wireless and oxygen equipment, and two forward-firing machine-guns.

The wings of the Starling prototype were of RAF 30 section, a biconvex profile which, among other characteristics, had a centre of pressure which remained practically stationary throughout a large range of incidence. Taking advantage of this peculiarity, Lloyd designed the Starling wings with deep front spars calculated to take most of the loads supplemented by very light rear spars which amounted to little more than substantial stringers. For the same reasons the two flying wires, stemming from the bottom wing roots, met at the top of the front interplane struts. Such small loads as might be applied to the rear spars were transferred to the more robust front spars through the N-type interplane struts.

Structurally the Starling followed the usual Armstrong Whitworth practice, with a bolted steel-tube fuselage and with wing spars built up from

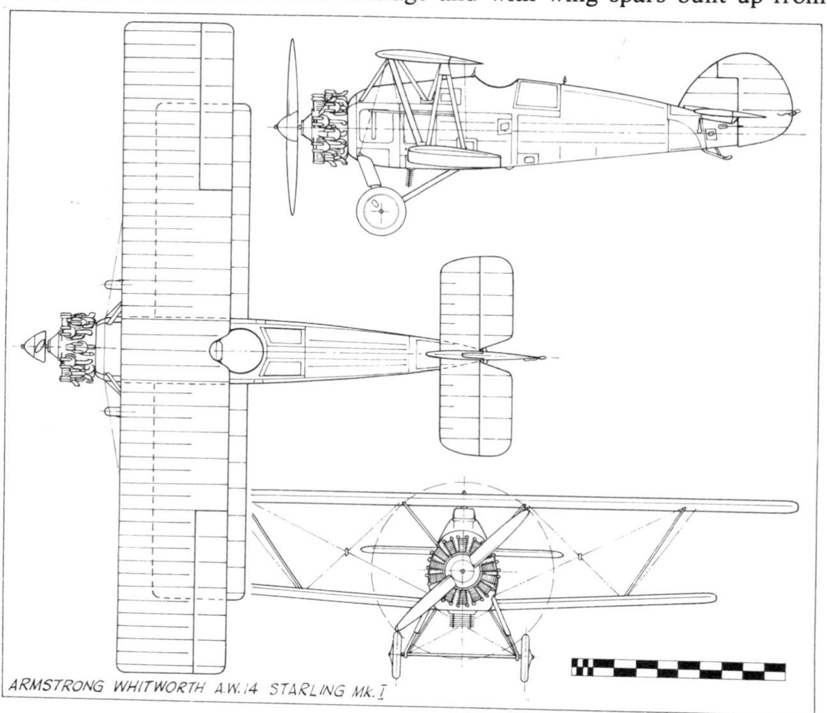

steel strip. Exceptionally, in the case of the Starling, the wing ribs were made of wood. This may have been because the use of the RAF 30 wing section was, to some extent, experimental, and the use of wooden ribs would make it easier and cheaper to alter the wing section. This change was, indeed, found to be necessary after initial trials had quickly revealed that the aircraft suffered from poor lateral control at the stall, coupled with a sudden, violent, and quite unacceptable, wing drop.

After these preliminary tests, the aircraft was returned to the makers and eventually reappeared, this time with the civil registration G-AAHC, at the Seventh International Aero Show held at Olympia, in

The Starling J8027, registered as G-AAHC, with new wings and a Townend ring, was shown at the Aero Show at Olympia in 1929. (*Flight International 6152*)

Another view of the Starling Mk.I prototype in its original form. (*Courtesy A. Campbell-Orde*)

July 1929. By now it had a new set of wings having the same overall dimensions but with a Clark YH wing section, another, but less pronounced, bi-convex profile. The new wings included slots, some 3 ft 8 in long, built into the leading edge of the upper wing opposite the ailerons. These slots were cut out of the wing section some distance behind the leading edge, which was left intact. Other modifications included the fitting of a more powerful Jaguar IV engine and a Townend ring cowling.

At the beginning of July 1929, just before its appearance at Olympia, the modified Starling had been put through a series of tests at Farnborough, first with the slots covered by fabric, and then with them open. The tests involved holding the aircraft in a stall with the stick held back at an airspeed of about 60 mph with the aircraft losing height at the rate of about 1,800 ft/min. In this stalled condition, with the slots covered, there was a tendency to drop a wing in either direction, and the ailerons were found to be ineffective, a deficiency that was partially offset by the large and powerful rudder. With the slots uncovered, the lateral stability was improved and the wing could be slowly raised by aileron, but the control of the stall was judged to be poor compared with the best examples of slotted-wing aircraft. The main conclusion drawn from the trials was that the slots were too short to be fully effective.

Later in the same year tests were undertaken at Farnborough with the same aircraft to determine the maximum lift coefficient of the Clark YH wing section. Using a swivelling pitot tube and a trailing static-head to ensure accurate speed measurement, the lift coefficient was measured at angles of incidence ranging between 9 deg and 29 deg. The figures which emerged for the Starling were lower than those obtained in wind-tunnel tests on the Clark YH wing in America, and they were also lower than the best results obtained with the similar RAF 34 wing section tested on a Bristol Fighter. Apart from the relatively poor lateral control, the Starling Mk.I with the Clark YH wings had, according to its makers, a fairly good

The Starling J8027 being demonstrated to the press in the summer of 1928.
(Flight International 6154)

The A.W.XIV Starling Mk.II which bore little or no resemblance to the Mk.I version. (*Courtesy A. Campbell-Orde*)

performance. Its maximum speed, attained at 15,000 ft, was 177 mph, and it could climb to 20,000 ft in $17\frac{1}{2}$ minutes.

No precise date has been found for the completion of the second Starling, the Mk.II J8028, but it is probable that it did not appear until late in 1929. As already mentioned, this aircraft differed in many respects from the Mk.I; the fuselage was more finely tapered and the undercarriage was taller in order to provide clearance for the large propeller fitted to the geared and moderately supercharged Panther engine. But the main difference lay in the wing structure: the Mk.II had a large top wing and a much

Another view of the Starling Mk.II carrying the marking A-1.

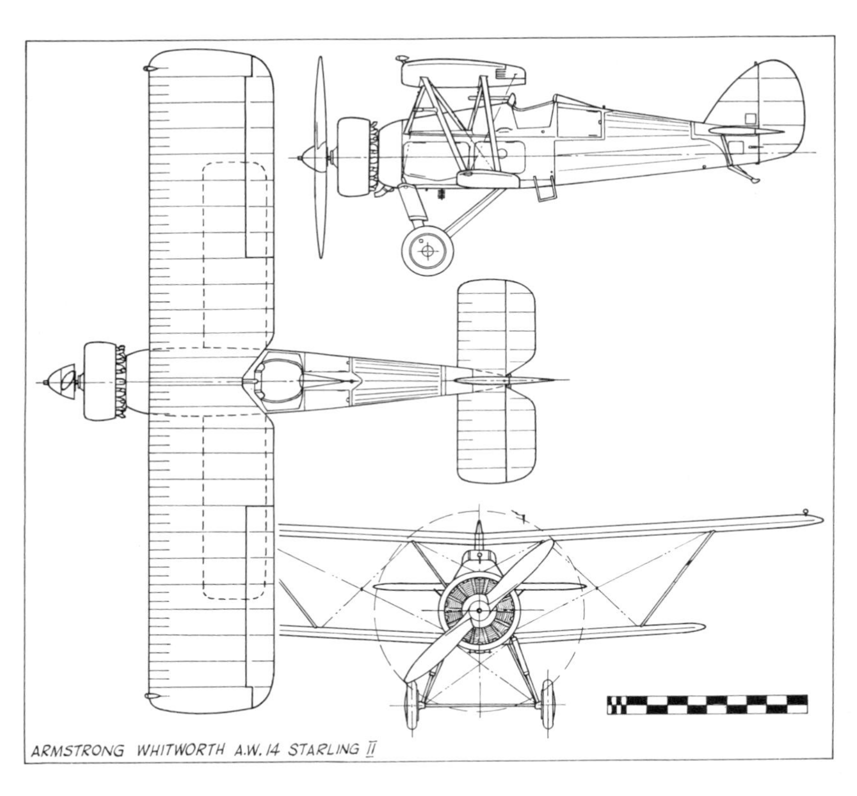

The Starling Mk.II with a new set of narrow-chord wings and renumbered A-2. (*Courtesy P. Jarrett*)

A three-quarter rear view of the Starling Mk.II with narrow-chord wings. (*Courtesy P. Jarrett*)

smaller lower wing, the relative proportions of which were more reminiscent of the Siskin IIIA, although the Starling lower wing had two spars. Only in the use of the Clark YH wing section did the Mk.II follow the lead of the Mk.I.

The Starling Mk.II was flown in two versions, but whether there were one, two or three examples of the type is open to doubt and is also, to some extent, a matter of opinion. On the face of it, there were three aircraft, J8028, A-1 and A-2, but from an examination of photographs it seems virtually certain that A-1 and A-2 were the same aircraft as regards the fuselage and undercarriage but fitted with alternative sets of wings, while from other photographs it would appear further that J8028 and A-2 were also one and the same aircraft. On the other hand, the works record gives three constructor's numbers, 455 for J8028, 459 for A-1 and 460 for A-2, but this evidence is not conclusive because of the company's habit of occasionally allotting new constructor's numbers when modification work was undertaken: the matter remains in doubt.

The Starling Mk.II, A-2, was later given the RAF Service number J8028.

With the marks A-1 the aircraft was flown with wide-cord wings as a fleet fighter, while as A-2 it was classed as an interceptor fighter and had the narrow-chord set of wings. In this configuration it may have been intended to meet specification F.9/26. Just when the change in the wings took place is not certain; the only evidence on the matter consists of two company drawings, one of each version, dated respectively January and February 1930. Little is known about the fate of either Starling and there was no further development of the type except in so far as its influence was evident in the next fighter produced by the company.

A.W.XVI

This was the unnamed A.W.XVI, which first flew late in 1930, the prototype aircraft bearing the serial S1591. This aircraft was designed to specification N.21/26 for a naval fighter, and it was tested at Martlesham Heath and then attached for trials to No.402 Flight, Fleet Air Arm. The second prototype A.W.XVI, initially bearing the mark A-2, first flew in the autumn of 1931. It was demonstrated to the Press by Alan Campbell-Orde on 6 October, 1931, and was then sent to Martlesham for official trials as a zone fighter to specification F.9/26. The A.W.XVI was a clean aeroplane with considerable refinement in its detail design aimed at cutting down resistance. It was claimed by the makers, perhaps with some justification, to have been the world's fastest single-seat fighter with an air-cooled engine: the final qualification was necessary because already the potentialities of the close-cowled liquid-cooled engine were becoming all too apparent.

In the event, there seems little doubt that the A.W.XVI's chances of

The prototype A.W.XVI built as a naval fighter to specification N.21/26. The aircraft carried the crest of No.402 Flight, Fleet Air Arm.

The second A.W.XVI, bearing the marking A-2, being demonstrated at Whitley Abbey in October 1931. (*Flight International 10872*)

success and, indeed, those of its successor the Scimitar, were spoilt by their engines. The Jaguar Major, or Panther, as it was later renamed, was a developed version of the Jaguar and had been stretched beyond the reasonable limits of that basic design. As a consequence, it was never able to achieve the high standard of reliability enjoyed by the original type. The story goes that the company received a letter from the Air Ministry to the effect that the A.W.XVI would have been ordered in quantity had it had a better powerplant. Be that as it may, it is certainly true that John Lloyd argued vigorously with Siddeley against the use of the Jaguar Major in the A.W.XVI and, as related elsewhere, was dismissed for his pains; fortunately his absence was short-lived, but Siddeley's inflexible engine policy remained unchanged.

The A.W.XVI bore a strong family resemblance to the A.W.XIV Mk.I, but had better lines and a less humpbacked appearance in profile. As with the modified A.W.XIV, the wings were of Clark YH section, of unequal span and chord, and supported by N-type interplane struts with normal wire bracing. As compared with its predecessors, the A.W.XVI had been cleaned up by the fitting of an internal engine-driven electrical generator, the suppression of the navigation lights within the wingtips, the careful fairing of the interplane, centre-section and undercarriage strut ends, and the fitting of wheel spats. The engine was enclosed by a Townend ring fixed to the cylinder heads, with an inner deflector ring bolted to the gear casing. Armament consisted of two Vickers guns firing through the propeller arc, and racks for four light fragmentation bombs under the wings. Other standard equipment included a radio-telephone set mounted behind the cockpit, oxygen equipment, Sutton harness for the pilot, and electrical circuits for heating, lighting and the radio. The framework of the A.W.XVI was of metal, with the fuselage fabricated from steel tubing and the wing spars and ribs built up from high-tensile steel strip. For perhaps the first time in an Armstrong Whitworth all-metal aeroplane, a morsel of duralumin found its way into the main structure in the shape of nose ribs in the wings. Another innovation was the fitting of wheel brakes, with differential control actuated by foot pedals mounted on the rudder bar.

After the first tests with the prototype at Martlesham Heath, and further trials with the second aircraft, there was some criticism of the controls,

The A.W.XVI A-2 was subsequently registered G-ABKF.

which exhibited a certain lack of harmony. As a result, the area of the fixed fin was increased and the horn balance on the rudder eliminated, and the size of the elevators was increased by extending the chord. Following these alterations the Martlesham pilots reported, in September 1932, that the aircraft's controls were greatly improved, although still not completely in harmony; the ailerons, although providing good control at the stall, were still light in comparison with the other controls, a characteristic that was found to be somewhat disconcerting at high speed. Both the rudder and elevators were improved, although the former was now slightly less effective at the stall. Spinning trials were satisfactory, but it was noted that reversal of the controls was necessary for recovery. The aircraft was steady in a terminal-velocity dive and reached a true speed of 350 mph. The conclusion was that the A.W.XVI would make a satisfactory zone

The A.W.XVI was well liked at Martlesham but the unreliability of the Panther engine weighed against it.

fighter, being very manoeuvrable in the air and on the ground, easy to land and take-off and pleasant to fly. The Martlesham performance figures indicated a top speed of 195 mph true at 14,500 ft (that is, about 2,500 ft above the rated altitude of the Jaguar Major engine), with the ability to climb to 20,000 ft in 18 min. The stalling speed was 55 mph.

In November 1932 the second prototype, still bearing the mark A-2, underwent 'ease of maintenance trials' at Martlesham Heath. As a result it

Another view of the A.W.XVI A-2. The engine was a Jaguar Major, later renamed Panther. (*Flight International 10865*)

Another view of the A.W.XVI.

The A.W.XVI with modified fin, revised exhaust system and a simplified Townend ring. (*Courtesy P. Jarrett*)

The A.W.XVI with a double Townend ring.

was judged to be good for ordinary daily maintenance, although the time taken to change an engine, which took two men $14\frac{1}{2}$ hr, was considered to be rather excessive. On the other hand, the airframe was found to be satisfactory; a lower mainplane was changed in 2 hr 10 min and a new petrol tank fitted in 1 hr 40 min. The specification F.9/26 was for a fighter to replace the RAF's Siskins and Gamecocks, and the A.W.XVI was in

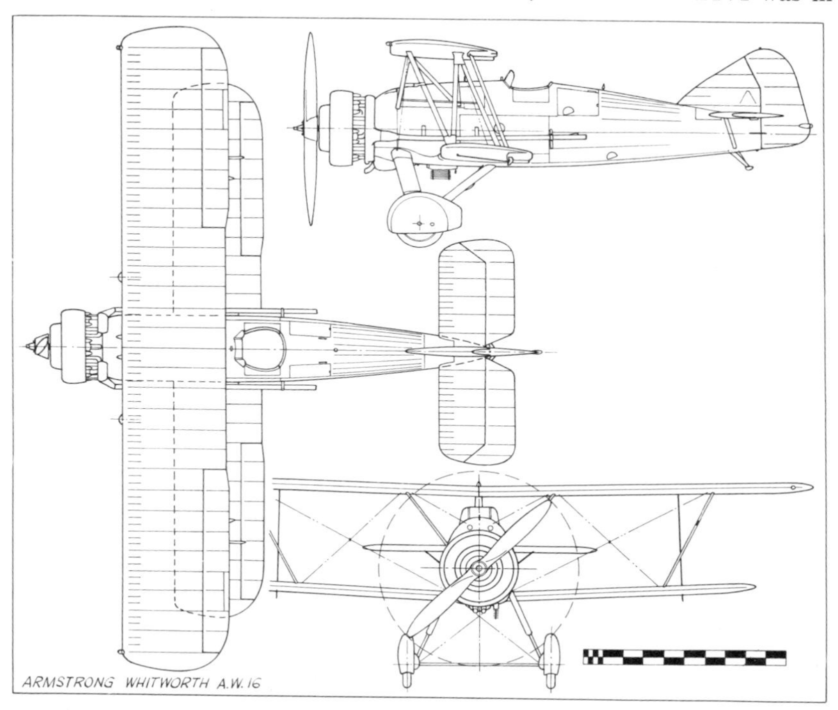

competition with, among others, the Boulton Paul Partridge, the Bristol Bulldog, the Gloster S.S.18 and the Hawker Hawfinch. The thoroughness of the official trials, outlined above, may be taken as an indication of how near the A.W.XVI came to being ordered: in the end it was the Bulldog that won. The only order received for the A.W.XVI came from China: according to the Armstrong Whitworth production list there was an allocation of sixteen works numbers for the Chinese order but only four were delivered. The first, G-ABRH, was test flown in June 1931, and this aircraft, together with the second and third, registered G-ABRI and G-ABRJ, were despatched to China in early 1932, whilst the fourth aircraft, G-ABZL, was first flown in October 1932 and, according to the company's list, was shipped to China in January 1933.

The Chinese order was negotiated through the agency of the Far East Aviation Co Ltd, of Hong Kong, whose managing director was the British test pilot and writer R. Vaughan-Fowler. The aircraft were operated by the

Cantonese Air Force and were used in battle against the Japanese. In England during 1932, the second prototype, originally A-2 but by now registered as G-ABKF, was used for a number of demonstrations flown by Alan Campbell-Orde. In May 1932 he put up an impressive performance at the Coventry Aero Club meeting at Whitley, and this was followed by another at Heston aerodrome during the meeting of the Household Brigade Flying Club. In July a similar demonstration was given at Whitley before the Parliamentary Air Committee.

Towards the end of 1932, Sir Alan Cobham, as an extension of his National Aviation Day campaign, made arrangements to take a team of pilots and a variety of aircraft on a tour of South Africa. By arrangement with Armstrong Whitworth the A.W.XVI G-ABKF was included, and it was flown throughout the tour by Charles Turner-Hughes. During the two months of the tour, which opened at Wingfield, the aerodrome for Cape Town, on 1 December, 1932, the team visited some sixty places, many of which posed problems of great heat combined with sandstorms, wind and thunderstorms. The A.W.XVI was the first high-speed fighter to be seen in the Union and the skilful exhibitions put up by Turner-Hughes made a great impression on civilians and Service people alike. On one occasion, during a demonstration at Germiston, the A.W.XVI nearly met with disaster: when flying low across the airfield at about 250 mph, it hit a bird and a large rent appeared in the fabric of the lower wing. Fortunately, Turner-Hughes was able to land before the tear spread catastrophically. After returning to England with Cobham, Turner-Hughes was asked by Armstrong Whitworth to demonstrate the A.W.XVI at the second SBAC Display at Hendon in June 1933. His performance, in G-ACCD, was watched by Armstrong Whitworth's general manager S. W. Hiscocks, who subsequently offered Turner-Hughes the job of test pilot.

The A.W.XVI G-ABKF, back from Africa, flew on 24 October, 1933,

The A.W.XVI G-ACCD at Hendon aerodrome for the SBAC Exhibition held in June 1933. (*Flight International 13271*)

In 1933 the A.W.XVI, G-ABKF, was used for flight development of the experimental fifteen-cylinder Hyena engine. Alternative types of cowling were tested in an effort to overcome cooling problems. (*Courtesy A. Campbell-Orde*)

for the first time with a new and experimental engine then being developed by Armstrong Siddeley. This was a fifteen-cylinder affair known as the Hyena; it was, in effect, three five-cylinder radials mounted in line on a common crankcase. Little is known about the performance of this engine except that it was said to be somewhat heavy for its power and that difficulty was experienced with the cooling of the rear cylinders. Several types of close-fitting cowling were tried on the A.W.XVI, but in spite of numerous modifications, the overheating troubles were not cured. Two Armstrong Whitworth projects were designed to take the Hyena engine, the A.W.21, a low-wing monoplane fighter (for which the Panther engine was also considered) and the A.W.28, which was essentially an A.W.XVI with the fuselage lengthened to compensate for the heavier engine. However, with the abandonment of the Hyena engine, both these projects failed to materialize.

Front view of the A.W.XVI with the Hyena engine.

The prototype A.W.35 Scimitar; in fact, a much-modified A.W.XVI with the same registration.

A.W.35 Scimitar

The next, and last, of the Armstrong Whitworth biplane fighters was the A.W.35 Scimitar, which first flew, piloted by Turner-Hughes, on 25 June 1934. The Scimitar was a modified A.W.XVI, and the prototype aircraft was, in fact, the A.W.XVI G-ACCD, which, as already recounted, was flown at the 1933 SBAC Display. When it emerged in 1934, the new aircraft, which still retained the markings G-ACCD, had a taller, split-axle undercarriage with smaller wheels and wheel spats, and telescopic struts embodying a combination of oleo shock-absorbers and coil-steel springs. The fuselage fairing in front of the pilot's seat was stepped down to meet a long-chord cowling enclosing the supercharged Panther VII engine. An alternative powerplant offered by the makers was the supercharged Tiger, but it is doubtful whether this engine was ever fitted. Other alterations from the original A.W.XVI involved some local strengthening and small changes in the size of the fin and elevators. With the Panther VII engine, which developed 640 hp at 14,000 ft, the top speed of the Scimitar at that height was 221 mph, and the aircraft could climb to 20,000 ft in under twelve min. The stalling speed was 60 mph. The Scimitar was designed to meet specification F.7/30 and was intended, when suitably equipped, for use as an interceptor, a day-and-night fighter or a shipboard fighter. It was in competition with, among others, the Vickers Jockey, the Hawker High Speed Fury and the Gloster Gladiator, which latter eventually won the contract. According to some opinions, the Scimitar was as good as, if not better than, the Gladiator and, like the A.W.XVI before it, might well have been ordered but for its unsatisfactory engine.

The first Scimitar, G-ACCD, and the second, G-ADBL (which first flew on 18 March, 1935), were A.W.XVI conversions, and the only other examples of the type to be built were four aircraft sold to the Norwegian Army Air Service and delivered at the beginning of 1936; before that, one of the aircraft, serial number 405, went to Martlesham Heath for trials in August 1935 and again in the following November. The Norwegian Scimitars, which were fitted with Panther XI engines, may also have been converted A.W.XVIs, but it is more likely that they were built as Scimitars from scratch, in which case they probably incorporated the modified form of fuselage construction consisting of welded tubes in the form of a Warren truss which was specified in a technical description issued by the company. The Norwegian order, which followed a demonstration of G-ACCD to the Norwegian authorities, included a licence agreement for the aircraft to be built by the Army Aircraft Factory at Kjeller, near Oslo. Trials in Norway showed, among other things, that the undercarriage needed strengthening for use with skis, and this, added to the fact that no further production was planned by Armstrong Whitworth, led to the cancellation of the licensing agreement soon afterwards. The four Norwegian Scimitars are said to have remained in service, in the training rôle, until the outbreak of war in 1939.

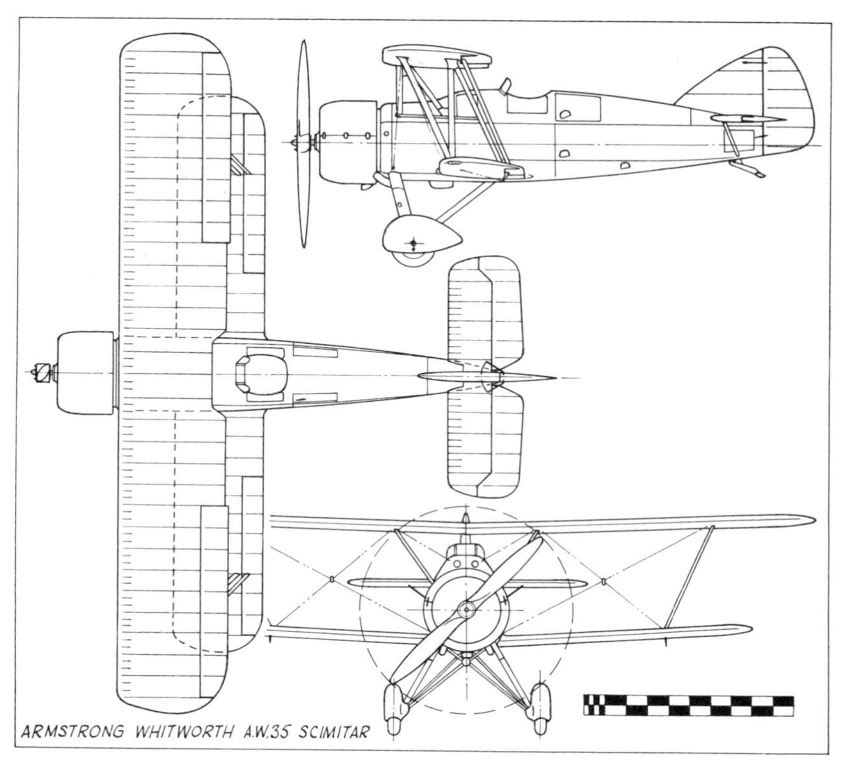
ARMSTRONG WHITWORTH A.W.35 SCIMITAR

The Scimitar, with a Panther engine, had a top speed of 221 mph at 14,000 ft.

By the time the Norwegian order was fulfilled, the company had become heavily involved with the Whitley bomber and interest in the Scimitar flagged: no further development took place and the last aircraft, G-ADBL, which had been used as the company's demonstrator, was put into storage at Whitley. Here it survived throughout the war only to be unceremoniously disposed of for scrap in October 1958.

Three of the four Scimitars delivered to the Norwegian Army Air Service. (*Flight International 12002S*)

A.W.XIV Starling Mk.I

Dimensions: Span 31 ft 4 in (9·55 m); length 25 ft 2 in (7·67 m); height 10 ft 6 in (3·20 m); wing area 246·4 sq ft (22·86 sq m).

A.W.XIV Starling Mk.II

Dimensions: Span 34 ft 3 in (10·44 m); length 24 ft 9 in (7·54 m); height 11 ft 10 in (3·61 m); wing area 258·5 sq ft (23·99 sq m); wing area, fleet fighter, 292·4 sq ft (27·17 sq m).

A.W.XVI

Dimensions: Span 33 ft (10·06 m); length 25 ft 6 in (7·77 m); height 11 ft (3·35 m); wing area 261·35 sq ft (24·28 sq m).

A.W.35 Scimitar

Dimensions: Span 33 ft (10·06 m); length 25 ft (7·62 m); height 12 ft (3·66 m); wing area 261·35 sq ft (24·28 sq m).

	A.W.XIV Starling Mk.I *385 hp Jaguar VII*	**A.W.XVI** *500 hp Panther IIIA*	**A.W.35 Scimitar** *640 hp Panther VII*
Max weight:	3,095 lb (1,404 kg)	4,067 lb (1,845 kg)	4,100 lb (1,860 kg)
Empty weight:	—	2,795 lb (1,268 kg)	2,956 lb (1,341 kg)
Max speed			
Sea level:	—	—	178 mph (286 km/hr)
10,000 ft (3,048 m):	173 mph (278 km/hr)	203 mph (327 km/hr)	208 mph (335 km/hr)
15,000 ft (4,572 m):	177 mph (285 km/hr)	194 mph (312 km/hr)	221 mph (354 km/hr)*
20,000 ft (6,096 m):	161 mph (259 km/hr)	187 mph (301 km/hr)	215 mph (346 km/hr)
Stalling speed:	—	55 mph (89 km/hr)	60 mph (97 km/hr)
Climb			
to 10,000 ft (3,048 m):	7 min	8·7 min	5·25 min
to 15,000 ft (4,572 m):	11·5 min	12·6 min	8 min
to 20,000 ft (6,096 m):	17·5 min	18 min	11·75 min
Service ceiling:	27,600 ft (8,412 m)	28,650 ft (8,733 m)	31,600 ft (9,632 m)
Endurance:	—	2 hr	2½ hr

* at 14,000 ft (4,267 m)

Some Peacetime Prototypes

Between the two wars the British aircraft industry built a great quantity of aircraft prototypes to meet a series of official requirements ranging over the whole spectrum of operational needs. It was always clear that only a small percentage of such creations could have any chance of a repeat order, but those were easy-going times and new aircraft could be designed, built and tested in a matter of months, and at a cost of a few thousand pounds. Although shortage of money meant that the peacetime Royal Air Force did not always benefit at once from the latest developments, the adopted policy did mean that the design staffs were at least kept in being and that there was some semblance of continuity in the development of engines and aircraft.

The four Armstrong Whitworth aircraft dealt with in this chapter all joined the great assemblage of unsuccessful competitors for government orders. None of the four got beyond the prototype stage and they were thus of no particular significance in the wider context of the company's history; nevertheless, each had a contribution to make to the technical progress at Coventry, and their interest lies more in their technical features than in their brief operational lives.

Awana

The first of the four, the Awana troop transport, was also the first true Armstrong Whitworth aircraft, as opposed to a Siddeley Deasy product, to fly from Whitley. The A.W. system of numbering (such as it was) had not yet been adopted, but it would seem in retrospect that this aircraft should qualify for the honour of being A.W.1.

For its time, the Awana was a very large aeroplane with biplane wings exceeding a hundred feet in span; it was designed to carry twenty-five troops and was fitted with two Napier Lion engines, each rated at 450 hp. In this respect it was unique among the early Armstrong Whitworth designs in as much as some fifteen years were to pass before another of the company's aircraft was to emerge with engines originating outside the Siddeley organization. The Awana was designed to meet an official specification numbered 5/20; it was in competition with the Vickers Victoria and two prototypes of each were ordered by the Air Ministry in 1921. Oddly, due no doubt to a mental aberration in official quarters, the first Awana appeared in June 1923 bearing the serial number J6860, the number correctly allocated to the first Victoria, which had been flying since the previous August. The correct number for the Awana, J6897, was

The Awana troop transport first flew in 1923. It did not go into production. (*Royal Aeronautical Society*)

soon substituted, but not before photographs, which subsequently appeared in the technical press, had been taken.

The Awana was of mixed construction with a fuselage built of steel tubes, wire-braced and fabric-covered, and with wings of the normal type with wooden spars and ribs. The engines were mounted ahead of the lower wing and were neatly cowled; cooling was by honeycomb radiators which were hinged so that they could be lowered into the slipstream or raised flush with the underside of the cowling. Outboard of the engines the extension wings, with three sets of interplane struts on either side, were arranged to fold. For ease of manufacture and transport, the top wing was divided into five sections, the centre section and the two extension wings, each of which was split inboard of the aileron; the bottom wing was similarly divided, except that the centre section was also split into two

The Awana was designed to carry twenty-five troops. The wings spanned more than 100 ft and could be folded. (*Royal Aeronautical Society*)

The second Awana, J6898. The aircraft weighed 18,450 lb fully loaded and had a top speed of 97 mph. (*Courtesy P. Jarrett*)

sections. The Awana's tailplane was of the biplane type, with a central fin and three balanced rudders. What appeared to be a pair of horn-balanced elevators on the top tailplane were, in fact, trimming surfaces, the true elevator being on the bottom plane. Two separate V-type undercarriages, each with two wheels and with oleo-pneumatic shock-absorbers incorporated in the front struts, were located under the engines. Fuel was contained in three cylindrical tanks, each holding 64 gal, set below the fuselage within an aluminium fairing, while above each engine, mounted under the top wing, was a 50-gal gravity tank. Fuel was supplied to the gravity tanks from the main tanks by windmill-driven pumps. The passengers were provided with hammock-type seats supported on cables, and entry was through a trap door in the floor of the cabin. The crew of two were situated in open cockpits in the nose, with the pilot in front on the port side and the navigator, or W/T operator, immediately behind; lateral control was by a wheel mounted on the control column, but no provision was made for dual controls.

The prototype Awana, with its incorrect serial number, made its first flight, piloted by Frank Courtney, on 28 June, 1923. Courtney recalls that it proved to be very much the conventional aircraft with flight characteristics which were adequate without being in any way remarkable. In the autumn of 1923 the Awana, now with its correct serial number, underwent official trials at Martlesham Heath and, in a report dated October 1923, the top speed at 1,000 ft was quoted as 97 mph, with an endurance of $4\frac{1}{4}$ hr at 85 mph. The initial rate of climb was just over 300 ft/min and the service ceiling was 8,000 ft. The report stated that the aircraft was not easy to taxi and, on fairly sharp turns, the inner undercarriage appeared to be under heavy strain. In the air the Awana was said to have pronounced longitudinal stability at all speeds and power settings, while control,

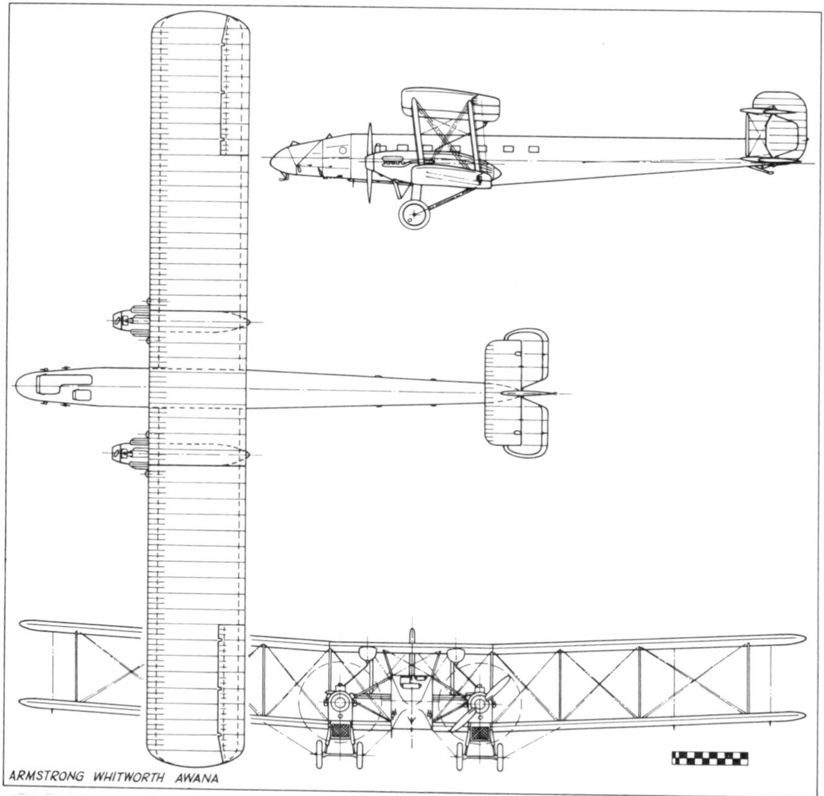

although moderately good at normal speeds, was definitely poor for landing. It was suggested that this fault might be cured by transferring the elevators to the top plane of the biplane tail. Lateral stability was considered satisfactory, although there was a tendency for a wing to drop at low speeds, and the response to the ailerons was slow. The view from the pilot's seat was classed as excellent, but dual seating and controls would have been preferred.

There was some criticism concerning the design and construction of the aircraft: the gravity fuel tanks under the top wing had no filler caps and had to be filled on the ground by hand pumps from the main tanks, a process which took more than an hour. More fundamental was the complaint that the steel-tube fuselage appeared to be too lightly constructed and too flexible, with the result that it required continual inspection and re-rigging. Other points noted were that there was insufficient clearance between the propeller tips and the side of the fuselage, which caused the celluloid windows to crack; that the flooring of the baggage compartment was not satisfactory; and that the tailskid was not strong enough. Finally, it was considered that the Awana would be difficult to maintain in service.

When the prototype Awana first appeared it carried the incorrect Service number J6860; this was subsequently altered to J6897.

By January 1924 the first Awana was reported to be lodged at Grain Island pending its transport to Farnborough for storage; meanwhile the second aircraft, J6898, had arrived at Martlesham Heath for further tests. This aircraft incorporated some of the improvements suggested after the first tests, notably an alteration to the angular setting of the aileron relative to the wing incidence, which had the effect of improving the lateral control. Nevertheless, in a document dated 23 January, 1924, a member of the Air Ministry Directorate of Research wrote that to incorporate all the modifications necessary to make the Awana really satisfactory would be very expensive; his conclusion was that although the Awana had a better performance than the Victoria, particularly as regards take-off and landing, the lightweight construction of the Awana's fuselage and undercarriages would probably lead to trouble in service. A further comment indicated that the large size of the Awana was a disadvantage, and that the arrangements for accommodating the troops were not as good as those of the Victoria. This document also made mention of an experimental fuselage of a different type which was being built for the Awana as '. . . an experiment in metal construction'. It was, however, suggested that it would be very expensive to fit this fuselage to the aircraft and that it might be better to use it for tests to destruction as originally intended. No details of this fuselage have come to light, and it can only be concluded that it represented a further improvement in the braced tubular type of structure which was to be a feature of all succeeding Armstrong Whitworth aircraft until the late 1930s.

In the end, the Vickers Victoria was chosen for production and the two Awanas passed quietly from the scene, with no known record of their ultimate fate. The effort put into them was not, however, entirely wasted: the experience gained in building the Awana was applied successfully in the design of the civil Argosy of 1926, which incorporated many features stemming directly from the Awana.

A.W.19

The so-called 'general purpose' aircraft, much in evidence in the years between the wars, was greatly favoured by an Air Ministry which was always short of money. Designed to perform a number of differing operational rôles, this type of aircraft was undoubtedly useful in peacetime but, like all compromises, it excelled at nothing and would have been hopelessly outclassed in any warlike activity more demanding than keeping a few rebellious tribesmen in order. By 1931 the time had come to plan for a replacement of the Westland Wapiti, and a specification, G.4/31, was drawn up with this object in view. It was issued in July 1931 and called for a two/three-seat aircraft suitable for army co-operation, reconnaissance, day and night bombing, and dive-bombing; later in the year the ability to carry a torpedo was added to the requirements. In spite of the design problems posed by this multiplicity of duties, the project was a tempting one for the manufacturers because, judging from past experience, the successful all-rounder would not only qualify for a sizable order initially, but would probably remain in production for a number of years. In fact, twelve companies tendered for the G.4/31 specification and no less than thirty different designs were submitted. Three of these firms received contracts for prototypes and five others decided to compete with private-venture entries.

An unusual view of the A.W.19 general-purpose biplane being prepared for its first flight in February 1934. (*Courtesy A. Campbell-Orde*)

Among the private-venture aircraft was the Armstrong Whitworth A.W.19, a large biplane of fairly conventional design with a fuselage that filled the gap between the upper and lower wings, which latter were cranked upwards at the centre section. The pilot was seated high up ahead of the top wing from where his view for dive-bombing and torpedo attack was exceptionally good. Aft of the wings was a gunner's cockpit with a sliding cowling for the protection of the occupant when his gun was not in use; between the two cockpits was a roomy cabin for the observer-navigator. A split undercarriage allowed for the carriage of an 18-inch torpedo. In their specification the Air Ministry had expressed a preference for an air-cooled engine, and Armstrong Whitworth, true to tradition, chose an Armstrong Siddeley engine, the Tiger IV, a geared and moderately supercharged motor which developed a maximum of 810 hp at 6,500 ft.

The construction of the A.W.19 followed conventional Armstrong Whitworth practice; the fuselage was built up of high-tensile steel tubing, with the front portion covered with detachable aluminium panels and the rear portion with fabric. The wing spars were fabricated from rolled-steel strip and were separated by tubular compression members. An innovation for Armstrong Whitworth was the use of light alloy for the construction of the wing ribs. The wing section was a modification of Clark YH, with the thickness/chord ratio increased by 2½ per cent. Ailerons were fitted to all four wings and the top wing carried auto-slots. Armament consisted of a single fixed Vickers ·303 machine-gun firing forward under the control of the pilot, and a Lewis gun, also of ·303 calibre, mounted on a ring for the rear gunner. The aircraft was designed to carry a K-type torpedo weighing some 2,000 lb, although, as an alternative, a 1,000-lb bomb could be carried in its place. There were also bomb

The A.W.19 climbing away from Whitley Abbey aerodrome. The engine was a Tiger VI. (*Flight International 10439S*)

The divided undercarriage of the A.W.19 enabled it to carry a torpedo, one of the many requirements of specification G.4/31. (*Flight International 10447S*)

racks under the lower wings which could accommodate a selection of smaller bombs totalling the same weight. The specification called for the ability to carry a torpedo up to 14,000 ft or a bomb load of 500 lb up to 20,000 ft. The Service equipment was to include appliances to cover almost every contingency: air bags in the fuselage to keep the aircraft afloat in a forced landing were supplemented by an inflatable dinghy, with an emergency radio and distress signals, stowed in the upper wing. Electrical equipment included a wind-driven generator to feed the W/T and R/T radio and heating circuits for the crew and the torpedo. The standard equipment specified included wingtip flares and provision for smoke floats and a camera; provision was also to be made for a message pick-up hook to be fitted in place of the torpedo.

The A.W.19 was first flown with the marking A-3, but was subsequently given the RAF Service number K5606. (*Flight International 10441S*)

Another air-to-air view of the A.W.19, a photograph taken through a Perspex window. (*Courtesy A. Campbell-Orde*)

The A.W.19 first flew on 26 February, 1934, with Campbell-Orde at the controls; initially it carried the mark A 3, but in 1935 it was acquired by the Air Ministry and given the serial number K5606. It first went to Martlesham Heath on 6 April, 1934, and, for its size and weight, it had a good performance but it suffered from persistent engine overheating. It was judged to be easy to fly with good stability under all conditions of load. By the time the A.W.19 was ready for trials there was no chance of an order for it or for any of its rivals, a situation for which the Vickers company was responsible: in addition to their official contract prototype aircraft, they had built, as a private venture, a monoplane constructed on the geodetic principle, and this aircraft was so promising that a new specification was written around it and, as the Vickers Wellesley, it was

The A.W.19 was eventually used as a test-bed for developing the Tiger engine for the Whitley bomber. (*Flight International 10448S*)

There was no production order for the A.W.19 and only one was built. (*Flight International 10440S*)

ordered into production. Thus, the G.4/31 specification, already three years old, was rendered obsolete and the aircraft built by Bristol, Fairey, Handley Page, Hawker, Parnall and Westland, as well as the A.W.19, became superfluous. The A.W.19 was returned to Armstrong Whitworth for use as a test vehicle for Tiger engine development, a task also undertaken by the Fairey G.4/31 K3905, at Whitley Abbey. In 1935 the A.W.19 was fitted with a Tiger VI engine and a year later trials were undertaken with a Tiger VII; these continued until the aircraft was scrapped in June 1940.

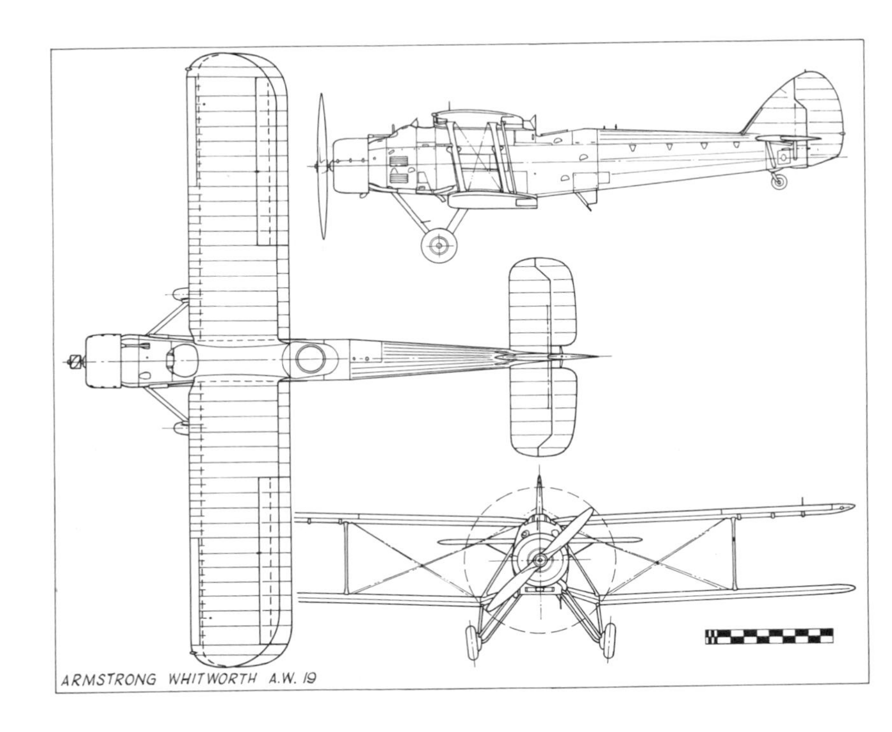

A.W.23

Another 'one-off' prototype to emerge from the Coventry factory was the A.W.23 bomber-transport of 1935. This aircraft was notable for a number of reasons, the most important being that from it stemmed the Whitley bomber: in addition, it marked the first significant break-away by Armstrong Whitworth from the methods of construction which had remained basically unchanged since the first all-steel Siskin of 1923. It was also the first of the company's aircraft to have a retractable undercarriage and the first twin-engined machine to be built at Whitley since the previous military transport, the Awana, twelve years before.

The A.W.23, the Handley Page 51 and the Bristol Bombay, were all designed to meet the Air Ministry specification C.26/31, which outlined requirements for an aircraft capable of carrying troops or bombs, as required. Competition between the three contenders was keen, and all three aircraft flew within two months of each other in 1935; the results were close and, in the opinion of some company people, the A.W.23 only narrowly missed being ordered. The favourable impression created by the Armstrong Whitworth aircraft (it was the only one of the three which had a retractable undercarriage) led to the decision that the type should be further developed, a policy which resulted, eventually, in the Whitley. It

The A.W.23 bomber-transport was designed to specification C.26/31.

thus happened that both the H.P.51, which was later developed into the Harrow bomber, and the A.W.23, more extensively redesigned into the Whitley, received much larger production orders than did the Bombay, which was the winner of the original bomber-transport competition.

The most notable design feature of the A.W.23 was the use of light alloy for the construction of the main spar of the cantilever wing. This was a box structure with flanges of sheet metal corrugated spanwise with webs of the same material corrugated vertically. The box structure so formed was stiffened by an internal bracing of steel tubes. The covering of the forward

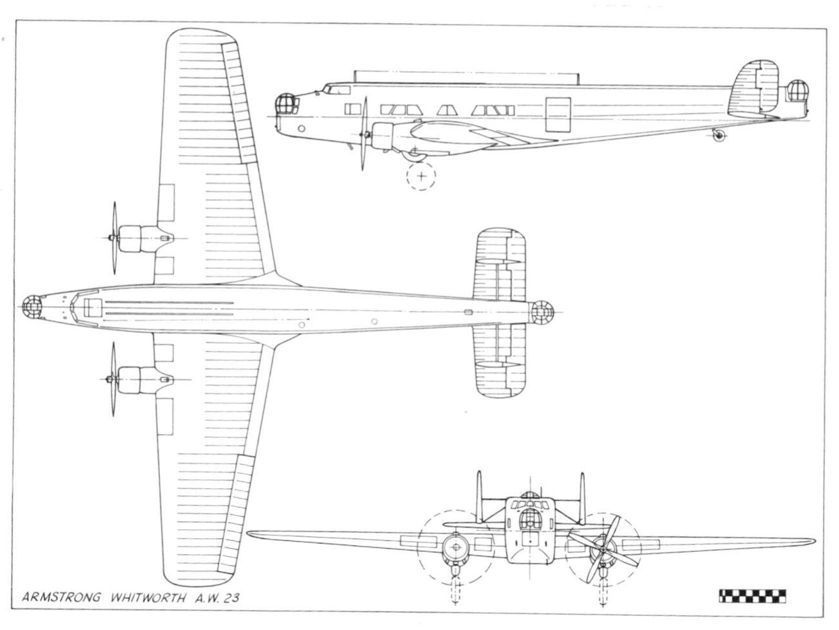

The wing of the A.W.23 undergoing a test to destruction in 1936.

part of the wing was of unstressed metal sheet which extended back as far as the rear face of the spar; aft of this point fabric covering was employed. This new type of wing construction, which was the subject of a company patent, was employed also in the Whitley, whose wing was virtually a replica of that of the A.W.23, being of similar outline with only a slight reduction in span and chord. The low-set tailplane, with its twin fins and rudders, was another feature of the A.W.23 which was reproduced in the Whitley. The fuselage of the A.W.23 was built in the conventional Armstrong Whitworth manner, with braced steel tubing covered with fabric.

The retractable undercarriage, which consisted of two independent single-wheel units, was folded by hydraulic power upwards and forwards into the fairings behind the engines. These were a pair of Tiger VIs, each developing 810 hp. When first flown, the A.W.23 was fitted with four-blade wooden propellers, but later the two-position variable-pitch type were substituted.

The A.W.23 was the first Armstrong Whitworth type to have a retractable undercarriage, here seen extended. (*Courtesy A. Campbell-Orde*)

The A.W.23's wooden propellers, seen in this photograph, were later replaced by variable-pitch units.

The A.W.23, with the serial number K3585, was first flown on 4 June, 1935, with Campbell-Orde in charge, and it made its first public appearance among the new and experimental aircraft at the RAF Display at Hendon on 29 June, 1935. On test, the aircraft performed well and was pleasant to handle, but two incidents took place during the maker's trials at Whitley. The first occurred on 9 March, 1936, when the port motor cut at 200 ft just after take-off; with the starboard engine at full throttle and the propeller in fine-pitch, the aircraft was just able to maintain altitude and, after a wide circuit, a successful approach and landing was made on the aerodrome. Unfortunately, the single hydraulic pump was actuated by the wind-milling port engine and, as a consequence, the pressure in the system was insufficient to lock the port undercarriage; as a result, this folded up just before the aircraft came to rest. The port wing touched the ground, but damage to the aircraft was slight and it was soon flying again. Sometime

In preparation for the first flight, the A.W.23, so far un-numbered, undergoing engine runs in front of the flight hangar at Whitley Abbey aerodrome.

In addition to the Service number K3585, the A.W.23 was given the number 8 for the RAF Display in 1935.

later, during a routine test flight, a large section of fabric became detached from the fuselage side; fortunately, it blew clear instead of wrapping itself round the tailplane. Campbell-Orde recalls that his chief emotion was one of surprise that the A.W.23 seemed to fly as well without the fuselage fabric as with it, and he experienced no difficulty in bringing the aircraft in to a normal landing.

After a period of storage at Baginton, the A.W.23 was lent by the Air Ministry to Flight Refuelling Ltd for use as a tanker aircraft. In this capacity the A.W.23 was eventually granted civil status and given the registration G-AFRX. Its adaptation to the rôle of tanker aircraft involved the installation of an additional fuel tank in the fuselage, a hose reel mounted over a hatch in the fuselage floor and the fitting of a large Perspex panel in the side of the fuselage to improve the view for accurate formation flying. In the summer of 1937 the A.W.23, together with the Handley Page 51 (which had also been lent to Flight Refuelling Ltd), gave a demonstration of the technique to officials at Farnborough. Afterwards the A.W.23 was used to test the practicability of making contact and transferring fuel by day and by night and in bad weather, in connection with Imperial Airways' proposed experimental Atlantic flights with Short C class Empire flying-boats. These tests culminated in successful trials over Southampton Water using the A.W.23 to refuel the flying-boat *Cambria*, the first operation taking place on 20 January, 1938.

The A.W.23 failed to get a production order, but it was further developed into the Whitley bomber.

The method used was known as the 'ejector system', and involved the receiving aircraft (the 'calf') trailing a weighted line from a refuelling aperture in the extreme tail. Meanwhile, the tanker aircraft (the 'cow') positioned itself on the starboard quarter and a little below the calf aircraft. From this position a line-throwing gun in the cow aircraft was fired into the parabola of the calf's weighted line; as the ejected line lost momentum it trailed rearwards and made contact with the calf's line, finally engaging with a grapnel at its extremity. It then became a simple matter for the joined lines to be used to haul across the refuelling hose from the cow aircraft. Although the system might be thought to be a trifle chancy, in practice it worked well and was used with consistent success during sixteen experimental Atlantic crossings made by Imperial Airways during 1938. By then, however, the A.W.23 had been superseded as a flight-refuelling cow by a number of Handley Page Harrows and, as war approached, the A.W.23 was once more put into storage, this time in one of the hangars at Flight Refuelling's base at Ford aerodrome in Sussex, and it was here that the aircraft was totally destroyed during an air raid on 18 August, 1940.

A.W.29

The last of the four aircraft to be dealt with in this chapter, the A.W.29, must be classed as a failure due to the over-stretching of the company's available facilities. Designed as a two-seat, single-engined day bomber, the A.W.29 was intended to meet specification P.27/32 issued in April 1933, but, while the design was under way, the company embarked on two other designs, the Whitley bomber and the Ensign airliner, both of which were given priority over the A.W.29. It soon became obvious that both the design staff and the factory facilities were inadequate to cope with both these large aircraft, and it was thus inevitable that the A.W.29 should have been pushed into the background. By the time the aircraft was eventually completed late in 1935, its rival, the Fairey Battle, which had flown some nine months earlier, had already been selected for large-scale production. The fact that, in war, the light day-bomber concept proved to be a disastrous mistake, while the Whitley, although by then obsolete, proved to be successful, may, in retrospect, have been seen as offering some moral justification for the course adopted by Armstrong Whitworth.

The intention behind the P.27/32 specification was to produce a light bomber capable of carrying a bomb load of 1,000 lb for a distance of 1,000 miles at a speed of 200 mph. This configuration seemed to lend itself to the current concept of a specialized mailplane and, when the design was first laid out in 1933, drawings were prepared for a version with a mail compartment situated over the wing centre section and with the pilot placed well aft of the wing in an open cockpit; nothing came of this project. Construction work on the light bomber started some time in 1934, and the design incorporated some novel features, the most notable of which was

Designed as a 200-mph day bomber, the A.W.29 was built to specification P.27/32.

the light-alloy monocoque rear fuselage, the first time this method of construction had been adopted by Armstrong Whitworth.

The monocoque fuselage extended aft from the wing centre section, while the forward part of the fuselage, containing the pilot's seat and the engine bearers, was a built-up framework of steel tubing covered with light-alloy panels. Both sections of the fuselage were bolted to the large box spar which formed the basis of the tapered, cantilever wing. This spar, built of light alloy, was similar to that used in the A.W.23 and, as in that aircraft, the forward half of the wing, from the leading edge as far back as the rear face of the spar, was covered with duralumin sheet, while aft of the spar the covering was of fabric. The tailplane was a cantilever structure, fabric covered except for a metal leading edge. The ailerons were Frise-balanced, while the rudder and elevators were fitted with servo-tabs which also acted as trimmers. The split flaps on the wing trailing edge extended from inboard of the ailerons to the fuselage. The undercarriage consisted of two units, each with one wheel, which retracted backwards into the wing root, which was increased in thickness on its underside to provide the

The fuselage of the A.W.29, aft of the wing, was of monocoque construction, the first to be so built by Armstrong Whitworth.

necessary space. The doors which enclosed the undercarriage left a small segment of the wheels exposed.

The increase in the thickness of the wing centre section also served to accommodate the bomb load which was carried in compartments faired over with spring-loaded doors which opened under the weight of the falling bombs. The war load could be made up of two bombs of 500 lb, four of 250 lb or eight smaller bombs of 112 lb or less. Defensive armament consisted of the usual fixed Vickers gun firing forward through the propeller arc, while a single Lewis gun, mounted in an Armstrong Whitworth manually-operated turret, was provided for the second crew man who combined his duties as gunner with those of W/T operator, observer and

The retractable undercarriage of the A.W.29.

bomb-aimer. The two crew members were separated by all of twelve feet and could communicate only by telephone or, if that failed, by written message passed by a string through a tube linking the two cockpits. During the early design stage in the autumn of 1933, there was a suggestion that the pilot should be accommodated in an open cockpit but, as built, the aircraft was fitted with an elaborate glazed canopy. The engine of the A.W.29 was a Tiger VIII with a two-speed supercharger; the power developed was 920 hp for take-off, with a maximum of 810 hp at 14,700 ft. The propeller was a three-blade two-position unit of Hamilton Standard design.

The estimated performance figures for the A.W.29 indicated that the maximum speed would be 225 mph at 14,700 ft, and 187 mph at sea level, while the rate of climb was given as 1,000 ft/min; the range was quoted as

Because of priority given to the Whitley bomber, the A.W.29 was delayed, and it did not fly until December 1936.

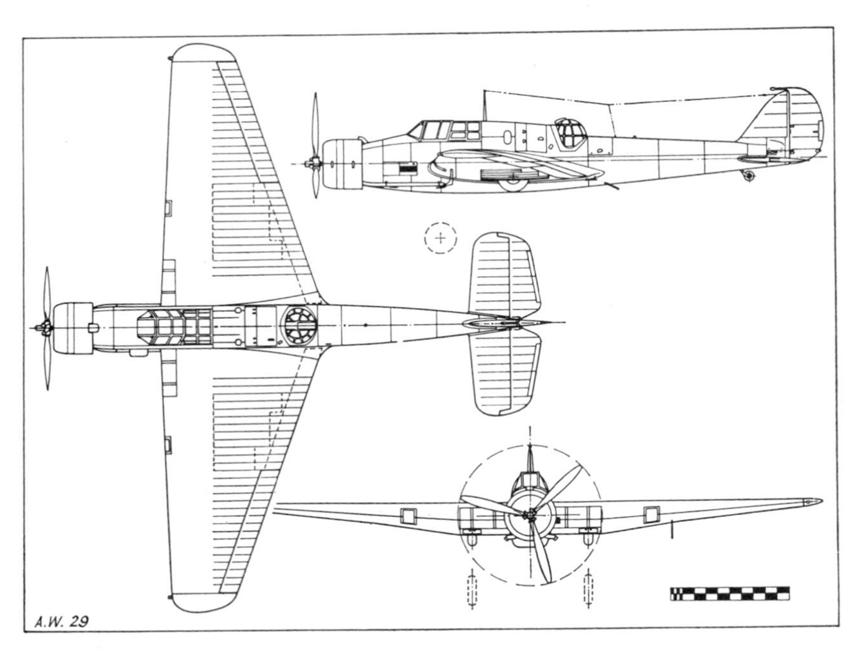

The engine of the A.W.29 was a Tiger VIII of 920 hp. (*Courtesy P. Jarrett*)

685 miles. These figures were never substantiated because the flying life of the A.W.29 was too short for measurement to be undertaken. The first flight, made by Turner-Hughes, took place on 6 December, 1936, and it was not long after this that another pilot was forced to land the aircraft with the undercarriage retracted. By now, there was no hope of a production order and, with all the available resources concentrated on the Whitley, and to a lesser extent on the Ensign, there was little incentive to devote the time and effort required to repair the A.W.29 and it never flew again. At a later date, some work was done towards modifying the aircraft to serve as a flying test-bed for the Armstrong Siddeley Deerhound engine then under development, but the work had not proceeded far before it was decided to use the Whitley for this task, and the remains of the A.W.29 were put on the scrap heap.

The split flaps of the A.W.29, the first to be fitted to an Armstrong Whitworth aircraft.

Awana

Dimensions: Span 105 ft 6 in (32·16 m); length 68 ft (20·72 m); height 20 ft 3 in (6·17 m); wing area 2,300 sq ft (213·68 sq m).

A.W.19

Dimensions: Span 49 ft 8 in (15·14 m); length 42 ft 2 in (12·85 m); height 13 ft (3·96 m); wing area 654 sq ft (60·78 sq m).

A.W.23

Dimensions: Span 88 ft (26·82 m); length 80 ft 9 in (24·61 m); height 19 ft 6 in (5·94 m); wing area 1,308 sq ft (121·51 sq m).

A.W.29

Dimensions: Span 49 ft (14·94 m); length 43 ft 10 in (13·36 m); height 13 ft 3 in (4·04 m); wing area 458 sq ft (42·55 sq m).

	Awana	**A.W.19**
	Two 450 hp Napier Lion	*810 hp Tiger VI*
Max weight:	18,450 lb (8,373 kg)	8,750 lb (3,969 kg)
Empty weight:	10,000 lb (4,536 kg)	4,298 lb (1,950 kg)
Max speed		
1,000 ft (305 m):	97 mph (156 km/hr)	—
6,000 ft (1,829 m):	92 mph (148 km/hr)	163 mph (262 km/hr)
15,000 ft (4,572 m):	—	152 mph (245 km/hr)
Climb to		
5,000 ft (1,542 m):	19·7 min	—
10,000 ft (3,048 m):	—	8·8 min
15,000 ft (4,572 m):	—	16·6 min
Service ceiling:	8,000 ft (2,438 m)	21,000 ft (6,400 m)
Range:	360 miles (579 km)	—

	A.W.23	**A.W.29**
	Two 810 hp Tiger VI	*920 hp Tiger VIII*
Max weight:	24,100 lb (1,093 kg)	9,000 lb (4,082 kg)
Empty weight:	—	—
Max speed		
Sea level	—	187 mph (301 km/hr)
6,000 ft (1,829 m):	175 mph (282 km/hr)	206 mph (332 km/hr)
14,700 ft (4,481 m):	150 mph (241 km/hr)	225 mph (362 km/hr)
Climb to		
10,000 ft (3,048 m):	19 min	11 min
15,000 ft (4,572 m):	—	16·8 min
18,000 ft (5,486 m):	—	20 min
Service ceiling:	20,000 ft (6,096 m)	21,000 ft (6,400 m)
Range:	900 miles (1,448 km)	685 miles (1,102 km)

The Argosy Mk.I, *City of Glasgow*, one of three which went into service with Imperial Airways in 1926 and 1927.

Imperial Transports

Between the two wars Armstrong Whitworth built three types of multi-engined airliners and, although each in its way represented a technical step forward, they were all built to the rather specialized requirements of Imperial Airways and, as a consequence, they unfortunately failed to find favour with other airlines.

Argosy

The first of the Armstrong Whitworth airliners was the Argosy, a three-engined aircraft with accommodation for twenty passengers and an operating crew of two: it was one of several new types ordered by Imperial Airways in 1925 in accordance with their new policy of using only multi-engined aircraft. The Argosy, for which there is no identifiable A.W. type number, was originally designed to a specification, drawn up in 1922, for a 'Middle East' aircraft with three air-cooled engines and capable of flying 500 miles against a headwind of 30 mph. Later, having decided that the Armstrong Whitworth design would be suitable also for its European routes, Imperial Airways placed an order for two aircraft, and this was backed up by an order from the Air Ministry for a third.

The *City of Birmingham*, the first Argosy Mk.I to be delivered to Imperial Airways.

The Argosy was a large biplane with three 385 hp direct-drive Jaguar engines, one mounted in the nose and the other two in the conventional position between the wings. No fuel was carried in the fuselage, the two tanks being situated beneath the top centre section. The angular box-shaped fuselage, which carried a biplane tail with three fins and rudders, was of steel-tube construction covered with fabric, along the lines already devised for the Siskin and the Atlas. The cabin section of the fuselage had a wooden floor which also served to brace the structure, while fabric was used to line the walls and roof of the cabin which was in consequence somewhat noisy. The twenty passengers were seated in a spacious compartment measuring 29 ft long, 4 ft 6 in wide and 6 ft 3 in high; there was a central gangway and an opening window beside each seat. At the rear of the cabin was a lavatory and behind that a large baggage compartment with an exterior door; another, smaller, freight hold was located forward under the pilot's cockpit.

The wings, except for the centre section, were of wooden construction, fabric-covered, with ailerons on all four planes. Both the top and bottom centre sections had steel spars, the top one being supported above the fuselage by tubular steel struts arranged in the shape of a W when seen from the front; the bottom centre section carried the wing-engine structure and from it depended the two-wheel undercarriage. This consisted of two Vs under the wing engines, each having oleo-damped, coil-spring shock-absorbers and axles hinged to a pyramid of steel struts under the fuselage. When first delivered, the Argosies were painted in the current Imperial

Airways livery of silver-doped wings and a dark blue fuselage with silver lettering; later, during 1927 and 1928, the colour scheme was changed to a silver fuselage with very dark blue edges and lettering. The first three Argosies were G-EBLF *City of Glasgow*, G-EBLO *City of Birmingham* and G-EBOZ *City of Wellington*. This last aircraft was later renamed *City of Arundel.*

Captain F. L. Barnard of Imperial Airways tested the first of the Argosies on 16 March, 1926, and this is believed to be the aircraft's first flight; other tests followed on the 19th, 20th and 24th of March. The second aircraft, G-EBLO, flew for the first time on 18 June, 1926, again with Barnard at the controls. This was the first aircraft to be delivered to Imperial Airways, who received it in July 1926. The third aircraft, that ordered by the Air Ministry, was delivered to Imperial Airways in March 1927. The Argosy's first service flight was made by the *City of Birmingham*, which flew from Croydon to Paris on 16 July, 1926; later the Argosies were employed also on the routes between London and Brussels and Cologne. In October 1926 the *City of Glasgow* was demonstrated before representatives of the Dominion Conference at Croydon Airport,

The interior of the Argosy; accommodation was provided for twenty passengers.

The Argosy, *City of Glasgow*, over London.

and *Flight* reported that '. . . the way this machine leaps off the ground and climbs almost like a scout is truly amazing'.

The introduction of the Argosy resulted in a significant boost to Imperial Airways' traffic figures, particularly on the London–Paris route. During most of the summer of 1926 the British company had been carrying forty per cent more passengers than the competing French airline; by October, with the Argosy in service, they were carrying one hundred per cent more than their rivals on the Paris route. Costs were also dramatically reduced; the airline's own figures showed that the cost per ton-mile-capacity for the Argosy was 9p (1/10d) against 14p (2/10d) for the Handley Page W10 and 21p (4/2d) for the D.H.34. The roomy cabin of the Argosy—it was more spacious than that of any of its contemporaries—was put to good use by Imperial Airways when, on 1 May, 1927, they inaugurated the *Silver Wing* service on the London–Paris route. This 'luxury' lunch-time flight boasted a cabin steward and a buffet bar; the service operated from both Croydon and Le Bourget, departing at 12 noon with a flight time of two-and-a-half hours. Fifty minutes was allowed for the coach journey between the West End of London and Croydon Airport. In a tariff published in October 1928 the single fare was quoted as £4.15s, which represented an increase of £1 on the fare for the ordinary morning service.

In June 1928 Imperial Airways stated that they were contemplating the operation of a service to Scotland, and that a trial would be made to see how such a service would compare with the existing railway journey. The test took place on 15 June, with two groups of passengers, one of which left Croydon in the *City of Glasgow* at 10 a.m., and the other steaming out of King's Cross station at the same time in the *Flying Scotsman*. The Argosy made intermediate stops at Bircham Newton and Cramlington, near Newcastle, and arrived at Turnhouse aerodrome, Edinburgh, just 15 minutes before the train pulled in to Waverley station. Not surprisingly, no more was heard of the suggested air service to Scotland. In the meantime the Argosies had been working hard on their legitimate business; figures published by Imperial Airways showed that by 8 December, 1928, the three Argosies had flown a total of 4,862 hours, equivalent to some 437,500 miles, and that the first to go into service, G-EBLO, had built up a total of 1,843 hours in just over 28 months. These figures were good by the standards of the day and Imperial Airways further stated that the Argosy was the first of their aircraft to pay its way. They gave proof of their satisfaction by placing a repeat order in 1928, firstly for three, shortly increased to four improved Argosies.

The Argosy Mk.II differed from its predecessors in having the more powerful geared Jaguar IVA engine which developed 410 hp. The rear

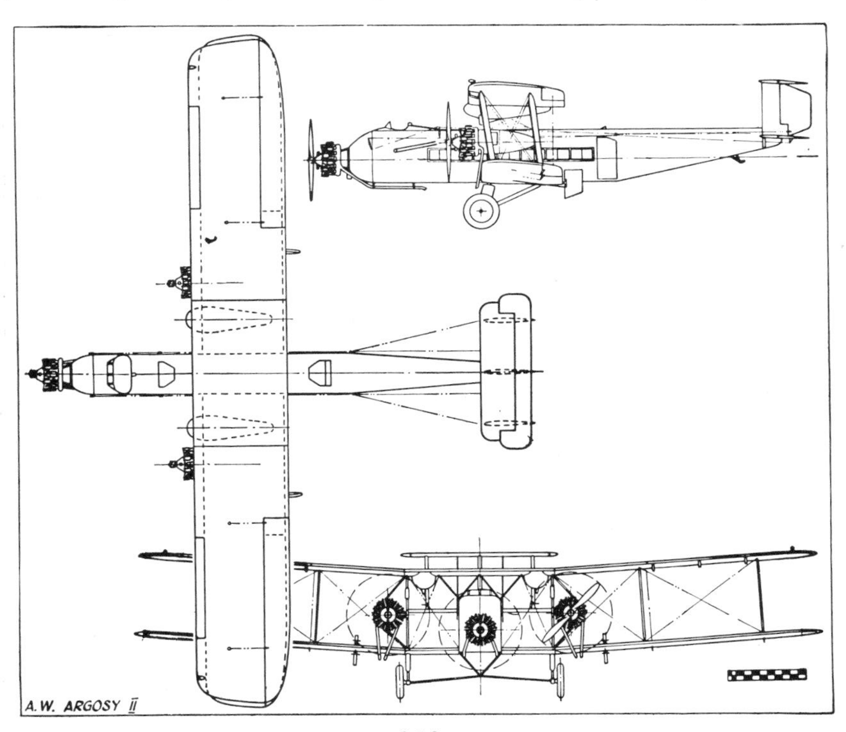

The Argosy Mk.II had geared Jaguar engines and Townend-ring cowlings.. (*Royal Aeronautical Society*)

cowling of the engines was of improved streamline shape and, on delivery, the engines themselves were fitted with Townend rings, but these were soon discarded when the aircraft went into service. Other changes were the fitting of automatic wingtip slots on the top wing, and an increase in the fuel capacity to 360 gal, enough for a flight of 520 miles. Another innovation was the novel method of operating the ailerons which was, in effect, an extension of the aileron balancing system used in the Wolf. In the case of the Argosy II, the ailerons themselves were unbalanced and were operated by servo flaps placed vertically behind the trailing edge of the lower wing.

The Argosy Mk.I, G-EBOZ, in the flight hangar at Whitley Abbey aerodrome. The photograph shows it in the original dark blue livery of Imperial Airways. (*Courtesy A. Campbell-Orde*)

These flaps, which looked like rudders, were pivoted on the ends of outriggers which were themselves pivoted on a vertical axis positioned between the wing spars. An angular displacement of the flaps, brought about by the pilot operating his lateral control wheel, caused the outriggers to move through an angle, and it was this lateral movement of the outriggers which, through connecting cables, moved the ailerons. The apparatus was somewhat untidy in appearance, but it enabled the stick loads to be adjusted to any desired degree of lightness without the risk of over-balancing the controls. It also conferred a measure of automatic stability in that any sideslip had the effect of operating the servo flap and thereby applying corrective aileron.

After many years of frustrating international negotiations, all seemed set, in 1929, for the opening of the first Empire air mail route from London to Karachi, then part of India. In fact, there were still further frustrations to come later due to the intransigence of Italy and Persia, but these new problems still lay ahead on 30 March, 1929, when, punctually at 10 a.m., the Argosy *City of Glasgow* carrying 364 lb of mail, left Croydon *en route* for Paris and Basle, the first sector of the route to India. The Argosy's part in the grand scheme was only a comparatively modest one: at Basle the mail was transferred to a train for conveyance to Genoa from where it was taken on by Short Calcutta flying-boat to Alexandria. From Egypt, de Havilland Hercules aircraft took the mail across the desert to Baghdad and thence along the shores of Persia and Baluchistan to Karachi. The journey took six days, as against fifteen days by land and sea, and the single fare, including meals and hotel accommodation *en route* was £130.

The Argosy G-EBOZ, now named *City of Arundel* and painted silver with dark blue lining, on Khartoum aerodrome.

Following the delivery of the four Mk.II Argosies, G-AACH *City of Edinburgh* (May 1929), G-AACI *City of Liverpool* (June 1929), G-AACJ *City of Manchester* (July 1929), and G-AAEJ *City of Coventry* (August 1929), the three Mk.I aircraft were re-engined with the Jaguar IVA geared engines and two of them, G-EBLO and G-EBOZ, were transferred to Cairo for the opening of the first section of the air mail route to Cape Town. This occurred on 28 February, 1931, when the first passengers and mail for Africa were flown out of Croydon in an Argosy. The event lost some of its drama because the Argosy used was the self-same aeroplane that was operating the London–Karachi service which, by now, was routed through Germany and the Balkans to Athens, where the flying-boats took over. From Cairo the Argosies operated the service down the Nile to Khartoum, a distance of about 1,000 miles which was covered in two days with a night stop at Aswan. The use of the Argosy on this section of the route was necessary because of the late delivery of the new Handley Page 42 airliners.

The African service got off to a bad start, with repeated delays caused by a number of mishaps which greatly aggravated the basic shortage of aircraft. In March 1931 the *City of Birmingham* suffered an engine seizure at Kareima, and later the same month an unspecified Argosy damaged its undercarriage at Khartoum. In June the situation was made still worse by the loss of the *City of Birmingham* which made a forced landing just outside the aerodrome at Aswan; there were no injuries to crew or passengers but the aircraft was written off, and the remaining Argosy Mk.I, the *City of Glasgow*, had to be sent out from England as a replacement.

The transfer of the third Argosy to Africa added considerably to Imperial Airways' difficulties in Europe, a situation which was still further complicated by an accident to the *City of Edinburgh* at Croydon. This occurred during a pilot's qualification test; at that time, commercial, or 'B'-Licence, pilots were required to have their licences endorsed for each type

In service, the Argosy's engine cowlings and exhaust rings were removed, although the extension pipes and heater muffs were left in place on the fuselage. (*Royal Aeronautical Society*)

A dramatic view of an Argosy Mk.II taking off.

of aircraft, and in order to qualify for a new type six take-offs and landings, three at light weight and three fully loaded, had to be made to the satisfaction of the inspector. On 22 April, 1931, a pilot undergoing the test had completed his six landings, but not being completely satisfied with his last touch-down, opened up for one more try. Unfortunately, the starboard engine failed to pick up and the aircraft swung violently towards the aerodrome fence. There was not room to take-off on two engines and, without brakes, there was insufficient distance in which to stop; the aircraft ploughed through the fence and, conveniently, finished up in the middle of a dump for old aeroplanes. The pilot was unhurt, but the Argosy caught fire and was destroyed.

In 1931 a Royal journey by airliner was still sufficiently novel to be noteworthy, and in April the Argosy came into the news when the Prince of Wales, later to become King Edward VIII, and Prince George, Duke of Kent, flew home from Bordeaux, on the last stage of a journey from South America, in the *City of Glasgow*. The interior of the aircraft had been re-arranged to provide a stateroom for the princes and another compartment for their staff. Interest was added to the event by the fact that the Argosy flew direct from Paris to Windsor, where a landing was made on Smith's Lawn in Windsor Great Park.

After many years of service during which no passenger had been injured, the one and only fatal accident to an Argosy occurred on 28 March, 1933. The *City of Liverpool*, while *en route* from Brussels to London, caught fire in the air near Dixmude in Belgium: it was seen descending from about 2,000 ft with smoke pouring from it, but, at about 200 ft from the ground, the fuselage broke in two and the aircraft crashed,

The Argosy Mk.II, *City of Edinburgh*. This aircraft was burnt out on the ground at Croydon Airport in 1931.

killing all the three crew and twelve passengers. The mail and a quantity of silver bullion were found scattered some distance from the scene of the crash. From the evidence of the wreckage it was clear that the fire originated in the lavatory or at the extreme rear of the cabin, and Imperial Airways' experts concluded that it was due either to deliberate sabotage, accidental firing by a passenger or spontaneous ignition in the baggage.

The arrival in service of the Handley Page 42s enabled the two Argosies G-EBLF and G-EBOZ to be brought back from Africa towards the end of 1933 for employment on the European routes, where they continued to operate until they were finally withdrawn in 1934. Of the two surviving Argosy Mk.IIs, the *City of Coventry* was withdrawn from service in 1935 and 'reduced to produce' at Croydon, while the *City of Manchester*, the last of the breed, was sold to United Airways in July 1935 and was used by them during the summer of 1936 for giving joy-rides from Stanley Park aerodrome, near Blackpool.

The first Argosy Mk.II, *City of Edinburgh*, showing the aileron-operating flaps on the lower mainplane. (*Courtesy A. Campbell-Orde*)

A.W.XV Atalanta

Imperial Airways' experience with the Argosy and the other three-engined aircraft tended to show that this number of engines did not provide complete immunity from forced landings due to engine failure, and, in 1929, the airline made a decision to standardize on four-engined aircraft. This, therefore, was made a condition in an Imperial Airways' specification, issued in 1930, for an aeroplane to serve between Kisumu in Kenya and Cape Town. The specification stipulated that the aircraft, with a payload of 3,000 lb, should be able to maintain an altitude of 9,000 ft with one engine stopped. It must also be able to operate from small, high and hot aerodromes, have a cruising speed of at least 115 mph and a range of 400 miles with the possibility of extending this to 600 miles if required. Accommodation was to be provided for nine passengers and a crew of three, with a large proportion of the payload being made available for mail and freight.

The first A.W.XV, bearing the name *Atalanta*; it first flew on 6 June, 1932.

When considering the best ways to meet the airline's requirements, John Lloyd weighed up the comparative merits of the monoplane against the biplane, which was then still very much in the ascendancy, at any rate among British manufacturers. One of the main reasons for this conservatism was that, with the knowledge then available, the biplane structure enabled a large wing area, and hence a low landing speed, to be achieved with much less weight than with the corresponding monoplane wing. On the other hand, Lloyd argued, the reliability which could be expected with the proposed four engines, and the large reserve of power to be provided, should make a rather higher-than-usual landing speed acceptable. If this principle was agreed, then a smaller wing and, indeed, a smaller and lighter aircraft could be envisaged—the greater aerodynamic efficiency of the monoplane wing more than making up for any small remaining weight penalty. In the light of subsequent developments and the acceptance of wing loadings and landing speeds undreamed of in 1930, these arguments may seem naïve, but at the time they were well ahead of current thinking, and the desire to limit landing speeds was then deeply rooted—and who shall say that this was wholly wrong?

Thus it came about that the second airliner to be built by Armstrong Whitworth, the A.W.XV Atalanta four-engined monoplane of 1932, represented a complete breakaway from the style of the earlier Argosy. The Atalanta was, for its time, an advanced design with every effort made to obtain performance in the most economical way, that is, by the reduction of drag. Indeed, with its clean lines and its neat, wing-mounted engines, the A.W.XV would not have looked too much out of place twenty years later: only its fixed undercarriage would have given it away, and even that was partially enclosed within the fuselage. The moderately-tapered thick-section cantilever wing was mounted on top of a well-streamlined fuselage of square section with rounded edges. The four 340 hp Double Mongoose

The extension wings of the A.W.XV had steel spars with wooden ribs and plywood covering.

engines were positioned on the leading edge of the wing and carefully faired into the wing profile. Lloyd remembers discussing this feature with Anthony Fokker who expressed the opinion that radial engines on the leading edge might be all right, but he wouldn't like to be the first to try it.

The success of Lloyd's efforts to reduce drag is evident from the fact that the total parasite drag of the Atalanta amounted to only 340 lb (as against 700 for the Argosy biplane) and of this figure, nearly one third was accounted for by the engine-cooling arrangements. Interference drag associated with the joints between the wing and the fuselage and the engine nacelles was minimal, a testimony to the careful wind-tunnel work which contributed to the design. Tests showed that the drag of the wheels and

The metal frame of the A.W.XV fuselage under construction.

spats amounted to some 25 per cent of that for the whole fuselage, a significant pointer to the value of the retractable undercarriage, a feature still looked upon with suspicion at that time in England.

The A.W.XV was of mixed metal and wood construction; the fuselage framework was built in three sections and, contrary to previous Armstrong Whitworth practice, the longerons and connecting struts were fabricated from steel strip formed into channel sections. The part of the fuselage containing the cabin was covered with three-ply wood carried on light stringers, while the rear portion of the fuselage was covered with fabric which was held off the main structure by rounded aluminium sheet at the four corners. The wing, also built in three portions, had two metal spars in the form of girders built up from channelled steel strip. In the centre-section portion, which contained the four engine mountings and the fuel tanks, the ribs were made of steel strip, whereas the ribs in the outboard sections of the wings were made of wood with a special type of fixing designed to allow for the expansion and contraction of the metal spars. The wing covering was of plywood back as far as the rear spar.

The engine selected for the A.W.XV was itself a comparatively new development; it consisted basically of two five-cylinder Mongoose radial engines joined together to make a ten-cylinder two-row engine, which, with moderate supercharging, developed a maximum of 375 hp at 4,500 ft. The new engine was at first called the Double Mongoose but was later renamed the Serval. The engine-mounting structure on the A.W.XV consisted of a bolted tubular framework fixed to the front spar with a fire-proof bulkhead

The mounting for one of the four Serval engines of the A.W.XV.

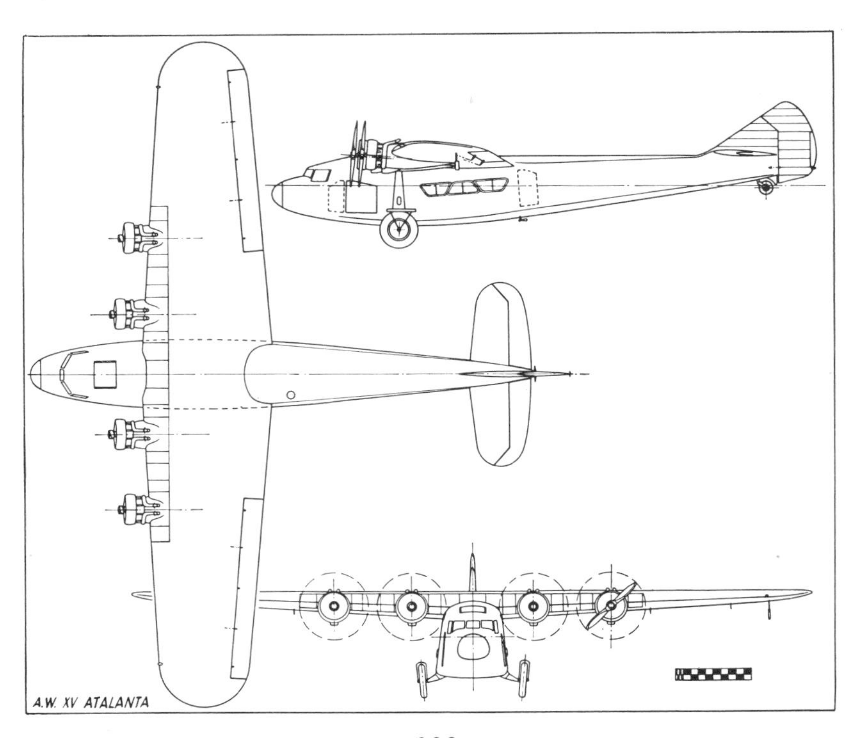

recessed in the leading edge of the wing. The two fuel tanks were also mounted in the leading edge, one between each pair of engines. In spite of the resulting small amount of fuel head, gravity feed to the engines was satisfactory.

As already mentioned, considerable ingenuity was shown in the design of the undercarriage, which consisted of two forged axles hinged on the fuselage centreline and projecting for rather less than half their length from its lower corners. The vertical movement of the axles was controlled by long telescopic struts located inside the fuselage and connecting the axles with the top longerons. Fairings fitted over the moving axles were so arranged that they married up smoothly with fixed fairings on the fuselage when the telescopic shock absorbers were fully extended in flight. The wheels, which were fitted with brakes having differential control, were almost totally enclosed in streamlined fairings but, when the aircraft entered service these were replaced by simple stone guards, the increased accessibility being considered worth the loss of about 6 mph in speed. The layout adopted for the undercarriage resulted in a comparatively narrow track and a rather small ground clearance, but these limitations do not seem to have caused any significant difficulty in practice.

The flight deck of the A.W.XV; on the right, the vertical shock-absorbing strut of the undercarriage which was enclosed within the fuselage.

When first delivered the A.W.XVs were furnished so that the payload could be divided almost equally between passengers and mail. Immediately aft of the cockpit, which was unusually large with accommodation for two pilots and a radio operator, was a mail compartment capable of holding a ton of mail. Behind this came a luggage hold and a steward's galley, and then came the passenger compartment furnished with nine seats arranged singly and in pairs and each with a table. In order to ensure the maximum

As equipped for the African route, the A.W.XV provided accommodation for nine passengers and up to a ton of mail. (*Courtesy A. Campbell-Orde*)

degree of comfort in tropical Africa, each passenger had much more space than was usual and special attention was paid to the ventilation of the cabin. At a later date, when the A.W.XVs were put on to other routes, more normal—and more profitable—seating arrangements were installed with accommodation for up to seventeen passengers.

The A.W.XV went straight into production 'off the drawing board', an unusual and rather daring procedure for those days, and the first aircraft, G-ABPI, made its maiden flight on 6 June, 1932. It was given the individual name of *Atalanta*, which duly became the Imperial Airways class name and, by common usage, the type name. The new airliner made its first public appearance at the SBAC Display held at Hendon aerodrome on 27 June, 1932, where its clean lines created a most favourable impression. The first aircraft, G-ABPI, went to Martlesham Heath for tests on 11 July, 1932, and received its certificate of airworthiness in August; two more A.W.XVs, G-ABTG and G-ABTH, were completed in September 1932 and the remaining five were all finished and certificated by April 1933. From the first, the A.W.XV proved pleasant and easy to fly, and no major modifications were called for. The lateral control was reported to be good and positive, and the elevators were light and effective in all conditions. The rudder, which was fitted with a servo-tab to lighten the control loads, showed symptoms of over-control at small angles of displacement, leading to some rudder oscillation; this only occurred at high speeds outside the normal operating range and was cured, at any rate to the satisfaction of the test pilots, by an arrangement of springs which confined the movement of the tab to large displacements of the rudder. During the investigation of this problem, a small hole was cut in the fuselage top so that Lloyd, by standing on the lavatory seat, could put his head outside and watch the rudder. The corrective device, claimed by the makers to be the first spring tab, proved to be unpopular with the airline pilots and was eventually discarded; in its place an adjustable friction damper was fitted to the rudder bar.

The A.W.XV had all the characteristics, not then familiar to many British pilots, of the thick high-lift-wing aircraft as built by Junkers and Fokker; the test pilot's report noted that, at take-off, the tail had to be kept low and the aircraft pulled off the ground at the right moment. On the glide the A.W.XV was sensitive to speed and attitude and, below a certain speed, it tended to sink rather suddenly. Other points noted were that the tail-wheel was prone to intermittent shimmying, a trouble that was cured by the fitting of another friction damper. On the other hand, the wheel brakes, still rather a novelty in British aircraft in 1932, were good, but in rain the cockpit leaked, especially at high speed. The main troubles encountered during the test flying resulted from high-frequency vibration of the Double Mongoose engines; this caused the bracing wires in the engine mounts to break and the oil tanks, mounted behind the engines, to split. The worst

The A.W.XV G-ABPI coming in to land at Whitley Abbey aerodrome after an early test flight. (*Flight International 11721*)

effects of the vibration (although, presumably, not the vibration itself) were overcome by replacing the wires with steel tubes and by providing rubber mounts for the oil tanks. Performance measurements by the makers and by Imperial Airways proved the aircraft to be eminently satisfactory and up to its guaranteed performance; the cruising speed was measured as 118 mph, true, at 9,000 ft, and at full weight the aircraft took off in 375 yards and climbed from ground level at 550 ft/min. With one engine stopped it easily maintained an altitude of 9,000 ft, and with the engines throttled back it stalled at an indicated airspeed of 51 mph. The best performance was above 5,000 ft, below which the engines had to be throttled back to avoid exceeding the maximum permissible boost of 4 lb/sq in. From the passenger's point of view, the cabin was found to be well ventilated and quiet, and the cane chairs, with adjustable backs, were comfortable.

Imperial Airways' first A.W.XV service was flown by G-ABPI, then named *Atalanta*, which operated the Brussels–Cologne service on September 26, 1932.

The four-engined monoplane layout of the A.W.XV was, in 1932, well ahead of its time.

By September 1932, the first two A.W.XVs, G-ABPI *Atalanta* and G-ABTG *Amalthea*, were at Croydon undergoing acceptance tests and crew training with Imperial Airways and, on 26 September, *Atalanta* flew a service to Brussels and Cologne; on the same day the third aircraft, G-ABTH *Andromeda*, was delivered to the airline at Croydon. From then on, until the beginning of 1933, the A.W.XVs were used intermittently on the London–Brussels service and then on the London–Paris–Basle–Zürich route. In the meantime the first aircraft, G-ABPI, was returned to Coventry for minor modifications and while there it suffered the indignity of a forced landing brought about, ironically enough, by a simultaneous loss of power in all of its four engines. This accident occurred on 20 October, 1932, and was caused by fuel starvation resulting from the use of

The first A.W.XV *Atalanta* after its forced landing at Whitley Abbey on 20 October, 1932.

an experimental type of fuel-tank vent. The failure occurred just as the aircraft had cleared the aerodrome boundary on take-off and the pilot, Alan Campbell-Orde, had no alternative but to put the aircraft down as best he could on a small hillock bordering the airfield. In the heavy landing which resulted, the undercarriage collapsed and the centre section of the fuselage was badly damaged. Campbell-Orde was unhurt but, unfortunately, his co-pilot Donald Salisbury Green, while endeavouring to trace the trouble, received injuries which eventually put an end to his career as a test pilot. Armstrong Whitworth went to considerable lengths to conceal details of this accident to G-ABPI which was, in fact, no reflection on the type's integrity. Such reports as did appear in the Press spoke of 'minor damage' and, in a further effort to avoid publicity, the name *Atalanta* was transferred to G-ABTI, the fourth aircraft, in the hope, probably justified, that few would notice that the P in *Atalanta*'s registration had changed into a T. After repair G-ABPI re-appeared as *Arethusa*.

After the accident in October 1932, the name *Atalanta* was transferred to the fourth production aircraft, G-ABTI.

The newly-named *Atalanta*, G-ABTI, was delivered to Imperial Airways on Christmas Eve 1932 and left Croydon on 5 January, 1933, on a proving flight to Cape Town, where it arrived on February 14. The crew consisted of Campbell-Orde with Capt L. A. Egglesfield of Imperial Airways as far as Cairo, and with Capt H. W. C. Alger, of Imperial Airways, from there to Cape Town. Demonstrations and crew training took place at points along the route, and the flying time totalled 71 hr. At the conclusion of the exercise *Atalanta* remained in South Africa, based at Germiston, ready to go into service; here she was joined by G-ABTG *Amalthea*, G-ABTH *Andromeda* and G-ABTJ *Artemis*, all of which left England for their new base during February 1933. The intention was that the A.W.XVs should replace the D.H.66 Hercules aircraft on the Kisumu–Cape Town section of the route, and all four of the A.W.XVs were soon in operation. However, right from the start, the Atalanta class aircraft were found to be too small for the existing traffic, and the D.H.66s were often called upon to help out.

The A.W.XV G-ABTH *Andromeda* being refuelled at Khartoum.

During the 1920s Imperial Airways had been formulating plans for the opening of the air route to India and Australia, and a service between London and Karachi was inaugurated in the spring of 1929. Subsequently, negotiations with the Government of India led to the formation of a new company known as Indian Trans-Continental Airways, which would share the route across India with Imperial Airways. Another, much later, agreement, with Australia, stipulated that the section of the Australia route from Singapore onwards should be the responsibility of an Australian airline company.

Astraea, G-ABTL, about to leave Croydon Airport on 29 May, 1933, for a survey flight to Australia. On board was Major H. G. Brackley, air superintendent of Imperial Airways (second from the left). The pilot was Captain A. R. Prendergast (second from the right).

By the time the A.W.XVs were being delivered, Imperial Airways had decided that the type should be used on the proposed extension of the route beyond Karachi, and to this end G-ABTL *Astraea* left Croydon on 29 May, 1933, on a proving flight to Australia. In fact, the flight was organized mainly for the purpose of showing off the A.W.XV in Australia and persuading Hudson Fysh, the managing director of QANTAS, to adopt the type for the Australian section of the route, the contract for which his company was, at that time, making a bid. In his negotiations with Imperial Airways during 1933, Hudson Fysh had shown little enthusiasm for the A.W.XV, considering it too expensive for his purpose and not fast enough. He believed that speed was more important than comfort and, at one time, expressed the opinion that the best type of aircraft for the Darwin–Brisbane route would be a fast single-engined four-seater. Although he later modified his views, he did not choose the A.W.XV but placed the order with the de Havilland company for the D.H.86. The proving flight with *Astraea* was accomplished with a minimum of trouble; across India stops were made at Cawnpore and Allahabad and so on to Calcutta. From there onwards, the flight met with severe monsoon conditions and stops were made at Akyab, Rangoon and Bangkok, where the aerodrome was flooded. On the last lap to Australia across the Timor Sea, headwinds of more than 30 mph made a refuelling stop desirable on Bathurst Island, after 5½ hours flying, before flying on to Port Darwin. While in Australia *Astraea* visited Brisbane, Canberra, Sydney and Melbourne and, as the first large airliner to be seen in Australia, it was received with enthusiasm at every stop.

The first A.W.XV, G-ABPI, now named *Arethusa*, at Calcutta after transfer, as VT-AEF, to Indian Trans-Continental Airways.

In the meantime, on 1 July, 1933, *Arethusa* had left Croydon to inaugurate the first through mail to Calcutta. On arrival in Karachi she joined Indian Trans-Continental Airways and assumed the Indian registration VT-AEF. She left Karachi on 7 July to open the new mail route through to Calcutta carrying six passengers and some 500 lb of mail. She was three hours late arriving in Calcutta the following day, a delay attributed to the enthusiasm of the crowds encountered *en route*. On the return flight from Australia, *Astraea* left Port Darwin, with Hudson Fysh as a passenger, on 10 July, and, with following winds, made good time across the Timor Sea, averaging 140 mph to Koepang. After a trouble-free journey to Singapore, the aircraft again encountered monsoon weather on the way to Calcutta but managed, nevertheless, to arrive on schedule on 16 July, ready to take on the westbound mail run to Karachi, due out the following day; in fact the flight was delayed for 24 hours by even worse weather.

The last A.W.XV to come off the line was G-ABTM *Aurora*, which was completed in April 1933. One of its first commitments was to visit Brussels, on 10 June, at the request of the King of the Belgians, who, with the Queen, flew for about an hour in the aircraft. Soon after, *Aurora*

Atalanta, G-ABTI, after a forced landing somewhere in India during 1938.

departed for her new base at Karachi and, like her sister ship *Arethusa*, was handed over to Indian Trans-Continental Airways with the new marks VT-AEG. These two aircraft, together with *Astraea* and G-ABTK *Athena*, both of which remained registered with Imperial Airways, thereafter maintained a twice-weekly service between Karachi and Calcutta until the further extension was opened to Rangoon on 23 September, 1933, and to Singapore starting with the service out of London on 9 December, 1933; the first service in the other direction left Singapore on December 31.

The through service to Australia was started in December 1934, with Qantas Empire Airways' D.H.86s responsible for the eastern section of the route beyond Singapore. However, because of a delay in the delivery of the Australian airline's D.H.86 aircraft, the Atalantas flew through to Darwin for the first few weeks. In 1938, there arose the possibility of an air service connecting Burma with southwest China, and Imperial Airways was asked by the British Air Ministry to organize a survey flight over the route between Akyab and Kunming in Yunnan province, a total distance of more than 700 miles. As the airfield at Kunming was some 6,000 ft above sea level, an aircraft with supercharged engines was needed, and the A.W.XV was the only one available in the area. Preparations for the survey flight went ahead, including the fitting of an extra 124-gal fuel tank, taken from a Westland Wapiti, into the forward freight hold of *Andromeda*. However, in June 1938, when all was ready, the Chinese changed their minds and banned the flight; the project was therefore deferred until another change of mind occurred in China, and the plans were revived in the early months of 1939. The survey flight eventually took place in March 1939 when *Artemis*, presumably with the Wapiti tank in her hold, left Rangoon on the first of the month and, after a night stop at Lashio, near the Burmese border, arrived at Kunming the following day. The return flight was made on 3 and 4 March, with another night stop at Lashio. The pilot's report was not encouraging: the airfield at Lashio was not considered suitable for

The clean lines of the A.W.XV are well illustrated in this head-on view. (*Courtesy A. Campbell-Orde*)

regular use, the meteorological service was virtually non-existent, and the air service could not operate without much improved radio facilities. In addition, the A.W.XV was not suitable for the route, having neither the speed to combat the high winds sometimes encountered, nor the ceiling necessary to cross the mountains at a safe altitude of between 17,000 ft and 20,000 ft.

In the years between the wars there were incidents and accidents which depleted the A.W.XV fleet. On 27 September, 1932, *Arethusa* made a precautionary landing at Ostend aerodrome after experiencing intermittent engine failure caused by the uneven emptying of the fuel tanks and the mishandling of the fuel cocks. The aircraft undershot on the approach and touched down just outside the aerodrome boundary and was slightly damaged. Another landing accident, this time to *Astraea*, occurred at Rangoon on 2 November, 1935; after landing downhill in bad weather and on a wet surface, the aircraft skidded sideways through a boundary fence, but the damage was not extensive and the aircraft was serviceable within three weeks. On 10 February, 1936, *Artemis* was damaged at Pietersburg when the aircraft became partially stalled and sank to the ground outside the aerodrome after trying to climb too steeply following an uphill take-off at night; *Artemis* was subsequently repaired. Another incident, at Delhi on 29 September, 1936, resulted in the complete destruction of *Athena* by fire due to an explosion following the accidental use of a bottle of oxygen, instead of a bottle of air, for starting the engines. Two years later, on 27 July, 1938, the first fatal accident to an Atalanta class aircraft occurred when *Amalthea* flew into a hillside just after taking-off from Kisumu. She was bound for Alexandria on transfer to India; there were no passengers on board, but the crew of four lost their lives. Another temporary casualty was *Atalanta*, which had been transferred from Africa to India in 1933. She was damaged in a forced landing at Jhansi some time in 1938, but was subsequently repaired. Finally, in May 1939, *Andromeda* was taken out of service and dismantled at Alexandria after damaging a wing main spar.

In the spring of 1936 the Imperial Airways African service was reorganized to terminate at Johannesburg and, as the Short C-class flying-boats started into service in 1937, the A.W.XVs were gradually phased out in Africa, the last A.W.XV service out of Johannesburg being flown by *Amalthea* which, with mails only, left on 7 June, 1937. Subsequently, both *Amalthea* and another A.W.XV, said to have been *Astraea*, were hired to Wilson Airways for use by that company on a shuttle service between Kisumu and Nairobi, and this arrangement lasted until 1 July, 1938, when the two A.W.XVs were replaced by D.H.89A Dragon Rapides. With the ending of the A.W.XV operations in Africa, it had been the intention that *Amalthea*, *Astraea* and *Artemis* should join *Aurora*, *Arethusa* and *Atalanta* at Karachi. As already recounted, *Amalthea* was lost before she could leave Africa; but *Artemis* and *Astraea* duly arrived in India and took up their duties with Imperial Airways' No.3 Operating Division on the eastern route in 1938.

Aurora, originally G-ABTM and later VT-AEG, flying with the Indian Air Force as DG454. (*Ministry of Defence*)

After the outbreak of war in 1939, all five of the A.W.XV aircraft were taken over by the newly-formed British Overseas Airways Corporation and, in October 1940, Air Headquarters in India suggested to the Air Ministry in London that the five aircraft, together with the pilots and ground staff stationed at Karachi, which at that time were standing idle, could be usefully employed by a bomber-transport or coastal-reconnaissance squadron. At the time the Indian Government was considering a suggestion from BOAC that the A.W.XVs should be allowed to operate a twice-weekly service between Karachi and Delhi. In the end, as the RAF requirement was not yet urgent, permission for the operation of the Karachi–Delhi service was granted in November 1940. However, in March 1941 all five aircraft were impressed into the RAF, *Atalanta* and *Artemis* on 5 March and *Astraea*, *Arethusa* and *Aurora* on 7 March.

Another view of *Aurora* in Indian Air Force colours. For reconnaissance purposes, an additional window was cut in the forward fuselage. (*Ministry of Defence*)

They were soon put to good use; in April some of them were called upon to fly reinforcements to Shaibah during the Rashid Ali rebellion in Iraq, and later at least one of the aircraft was used to evacuate civilians from the RAF base at Habbaniyeh.

After Japan entered the war in December 1941, the five A.W.XVs were handed over to the Indian Air Force and were added to No. 1 Flight of No. 101 GR Squadron which used them for coastal-reconnaissance duties from a base at St Thomas' Mount, Madras. The aircraft were modified internally for their new duties and some machines were fitted with an additional window in what had been the forward freight compartment. The first casualty with the Indian Air Force occurred in April 1942 when *Aurora*, now bearing the military serial number DG454, force-landed in a swamp near Calcutta and, as the terrain made salvage impossible, the aircraft was burnt on the site. The next aircraft to go was *Atalanta*, now DG451, which swung off the runway when landing at St Thomas' Mount on 28 August, 1942; the aircraft caught fire and was destroyed after hitting a pile of earth. For reasons unknown, *Astraea*, now DG450, was withdrawn from service in September 1942, and she was probably cannibalized for spares before being finally struck off charge in November 1943. Following the accident to *Atalanta*, it is believed that the two surviving aircraft, *Arethusa* (DG453) and *Artemis* (DG452), were used as freighters until both were struck off charge at the beginning of June 1944.

For its time, the A.W.XV had many good points but by the time it was completed it was already too small both for the task for which it was originally built and for any hope of success in world markets. For their part, Armstrong Whitworth gave consideration to possible variations of the basic type; in 1931 a seaplane version with a larger cabin, but with the wing span reduced by six feet, was proposed, but for what purpose remains obscure. In 1933 the company announced an A.W.XV Mk.II. With four

Jaguar engines each of 450 hp, this aircraft was calculated to have a cruising speed of 135 mph and a payload of 5,170 lb, made up of twenty passengers, freight and mail; another proposal evaluated in 1934 was a similar aircraft powered by two 800 hp Tiger engines. These variants probably represented a last attempt to make a saleable aircraft but, without a significant increase in carrying capacity, a more powerful A.W.XV could hardly have offered many attractions from the point of view of operating economy. In any case, by the middle of the 1930s, Imperial Airways were already thinking along different lines.

A.W.27 Ensign

As a result of the British Government's stated intention to send by air all first-class mail for Empire countries on the routes to South Africa and Australia, Imperial Airways drew up plans in 1934 for a fleet of new aircraft to meet this commitment. The bulk of the new fleet was to consist of Short flying-boats, but there was also a requirement for a large landplane airliner to serve in Europe and on the Eastern route. Imperial Airways approached Armstrong Whitworth regarding this aircraft, and the company agreed to submit their proposals in accordance with the airline's specification of May 1934 for an 'Empire route airliner'. Several alternative designs were considered by Lloyd, including low-wing monoplanes with both three and four engines, but G. E. Woods Humphery, the managing director of Imperial Airways, insisted on a high-shoulder-wing layout, as this was thought to be popular with passengers, and four engines were chosen in line with the airline's policy.

The final specification drawn up by Armstrong Whitworth in October 1934 stated that in the proposed design care had been taken to avoid wing flutter and tail buffet; to this end special attention had been given to the disposition of the tail in relation to the wing, and to the design of the wing fillets to avoid trouble due to eddies from the wing when stalled. Other steps taken to prevent flutter were the mass balancing of the controls and

The A.W.27 Ensign, G-ADSR, the first of a fleet of twelve, later increased to fourteen, ordered by Imperial Airways.

the design of a very stiff fuselage structure. The original intention had been to use 'two-speed' Tiger engines and wooden propellers, but the difficulties experienced with the development of this type of engine and the appearance of the two-position propeller, which offered an easier solution, led to the substitution of engines with normal gearing. In the specification the wing structure was described as being exactly similar to that being employed in '... current Air Ministry contracts', with the main spar being built in three portions, the centre one supporting the engines and the two independent fuel tanks situated in the leading edge. The performance guarantees included a cruising speed of 155 mph at 5,000 ft, and a take-off run of 320 yards.

The official order for the first A.W.27 was placed by Imperial Airways in a letter to Armstrong Whitworth dated 22 September, 1934. The price agreed was £70,000, made up of £27,000 as the cost of design and £43,000 as the cost of manufacture: delivery was to be within two years. On 29 May, 1935, a further order for eleven A.W.27s was placed at a price of £37,000 each, two to be delivered by May 1936 and the remainder at the rate of one a month starting in March 1937. Finally, on 19 January, 1937, two more aircraft were ordered at £39,766-13s-4d each, these to be delivered at monthly intervals after those ordered in May 1935. In retrospect, it may be questioned whether Armstrong Whitworth were altogether wise to accept this order for a large and complicated airliner at the time when the Whitley bomber was being ordered into production. In the event, it soon became clear that the Coventry factory would not be large enough to cope with the production of both types: this handicap was to some extent overcome by arranging for the airliners to be erected in the Air Service Training shops at Hamble, but the problems facing the company's

The A.W.27 aircraft were assembled in the workshops of Air Service Training at Hamble.

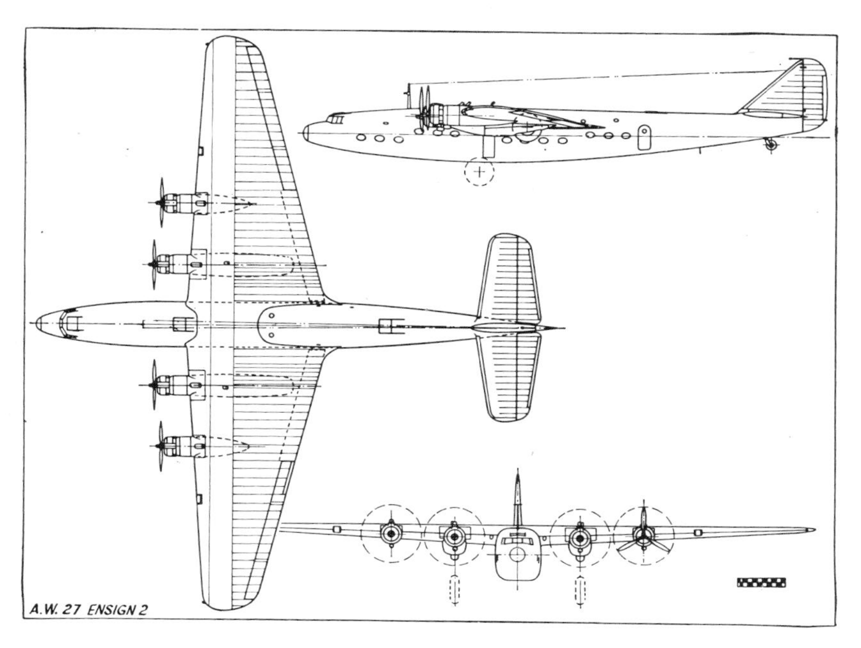

design staff were not so easily overcome. The RAF expansion programme was gathering way and there was, at the time, a shortage of suitably qualified people. As it turned out, the build-up of orders for the Whitley and the increasing priority given to that aircraft, inevitably led to some neglect of the A.W.27 with, as will be seen, disastrous results to that aircraft's production programme.

The A.W.27, given the class name Ensign by Imperial Airways, was the largest airliner to be built in Britain before the war. Two versions were proposed, one with seats for forty passengers for use in Europe, and the other for the Eastern route accommodating twenty-seven passengers by day and twenty by night in sleeping berths. The two versions came to be known as the Eastern and Western types, but, except for the interior arrangements, both were identical. Power was supplied by four 800 hp Tiger IX geared and moderately supercharged engines mounted on the leading edge of the wing. For ground use the aircraft was equipped with a small petrol engine driving a generator to provide current for lighting and the radio and to charge the main batteries. The A.W.27's wing was a cantilever structure built round a large box spar of light-alloy construction stabilized by internal bracing tubes. To the spar were attached the front and rear rib sections, the leading edge as far back as the rear face of the spar being covered with sheet metal, while the trailing edge, aft of the spar, was fabric covered. Split trailing-edge flaps extended from the ailerons to the outboard engines. Each engine was supported on a tubular framework with flexible rubber mountings and was enclosed in a long-chord cowling.

The massive box spar of the A.W.27 in place on the fuselage. (*Flight International 15181S*)

The long, slender oval-section fuselage was of light-alloy, stressed-skin monocoque construction with transverse frames and longitudinal stringers. The top of the fuselage was recessed in the area of the wing, and the floor was strengthened by a substantial system of tubular girders. The high-wing arrangement of the aircraft posed some problems in the design of the retractable undercarriage, which, with its wheels of 6 ft 3 in diameter, was the largest made up to that time. It was designed and made by Armstrong Whitworth, but the hydraulic jacks were supplied by Automotive Products, who also provided the other twelve jacks in the aircraft which were used for operating the wing flaps, the undercarriage wheel doors and to lock the undercarriage in the raised position. The undercarriage legs retracted backwards into fairings behind the inboard engines; they were designed to be raised in $1\frac{1}{4}$ min, but this time was seldom achieved and, in practice, it was found that the two legs retracted unevenly.

The interior arrangement of the Eastern version was such that either chairs or bunks could be fitted, the changeover, including the installation of the partitions and curtains etc, being possible, allegedly, within 15 min. The seats and backs of the day-time chairs were used to form part of the mattresses for the bunks; they also served the purpose of flotation gear, thus complying with the current regulations for flight over open water. The interior of the Eastern type was divided into three passenger compartments with a central section between the forward and midships cabins. This central section contained a large freight compartment, a pantry, a lavatory, and a mail compartment, all situated on the starboard side; on the port side was a so-called promenade deck which was, in fact, a narrow passage 1 ft 7 in wide connecting the forward and aft cabins. In the Eastern type each of the three passenger compartments contained nine seats; in the Western version the forward, midships and aft main compartments each accommodated twelve passengers. Aft of the main rear cabin was a small four-seat coupé. Smoking was allowed in the forward cabin of both versions. The intention was that the crew of the Eastern type should consist of two pilots, a wireless operator, a flight clerk and a steward; on the Western type a second steward would be carried instead of the flight clerk.

When the original order was placed in September 1934, it was expected that the first A.W.27 would be flying during the second half of 1936, but the delaying factors already referred to, plus the innumerable changes in detail demanded by Imperial Airways at every stage in the design and construction, resulted in the first aircraft being nearly two years late. It was

The flight deck of the A.W.27 in the course of construction. (*Flight International 15179S*)

on Sunday, 23 January, 1938, that the prototype aircraft, G-ADSR, taxied across the road that separated the AST workshops from the aerodrome at Hamble. On the morning of the following day Turner-Hughes, assisted by Eric Greenwood, made four ground runs to get the feel of the controls and to test the brakes; on the fifth run the aircraft was taken-off after a run of 16 sec. On this flight, which lasted for about 15 min, the undercarriage was not retracted, but all went well except that the rudder control was found to be extremely heavy, needing the combined efforts of both pilots to achieve any significant displacement. After two days spent in adjusting the rudder servo-tab and swinging the compass, Turner-Hughes again took the aircraft off, retracted the undercarriage, and flew to Baginton aerodrome where the maker's tests were to be undertaken.

Not much is on record about the trials at Baginton, but, by a strange coincidental repetition of history, the prototype, now bearing the name

The high wing of the A.W.27 resulted in a very large undercarriage; the wheels were 6 ft 3 in diameter. (*Flight International 15180S*)

Ensign, very nearly suffered the same fate as had *Atalanta* before it. During a test flight on 8 March, 1938, all four engines stopped together; fortunately the aircraft was at a good altitude and Turner-Hughes was able to glide to the RAF aerodrome at Bicester where he made a successful 'dead-stick' landing, no mean feat considering the size of the aircraft and its comparative lack of manoeuvrability. As was the case in the earlier *Atalanta* incident, the *Ensign*'s engines stopped because of fuel starvation, due to an error in the setting of the fuel cocks. Another trouble which developed later, and which baffled the engineers for some time, was the intermittent jamming of the elevator controls. This, fortunately, occurred only at altitude and it could never be reproduced on the ground; this was not surprising because it was eventually found to be due to low temperatures at altitude making the fuselage shrink slightly with the result that the elevator control wires, running above one another down the length of the fuselage, became slack. This allowed two adjacent wire connectors, one on each wire, to foul each other, causing a momentary jamming of the controls. Needless to say, suitable modifications were quickly introduced to rule out the possibility of these incidents recurring.

The first A.W.27 being wheeled out for initial engine runs at Hamble aerodrome, towards the end of 1937.

At the conclusion of the maker's trials in the early part of June 1938, *Ensign* was sent to Martlesham Heath, and it soon became apparent to the RAF pilots that the aircraft was underpowered. Flown initially at an all-up-weight of 49,000 lb, it left the ground after a take-off run of 350 yards. The raising of the undercarriage took $1\frac{1}{2}$ min and the initial climb was consequently slow; it took one minute to reach 500 ft and three minutes to reach 1,600 ft. In level flight at 7,200 ft, *Ensign* reached a true airspeed of 200 mph, and with two engines shut down height could be maintained at 6,000 ft, but only if the flaps and undercarriage were retracted. With these appendages lowered and one engine throttled, level flight could be maintained at 2,000 ft. Generally speaking, the handling characteristics were deemed to be good, with elevators and rudder reasonably light and the ailerons effective but somewhat heavy; the tail-trimming gear was criticized as being too powerful and sensitive. There were some troubles during the trials: sparking plugs tended to oil up badly during slow running and, in one case, caused an engine to cut out during take-off. Another engine failed due to oil-scavenging trouble and had to be replaced, and a panel of fabric twelve feet long, used to cover the main-spar joint on the star-

The first Ensign, G-ADSR, made its maiden flight on 24 January, 1938.

board wing, came adrift during flight, having torn away at the point where it met the metal skin of the leading edge.

At the conclusion of the Martlesham trials the A.W.27 was recommended for a certificate of airworthiness at an all-up weight of 49,000 lb, subject to certain alterations and additions being made. These included a modified form of fixing for the fabric of the trailing edge, the gearing down of the elevator trimming system, the provision of a clear-view panel for the pilot and the fitting of an engine-driven compressor to charge the air bottle of the wheel-brake system. In addition, an alteration was called for in the control locks, which were provided for the rudder and elevator only, each linked direct to the inboard throttle levers. Other criticisms calling for rectification concerned the passenger-escape hatches and the fact that oil fumes percolated through the centre section of the wing into the front freight compartment.

On its second flight, on 26 January, 1938, *Ensign* was flown to Baginton aerodrome where flight trials took place.

The certificate of airworthiness for G-ADSR was granted at the end of June before the required modifications were carried out, and she returned to Martlesham in the following month for further tests with slightly larger propellers, but the climb with these propellers was not significantly better. At that time the necessary modifications had not been completed and *Ensign* visited Martlesham again in October 1938 for a further check following which the modifications were passed as satisfactory. It was noted during these numerous visits that the aircraft's controls varied in weight from test to test, but this was considered to be due to variations in the adjustment of the rigging.

Ensign first visited Croydon at the beginning of July 1938 and made a quick trip to Paris before returning to Coventry, but it was not until 24 October that year that the *Ensign* went into *ad hoc* service on the London–Paris route, following a demonstration flight over the route on October 20.

The Ensign G-ADSU *Euterpe* being loaded at Croydon Airport with the 1938 Christmas mail for Australia.

In December three of the new aircraft, G-ADSS *Egeria*, G-ADST *Elsinore* and G-ADSU *Euterpe*, were pressed into service as relief aircraft to help carry the heavy Christmas mail to Australia. None of the three aircraft got there: *Egeria* was grounded at Athens for an engine change, and *Elsinore* suffered the same fate at Karachi; what happened to *Euterpe* is not clear, but she, too, failed to get beyond India. On the return flight *Elsinore* had to have her undercarriage lowered by hand, which meant that it could not be retracted again until she went into the shops; thus, the last 2,500 miles of the journey home was flown with the wheels down. *Elsinore*'s pilot complained that the aircraft's fore-and-aft stability was bad and that the mixture control was difficult to adjust with the result that the fuel consumption varied between 124 and 174 gal/hr. After the fiasco of the Christmas mail, Imperial Airways withdrew the A.W.27s from service, and the five aircraft so far delivered were returned to Coventry for something to be done to improve both reliability and performance.

Armstrong Whitworth were already working on the problem and, in April 1939, G-ADSW *Eddystone*, the sixth aircraft off the line, emerged with the more powerful Tiger IXC engine which developed an extra 55 hp with the take-off boost raised from $2\frac{1}{2}$ to $3\frac{1}{2}$ lb/sq in. In addition, constant-speed propellers had replaced the previous two-position type. Other alterations included a reduction in the area of the rudder and the elevators and a modification of the control runs to reduce friction. At the end of April the modified *Eddystone* went to Martlesham Heath for further evaluation; this time the tests were made at an all-up weight of 48,500 lb and, as might be expected, the combination of more power, more efficient propellers and a reduction in weight, resulted in an improvement in the climb performance. In the first minute after take-off *Eddystone* climbed to 800 ft and reached 2,800 ft in three min. The rudder and elevators were found to be lighter, but the ailerons of *Eddystone*, although not modified in any way, were heavier than those of *Ensign*. Laterally, the aircraft was found to be neutrally stable, with the result that it wallowed badly in rough weather and required hard work with the ailerons to keep it level. In contrast to *Ensign*, *Eddystone* was judged to be longitudinally unstable, a difference that was thought to be due to the reduction in the control-circuit friction. As a result of these trials, the airworthiness certificate for the A.W.27 was amended to a reduced all-up weight of 48,500 lb.

Delivery of the modified aircraft began in the summer of 1939, *Ensign* returning to Croydon on 12 July and G-ADSV *Explorer* on 18 July, with G-ADSZ *Elysian* and G-ADSX *Ettrick* following shortly after. But there were further troubles: all the aircraft suffered from inefficient oil-coolers and some had troubles with the constant-speed unit of the airscrews. On the other hand, some improvement in the reliability of the engines had been achieved. This was due to various factors: in the first place the new constant-speed airscrews prevented over-speeding of the engines, and the incorporation of automatic mixture control avoided careless adjustment by the pilots. A modification to the priming system prevented flooding of the cylinders with petrol which, in the past, had caused hydraulic locks and the fracture of cylinder barrels, while the use of bolts instead of studs cured the constant failure of the rocker-arm brackets. Finally, the improved training of the pilots in the technique of engine handling was having its effect on reliability. But the technicians of Imperial Airways had already decided that, although the Tiger-powered aircraft might be suitable for European operations, they would not meet the requirements of the Eastern route, and that in the hottest conditions in the Middle East the take-off weight of the A.W.27 would have to be reduced by at least 1,500 lb. A change of powerplant was thus seen to be essential and, as early as May 1939,

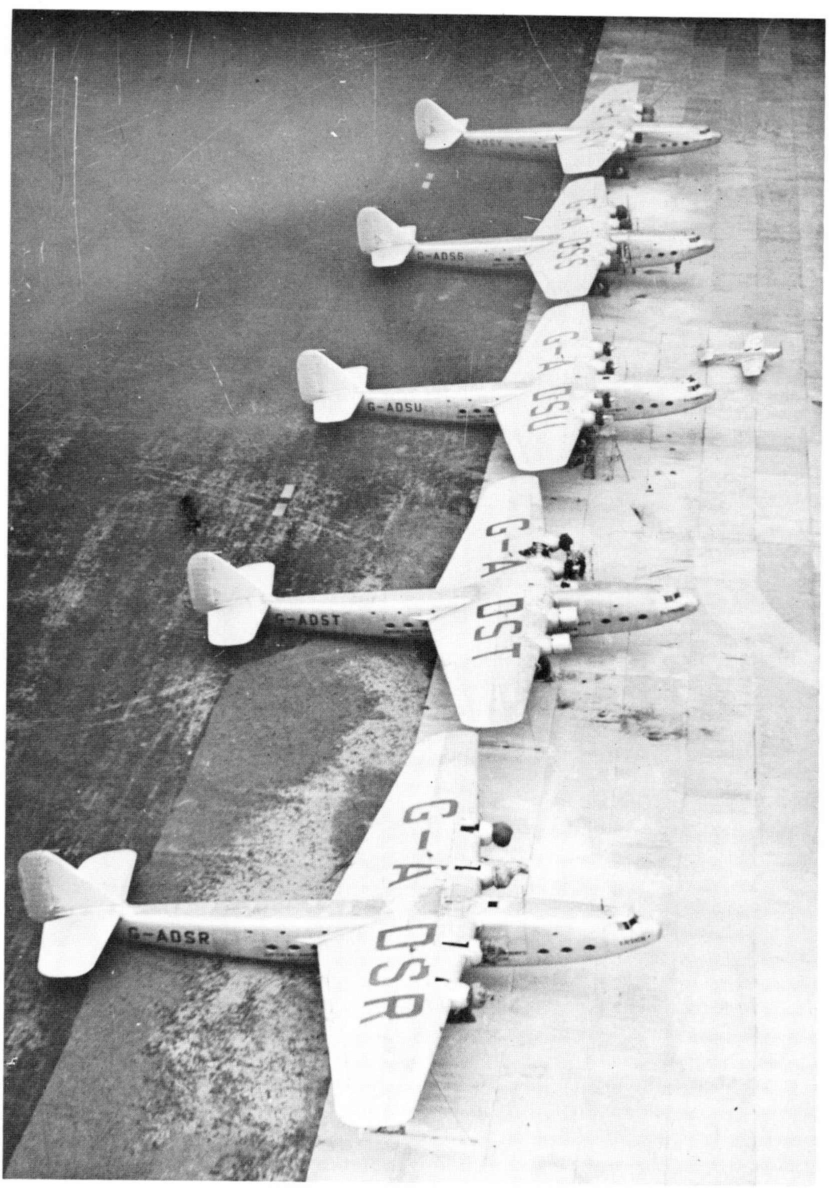

From the top: *Empyrean*, *Egeria*, *Euterpe*, *Elsinore* and *Ensign*.

consideration was being given to the relative merits of the Wright Cyclone GR-1820-G-102A and the G-202 engines.

By the end of August 1939, eleven Ensign class aircraft had been delivered to Imperial Airways; four of these, *Eddystone*, *Ettrick*, *Empyrean* (G-ADSY) and *Elysian*, were of the Western type, with the remaining seven, *Ensign*, *Egeria*, *Elsinore*, *Euterpe*, *Explorer*, *Euryalus* and *Echo*, destined originally for the Eastern route. It had been intended that four of the eastern aircraft should be allocated, like the Atalantas before them, to Indian Trans-Continental Airways with Indian registration marks and new names. In the event, this never happened, and no A.W.27s reached India before the outbreak of war. Only one aircraft actually emerged from the factory with Indian marks; this was *Euryalus* which briefly carried the registration VT-AJG, but this had been replaced by G-ADTA by the time she was delivered in August 1939.

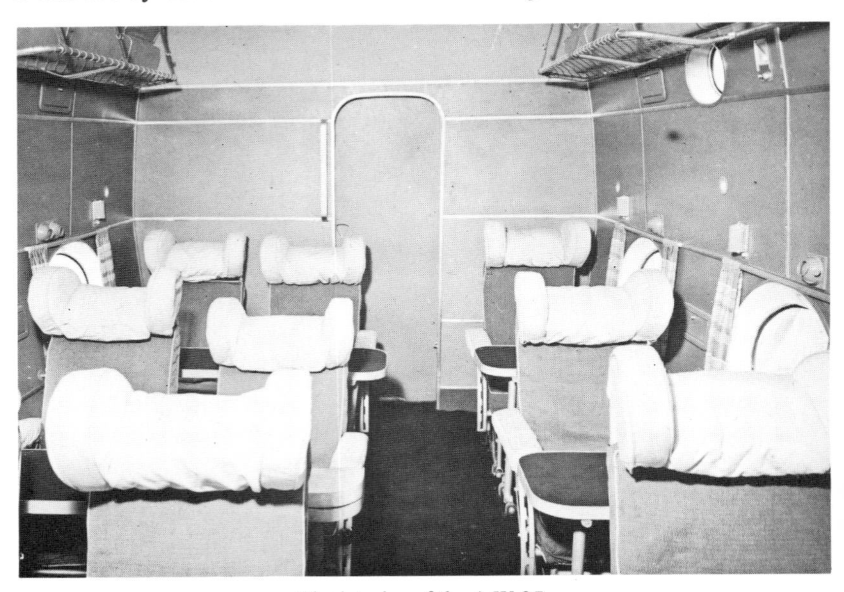

The interior of the A.W.27.

On the eve of the war, a certain amount of chaos was evident at Croydon when, according to a pre-arranged plan, all civil aircraft were being evacuated to Whitchurch aerodrome near Bristol. For some reason, perhaps because of congestion at Whitchurch, seven of the A.W.27s were diverted to Baginton on 1 September, and great confusion was caused because nobody quite knew why they had been sent there; the pilots thought they had come up for new engines to be fitted, but this was not so. Most put out by their arrival was the aerodrome manager at Baginton, who complained bitterly to the authorities that the presence of seven large, bright silver aeroplanes on the aerodrome completely ruined his camouflage scheme; the matter was eventually resolved, and the A.W.27s left for Whitchurch where they should have been sent in the first place. Meanwhile, the aircraft left behind at Croydon were soon usefully employed, and it was an A.W.27 that had the distinction, on 2 September, of carrying the first batch of RAF officers to leave the country for France. The aircraft made two journeys, each with thirty officers and men with their equipment. As the organization at Whitchurch settled down and the motley collection of aircraft were allocated duties, it was decided, in view of continual trouble with the Tiger engines, that sending the A.W.27s further afield than France could not be contemplated. It was not to be long before this cautious policy was forgotten, but in the meantime the principal duty allotted to them was the operation of a twice-daily service between Heston aerodrome and Le Bourget. This service began in October 1939 and continued until more important tasks arose after the Germans invaded Belgium and Holland in the spring of 1940. By this time the planned merger between Imperial Airways and British Airways had led, in November 1939, to the formation of the British Overseas Airways Corporation, to whom passed the ownership of the twelve A.W.27s then completed.

The first casualty to the Ensign fleet occurred in December 1939 when *Euterpe*, on a flight to Doncaster, overran the aerodrome boundary at Chipping Warden and wrecked her undercarriage; the damage was severe, but she was dismantled and returned to Hamble and eventually repaired. More serious were the casualties suffered by the fleet after the fighting started in earnest. Following the German break-through, the A.W.27s were used to carry supplies to the British Army in France, and it was during this phase that the first aircraft of the fleet were lost. On 23 May, 1940, a collection of transports including five A.W.27s, a DC-3 and two Savoia Marchetti airliners belonging to Sabena, left Croydon for Merville, their 'war station' situated some 30 miles south of Dunkirk. With an escort of Hurricanes they arrived safely, but, while engaged in unloading their stores, the escorting fighters were attacked by a squadron of Messerschmitt Bf 109s. After driving off the enemy the Hurricanes left for home, their ammunition exhausted; no sooner had they left than more Messerschmitts appeared and proceeded to shoot up the transports on the ground with the result that *Elysian* was set on fire and burnt out. The other four A.W.27s managed to take-off successfully, but *Echo* arrived back at Heston with a damaged tailplane. *Euryalus* ran into more trouble; on the way to the coast she was fired on from the ground and again attacked by an enemy aircraft. She was damaged and, before long, the port inner engine had to be shut down through lack of oil. The captain set course for Hawkinge aerodrome and kept down to about 300 ft in the hope of avoiding further attack. Later, when approaching the English coast, the starboard inner engine also failed, and the captain decided on an immediate landing at Lympne aerodrome. By now the aircraft, with two engines stopped, was down to 100 ft above the ground, and the captain wisely refrained from lowering the undercarriage

Ettrick, G-ADSX, at Croydon Airport.

until the last moment and, as luck would have it, only one leg was fully extended when the aircraft touched down. No one was hurt, but the damage to the aircraft was considerable; she was dismantled and taken to Hamble for repairs but eventually, in November 1941, it was decided to cannibalize her so that *Euterpe*, damaged at Chipping Warden, could be repaired.

The next to go was *Ettrick*, which was caught in an air raid and damaged while on the ground at Le Bourget Airport on 1 June, 1940. She had to be abandoned and was eventually repaired and used by the Germans; they too, apparently, did not think a great deal of the Tiger engines which they replaced with Daimler-Benz liquid-cooled motors. During the Battle of Britain, the A.W.27s were employed in assisting with the movement of fighter squadron personnel about England, and it was during this time that *Endymion* was hit and burnt out on the ground during an air raid on Whitchurch aerodrome on 24 November, 1940. *Explorer*, *Empyrean* and *Echo* also suffered superficial damage from bomb splinters during this raid.

After a disappointing start, the Ensign class aircraft had gone far to retrieve their reputation by their good service during the early stages of the war, and this, coupled with the acute shortage of transport aircraft, resulted in top priority being given to the completion of the two aircraft ordered at the end of 1936. Work on these had been slowed down in 1938 because of a proposal put forward by Imperial Airways that the A.W.27 should be used as the lower component of a composite aircraft similar to the Short *Maia* and *Mercury*, the 'pick-a-back' aircraft successfully tested in February 1938. The suggestion was that the last four A.W.27s should be so converted, but in January 1939 Armstrong Whitworth informed Imperial Airways that, lacking a positive decision, it was by then too late to convert the eleventh and twelfth aircraft and that work on the thirteenth and fourteenth was virtually at a standstill pending instructions one way or the other. The scheme was eventually abandoned, but work on the last two A.W.27s was again held up at the beginning of the war until the importance of transport aircraft was emphasized by the events of 1940.

The popularity of the A.W.27s at this time was largely due to their spacious interiors and their ability to use comparatively small, grass airfields; however, they were still underpowered, and the Tiger engines, in spite of improvements introduced, were still far from perfect. It is, perhaps, a measure of the A.W.27's potential as a war transport that it was regarded as worthwhile to fit them with more powerful engines at a time when the industry was stretched to the limit. Thus it came about that when the worst of the pressure of the Battle of Britain was over, the decision was taken to fit the A.W.27s with four Wright Cyclone GR-1820-G-102A engines which together would provide something like an additional 1,000 hp for take-off. The Cyclone was certainly a better engine than the Tiger, but all the same, as will be seen later, the choice was not an entirely happy one.

Egeria and another in wartime service.

The first aircraft to have the new engines was G-AFZU *Everest*, one of the last two aircraft on which work had restarted in 1940, and this, the prototype A.W.27 Mk.II, made its first flight on 20 June, 1941, piloted by Turner-Hughes. *Everest* went through her test routine and was delivered to BOAC within four days of her first flight, and she was followed at the end of October by G-AFZV *Enterprise*, the fourteenth and last of the type.

With the improved performance provided by the Cyclone engines, the A.W.27s were now deemed to be suitable for operating in hot climates, and they were consequently allocated to the Middle East theatre for service on the important supply route then being organized between the West African ports and Egypt. The ferrying of the first aircraft started late in 1941, and one of the first, if not the first, of the Mk.IIs to leave for Cairo was *Everest*, which departed on 9 November, only to be attacked and badly damaged by an enemy aircraft over the Bay of Biscay. *Everest* was fortunate to be able to return to England where she was repaired and delivered successfully on the second attempt. *Enterprise*, which left for Bathurst in February 1942, was not so lucky: while flying south from Gibraltar along the west coast of Africa, engine trouble developed. First, the port inner engine was shut down because of leaking oil; soon afterwards the port outer engine was throttled back for the same reason, and when the starboard inner developed similar symptoms, the captain decided to land on the first suitable stretch of desert. This he did, with the wheels up, at a point about 300 miles north of Bathurst near the town of Nouachott on the coast of French West Africa. After landing, the radio operator was able to make contact with the Bathurst base and a Sunderland flying-boat was sent to rescue the crew. At the subsequent enquiry it was concluded that the trouble was caused by the crew, lacking proper measuring arrangements, having pumped too much oil into the engines from the extra tanks fitted for the flight. *Enterprise*, which was not badly damaged, was subsequently salvaged by the French and flown back to France; later she was seized by the Germans, fitted with Daimler-Benz engines and put back into service.

Explorer in camouflage. In spite of its numerous shortcomings, the Ensign class gave good service and the type was never involved in a fatal accident.

During the long-drawn-out campaign in North Africa, the A.W.27s performed useful work on the supply route across Africa and on the route between Cairo and Asmara in Eritrea, where, as an insurance against the possible loss of Egypt, a large overhaul base had been established. When North Africa was finally cleared of the enemy in May 1943 and the Mediterranean was open again to Allied shipping, the trans-African route lost its importance, and the Ensign fleet, now based in Cairo, was transferred to the Cairo–Calcutta service, the task for which the Eastern-type aircraft had been destined in the first place. By the beginning of 1944, the surviving A.W.27s were being worked hard. *Ensign*, which had been damaged at Lagos in 1942 when her undercarriage was retracted on the ground, was withdrawn from service in September 1944 at Almaza aerodrome, Cairo, because there was insufficient labour available to undertake the considerable work necessary for renewal of her certificate of airworthiness. Because of overhauls and routine maintenance of the other aircraft of the fleet, there were seldom more than five or six machines available to maintain the thrice-weekly service between Egypt and India, a journey that was scheduled to take 2½ days, and in spite of the energetic work put in by the engineers, the A.W.27s were beginning to show their age. Circumstances often dictated the use of inferior materials during overhaul—on one occasion a windscreen blew in because the wrong type of wood was used in the mounting—and difficulty was also being experienced with the Cyclone engines because the GR-1820-G-102A version had by now gone out of production and spares were virtually unobtainable. The pilots still complained about the aircraft's slow rate of climb, the poor fore-and-aft stability and the fact that the machine was heavy to fly, which, coupled with the unreliability of the auto-pilot, made the task extremely tiring. One possible explanation put forward for the longitudinal instability was a disturbance of the airflow over the tail caused by the fabric of the wing becoming slack due to heat and moisture.

The mounting list of troubles and complaints led, at the beginning of 1945, to the local representative of the Air Registration Board making a verbal recommendation that the A.W.27s should be withdrawn from service as soon as possible. However, BOAC could not accept the suggestion because there was no possibility of obtaining replacement aircraft to carry the urgent war loads then being lifted by the A.W.27s. This action by the local ARB man appears to have been the beginning of a long, three-cornered argument, centred around the Ensign class aircraft, between the Air Ministry and BOAC in London and the pilots and engineers in Egypt—all with essentially valid but entirely different points of view. The pilots found the aircraft difficult, if not actually dangerous, to fly; the engineers complained at the enormous effort necessary to maintain them, quoting that renewals of certificates of airworthiness were absorbing anything from 20,000 to 70,000 man-hours but, at the same time, stoutly maintaining that those aircraft which had been recently overhauled were in a first-class condition. At home there were the officials of BOAC, some of whom nursed a lingering prejudice against the Ensign class aircraft and would like to have been rid of them but could not do without them while the war lasted. Finally, there were the men at the Ministry, far removed from the operational problems being coped with east of Suez, who thought mainly of the possible potential of a fleet of large transports at a time when such aircraft were worth a good deal more than their weight in light alloy. Later, in January 1945, the ARB wrote officially to BOAC expressing the hope that the aircraft would be withdrawn within the next twelve months and, in March, BOAC themselves asked the Ministry to agree that all the nine existing aircraft should be written off before the next monsoon. But the Ministry officials were reluctant to agree and countered with the suggestion that the aircraft should be brought home for possible use as airliners after the war had ended.

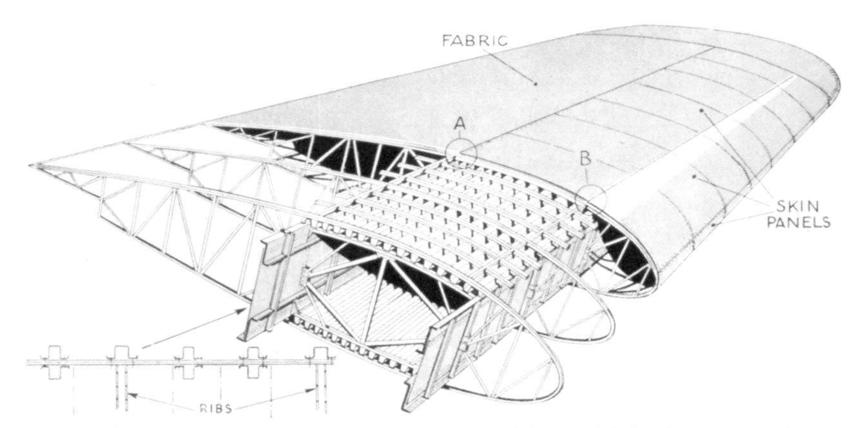

A drawing in an Armstrong Whitworth brochure of the A.W.27's wing construction.

The argument dragged on throughout 1945; in August it was decided that Lloyd from Armstrong Whitworth and a man from BOAC should go to Cairo to assess the state of the aircraft, and at the beginning of December the Ministry of Civil Aviation asked BOAC to fly one of the A.W.27s home so that an estimate could be made of the cost of reconditioning and fitting them with Cyclone 208A engines in place of the 102A type installed in 1941. BOAC seized on this chance to bring to an end their expensive Ensign class operation and replied that the last A.W.27 Indian service would be 22E276 leaving Calcutta on 1 January and terminating in Cairo on 4 January, 1946, and that thereafter they would like to arrange for as many as possible of the A.W.27s to be flown home without delay. This was agreed, and the first aircraft, *Eddystone*, left Cairo for England on 1 January, 1946. But she did not get far: one undercarriage leg refused to come down and the aircraft made a belly landing at Castel Benito aerodrome, Tripoli. It therefore transpired that the first aircraft to arrive back in England was *Empyrean* which left Cairo on 4 January and had arrived at Hamble, via Hurn, by 14 January. Two more aircraft, *Echo* and *Elsinore*, left Egypt on 29 January and 6 February respectively, and these were followed by *Egeria*, which left on 18 March, *Explorer* which was in England by 5 April, and *Everest* which did the journey some time during the month of May. Meanwhile, on 11 February, 1946, the Ministry of Civil Aviation reluctantly agreed that *Ensign* and *Euterpe* should be reduced to produce at Almaza; they really had no choice, because *Ensign* had already been extensively cannibalized and *Euterpe*, after standing idle since February 1945, had also contributed many spares to help the others get home.

But it was all rather a wasted effort: in spite of the persuasive arguments put forward by the Ministry, nobody, once appraised of the possible cost of overhaul, would contemplate the use of the A.W.27s on the civil routes.

At one time BEA toyed with the idea of using them, at a reduced weight, on the London–Paris route, but that project, too, fell through on the score of expense. At last the Ministry officials were forced to admit defeat, and on 10 May, 1946, they wrote to BOAC agreeing that all the A.W.27s should be officially struck off charge, including *Ensign* written off some time before, and *Euterpe*, disposed of with effect from 15 February, 1946. The honour of being the last A.W.27 to fly fell, therefore, to *Eddystone*: she had been flown back to Almaza in April after her wheels-up landing at Castel Benito and, in a last burst of activity before they left for home, the rearguard engineers in Cairo made her serviceable for the flight home which began on 3 June, 1946, and finished, like those of her sister ships, at Hamble *en route* for the scrap-heap.

In spite of the useful and even distinguished part played by the type during the war, the A.W.27 could not by any standards be described as an unqualified success: the fleet was kept serviceable only at great expense and, by the end of the war, was virtually worn out, although the most that any one of the aircraft had flown was a mere 3,720 hours. BOAC, no doubt soured by their early experience, and particularly by the fiasco of the 1938 Christmas mail flights, were, perhaps, unduly prejudiced against the type all along, and it is interesting to speculate what might have happened had the war not intervened; it is possible that the corporation might have rejected the fleet outright. On the other hand, from the maker's point of view, it was perhaps unreasonably optimistic to expect that such a large and complicated aircraft could be built and put into service without considerable development. Had there been an opportunity to produce a modified version with, among other improvements, better engines, a fully-metal-clad wing and an undercarriage that retracted more smartly, it is possible that the type might have been successful. But by the end of the war it was too late, and it is now clear that a refurbished A.W.27 could not have lasted for long: the airliner that could land slowly in a short distance was already obsolete, and it could not compete economically with the faster aircraft for which long runways had become available. From then on the runways were to be extended, and extended again, to suit aircraft demands, and more than two decades were to pass before circumstances once again suggested that it might be more realistic to reverse the trend and make the aircraft conform to the runway.

Argosy Mk.I
Dimensions: Span 90 ft 8 in (27·64 m); length 65 ft 10 in (20·07 m); height 19 ft 10 in (6·05 m); wing area 1,886 sq ft (175·22 sq m).

Argosy Mk.II
Dimensions: Span 90 ft 4 in (27·53 m); length 67 ft (20·42 m); height 20 ft (6·10 m); wing area 1,873 sq ft (174·01 sq m).

A.W.XV Atalanta
Dimensions: Span 90 ft (27·43 m); length 71 ft 6 in (21·79 m); height 14 ft (4·27 m); wing area 1,285 sq ft (119·38 sq m).

A.W.27 Ensign Mks.I & II
Dimensions: Span 123 ft (37·49 m); length 111 ft (33·83 m); height 23 ft (7·01 m); wing area 2,450 sq ft (227·61 sq m).

	Argosy Mk.I *Three 385 hp Direct-Drive Jaguar*	Argosy Mk.II *Three 410 hp Geared Jaguar IVA*
Max weight:	18,000 lb (8,165 kg)	19,200 lb (8,709 kg)
Empty weight:	—	12,090 lb (5,484 kg)
Payload:	4,500 lb (2,041 kg)	5,000 lb (2,268 kg)
Max speed:	110 mph (177 km/hr)	110 mph (177 km/hr)
Cruising speed:	90–95 mph (145–153 km/hr)	90–95 mph (145–153 km/hr)
Take-off distance:	1,050 ft (320 m)	900 ft (274 m)
Climb to 3,000 ft (914 m):	5 min	4·5 min
Accommodation:	20 passengers	20 passengers
Range:	330 miles (531 km)	520 miles (837 km)

	A.W.XV Atalanta *Four 340 hp Serval III*
Max weight:	21,000 lb (9,525 kg)
Empty weight:	14,832 lb (6,727 kg)
Payload:	5,500 lb (2,495 kg)
Max speed at 3,000 ft (914 m):	156 mph (251 km/hr)
Cruising speed at 9,000 ft (2,743 m):	118 mph (190 km/hr)
Stalling speed:	51 mph (82 km/hr)
Take-off distance:	1,125 ft (343 m)
Climb to 9,000 ft (2,743 m):	21·5 min
Service ceiling:	14,200 ft (4,328 m)
Accommodation:	9–17 passengers
Range:	640 miles (1,030 km)

	Ensign Mk.I *Four 850 hp Tiger IXC*	Ensign Mk.II *Four 950 hp Wright Cyclone*
Max weight:	48,500 lb (2,199 kg)	55,500 lb (15,175 kg)
Empty weight:	32,920 lb (14,932 kg)	36,590 lb (16,597 kg)
Payload:	9,500 lb (4,309 kg)	12,000 lb (5,443 kg)
Max speed at 7,200 ft (2,195 m):	200 mph (322 km/hr)	208 mph (338 km/hr)
Cruising speed:	170 mph (274 km/hr)	180 mph (290 km/hr)
Stalling speed:	68 mph (109 km/hr)	—
Take-off distance:	1,140 ft (347 m)	—
Climb to 1,000 ft (305 m):	1·2 min	1·1 min
Climb to 3,000 ft (914 m):	3·2 min	—
Service ceiling:	22,000 ft (6,106 m)	24,000 ft (7,316 m)
Accommodation:	Western 40 pass. Eastern 27 pass.	—
Range:	860 miles (1,384 km)	1,370 miles (2,205 km)

The A.W.38 Whitley prototype which first flew from Whitley Abbey aerodrome on 17 March, 1936. (*Ministry of Defence*)

The Whitley and the Albemarle

A.W.38 Whitley

Armstrong Whitworth's greatest contributon to aviation was undoubtedly the A.W.38 Whitley heavy bomber: not only was it perhaps the best known of the company's aircraft, but it was also built in greater numbers than any other Armstrong Whitworth design to emerge from either Newcastle or Coventry.

The Whitley was designed to the Air Ministry specification B.3/34 issued in July 1934 and was clearly a descendant of the A.W.23 bomber transport, although there were significant differences. The light-alloy box spar devised for the A.W.23 was used again in the Whitley, but the A.W.23's low-wing configuration was changed to the mid-wing position in the Whitley. The biggest departure from normal Armstrong Whitworth practice was in the fuselage, which was of light-alloy monocoque construction, a radical departure from the company's traditional method of steel-tube construction used consistently since the days of the first metal Siskin. Designed as a heavy bomber as part of the rearmament programme initiated by the British Government in 1934, the Whitley was put into production off the drawing board, the go-ahead being given in June 1935. This was followed by a written order for eighty aircraft, placed in August of the same year. The prototype Whitley, K4586, was first flown on 17 March, 1936, from Whitley aerodrome and the pilot was Alan

The prototype Whitley, flown by Campbell-Orde, coming in to land at the end of its first flight. (*Courtesy A. Campbell-Orde*)

Campbell-Orde; like the A.W.23, the Whitley was powered by two Tiger engines, in this case the Mk.IX, driving the newly-introduced, three-blade two-position de Havilland propellers. A second Whitley prototype, K4587 (to specification B.21/35), was also built, and this aircraft had the more powerful Tiger XI engine. The second aircraft was first flown on 24 February, 1937, by Charles Turner-Hughes. The Whitley made its first public appearance at the RAF Display at Hendon on 27 June, 1936, when K4586 was included among the new and experimental aircraft.

When the A.W.38 design was first finalized, wing flaps were a relatively unknown quantity, and in order to keep the landing speed low, the wing of the Whitley was given a large angle of incidence relative to the fuselage: in fact, flaps were added at a later stage, but by then it was too late to alter the wing setting. The large wing incidence, which was retained through all the Whitley variants, accounted for the characteristic nose-down attitude which made the Whitley so easily recognizable in flight. The combination of the large angle of incidence and the split flaps kept the Whitley's landing speed very low, a feature which made it eminently suitable for operation at night.

The second prototype Whitley, K4587, had more powerful Tiger engines and a smal amount of dihedral on the wings. (*Imperial War Museum MH3410*)

Constructionally, the Whitley was, as already mentioned, a considerable break-away from previous Armstrong Whitworth practice, and it was also the first aircraft with a stressed-skin fuselage to go into production for the RAF. The fuselage was built up with light-alloy sheet supported by longitudinal stringers and transverse frames and was fabricated in three sections, a nose portion, a main centre portion integral with the centre section of the wing, and a rear portion attached aft of the tailplane. The straight lines of the fuselage, and hence its rather box-like appearance, were the

The prototype Whitley under construction.

result of a decision to avoid as far as possible the use of double-curvature skin panels. The wing, also divided into three sections, consisted basically of a large light-alloy box spar of corrugated sheet metal internally braced with a structure of tubing. The leading and trailing edges of the wing were built up on rib sections attached to the spar, the leading edge and the spar itself being covered with sheet metal, whilst the trailing edge, aft of the spar, was fabric covered. As originally built, the cantilever wing had no dihedral angle, but subsequently, during the building of the first production batch, the wing extensions were given a dihedral angle of 4 deg. The low-set tailplane was of similar construction with fabric-covered elevators and twin fabric-covered fins and rudders. The undercarriage consisted of two single-wheel units which retracted upwards and forwards into the base of the engine nacelles, the shock-absorbers being compressed during retraction to economize space. When the undercarriage doors were closed after retraction, a small portion of the wheel was left protruding in order to minimize damage in a wheels-up landing. It speaks well for the basic design of the Whitley that no major structural alterations were necessary to take care of the increasing weight of the aircraft which, during its life, rose by more than 12,000 lb.

Fuel totalling 519 gal was carried in three tanks, two located in the leading edge of the wings, each of which contained 182 gal, and another, containing 155 gal, situated in the top of the fuselage over the wing centre-section. Additionally, arrangements were made for the quick installation of long-range tanks, with a capacity of 132 gal, in the forward bomb bay. The bomb load, which could amount to 3,360 lb, was distributed between two bays in the fuselage and in numerous small compartments in the wings. Defensive armament was carried in two Armstrong Whitworth manually-operated turrets, each with a single Vickers ·303 machine-gun, mounted in the nose and tail positions.

In the early part of 1938, while Whitley IIIs were going through the shops at Coventry, the company designed and built a wing for the aircraft made principally of wood: the idea was that, in an emergency, fresh sources of material and labour could thus be tapped. At the time it was thought that there would be difficulty in designing a wooden wing strong enough, especially as regards torsional stiffness, to stand up to the speeds then

The undercarriage and engine mounting of the Whitley. The fuel tanks can be seen in the wing leading edge.

The tail unit of the Whitley and the manually-operated Armstrong Whitworth gun turret.

contemplated. For this reason, the wooden box spar of the wing was strengthened by an internal bracing of steel tubes. The wooden wing, which was interchangeable with the standard article, was apparently never flown, but it was claimed that, without altering the wing area, the space available for fuel was increased and that the bomb load could be stepped up by some 2,800 lb.

The prototype Whitley, K4586, underwent trials at Martlesham Heath during the autumn of 1936. Flown at a weight of 21,094 lb, the aircraft took-off in 286 yards at a speed of 69 mph; the landing run, using brakes, was 210 yards, and the distance to stop, landing over a 50-ft screen, was 425 yards, the touch-down speed being 63 mph. The take-off was described as normal and straightforward, except for a tendency to swing to starboard which, in some cases, needed full opposite rudder. The landing was easy and straightforward, and it was this, combined with the low landing speed, that made the Whitley popular with pilots. The level speed, as measured at Martlesham, was 192 mph, true, at 7,000 ft, the full-throttle height of the moderately-supercharged Tiger IX engine, and the climb to 10,000 ft took 15 min; the service ceiling was 19,200 ft. Criticisms of the Whitley were of a minor nature and were concerned mostly with the disposition of the flap, undercarriage and other controls in the cockpit. The fuel-tank venting system was criticized as being inadequate to cope with the high speed of the under-wing pressure refuelling system, a recently introduced technique.

The first production Whitley Mk.I. Aircraft of the first batch had no dihedral, but this was added retrospectively. (*Imperial War Museum MH4292*)

The first production Whitley, K7183, was delivered in the early months of 1937, with the second aircraft, K7184, being flown direct on 9 March from Baginton to No.10 Squadron, then equipped with Handley Page Heyfords and stationed at Dishforth aerodrome. Half-way through the first production batch, after thirty-four aircraft had been completed, the Whitley I gave place to the Mk.II version which had the Tiger VIII engine incorporating a two-speed supercharger. This was said to be the first time such a supercharger had been fitted to a military aircraft, and it gave a better climb and an improved performance at altitude. The first Whitley II was a modified Mk.I and the total production of this version amounted to forty-six aircraft. The Whitley III which followed differed mainly in the matter of armament, a power-operated Nash and Thompson turret with

A production Whitley Mk.I on test. Deliveries began in the early months of 1937.

The Whitley K8936 was the first production Mk.III aircraft; it had Tiger VIII engines, a power-operated nose gun turret and increased dihedral. (*Imperial War Museum MH5658*)

one machine-gun replacing the Armstrong Whitworth manually-operated turret which had previously occupied the nose position. A new feature, introduced to supplement the Armstrong Whitworth turret still retained in the tail position, was a retractable ventral turret located amidships and equipped with twin ·303 in Browning machine-guns. In addition, the bomb bays and racks were modified to take bigger bombs. Once again, it was a modified Whitley I (K7211) that was used as a prototype for the Mk.III, of which eighty were built.

The need for still more performance and greater reliability resulted in a decision to fit the Whitley with the Rolls-Royce Merlin engine. The first Whitley to be so fitted—and the first Armstrong Whitworth aircraft of Coventry origin, since the Awana of 1923, to have an engine of rival

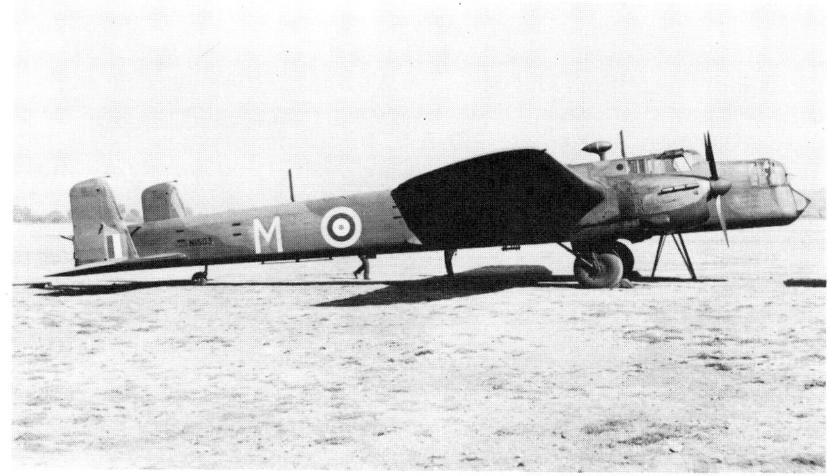

The Whitley Mk.V, with two Rolls-Royce Merlin X engines, was the most numerous variant, with a total of 1,466 built. (*Courtesy D. James*)

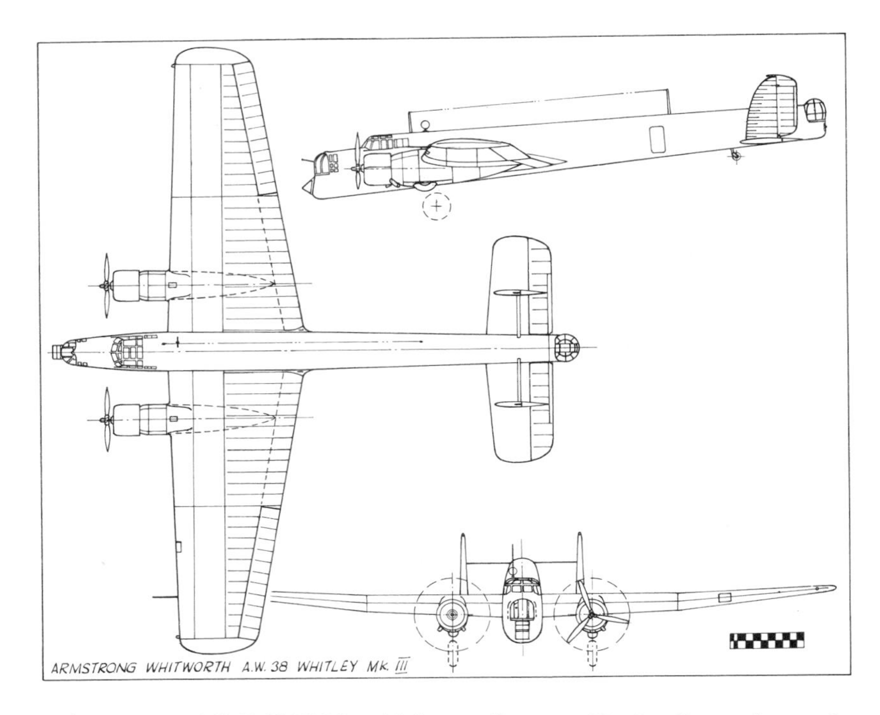

make—was a Mk.I, K7208, which was flown to Hucknall aerodrome for the purpose, and the first flight of this aircraft with the new powerplants took place successfully from Hucknall on 11 February, 1938: the second flight, a few days later, was brought to an abrupt conclusion by the seizure of one of the engines. Later, two other Whitley I aircraft, K7209 and K7211, were fitted with Merlin engines and used as test aircraft. During the months of April and May 1938, the Whitley K7208 underwent performance trials at Martlesham Heath aerodrome. The Merlin II engines, then fitted, developed 990 hp at 12,000 ft, with a maximum of 1,030 hp at 16,000 ft, while the aircraft, as tested, weighed 20,000 lb and was without its nose and tail turrets. At the full-throttle height of 16,000 ft, the Whitley's true airspeed was measured as 239 mph. The report stated that the aircraft's heating system was not satisfactory and that the engines were exceedingly noisy. This was thought to be due either to the ejector exhaust system or to the airscrews; as a result the Whitley was returned to Rolls-Royce for an investigation into the problem in co-operation with the RAE.

The production version of the Rolls-Royce-powered aircraft, the first of which flew on 5 April, 1939, was fitted with Merlin IV engines and was known as the Whitley IV. With this engine the performance of the production aircraft differed somewhat from that of the prototypes, and the revised official figures will be found on page 286. Another innovation in Mk.IV was the fitting, in the tail position, of a power-operated Nash and

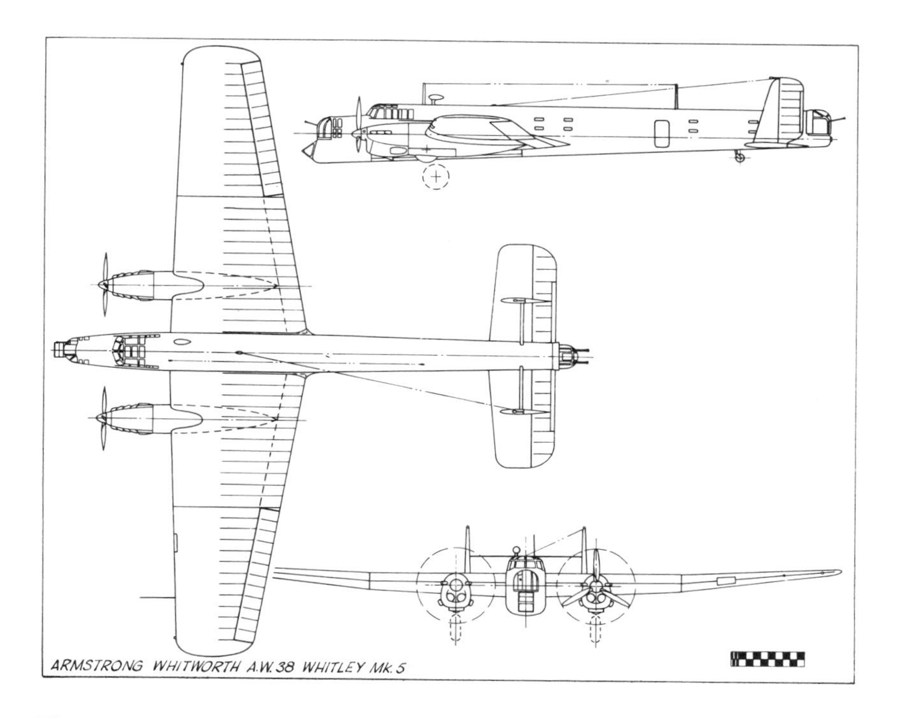

Thompson turret mounting four ·303 in Browning machine-guns—the first time a heavy bomber had been provided with such an effective rearwards defence. Other improvements included two additional fuel tanks in the wings, increasing the capacity by 186 gal and bringing the normal fuel load to 705 gal. A noticeable feature of the Mk.IV was the new 'chin' transparent panel which gave the bomb-aimer in the nose a wider view. Altogether forty Mk.IVs were built, but the last seven aircraft of the batch were fitted with the more powerful Merlin X engine and were known as Whitley IVAs.

During the years 1937 and 1938, when the likelihood of war was becoming ever more apparent, continuous efforts were made to improve the battleworthiness of the Whitley and to make it better able to meet the difficult tasks which clearly lay ahead. This process really culminated in the Whitley V, the version that was built in greater numbers than any other mark. The main features of the Mk.V, which was also powered with the Merlin X, included an extension of the rear end of the fuselage by 15 inches to give the rear gunner a wider field of fire on the beam. Another change at the back end was a modified fin with a straight leading edge in place of the curved variety of the earlier marks. The fuel capacity was again augmented to a normal total of 837 gal (which could be increased to 969 gal with extra tanks in the bomb bay). Another important improvement was the fitting of rubber de-icer boots to the leading edges of the wings.

The characteristic nose-down attitude of the Whitley in level flight is well illustrated in this photograph of a Mk.V aircraft. (*Courtesy D. James*)

In May 1940 the Whitley was one of the five aircraft to be given overriding priority by the newly-formed Ministry of Aircraft Production (the others were the Spitfire, the Hurricane, the Blenheim and the Wellington) and altogether 1,466 Whitley V's were built, the first examples coming off the line during 1939 with first deliveries being made in August. When the war started there were 196 Whitleys of assorted marks with the RAF, serving with Nos.10, 51, 58 and 78 Squadrons. Shortly after the outbreak of war, the few available Mk.V aircraft were handed over to No.77 Squadron, which thus became the first operational squadron to use the latest version of the aircraft.

At the start of the war the Hampden and the Wellington were looked upon as being suitable for daylight attacks, while the slower Whitley was

The cockpit of the Whitley Mk.V. (*Courtesy H. A. Taylor*)

classed as a night bomber. The harsh lessons learned from the early raids on German shipping soon caused these daylight forays by the larger bombers to be abandoned, and they subsequently joined the Whitleys in the night-bombing force. Nevertheless, it was the Whitleys that performed the major share of the early night operations, and no time was lost in sending them into action. On the first night of the war, ten Whitleys from Nos.51 and 58 Squadrons penetrated to Hamburg, Bremen and the Ruhr, but the impact of the raid was somewhat diminished by the fact that the aircraft dropped nothing more lethal than propaganda leaflets. This was the first of many such leaflet raids, known by the code name of 'Nickle', during which the Whitleys visited Berlin, ranged far and wide over enemy

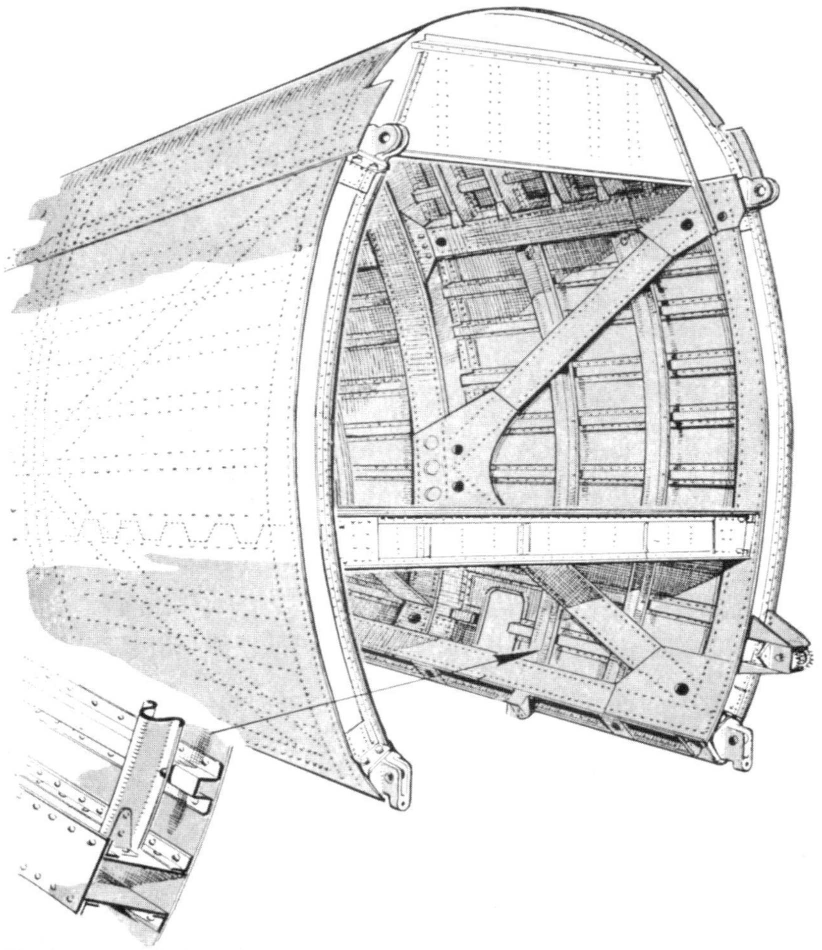

The Armstrong Whitworth type of monocoque construction used in the Whitley fuselage.

The fuselage of the Whitley Mk.V was extended by fifteen inches to give a wider field of fire for the rear gunner.

territory and, on one occasion, penetrating into Poland. The effect of the leaflets on the German population was probably negligible, but valuable operating experience was gained and, although the raiders seldom met with opposition from the Germans, the flights were often made hazardous by bad weather, and losses were, in fact, uncomfortably high.

The first bombs to be dropped by the Whitleys were aimed at mine-laying seaplanes taking-off from the Borkum air station located in the Friesian Islands. This attack took place during the night of 12–13 December, 1939, and subsequently many patrols were made in this area, and bombs were dropped on seaplane flare paths in an attempt to harass the seaplanes which, with their magnetic mines, were causing serious concern in Britain. It was during one of these sorties, on the night of 19–20 March, 1940, that the first bombs were deposited on German soil, as opposed to coastal waters and seaplane take-off areas. These were dropped by a combined force of Hampdens and Whitleys on the shore installations of the seaplane station of Hornum in the Friesian Islands, the Whitleys coming from Nos.10, 51, 77 and 102 Squadrons.

Bomber Command's Whitleys scored many other notable 'firsts': on the night of 10–11 May, 1940, within hours of the German invasion of the Low Countries, Whitleys of Nos.77 and 102 Squadrons dropped the first bombs on the German mainland; these were aimed at railway centres on the German supply routes to the Netherlands. In the following month the RAF marked Mussolini's entry into the war at midnight on 10 June, 1940, by staging a raid on Italian territory. Denied the use of French airfields by a government which was on the point of capitulating to the Germans, the thirty-six Whitleys, drawn from Nos.10, 51, 58, 77 and 102 Squadrons, refuelled in the Channel Islands on their way to Italy on the night of 11–12 June, but engine failure on some aircraft and bad weather over the Alps caused the majority of the raiders to turn back and, in the event, only thirteen aircraft succeeded in reaching their targets in Genoa and Turin. More dramatic still was the raid during the night of 25–26 August, 1940, when the Whitleys of Nos.51 and 78 Squadrons shared with Hampdens and Wellingtons the dropping of the first bombs to fall on Berlin.

From then on the Whitleys, in company with the growing force of Wellingtons, continued to carry the offensive into the heart of Germany. These early raids were, in fact, not very damaging to the enemy: post-war studies revealed that during the twelve months from May 1940 to May 1941, nearly half the bombs dropped at night on Germany fell in open country. But valuable experience was being accumulated and scientific aids to more accurate navigation were soon to change the picture dramatically. But before this happened, the Whitleys were retired from Bomber Command, their last operation with that command being an attack on

Whitley Mk.V aircraft of No.102 Squadron, RAF; in the foreground is N1421. (*Imperial War Museum C921*)

Ostend harbour during the night of 29–30 April, 1942, although some Whitleys, brought in from Operational Training Units, took part in the famous '1,000 Bomber' raid on Cologne on the night of 30 May, 1942.

But the Whitley's wartime activities were by no means confined to service with Bomber Command: soon after the outbreak of war, at the end of September 1939, No.58 Squadron was temporarily transferred to Coastal Command and based at Boscombe Down aerodrome from whence the squadron's Whitleys undertook anti-submarine patrols over the English Channel. The squadron returned to Bomber Command in February 1940, but two years later it was again called upon to assist Coastal Command, this time by patrolling the Western Approaches, based first at St Eval and later at Stornoway aerodrome in the Outer Hebrides. Other Whitley bomber squadrons which from time to time helped out with maritime duties were No.51, which patrolled the Western Approaches from May 1942 until the following October, and No.77 which, during the same period, flew against submarines in the Bay of Biscay. These long ocean patrols were not without their dangers, both from enemy action and from unpredictable weather, and losses were frequent. A Whitley unit used

A Whitley Mk.VII, one of a number built for maritime reconnaissance duties with RAF Coastal Command. (*Imperial War Museum MH4295*)

for anti-U-boat duties, and maintained by No.10 (Bomber) Operational Training Unit, lost thirty-five aircraft in the twelve months ending July 1943; during this time they flew some thirty-five sorties each week and accounted for one submarine sunk and four others damaged.

With its ample range and good load-lifting capacity, the Whitley was well suited to the maritime reconnaissance rôle, and it was soon adopted for this duty in its own right, being used to re-equip No.502 (General Reconnaissance) Squadron at Aldergrove aerodrome, near Belfast, in the autumn of 1940, and No.612 (GR) Squadron in the following year. To begin with, these two squadrons used the standard Whitley bomber, but their success with Coastal Command led to the development of a more specialized version known as the Mk.VII (the designation Mk.VI was allotted to a projected Pratt & Whitney powered version proposed in case the supply of Merlin engines became critical: in fact, this never happened and the Mk.VI never left the drawing board).

The new Whitley VII joined Coastal Command during 1942 and the first sinking of an enemy submarine by a Whitley VII occurred in the Bay of Biscay on 30 November, 1941, when an aircraft of No.502 Squadron bombed and sank the *U-206*. The Whitley VII was basically a Mk.V with the fuel capacity raised to a total of 1,100 gal by the addition of four auxiliary tanks located in the rear fuselage and two in the front bomb bay. The essential equipment of the Mk.VII consisted of the new long-range ASV Mk.II air-to-surface radar. The Whitley VII was the first operational aircraft to carry this new equipment, and the crew of the aircraft was increased to six by the addition of a radar operator. The higher all-up weight of the Mk.VII and the extra resistance caused by the five radar masts strung out along the top of the fuselage, reduced the speed of the aircraft, but the range was stepped up to a maximum of some 2,300 miles. Production of the Whitley VII amounted to 146 aircraft and, in addition, a number of Mk.Vs were also converted to Mk.VIIs; the type remained in service with Coastal Command until early in 1942.

As Whitleys became more plentiful they were adapted to other rôles. In 1940 the type was chosen to equip the Central Landing School, which later became No.1 Parachute Training School, based at Ringway aerodrome near Manchester. At first, Whitley IIs were used, and it was from these that the early experiments in dropping parachute troops were conducted, but eventually all marks of Whitley, except the Mk.VII, were used by the school, which played a major part in building up the 'Red Beret' paratroop units of the British Army. In 1941 the Whitley V was adapted as a glider tug. At first the towing gear was fitted in place of the rear turret; later the turret was replaced and the towing point transferred to a substantial yoke fitted below the base of the turret. In September 1942 a Whitley V was

A Whitley Mk.II, K7262, in use as a paratroop trainer. The occasion was a demonstration before HM King George VI given in May 1941. (*Imperial War Museum H9955*)

used at Farnborough for tests involving the towing of two General Aircraft Hotspur training gliders, each weighing 3,600 lb, and these trials were followed in October 1942 by tests with an Airspeed Horsa glider at weights varying between 10,000 lb and 14,500 lb. In June 1943 further tests were made at the RAE with a Whitley V (EB356) as a result of which the all-up weight of the Whitley V, when used as a glider tug, was fixed at 23,170 lb.

The training of glider-tug pilots took place on Whitleys attached to No.21 Glider Conversion Unit based at Brize Norton aerodrome, and Whitleys were used to equip three squadrons of No.38 Wing, Nos.195, 296 and 297, formed in 1941 and 1942 for the transport of airborne forces. Meanwhile, Whitleys of Bomber Command were used to drop paratroops in Italy on an operation staged on 10 February, 1941, and aimed at destroying an aqueduct at Tragino in the south of the country. The aqueduct supplied water to Taranto, Brindisi and Bari, ports which were then being used by the Italians in their campaign against Greece. The paratroops were dropped from five Whitleys which, with two others used to create a diversion, had taken-off from Malta. The parachutists succeeded in destroying the aqueduct before being captured by the Italians, and the attack caused consternation among the enemy, although it is said to have had no noticeable effect on the supplies of water to the Italian troops. Of more practical value was another Commando raid in which Whitleys also played a part, in February 1942. During the previous year the Germans had set up a new type of anti-aircraft radar on a cliff top at Bruneval, on the French coast near Le Havre, and the British, anxious to learn more about this latest development in German radar technique, mounted an

The Whitley Mk.V was used at Farnborough for glider-towing experiments; note the towing yoke at the tail and the RATOG containers under the wing.

A Whitley V tug towing an Airspeed Horsa.

expedition to capture the new installation. The operation, known by the code name 'Biting', involved twelve Whitleys of No.51 Squadron which took off from Thruxton aerodrome on the night of 27–28 February, 1942, and carried paratroops and radar specialists to the site of the station. All but two of the Whitleys dropped their men in the right place and, while the troops held the enemy at bay, the experts, under continuous and accurate machine-gun fire, first photographed the apparatus, then dismantled it and took away the vital parts and finally blew up the remains. With their booty, and some prisoners, they then withdrew to the beach and were taken off by the Royal Navy; the total British casualty list amounted to fifteen.

From the first moment of their invasion, the German troops in occupied Europe were continuously harassed by Resistance groups which grew in strength and ingenuity as time went on. Naturally, every possible help and encouragement was forthcoming from Britain, and in the summer of 1941 and early in 1942 two 'Special Duty' squadrons, Nos. 138 and 161, were formed for this purpose. By the spring of 1942 these two squadrons, both based at Tempsford aerodrome, near Bedford, had a combined fleet consisting of twelve Whitleys together with a number of Westland Lysanders and other assorted types of aircraft. The main task of the Whitleys was the dropping of agents (many of whom would be picked up later by the Lysanders) and supplies of arms and other requisites to the Resistance groups. The operations eventually became highly organized, with radar beacons ('Rebecca' on the ground and 'Eureka' in the aircraft) being used to locate the dropping zones in the dark.

One of the fifteen Whitley Mk.V bombers which were used by BOAC to fly urgent supplies to Malta.

In May 1942, after the Whitleys of Bomber Command were withdrawn from front-line service, fifteen Mk.Vs were registered as civil aircraft (G-AGCF-K and G-AGDU-EC) and handed over to BOAC for use as freighters. In the event, only thirteen of these aircraft were actually used by the corporation, and these were converted by the removal of the gun turrets and the bomb gear and the fitting of extra fuel tanks in the bomb bays. The BOAC Whitleys were based at Gibraltar and used for flying supplies to Malta. This involved a seven-hour flight through the night and, as often as not, an arrival in Malta in the middle of an air raid. In spite of such distractions, the turn-round of the Whitleys had necessarily to be hurried so that they could get well clear of the island before daybreak. Even with an overload, the amount of freight that the Whitleys could carry from Gibraltar to Malta, a distance of more than 1,100 miles, was small, but supplies were so short in the island that anything was welcome, even although providing fuel for the Whitleys' return journey was a high price to pay. The Whitleys flew the route intensively until they were eventually replaced by more up-to-date and efficient aircraft. In spite of the fact that, as loaded for the Malta flights, they could not have remained airborne for long on one engine, no Whitleys were lost during these supply flights, and the only casualty was G-AGCI, which crashed into the sea on a test flight from Gibraltar. The accident was thought to be due to damage to the elevator control circuit sustained when the aircraft was parked with its tail into wind. After being withdrawn from the Malta run, the Whitleys were employed for a short time on the route between Leuchars aerodrome, in Scotland, and Stockholm in order to bring in urgently needed supplies of Swedish ball-bearings, but their performance was not good enough to evade the enemy fighters based in Norway and Denmark, and they were soon replaced by de Havilland Mosquitoes. After this, the useful life of the Whitleys as civil freighters came to an end, and they were all handed back to the RAF during the course of 1942 and 1943.

In the years immediately preceding the war, the Armstrong Siddeley company was busy developing a new high-power, twenty-one cylinder engine known as the Deerhound, a three-row radial with seven cylinders in each row. When the proposal was being discussed, both the engine designers and Lloyd suggested that an engine of the size contemplated should preferably be water-cooled, but Siddeley would have none of it, and insisted that the new engine should be air-cooled. The Deerhound engine had a swept volume of 38·2 litres and a compression ratio of 6·75 to 1; on the factory test-beds it developed 1,500 hp at 2,975 rpm and 5 lb/sq in boost pressure. It is known that the Folland 43/37 engine-test aircraft was intended to be used as the test vehicle for the Deerhound but, in fact, the

The Deerhound engine installed in the Whitley Mk.II K7243. Cooling air entered through the scoop under the spinner. (*Courtesy J. Rait*)

Another view of the Deerhound Whitley. The twenty-one cylinder engine developed some 1,500 hp (*Courtesy J. Rait*)

air testing was done in a standard Whitley II, K7243, which made its first flight with the new engine during the first week of January 1939.

The Deerhound Whitley continued to fly from Baginton on test, mostly piloted by John Grierson, who was then acting as test pilot for Armstrong Siddeley Motors. He recalls that the Deerhound engine was working reasonably well and that most of the delays that did occur were due to airframe unserviceability rather than engine troubles. Most of the difficulties with the Deerhound were due to overheating arising, in part, from the unusual reverse-flow cooling arrangement in which the air entered the cowling at the back of the engine by way of a large forward-facing scoop. It transpired that the Deerhound also had inadequate cylinder finning, and a new cylinder design had been prepared to overcome this failing; but, at that stage, development was halted following the destruction of the test Whitley in a fatal crash during the first week of March 1940. The accident was caused by the pilot, an RAF officer, taking the aircraft off the ground with the tail trim wound fully back, with the result that the pilot could not hold the nose down, and the aircraft stalled. The tail-trimming device on the Whitley was very powerful and the position indicator for the trim wheel could easily be misread. There had been a previous Whitley accident at Baginton when Sqdn Ldr M. J. Adam, of altitude record fame, had been killed in similar circumstances; at first it was thought that he had taken-off with the control locks in place but, after the Deerhound crash, it was realized that an incorrect tail-trim setting was the more likely cause of this accident.

Grierson himself had a narrow escape on 23 May, 1939, at the conclusion of a carburation test on a Whitley III, K8966. The test involved a prolonged flight at 18,000 ft and, to conserve his oxygen supply, Grierson had used it only intermittently during the flight. By the time the test was concluded he was, without realizing it, suffering from oxygen starvation, with the result that he started his descent by light-heartedly putting the Whitley into a stalled turn. In the rarefied air at 18,000 ft, the stall was vicious, and the Whitley dived away at high speed until the airspeed indicator went off the clock at 240 mph. During the dive the engines over-sped, the port one breaking up in the process; in addition, the nose hatch blew in and a portion of the fabric on the trailing edge of the starboard wing stripped off. Eventually, Grierson was able to ease the aircraft out of the dive and, with his full faculties once more restored at a lower altitude, he was able to make a safe landing.

The wing of Whitley K8966 partially stripped of fabric after a high-speed dive from 18,000 ft. (*Courtesy J. Grierson*)

One of the last Whitleys to be built, LA951, was retained by the company on its completion in 1943, and was used for general test and experimental flying. One of its main tasks was to act as a tug for the A.W.52G glider during its flight trials which started in 1945. Four years later, in March 1949, the veteran LA951, the last of the Whitleys to fly, was withdrawn from service and dismantled. It deserved a better fate; the Whitley had earned for itself an honourable place in the history of the RAF. Before the war the Whitley squadrons represented the world's first fully-trained night-bomber force, and, although already becoming obsolescent by September 1939, the Whitley formed the corner-stone of Britain's night-bombing offensive in the first years of the war. By so doing it laid the foundation for the RAF's night-bombing strategy and tactics which later played a significant part in the eventual victory. The fact that these early RAF night raids often did relatively little damage does not alter the fact that they had a powerful effect on the morale of both the British and the German populations in as much as they carried, by the only means then available, the war into the enemy's homeland and showed the German people that, even in adversity, the British people could still strike back.

A.W.41 Albemarle

The Whitley's reputation was gained doing the job for which it was designed: not so in the case of the Albemarle, a not very distinguished aeroplane, but one which in the end did have its moments of glory performing tasks far removed from its intended function. The aircraft which eventually became the A.W.41 Albemarle started life on the drawing boards of the Bristol Aeroplane Co as a twin-engined medium bomber designated the Bristol 155 and designed to specification P.9/38; this specification gave way, in due course, to B.17/38, and at this stage the design responsibility was transferred from the Bristol company to Armstrong Whitworth, with the concept altered to that of a reconnaissance-bomber to a new specification, B.18/38. Although almost entirely re-hashed by Lloyd at Coventry, particularly as regards structural design, the Albemarle seems to have retained some features stemming from its grandparentage—the nose, which bore a resemblance to that of the Bristol Blenheim IV, being a case in point.

The brief given to Armstrong Whitworth was a difficult one: as an insurance against a possible shortage of exotic alloys and the devastation of

The second prototype A.W.41 Albemarle, P1361. (*Imperial War Museum ATP10510D*)

The mock-up of the Albemarle. The design originated as the Bristol 155.

British aircraft factories, the A.W.41 was to be built mainly of wood and steel, and was to be extensively sub-contracted to a variety of firms whose skills would not be fully employed on other war work. The design was to be so engineered that it could be divided up into sub-assemblies which could be transported on a standard 60-ft 'Queen Mary' trailer. Lloyd succeeded in all these objectives, but at the expense of a somewhat heavy structure and a lengthy delay in getting the aircraft into production. The two prototype Albemarles, P1360 and P1361, were assembled at Hamble in the shops of Air Service Training Ltd, but production aircraft, originally to have been assembled by the Gloster Aircraft Co, at Brockworth, were in fact put together by a new company within the Hawker Siddeley Group known as A. W. Hawksley Ltd, also located at Brockworth, using sub-assemblies which, in the end, came from more than a thousand sub-contractors scattered throughout the country. Among the largest of these were Harris Lebus Ltd, the furniture makers, who made tailplane units; the Rover Car Co, who made the wing centre section; and MG Motors who were responsible for the front fuselage section.

The Albemarle was a mid-wing cantilever monoplane and was the first British aircraft with a nosewheel undercarriage to be built in quantity for the RAF. The power was supplied by two Bristol Hercules XI engines, each developing 1,590 hp, and driving de Havilland three-bladed fully-feathering hydromatic propellers. The fuselage, which was divided into three sections, consisted of four circular-section steel longerons with steel-tube bracing struts joined by bolted gusset plates. The covering was of

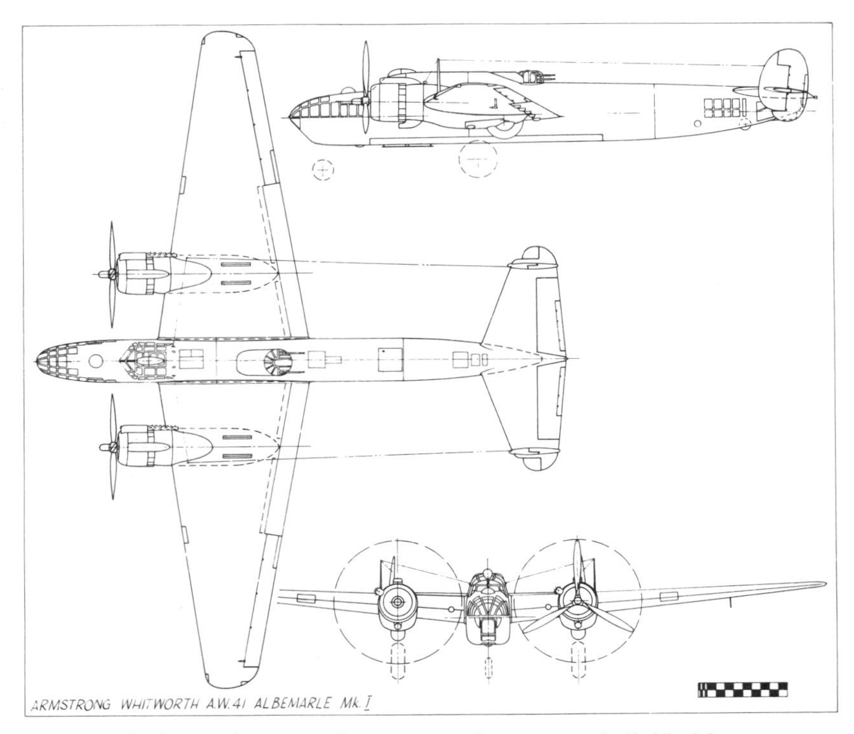

unstressed plywood mounted on spruce formers and divided into convenient sections which could be replaced in case of damage. The centre section of the wing was built in one piece running through the fuselage and was fabricated upon a girder of steel tubes which formed the base for the attachment of the nose and centre portions of the fuselage, the engine mounts, the main undercarriage legs and the extension wings. The wing centre section was covered with three-ply wood except for a portion of the leading edge where light-alloy sheet was used. The extension wings had two spars with spruce booms and plywood webs, the two spars being braced together with steel tubes; further torsional bracing was provided by the plywood upper and lower skins joining the spars. The Frise-type ailerons and the slotted flaps, the latter also designed to act as dive-brakes, were also covered with plywood, as were the tailplane, the elevators and the fins and rudders. The wing section was a modification of the Clark YH profile blending to Clark Y at the tips. Fuel was carried in four tanks, two in the fuselage holding 204 and 165 gal, and two in the wing centre section, each with a capacity of 200 gal, located between the spars on either side of the fuselage. In addition, three auxiliary tanks, each of 210 gal, could be fitted in the bomb bay.

As originally built for the reconnaissance-bomber rôle, the Albemarle was armed with a Boulton Paul electrically-operated, four-gun turret in the

A production Albemarle Mk.I, P1372, photographed in March 1942. (*Imperial War Museum MH4286*)

dorsal position, and a two-gun, manually-operated turret under the fuselage. Forward of the dorsal turret, which was offset to port to allow space for a passageway to the rear fuselage, was a fairing which retracted automatically when the turret was trained to fire forwards. In order to coordinate the defensive fire, it was proposed that a fire-controller should be carried, and this was the reason for the extensive transparent areas at the rear end of the fuselage. The ventral turret was soon dispensed with, but the dorsal turret was retained in the bomber version. A large bomb bay, with hydraulically-operated doors, extended from just aft of the cockpit to about halfway between the wings and the tail.

By the time that the production problems had been overcome, the Albemarle, apart from its relatively poor weight-lifting capacity, had been rendered obsolete as a bomber by the arrival in service of the larger four-engined aircraft. It was, therefore, decided to use the Albemarle, considerable numbers of which were by then coming off the production lines, as a special transport and as a glider-tug. For this purpose the four-gun dorsal turret was replaced by a two-gun, hand-operated version covered by a sliding hood, and a freight door was fitted in the starboard side of the fuselage. Extra space was made available in the fuselage by the removal of the rear fuselage tank and the bomb-dropping equipment. For glider towing a Malcolm-type quick-release hook was fitted to the rear extremity of the fuselage with a release handle for pilot operation.

The first Albemarle, P1360, was completed during the early months of 1940, and in March of that year Turner-Hughes conducted some taxi-ing tests at Hamble aerodrome. During these tests he reported that the aircraft showed little inclination to fly, but this was thought to be a characteristic, stemming from the unfamiliar nosewheel undercarriage. During further taxi-ing trials on 20 March, 1940, Turner-Hughes, in the course of one run, suddenly realized that he had gone too far and was travelling too fast to stop in safety and that he had left himself no alternative but to attempt a take-off. This he achieved, with the barest possible margin, after having used the full length of Hamble aerodrome: after keeping the aircraft in the

An Albemarle Mk.I with Bristol Hercules XI engines.

air with some difficulty, Turner-Hughes succeeded in making a circuit and landed back safely at Hamble. As a result of this experience, it was decided to add another ten feet to the wing span. This was done before the aircraft made its second, and more satisfactory, take-off from Hamble, on which occasion it was ferried up to Baginton for the flight-test programme. Subsequently, in September 1940, the prototype, P1360, was damaged when another Armstrong Whitworth pilot made a forced landing near Stratford-on-Avon after a piece of wing skin had come adrift in the air, but the aircraft was eventually repaired and flown back to Baginton by Turner-Hughes.

In June 1940 John Grierson started testing for Glosters at Brockworth and he was, in addition, given the task of testing the Albemarles coming off the Hawksley production line. According to him, the Albemarle was a very average aeroplane '... with no virtues and no vices'. The rudders were

The last production Albemarle Mk.I, V1599, formed the prototype for the S.T.Mk.I. (*Royal Aeronautical Society*)

judged to be somewhat over-balanced and Grierson, profiting from previous experience, decided that the fault lay in the thinness of the rudder trailing edge; his solution was to thicken up this part of the rudder by doping on a length of cord. Another trouble encountered during the test flying was a tendency for the engines to over-heat; this fault was never completely cured except by the doubtful expedient of raising the maximum permissible cylinder-head temperature from 280 deg C to 300 deg C. Official tests by the RAF showed that the take-off speed of the Albemarle, at an all-up weight of 36,500 lb, was 100 mph, with a single-engine minimum control speed of 130 mph. The stall, which occurred at about 80 mph with flaps and undercarriage down, was found to be gentle but was accompanied by a slight vibration and a considerable sink with a tendency to drop a wing. During recovery from the stall, the elevators were found to be relatively ineffective unless the throttles were partially opened. The maximum speed was measured at 265 mph at 10,500 ft, and the cruising speed was 170 mph with a range of 1,300 miles.

The cockpit of the Albemarle. (*Courtesy H. A. Taylor*)

Following the two prototypes, P1360 and P1361, production commenced with the Bomber Mk.I; after this production was confined to a series of variants divided into two main categories: with five marks of Special Transports, the S.T.Mk.I Series 1 and 2, the S.T.Mk.II, the S.T.Mk.V and the S.T.Mk.VI; and three marks of Glider Tugs, the G.T.Mk.I and the G.T.Mk.VI Series 1 and 2. In addition, there were single examples of a Glider Tug Mk.II and an Albemarle Mk.IV fitted with Wright Double Cyclone engines. Production details of these various categories will be found in Appendix C on page 376. The difference

The Albemarle G.T.Mk.I P1442. The towing hook is visible below the tailplane. (*Imperial War Museum MH4287*)

The Albemarle G.T.Mk.II V1600 with the four-gun dorsal turret removed. (*Imperial War Museum ATP12324D*)

The single example of the Albemarle Mk.IV, a version fitted with Wright Cyclone engines. (*Imperial War Museum ATP11295B*)

between the various marks was principally a matter of internal fitting and alterations to the armament. One major modification was made in 1943 in order to investigate the practicability of achieving 'hands-off' landings. The Albemarle was selected for these experiments because it was, at the time, the only British aircraft to meet the essential requirement of having been designed with a nosewheel undercarriage. For the tests a special undercarriage was fitted to the Albemarle V1599; it measured 12 feet long when fully extended and was designed to move backwards as well as upwards under landing loads. To make retraction possible, the long-travel shock-absorbers were compressed when the undercarriage was raised. Turner-Hughes first flew this special Albemarle on 8 November, 1943, and he found it quite feasible to let the aircraft fly itself on to the ground without any attempt by the pilot to check the descent. The experiment was considered to be a success, but only at the expense of considerable complication and a large weight penalty.

One of the ten Albemarles supplied to the Soviet Union. (*Imperial War Museum CH18401*)

In a burst of fraternal generosity, the British Government offered to supply ten Albemarles to the Soviet air force, and an RAF ferry training unit was formed at Errol aerodrome in Scotland for the purpose of training the Russian air crews who were to fly the aircraft to Russia. The crews arrived from Russia in March 1943, and it is believed that they remained at Errol for the best part of a year, during which time one of the Albemarles, flown by a Russian pilot, was lost in an accident. How many Albemarles eventually reached Russia and what their new owners did with them is not recorded, but the probability is that what they valued most was the acquisition of the Bristol Hercules engines, which they are said to have copied.

The first RAF squadron to receive the Albemarle was No.295, which was formed in the summer of 1942 for the transport of airborne forces in Horsa gliders, and the first Albemarle Glider Tugs joined the squadron in January 1943. The Albemarle was used operationally for the first time

Another Russian Albemarle, showing the freight door in the fuselage side. (*Imperial War Museum CH18402*)

during the invasion of Sicily—'Operation Husky'—on the night of 9–10 July, 1943, when Nos.296 and 297 Squadrons, which formed part of No.38 Wing, were engaged in the landing of glider-borne troops. Altogether, some 1,200 soldiers were involved in the airborne part of the exercise, the bulk of them being carried in American gliders towed by Douglas C-47s. The British contingent consisted of the 1st Airborne Division, part of which was flown in Horsa gliders towed by twenty-eight Albemarles and seven Halifaxes. Unfortunately, the airborne part of the invasion was something of a failure; the winds were unexpectedly strong and large numbers of troops were lost because the gliders were released too early over the sea. In fact, only twelve gliders, all towed by Albemarles and Halifaxes, reached their appointed objective, a river bridge to the south of Syracuse, and the successful capture of this bridge by a handful of troops in the face of constant counter attacks is one of the many minor epics of this campaign. Later in the battle for Sicily, on the night of 13–14 July, an airborne attack was mounted in an attempt to capture intact another bridge situated to the northwest of Catania. On this occasion the 1st Parachute Brigade and some Royal Engineers were carried by a force of 107 aircraft, including seventeen gliders towed by Albemarles and Halifaxes. Unfortunately, the Allied aircraft became mixed up in an air raid on the invasion fleet lying off the coast of Sicily, and the aircraft were scattered by anti-aircraft fire from the ships, which accounted for three of the Albemarles. In the end, thirteen gliders landed in the correct place and, despite the fact that only a small force was available, the bridge was eventually captured intact.

Albemarles played their part, too, in 'Operation Overlord', the invasion of Normandy on 6 June, 1944. Among the very first Allied troops to land in France on that occasion were men of the British 6th Airborne Division, who dropped by parachute near Caen soon after midnight in the first minutes of 'D-Day', and it was a flight of Albemarles of No.295 Squadron that acted as pathfinders for this action. Later, four squadrons of Albemarles towed Horsa gliders across the English Channel during the main assault which followed. Albemarles also took part in what was the largest airborne operation so far undertaken, the dropping of the 1st Airborne Division at Arnhem on 17 September, 1944. Two squadrons of Albemarles from No.38 Group towing Horsa gliders took part in this action. Altogether, four RAF squadrons used the Albemarle for transporting combat troops, either in towed gliders or as parachutists; in addition No.511 Squadron of Transport Command was equipped with Albemarles as freight carriers in February 1943. The type also formed part of the equipment of No.161 Squadron, which employed a variety of aircraft types for special duties such as those described earlier.

The final version of the special transport version, the Albemarle S.T.Mk.VI. (*Imperial War Museum ATP12994B*)

It was not the fault of the Albemarle that it was never called upon to fill the niche for which it was intended; there never was, fortunately, a critical shortage of light alloys, and the country's aircraft factories, although suffering their share of damage, were never remotely in danger of being wiped out. Had either of these contingencies in fact occurred, the Albemarle story might have been very different. In spite of the fact that it was never really fitted into the strategic picture, the Albemarle finally justified its existence by playing a useful part in the final and decisive battles of the war and, technically, if it did nothing else, it showed that extensive sub-contracting by firms entirely ignorant of aircraft construction could, given time, be made to work effectively. Albemarle production finally came to an end in December 1944, by which time 602 aircraft had been completed.

A.W.38 Whitley

Dimensions: Span (all marks) 84 ft (25·60 m); length (Mks.I, II, III and IV) 69 ft 3 in (21·11 m); height (all marks) 15 ft (4·57 m); wing area (all marks) 1,137 sq ft (105·63 sq m).

	Mk.I *Two 795 hp Tiger IX*	**Mks.II and III** *Two 845 hp Tiger VIII*	**Mk.IV** *Two 1,030 hp Merlin IV*	**Mk.V** *Two 1,145 hp Merlin X*	**Mk.VII** *Two 1,145 hp Merlin X*
Max weight:	21,660 lb (9,824 kg)	22,990 lb (10,428 kg)	25,900 lb (11,748 kg)	33,500 lb (15,196 kg)	33,950 lb (15,400 kg)
Empty weight:	14,275 lb (6,475 kg)	15,475 lb (7,019 kg)	17,250 lb (7,824 kg)	19,350 lb (8,777 kg)	19,600 lb (8,890 kg)
Military load:	3,365 lb (1,526 kg)	4,200 lb (1,905 kg)	—	7,375 lb (3,345 kg)	5,995 lb (2,719 kg)
Max speed at 16,400 ft (4,999 m):	183 mph (295 km/hr)*	209 mph (336 km/hr)	244 mph (393 km/hr)	230 mph (370 km/hr)	215 mph (346 km/hr)
Cruising speed at 15,000 ft (4,572 m):	163 mph (262 km/hr)	177 mph (285 km/hr)	220 mph (354 km/hr)	210 mph (338 km/hr)	195 mph (314 km/hr)
Climb to 15,000 ft (4,572 m):	27·4 min	23·5 min	16 min	16 min	22 min (to 12,000 ft (3,658 m))
Service ceiling:	19,200 ft (5,852 m)	23,000 ft (7,010 m)	—	26,000 ft (7,925 m)	20,000 ft (6,096 m)
Fuel capacity †:	519 Imp gal (2,359 lt)	519 Imp gal (2,359 lt)	705 Imp gal (3,205 lt)	837 Imp gal (3,805 lt)	1,100 Imp gal (5,000 lt)
Range with normal tankage:	1,250 miles (2,012 km)	1,315 miles (2,116 km)	1,250 miles (2,012 km)	1,500 miles (2,414 km)	2,300 miles with auxiliary tanks

A.W.41 Albemarle

Dimensions: Span 77 ft (23·47 m); length 59 ft 11 in (18·26 m); height 15 ft 7 in (4·75 m); wing area 803·5 sq ft (74·65 sq m).

	Two 1,590 hp Hercules XI
Max weight Special Transport:	36,500 lb (16,556 kg)
Max weight Glider Tug:	22,600 lb (10,251 kg)
Max landing weight:	32,500 lb (14,742 kg)
Max speed at 10,500 ft (3,200 m):	265 mph (427 km/hr)
Cruising speed:	170 mph (274 km/hr)
Safety speed:	130 mph (209 km/hr)
Stalling speed:	80 mph (129 km/hr)
Service ceiling:	18,000 ft (5,486 m)
Normal fuel capacity:	769 Imp gal (3,496 lt)
Auxiliary tank capacity:	630 Imp gal (2,864 lt)
Range with normal tankage:	1,300 miles (2,092 km)

* 192 mph (309 km/hr) at full-throttle height of 7,000 ft (2,103 m).
† Most versions could be fitted with additional auxiliary tanks.

The Flying Wings

A.W.52G and A.W.52

Aircraft designers and aerodynamicists have long been attracted by the concept of the tailless aircraft or flying wing, in which the drag of the fuselage and tailplane are eliminated, and from time to time much money and effort have been expended in an endeavour to exploit the theoretical advantages of this configuration. J. W. Dunne was probably the first to try out the tailless formula with his 1909 aeroplane, but he was seeking automatic stability; later, between the wars, much study was devoted to the series of Westland-Hill Pterodactyls, and these were followed, after the Second World War, by the de Havilland 108 and the General Aircraft sweptwing gliders. More ambitious were the large Northrop XB-35 and XB-49 aircraft, which underwent prolonged testing in America, and the Armstrong Whitworth experiments, firstly with the A.W.52G glider, and then with the A.W.52 jet-propelled flying-wing aircraft of 1947.

The object of the Armstrong Whitworth designs was to combine the merits of the tailless layout with the equally attractive advantages of the laminar-flow wing. As far back as 1942, Lloyd was asked by the Directorate of Scientific Research of the Ministry of Supply to design a full-scale section of a wing suitable for laminar-flow drag tests in the wind-tunnel at the National Physical Laboratory. An essential prerequisite of such a wing was a surface in which variations from the smooth curve were limited to a few thousandths of an inch. This was achieved with a metal-skinned specimen having a span of 8 ft and a chord of 6 ft. When tested in the NPL tunnel, this wing maintained laminar flow for up to 60 per cent of the chord, with the result that the profile drag was reduced to about half the normal value. Later, Armstrong Whitworth built a wing with a NACA laminar-flow section to fit on to a Hurricane. By the use of special methods of construction, a surface smoothness to very fine limits was achieved on this wing, and, Lloyd recalls, gave very good results, but only for limited periods because the flies and dirt which adhered to the surface during flight were enough to cause a break-down of the laminar flow.

In spite of this difficulty, the attractions of laminar flow were sufficiently marked for experiments to be continued, and Lloyd calculated that the combination of a clean tailless layout and a laminar wing would result in a machine with a total parasite drag of about one-third of that for a normal aircraft. Such a promising prognosis led naturally to speculation about the possibilities of a jet airliner incorporating the two principles, and Lloyd had many discussions on the subject with J. L. Nayler of the NPL and with members of the quaintly-named 'Tailless Committee' of the Directorate of Technical Development. In the type of aircraft envisaged, everything would have to be located within the wing; it would thus be the minimum amount of head room for the passengers that would determine the wing thickness and, consequently, the size of the aircraft. On this basis it was reckoned that the span would need to be at least 160 ft, with a corresponding weight of some 180,000 lb to 200,000 lb. The use of jet engines, which would be completely buried, would eliminate the spoiling effect of propeller wash on the laminar flow over the wing. The structure weight of such an aircraft would be low, partly because of the absence of a fuselage and tail unit and partly because the spanwise distribution of the load would reduce the bending moments in the wing.

As a first step towards this visionary project, a design known as the A.W.50 was put in hand; this was to have been a sweptwing aircraft with a normal fin and rudder but no horizontal tailplane; the power was to have been supplied by four Metropolitan-Vickers ducted-fan jet engines. No other details of this design are now available, and the same lack of information applies to the A.W.51 design, which was to have been a one-third scale test vehicle for the A.W.50, built as a glider. However, second thoughts on the project brought about considerable modification to the design, and, in 1943, work was started on the A.W. 52G, another glider which was intended as a half-scale model of a powered aircraft, the A.W.52, which would itself be about half the size of the projected airliner. The purpose of the glider was to provide aerodynamic data and to explore the control and stability aspects of the tailless configuration. A glider was chosen in order to save time and, for the same reason, it was decided to build it mainly of wood. The wing of the A.W.52G, which was of a NACA section, was built

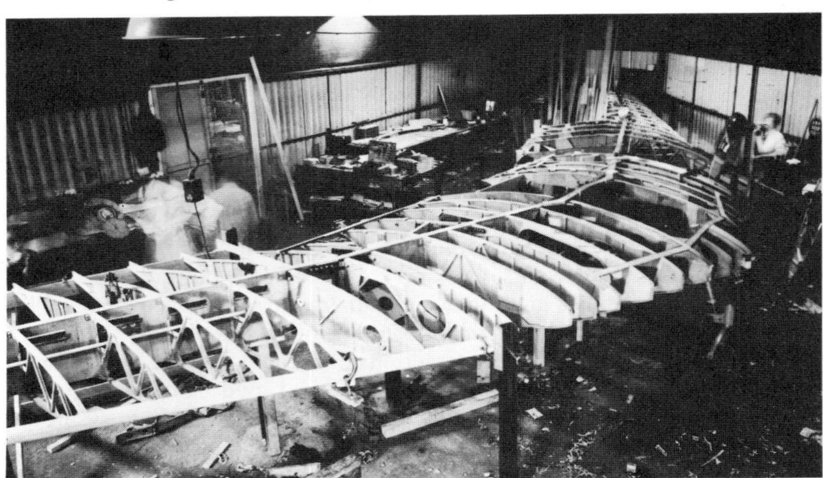

The A.W.52G under construction at Baginton, a photograph taken in August 1944.

The structure of the A.W.52G was mainly of wood.

in three portions, a centre section with a sweptback leading edge, and two outer portions, tapered, and with an increase in sweepback. The crew of two was carried in a nacelle built into the wing centre section with a transparent canopy rising from the upper surface of the wing. Control was by wingtip elevons which combined the functions of elevators and ailerons, working in unison for the former duty, and differentially for the latter. The elevons were hinged to the trailing edges of so-called 'correctors' which were, themselves, hinged to the wing. These correctors were used to

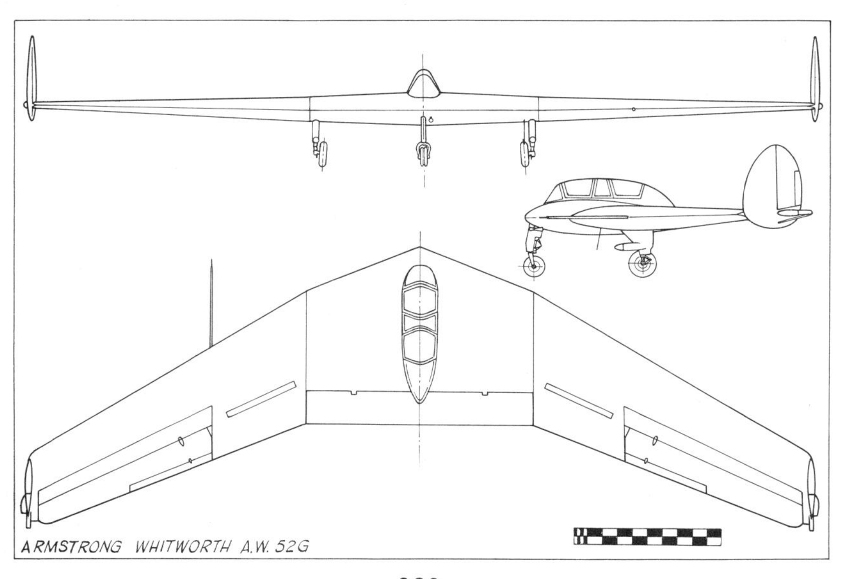

The completed A.W.52G, RG324, a photograph taken on 3 March, 1945, the day after the first flight.

provide for fore-and-aft trimming and to correct for the pitching moment caused by the operation of the Fowler flaps which occupied the trailing edge of the centre section. In addition, retractable spoilers, interconnected with the elevons, were fitted to the upper surface of the wing. Directional control was by fins and rudders mounted on the wingtips; these incorporated a differential control by means of which the outward-moving rudder travelled through a greater angle than the inward-moving surface. At the base of each rudder was a fairing housing an anti-spin parachute.

To prevent wingtip stall at low speed, boundary-layer control was provided over the outer sections of the wing. This was achieved by sucking the boundary-layer air into a slot situated in front of the elevons, thus preventing the break-away of the air flow over the wing and delaying the tip stall. The same effect could have been brought about by the use of automatic wingtip slots, but the fitting of these would not have been consistent with the laminar flow characteristics of the wing. Power for sucking the air into the slots was provided by wind-driven pumps mounted on the two main undercarriage legs.

Front view of the A.W.52G; the clean lines were broken only by the fixed undercarriage.

The wing structure consisted of a single box spar built of spruce and plywood with ribs of the same materials. There was, in addition, an auxiliary spar in the centre section to carry the loads of the nosewheel which, like the main gear, was not retractable. The leading and trailing edges of the wing were covered with wood, but the rest of the covering was of 'Plymax', the trade name for a product consisting of plywood and light-alloy sheet glued together.

Design work on the A.W.52G started in May 1942, the first wood was cut in March 1943, and on 2 March, 1945, the glider, flown by Turner-Hughes, was towed into the air by a Whitley for its first flight. On this first occasion the glider, which bore RAF roundels and the serial number

The unfinished cockpit of the A.W.52G, with its simple, but somewhat haphazard, instrument arrangement.

RG324, was released at 12,000 ft, but during test flying the normal release height was 20,000 ft, enabling the aircraft to stay airborne for about half an hour or more before landing back at Baginton. Flight tests with the glider confirmed most of the previous calculations regarding control and stability, and there was good agreement with the results of the wind-tunnel experiments. The only modification to the controls that was found necessary was the lowering of the gear ratio in the elevon circuit. At the end of a useful life that lasted for about two years, the A.W.52G was erected near the main gate of the Baginton factory, where it remained on display until, after some dilapidation, it was removed and broken up in the late 1950s.

The A.W.52G was able to remain airborne for about half an hour after being released at 20,000 ft. (*Charles E. Brown*)

The glider had provided useful information about the low-speed control and stability problems, but the high-speed development work could only be undertaken by a powered aircraft which, as mentioned previously, would itself be but a step towards the large six-jet airliner project already being actively studied by the company. In pursuance of this policy, the Ministry of Supply placed a contract with Armstrong Whitworth, towards the end of 1944, for two experimental aircraft to the Air Ministry specification E.9/44. Although primarily intended as research vehicles, the aircraft, if successful, were seen to have possibilities as fast mail carriers, and provision was made in the design for the accommodation of 4,000 lb of cargo. The A.W.52 was similar in outline to the glider and had a span of 90 ft and a designed all-up weight of 34,150 lb. The first aircraft had two Rolls-Royce Nene turbojets, each of 5,000 lb static thrust, and both aircraft were of all-metal construction. The engines were buried in the wing centre section on either side of the nacelle which projected ahead of the leading edge and which accommodated the crew of two, seated in

The A.W.52G airborne under tow.

tandem: the pilot only was provided with a Martin-Baker ejector seat. The crew compartment was pressurized to a maximum differential of 3½ lb/sq in, which gave a cabin pressure height of about 17,000 ft when the aircraft was flying at 31,000 ft. Fuel was contained in eight separate tanks, giving a total capacity of 1,700 gal for maximum range; normally only six of the eight tanks were used, these having a combined capacity of 1,245 gal. The wing had a thickness/chord ratio of 18 per cent tapering to 15 per cent at the tips, and the extension wings had a sweepback of 43½ deg at the leading edge. The wing section, which varied slightly from root to tip, was of a profile devised by the NPL which gave, in theory, laminar flow over about 55 per cent of the wing chord. The trailing edge of the centre section was occupied by a Fowler flap which was suitably dished to pass under the protruding jet-pipes.

The first A.W.52, TS363, with two 5,000 lb thrust Rolls-Royce Nene turbojets.

Control of the A.W.52 was basically similar to that of the glider; the elevons were hinged to the correctors as before and incorporated the so-called Irving-type balancing system in which the portion of the elevon surface ahead of the hinge was housed within a sealed pressure chamber located within the thickness of the corrector. The balancing forces were supplied by the pressure of the air which entered the chamber through ducts in the upper and lower surfaces of the wing. The end-plate fins and rudders were of the same type as those of the glider, having a similar differential movement. For the prevention of tip stalling, boundary-layer control was again employed with suction slots situated at about mid-chord ahead of the correctors. In the case of the A.W.52 the turbojets were used to provide the necessary suction. For this purpose the suction slots in the wing were connected by ducts to the engine air-intakes, where controllable flaps allowed the amount of suction to be regulated as required. Boundary-layer control was only brought into use at high angles of incidence, and matters were so arranged that the opening of the flaps in the air-intakes was

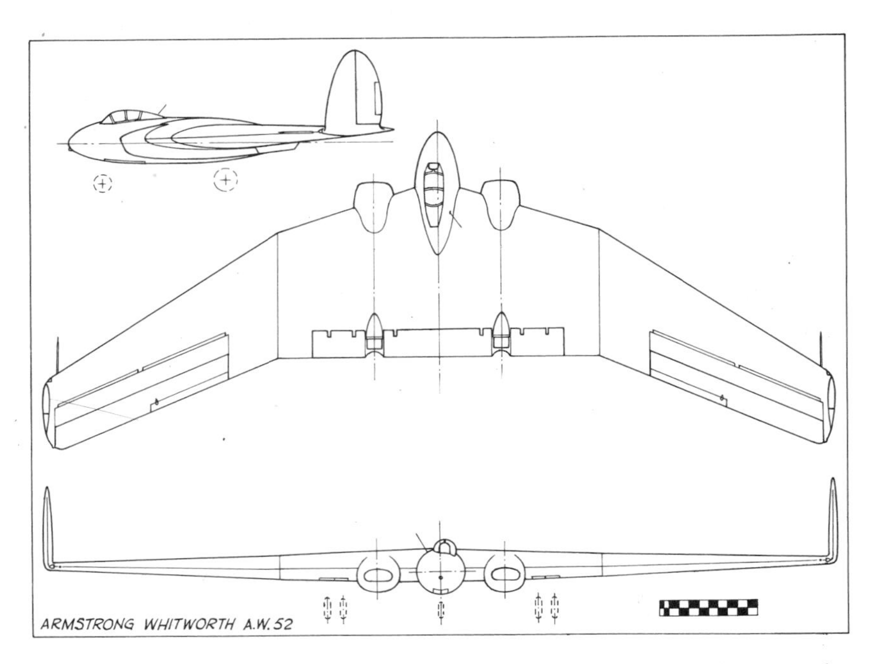

regulated either by the backward movement of the control column, or by the closing of the throttles, or by a combination of both.

In order to achieve the smooth wing surface necessary to maintain laminar flow, special methods of construction had to be devised. In effect, the system employed involved building the wing in two halves from the outside inwards. The top and bottom wing skins, already rolled to the correct profile, were held in external jigs accurately shaped to the correct wing section. To the inner surface of these skins were added spanwise stringers and the upper and lower halves, as appropriate, of the ribs and the torsion-box spar; finally, both sections were joined, resulting in a wing in which the surface variations everywhere measured less than two thou-

An unusual view of the second A.W.52, TS368. This aircraft had two 3,500 lb thrust Rolls-Royce Derwent turbojets.

The A.W.52, TS363, on test from Baginton aerodrome.

sandths of an inch. Other features of the A.W.52 were a retractable tricycle undercarriage and thermal de-icing of the wings, using hot gases drawn from the engine jet-pipes mixed with cold air entering from a scoop placed outside the engine cowling.

The A.W.52, with the serial number TS363, made its first flight from Boscombe Down aerodrome on 13 November, 1947, while the second aircraft, numbered TS368, which differed from the first only in that it was fitted with Rolls-Royce Derwent turbojets of 3,500 lb thrust, first flew on 1 September, 1948. The A.W.52, TS363, put up an impressive performance during its first public appearance at the SBAC Show at Farnborough in September 1948 but, on test, the results were, from the first, disappointing: although the Nene-powered version was capable of about 500 mph, true laminar flow was not achieved, and Lloyd came to the conclusion that it could not be maintained on a swept wing. Added to this was the natural disadvantage of the tailless type of aircraft in which the fore-and-aft control limitations resulted in the wing having a lower maximum lift coefficient than that of a normal aircraft. Because the A.W.52 did not have the long lever arm provided by the normal fuselage and tailplane, the down load on the elevons required to raise the aircraft's nose was necessarily large, and this tended to cancel out the lift obtained from the flaps. The result was a significant increase in the landing and take-off distance of the A.W.52 as compared with conventional aircraft with the same wing loading.

During a test flight of TS363 on 30 May, 1949, an asymmetric flutter developed in one wingtip, and this spread quickly across the whole span, shaking the entire aircraft to such an extent that the pilot, J. O. Lancaster, was forced to abandon ship, thus, incidentally, achieving the distinction of being the first person, at any rate in the United Kingdom, to use the

Martin-Baker ejector seat in an emergency. As luck would have it, the aircraft, left to its own devices, stopped fluttering and glided down to land itself in open country with relatively little damage. Following this incident, and in view of the disappointing results obtained, no further development of the flying-wing formula was undertaken by Armstrong Whitworth, who had by now turned their attention to the more conventional A.W.55 propeller-turbine airliner. The second A.W.52 was handed over to the Royal Aircraft Establishment at Farnborough, where it was used for experimental flying until it was finally disposed of in June 1954.

A.W.52G
Dimensions: Span 53 ft 10 in (16·41 m); length 19 ft 4 in (5·89 m); height 8 ft 4 in (2·54 m); wing area 443 sq ft (41·16 sq m).

A.W.52
Dimensions: Span 90 ft (27·43m); length 37 ft 4 in (11·38 m); height 14 ft 5 in (4·39 m); wing area 1,314 sq ft (122·07 sq m).

A.W.52

Two 5,000 lb-thrust Rolls-Royce Nene

Max weight:	34,150 lb (15,490 kg)
Empty weight:	19,660 lb (8,917 kg)
Max speed	
Sea level:	500 mph (805 km/hr)
36,000 ft (10,973 m):	480 mph (773 km/hr)
Rate of climb	
Sea level:	4,800 ft/min (24·4 m/sec)
20,000 ft (6,096 m):	3,000 ft/min (15·2 m/sec)
36,000 ft (10,973 m):	1,600 ft/min (18·3 m/sec)
Fuel capacity:	1,700 Imp gal (7,728 lt)
Range:	1,500 miles (2,414 km)

The A.W.55 Apollo as it appeared at the time of its first flight on 10 April, 1949.

The A.W.55 Apollo

At the end of the Second World War Great Britain found herself in possession of a highly skilled and technically advanced aircraft industry, but one which for five years or more had given hardly a thought to the problems of airliner design. On the other hand, as the war progressed, air transport had rapidly come into its own and from the handful of civil airliners possessed by Great Britain in 1939 had grown a great armada of military transports which, in the end, played a decisive part in the defeat of Germany and Japan. With minor exceptions, the growing demand for transport aircraft had, by agreement, been met by the United States aircraft industry, which thus found itself in a dominating position for meeting the big post-war demand for airliners. In this situation, the British aircraft industry was handicapped by the lack of continuity in the development of transport aircraft; on the other hand, the country had in the gas-turbine engine one valuable asset, in whose development Great Britain held a commanding lead over all other nations, including the United States.

At first the jet engine was generally considered to be a purely military power unit and, in America particularly, it was thought to be entirely unsuitable for commercial use because of its high specific consumption. However, in Britain some designers thought otherwise, but at first opinion was divided between the merits of the pure jet and the gas-turbine driving a normal propeller. Because this latter combination could promise a better specific fuel consumption, it was generally thought to be more suited to civil needs although it could not provide the high speeds which were possible with the straight jet engine. History shows that it was the pure jet that was to become predominant during the 1960s, with the propeller-turbine aircraft tending to fill a secondary rôle. Subsequent history has paid its due tribute to both schools of thought: the high-ratio by-pass, or turbofan, which seems likely to dominate the airliner pattern in the 1970s, represents a logical combination of the best features of the pure-jet and the propeller-turbine concept.

Although during the war Britain could spare no productive capacity for transport aircraft, the future needs of British civil aviation were given some theoretical study, and as early as 1942 the Government appointed a body of experts, which became known as the Brabazon Committee, to draw up proposals for the various types of aircraft likely to be required in peacetime. Among the committee's recommendations was the Brabazon Type II, an aircraft to carry 24 passengers and suitable for short and medium-haul duties in Europe. Two categories were suggested, one with piston engines and another to be powered by propeller-turbines. For this latter category both Vickers and Armstrong Whitworth submitted designs, and two prototypes of each were ordered by the Ministry of Supply in the spring of 1946: these aircraft eventually materialized as the Vickers Viscount and the A.W.55 Apollo.

The Armstrong Whitworth aircraft was designed to specification C.16/46, which called for an aircraft to carry 24 to 30 passengers for 1,000 miles at a cruising speed of 300 mph. At that early stage in gas-turbine development, there were divided opinions about the merits of the two types of engine compressor, the centrifugal type used in the Rolls-Royce Derwent and the de Havilland Ghost engines, and the axial type, which was at that time less well developed but which promised a much higher degree of efficiency than the cruder, but more robust, centrifugal blower. In the propeller-turbine field the two types were exemplified by the Rolls-Royce Dart with a centrifugal compressor, and the Armstrong Siddeley Mamba with its long, slender, axial-flow compressor. In theory, the latter was the engine with the greater development potential, and it is

The Apollo was designed to carry up to thirty passengers, to the requirements of specification C.16/46.

The first phase of Apollo test flying was undertaken with military markings and the Service number VX220.

not surprising that Armstrong Whitworth, with their strong sense of patriotism towards their sister engine company, should choose the Mamba as the powerplant for the A.W.55. On the other hand, Vickers chose the Dart for their Viscount project, thereby electing to play safe. In the event, Armstrong Whitworth were unlucky, and the Apollo's lack of success can, to a very large degree, be blamed on the failure of the Mamba engine, just as the success of the Viscount was due in a large measure to the outstanding qualities of the Dart engine. In passing, it is interesting to note that the reverse was true in the case of the pure-jet airliner; the first Comets used centrifugal-compressor engines, but these were soon replaced by the axial-flow type which, in the end, completely ousted those with the centrifugal blower.

The Mamba engine, as at first fitted to the Apollo, was designed to develop 1,010 shaft horse power plus 307 lb of jet thrust at take-off, and it was expected that, by the time the aircraft was in production, the developed engine would be capable of delivering 1,270 shp. When the Apollo first flew, the Mamba engine was actually developing about 800 shp for a weight of some 780 lb, and an attractive feature was its small diameter, which measured only 31 inches. The Mamba engine had an annular air intake surrounding the reduction-gear casing; from here air passed to the ten-stage compressor and thence into the six combustion chambers before passing out of the jet pipe via the two-stage turbine wheels. The reduction gear cut down the turbine-shaft speed of 15,000 rpm to a propeller speed of 1,450 rpm. The Mamba engine ran for the first time in April 1946, and first became airborne on 14 October, 1947, installed in the nose of an Avro Lancaster. In May 1948 it was flown in a Boulton Paul Balliol trainer, and it was later fitted experimentally to the Avro Athena and the Handley Page Marathon. In February 1948 the Mamba completed the 150-hour Ministry Civil and Military Type Test, and, on 25 August, 1948, successfully completed a 500-hour sealed endurance test under the super-

The development of the Apollo was hindered by trouble with the Mamba propeller-turbines.

vision of the Air Registration Board. These early tests seemed to augur well for the future of the engine, but it was not to be: when installed in the Apollo airliner a variety of difficulties arose, many of which proved incapable of solution within the life of the aircraft.

Early drawings of the A.W.55 show an aircraft with a span of 92 ft, and a relatively short fuselage, giving an overall length of 64½ ft. At a later stage in the design study, the length was increased to 68 ft and finally, as built, a further increase brought the overall length up to 71½ ft. During 1946, concurrently with the design of the Mamba-powered A.W.55, a proposal was drawn up for a pure-jet version, then known as the A.W.55 Mk.II. This was to have had four Rolls-Royce Derwent V turbojets, each developing 3,500 lb of static thrust. These engines would have given the aircraft an economical cruising speed of 375 mph at 25,000 ft and a range of 1,000 miles. The fuselage was to have been the same as that of the Mk.I, but a new wing of slightly shorter span and a redesigned undercarriage were proposed. Another suggested development was a stretched version with an extra 6 ft 8 in inserted in the fuselage to increase the seating capacity to 45 or more; as with the jet-powered variant, this proposal got no further than the drawing board, but for those operators preferring a piston engine installation—and there were many who were not yet convinced of the merits of the gas-turbine—a version of the standard A.W.55 was offered with either Rolls-Royce Merlin 35 or Pratt & Whitney Twin Wasp R-1830 engines.

As finally built, the A.W.55, at first named the Achilles, then the Avon and finally the Apollo, had an all-up weight of 45,000 lb with accommodation for 26 to 31 passengers. Notable features of the design included pressurization and air conditioning for the crew and passengers, thermal de-icing of the wings and tailplane, and constant-speed reverse-pitch and automatic-feathering propellers. The fuselage of the Apollo was of circular cross section with an internal diameter of 10 ft 2 in and was designed for a working differential pressure of $5\frac{1}{2}$ lb/sq in, enabling a cabin pressure height of 8,000 ft to be maintained at an aircraft altitude of 25,000 ft. The fuselage was constructed of duralumin sheet with riveted Z-section stringers and channel-section frames. The wing was built up around an extremely light and strong box spar consisting of two plate-web girders joined by wing skins which were themselves stiffened between the webs by an internal corrugated skin riveted to the normal outer skin panels of the wing. Six fuel tanks, three on each side, were located between the spar webs, and Fowler flaps, extending the full length of the wing inboard of the ailerons, were fitted. The tailplane was set high on the fin to keep it clear of the wing turbulence, and the elevators were aerodynamically balanced by the Irving shrouded system. This consisted of a plate projecting forward from the elevator hinge into a pressure chamber located within the thickness of the tailplane with ducts opening into the upper and lower surfaces of the tailplane; a similar system had been used on the A.W.52 flying-wing aircraft. Originally the rudder of the Apollo was to have been divided into two sections, the forward half coming into operation only after the rear half had reached its full angular displacement; the object of this arrangement was to provide sufficient rudder power to cope with two engines shutdown on one side, a difficult case with the Apollo because of the high power of the engines and their wide spacing relative to the centreline of the aircraft. In fact, the split rudder was not fitted, neither was another novel design feature, a gust-alleviating device by means of which both ailerons

The Apollo under construction; an interior view, looking forward.

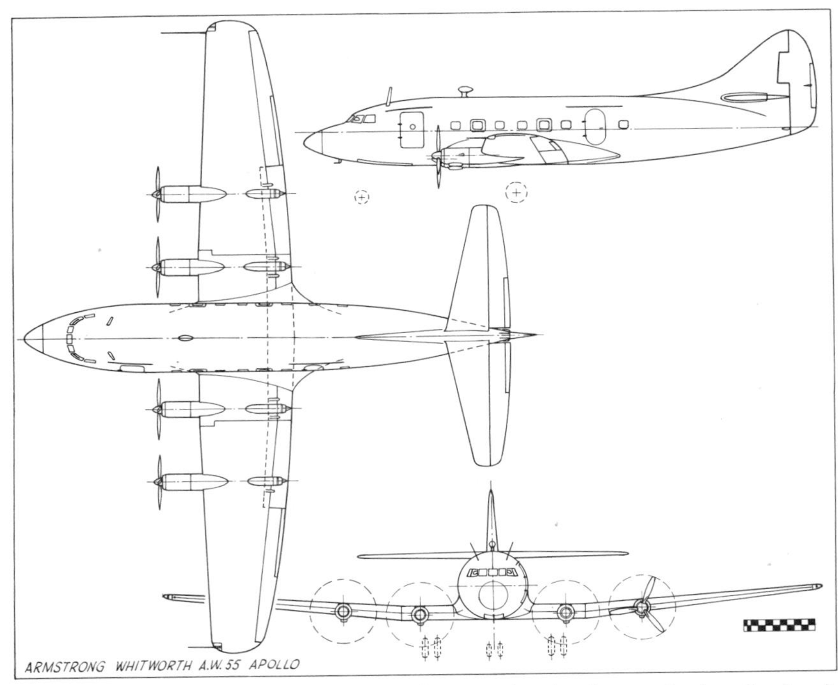

were allowed to deflect upwards under gust loads, thus reducing the loads imposed on the wing. There were twin wheels on each undercarriage unit and the main legs folded sideways, fighter fashion, into recesses in the centre section below the fuselage. This was necessary because the small diameter of the Mamba engine made it impossible to house the gear within the engine fairings in the normal way. The nosewheel retracted backwards into the fuselage in the conventional fashion. In the early specifications and brochures describing the Apollo, there was mention of a long-travel undercarriage to enable the aircraft '... to touch down unchecked from the normal glide path ... when landing on the beam'. This was presumably inspired by the early experiments with the Albemarle, but the proposal does not seem to have been pursued.

Construction work on the Apollo began early in 1948; two complete aircraft were put in hand, together with a third fuselage destined for ground testing. Pressurized aircraft were still a comparative novelty in Great Britain in 1948, and the testing of the extra fuselage was mainly concerned with pressurization trials. This test fuselage followed the prototype aircraft on to the one and only fuselage jig at Baginton, thus delaying the assembly of the second complete aircraft, but the importance attached to the pressurization tests was considered to be sufficient justification for adopting this policy. Under proof-pressure load tests, there was always a possibility that the fuselage might explode which, apart from

An Apollo test specimen in the water tank at Farnborough in October 1951. (*Royal Aircraft Establishment 95406*)

destroying the test specimen, would also obliterate the important evidence indicating where the initial failure took place. It was this consideration which led to the devising of the water-tank method of pressure testing; this was based on the premise that water, being virtually incompressible, does not store energy as is the case with compressed air, and therefore would not cause a catastrophic explosion if a failure of the fuselage skin occurred. The first Apollo test specimen consisted of the forward portion of the fuselage, the most critical section because of its irregular shape and the presence of large glazed areas around the flight deck.

The problem of providing a suitable water tank was solved at Baginton when somebody recalled an emergency hospital that had been built during the war in the form of a concrete dugout. This had subsequently been filled with earth, but it was now excavated, the top removed and the sides rendered waterproof; by this means, a tank capable of holding the 22-ft section of the fuselage and 27,000 gal of water was quickly made available. A steady source of supply for pumping water into the fuselage was necessary (which meant that a supply direct from the mains was not acceptable) and this was obtained by locating a header tank on the roof of a nearby factory building. The first tests involved raising the internal pressure of the fuselage to proof load, that is $1\frac{1}{3}$-times the normal working pressure which, in the case of the Apollo, amounted to $7\frac{1}{3}$ lb/sq in. The regulations called for this pressure to be held for $2\frac{1}{2}$ minutes without causing any set, or permanent distortion of the structure. This standard was easily achieved and, on a subsequent occasion, the internal pressure was taken up to 13 lb/sq in, 2·3 times the normal pressure, without damage to the fuselage. These fuselage pressure tests at Baginton are believed to have been the first to be conducted in a water tank, but it may be noted that this first use of the method was not then concerned with fatigue problems caused by pressure cycles; this aspect of cabin pressurization was not thought to be a problem until the Comet disasters of 1954 brought the phenomenon into prominence. At a later date, when the Apollo prototype had finished its flying life, it was returned to Baginton, dismantled, and used for cyclic pressure tests as part of a programme of research into this aspect of metal fatigue. During these later tests, the Apollo fuselage underwent 38,000 pressure reversals, equivalent to at least 60,000 hours or more than twenty years of airline flying, a striking enough testimony to the soundness of the aircraft's structural design.

The prototype Apollo, bearing RAF roundels and the serial number VX220, was ready for engine runs in March 1949; after the usual taxi-ing trials and high-speed ground runs, the aircraft made its first flight on 10 April, 1949. From the first there were problems; first and foremost, the Mamba engines were still in an undeveloped state, and it soon became apparent that successful running on the test-bed was no guarantee that the engine would perform equally well in the air. In order to avoid excessive jet-pipe temperatures, the output of the Apollo's engines had to be limited to 800 shp; in addition, the Mamba's compressor suffered from a tendency to stall. As a result, much of the Apollo's early test flying was devoted almost exclusively to engine development, but in spite of intense effort, these, and other engine problems, were never to be overcome in time to save the reputation of the aircraft. As it transpired, the Apollo's Mamba engines only achieved their promised rating of 1,000 shp for a short period towards the end of the flight-test programme before they had to be once again de-rated to 970 shp following a compressor-blade failure. Calculations had shown that, had the developed engines giving 1,270 shp ever become available, the economical cruising speed of the Apollo would have been 280 mph and the range 1,260 statute miles, as against the comparable figures of 270 mph and 1,130 statute miles with the 1,000 shp engines. On the other hand, the take-off power from the more powerful engines would have led to a considerable increase in the one-engine-out safety speed, and there would have been a slight loss of longitudinal stability. This factor arose because the length of the Mamba engine meant that the propellers were well ahead of the aircraft's centre of gravity, resulting in some degree of de-stabilization, an effect that would be aggravated by an increase in power.

Apart from the difficulties experienced with the engine, the aircraft itself presented problems. Due mainly, perhaps, to the rather short fuselage with its limited lever arm, there was some instability, both longitudinally and in azimuth, and there were deficiencies in the amount of elevator control; on the other hand, the pedal forces for the rudder were too high. These troubles were partly overcome by an increase in the span of the tailplane, a reduction in the chord of the rudder and an increase in the fin area,

In the early months of 1950, the Apollo appeared with an enlarged fin and civil registration.

alterations which were incorporated in the early months of 1950 after about a hundred hours of test flying had been completed. Another modification involved replacing the three-blade propellers on the inboard engines with four-blade units in order to cure a periodic vibration noticeable in the cabin; later, all the engines were fitted with four-blade propellers. Following these modifications, the Apollo, now registered as a civil aircraft with the marks G-AIYN, was granted a limited-category certificate of airworthiness on 30 October, 1950, which allowed it to carry non-fare-paying passengers. By now, the Mamba engines were permitted to operate at 920 shp for take-off, and the authorized all-up weight was 45,000 lb.

On 12 March, 1951, the Apollo flew to Paris, this being the first of a proposed series of proving flights called for in the contract with the Ministry of Supply. The flight was made from Baginton direct to Orly Airport at a cruising altitude of 11,500 ft; the elapsed time was 86 min, a saving of some 60 min on the current BEA Birmingham–Paris schedule.

The Apollo drawn up in front of the control tower at Farnborough aerodrome.

The return journey to Baginton, flown at 12,000 ft, was made in 78 min. Plans for further proving flights were deferred pending the completion of the test programme and the granting of a full certificate of airworthiness; in the event, they never took place. In July 1951, uprated Mk.504 engines were installed, these having an authorized take-off power of 1,000 shp, but towards the end of the same year the failure of an engine compressor put a stop to development flying until the spring of 1952, when new engines with modified compressor blades were fitted. Initially, these new engines were rated at only 970 shp for take-off.

An interior view of the Apollo, looking aft.

During 1950 an energetic sales campaign was initiated directed mainly at European airlines, and a number of individual route studies were undertaken for potential customers. These were mostly based on an aircraft first cost of £200,000, an annual utilization of 3,000 hr with depreciation spread over eight years. Using these and other assumptions, the direct operating cost, per aircraft nautical mile, was calculated as £96-16s for a stage length of 260 nautical miles. Unfortunately, no immediate sales were forthcoming and, as the test programme revealed the various shortcomings of the aircraft and its engines, the sales campaign lost much of its drive; by 1952 it was becoming abundantly clear that there was no commercial future for the Apollo and in June a decision was taken to discontinue the development of the type. At this time the second aircraft was still incomplete, but work was continued and it eventually made its first flight on 12 December, 1952, bearing the RAF serial number VX224. After two further flights in

The Apollo G-AIYN in a new livery and with four-blade propellers on the inboard engines; later, all four engines were so equipped.

December this aircraft was returned to the shops for fitting out, and it finally flew in its finished state in September 1953.

Both the Apollo aircraft had been paid for by the Ministry of Supply and, with the end of the development programme, they were both handed over to the Ministry and delivered to the Aeroplane and Armament Experimental Establishment at Boscombe Down. The first aircraft, which had by now reverted to VX220, was delivered on 24 September, 1952, after it had flown a total of about 300 hr, while VX224, which never carried its civil registration G-AMCH, was handed over on 15 October, 1953. At Boscombe Down, VX220 was employed as a test vehicle for the Decca Navigator system, and these trials continued until April 1953 when, after a total of some 400 landings, an undercarriage failure occurred. Undercarriage modifications were incorporated in VX224, but the prototype itself was not repaired and, in December 1954, it was dismantled and returned to Armstrong Whitworth where, as recounted earlier, it was used for further research into metal fatigue. Meanwhile, VX224 was delivered to Boscombe Down in October 1953 for tests and general handling trials, at the conclusion of which it was passed to the Empire Test Pilots' School at Farnborough aerodrome. It cannot be said that they received it with enthusiasm; the engines continued to give trouble and, during the nine months that VX224 was with the ETPS, from March 1954 until the following December, the aircraft flew a total of less than 20 hr. The last flight of VX224 took place on 14 December, 1954, after which it was handed over to the structural test department of the Royal Aircraft Establishment at Farnborough, who used the fuselage for another series of water-tank pressurization tests.

The question inevitably arises: would the Apollo, given efficient engines, have been able to compete successfully with the Viscount? The Apollo, like its rival, was too small to start with and would have had to be stretched, and a longer fuselage might well have helped to cure any residual control and stability problems. On the other hand, the Viscount had a head start,

The Apollo G-AIYN was handed over to the Ministry of Supply in September 1952 and reverted to the Service number VX220.

and it is difficult to avoid the suspicion that Armstrong Whitworth's preoccupation with lucrative military sub-contract work might well have diverted from the Apollo the drive and initiative which would have been essential to make it into a technical and commercial success.

A.W.55 Apollo

Dimensions: Span 92 ft (28·04 m); length 71 ft 6 in (21·79 m); height 26 ft (7·92 m); wing area 986 sq ft (91·6 sq m).

A.W.55 Apollo	
	Four 1,010 shp Mamba Mk.504
Max weight:	45,000 lb (20,412 kg)
Empty weight:	30,800 lb (13,971 kg)
Payload:	7,500 lb (3,402 kg)
Max speed:	330 mph (531 km/hr)
Cruising speed:	276 mph (444 km/hr)
Landing speed:	89 mph (143 km/hr)
Rate of climb at sea level:	1,500 ft/min (7·62 m/sec)
Service ceiling:	28,000 ft (8,534 m)
Fuel capacity:	970 Imp gal (4,410 lt)
Range:	940 miles (1,513 km)

The Argosy Again

Armstrong Whitworth's final venture into the civil aircraft field, and the last aircraft to carry the firm's name, was the Argosy freighter which emerged from the Bitteswell factory in 1958. During the somewhat protracted gestation period of this aircraft, the prospects for the British aircraft industry had altered dramatically as a result of a Government White Paper in 1957; this had the effect of switching the emphasis from manned aircraft to rockets and guided missiles. No longer, it seemed, were the aircraft manufacturers able to look forward to profitable long-run orders for the RAF or the Royal Navy, and it became clear that, in order to survive at all, the industry must look to a wider market for its products. It is, nevertheless, true that the Argosy was first considered as a military project. In 1955 the Air Ministry issued specification OR323 for a medium-range freight-carrying aircraft capable of lifting a load of up to 25,000 lb and having a range of 2,000 miles with a payload of 10,000 lb. It was a sign of the times that the specification laid emphasis on the need for the aircraft to meet the requirements of civil operators.

Late in 1955 Armstrong Whitworth set up a team to work on this project, and they came up with a design known as the A.W.66. This was a high-wing monoplane incorporating a truncated fuselage with a rear ramp and doors suitable for both ground loading and for the air-dropping of supplies. Power was to have been supplied by two 3,000 hp propeller-turbines, and the all-up weight would have been about 65,000 lb. In this design the tail surfaces were carried on two closely-spaced booms growing out of the sides of the fuselage. While studying the project Armstrong

The first A.W.650 Argosy takes-off for its maiden flight from Bitteswell aerodrome on 8 January, 1959.

A model of the A.W.66 project, representing the company's early thoughts on the layout for a freighter aircraft.

Whitworth undertook an extensive survey of both the civil and military potential markets. These studies indicated that the proposed RAF aeroplane was of a size and character that would be likely to interest many operators; on the other hand, it was equally obvious that there would need to be important differences between the military and the civil version. For civil operation, for instance, it would be essential to ensure the possibility of a quick turn-round, while there would certainly be no requirement for making air drops, an essential military need. The quick-loading requirement for civil operation was seen to call for full-section doors at both ends of the fuselage, necessitating a considerable measure of revision to the A.W.66 layout; there thus emerged another version of the aircraft to meet this civil need, and this was designated A.W.65. At the same time, during 1956, it was becoming clear that a shortage of money was likely to result in the abandonment of the OR323 project, and this brought about a reversal of the previous position; the emphasis was now on a civil freighter with military applications.

By September 1956 the prospects of a military order had, in fact, evaporated, and a decision was taken by Armstrong Whitworth to go ahead with the civil aircraft as a purely private venture. This time there were to be no half measures: plans were formulated for a batch of ten aircraft, with two additional test airframes, to be laid down without waiting for prototype trials. The new design, now designated A.W.650, differed in many respects from the original A.W.66 layout; four Rolls-Royce Dart propeller-turbines replaced the two engines previously specified, and two widely-spaced booms gave ample clearance for the sideways-opening doors which were located at both ends of the truncated, pressurized fuselage. This provided a completely unobstructed cargo space measuring 47 ft long and 10 ft wide at floor level, with a sill height only 4 ft off the ground to correspond to the height of the normal truck-bed level. The flight deck was situated high up in the nose above the freight compartment. At first the A.W.650 project was given the name Freightliner but, in July 1958, this was changed to Argosy.

Considerable design and development time was saved by the fortuitous fact that the design parameters of the Argosy's wing were found to be almost exactly the same as those of the existing Avro Shackleton. This basic wing design was therefore adopted for the new aircraft with such modifications as were necessary to allow for the different engine spacing, the mounting of the tail booms, the incorporation of thermal de-icing in the leading edge, and the fitting of large double-slotted flaps. The nosewheel undercarriage of the Argosy consisted of three elements, each of which, with its twin wheels, retracted backwards, the main legs being accommodated in the tail booms behind the engines and the nosewheel occupying a bulge under the fuselage. The engines fitted to the first batch of aircraft were Rolls-Royce Dart 526s and these, together with the engine mounts, were in all essentials the same as those used on the Vickers Viscount. The engines drove Rotol constant-speed fully-feathering reverse-pitch propellers. Provision was made in the design for the carriage of passengers instead of, or as well as, freight; the all-passenger version provided seats for 83 passengers arranged six-abreast at 32-inch pitch. With only 36 passengers in six rows of seats, there remained 188 sq ft of cargo space, the two sections being divided by a removable bulkhead. By 1958, when the

The Argosy mock-up in the Bitteswell factory.

Left, portions of the Argosy freight hold floor under construction; *right*, a section of the fuselage built for structural tests.

first aircraft was nearing completion, the designed all-up weight was quoted as 82,000 lb with a maximum payload of 28,000 lb.

During the design stage the Argosy was the subject of a very comprehensive test programme. Although the aircraft had to be tailored primarily for the quick handling and the carriage of bulky cargo in and out of short runways, some aerodynamic refinement was desirable, particularly in view of the estimate that a saving of one per cent in the profile drag could result in a saving to the operator of some £300 per year at 1958 values. To achieve the best possible aerodynamic shape within the limits set by other design considerations, many wind-tunnel experiments were made. Initially, the original 1928 low-speed wind-tunnel at Whitley was used; this venerable device, with its 5 ft by 4 ft throat, was able to accommodate a 1/13th-scale model of the Argosy and was quite adequate for a preliminary evaluation. Because the aircraft was a purely private venture, it was not possible to obtain time in the low-speed tunnels at Farnborough, but use was made of the tunnel operated by the Avro company at Woodford, which was large enough to hold a 1/10th-scale half-model of the aircraft. Still other tests were made with a 1/30th-scale model in the compressed-air tunnel at the National Physical Laboratory, in the tunnel belonging to Armstrong Siddeley Motors at Anstey, near Coventry, and in the small high-speed Armstrong Whitworth tunnel at Whitley. One of the more elaborate wind-tunnel models of the Argosy contained two electric motors for the purpose of driving the four small propellers, through bevel gears, at

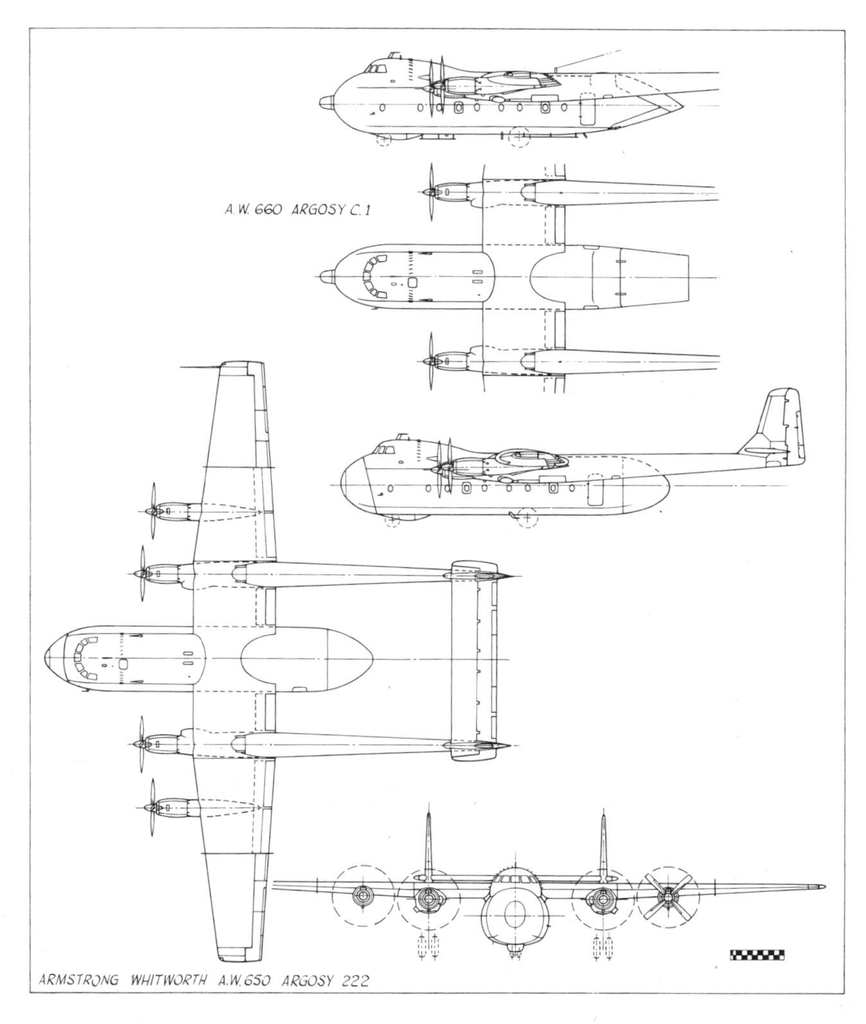

about 12,000 rpm. Altogether, some 2,320 wind-tunnel tests, occupying more than 1,370 hr of running time, were completed by December 1958.

As the design work progressed, a great deal of experimental testing was undertaken at Baginton on the various aircraft systems assembled as ground rigs within the factory. The largest of these was the fuel-system rig, which comprised a complete set of port wing tanks in a mock-up wing supported by a sling and two jacks to enable various aircraft attitudes to be simulated. Another rig for testing the hydraulic system was divided into three sections which dealt respectively with the main undercarriage, the nosewheel and the flaps; power for this rig was supplied by three standard aircraft pumps. Similarly, full-scale electrical test rigs, using actual aircraft

The first Argosy fuselage being transferred to the assembly shop in May 1958.

wiring and components, were used to evaluate the aircraft's three power systems, which operated at 28 volts, DC; 115 volts, AC; and 208 volts, AC. In addition, much useful experimental work was accomplished on a rig of the air-conditioning system, which comprised two cabin superchargers driven by a variable-speed DC electric motor. These rigs played an invaluable part in the design and development of the Argosy; not only did they enable the design staff to see how their theoretical ideas worked out in practice, but they allowed the engineers to become familiar with the systems in the most effective manner. Above all, a study of the rigs enabled many faults to be rectified cheaply and safely before the first aircraft left the ground.

As already mentioned, two complete Argosy airframes were built for

The first Argosy being assembled at Bitteswell.

the structural test programme; this was to enable both static strength tests and fatigue-life trials to be conducted simultaneously and completed by mid-1960, the target date for obtaining a certificate of airworthiness. In order to undertake this programme, more comprehensive than anything attempted previously by Armstrong Whitworth, a new structural-test laboratory was built at Whitley, the equipment of which included two new water-tanks, each with a capacity of 150,000 gal and capable of accommodating an Argosy fuselage. Other appropriate test equipment was provided for the wing, the tail-boom assembly, the tail unit and the undercarriage, as well as numerous other smaller sub-assemblies and components. These piecemeal tests culminated in proof-load tests and cyclic-pressure tests on the fuselage and on a complete aircraft in the water-tank. By May 1959, when the Argosy obtained a restricted certificate of airworthiness, the fatigue tests had covered all the critical loading cases and the aircraft in the water-tank had completed trials equivalent to 5,000 hr of airline flying.

The Argosy fuselage being put into the water tank for pressurization tests at Bitteswell aerodrome.

The task of designing and manufacturing the Argosy was, to some extent, shared among other member companies of the Hawker Siddeley Group. As already noted, the wing of the aircraft was derived from that of the Shackleton and it was, therefore, natural that the Avro company should undertake the design and construction of this component. The design of the tail surfaces, the wingtips and the outer engine nacelles was tackled by the

During pressurization tests the water was drained off periodically so that the fuselage could be inspected for cracks.

Gloster company, although the actual manufacture of these parts was done by Armstrong Whitworth, who also made the fuselage and the tail booms; the undercarriage was designed and constructed, outside the Group, by Dowty Equipment, Ltd. Work on the first aircraft began in 1957, with final assembly taking place at Bitteswell aerodrome. The first aircraft, G-AOZZ, was rolled out for engine runs on 21 December, 1958, and the first flight, with Eric Franklin at the controls, took place eight days behind schedule, on 8 January, 1959. The second aircraft, G-APRL, followed it into the air on 16 March and four more were flown before the end of the year, with the fifth aircraft emerging exactly on time. The first two aircraft, joined later by the third, G-APRM, were used for test and development flying and for performance measurement, the object being to obtain a certificate of airworthiness by the spring of 1960. All three aircraft were extensively instrumented and each one was allotted a definite rôle in the programme, the first being used mainly for general handling trials, the determination of the centre of gravity position and the establishment of the all-up weight at 82,000 lb (this was eventually stepped up to 88,000 lb). The testing of the radio and auto-pilot installation was also the task of this aircraft. The second aircraft was scheduled for engine and propeller-vibration trials and the testing of the engineering systems and, eventually, tropical trials. These took place in September 1959 at Khartoum and Nairobi, where, incidentally, the summer was the coldest and wettest experienced in Africa for half a century. The third machine was instrumented for performance measurement, and also for evaluating airframe loads during flight.

In the six months following the Argosy's first flight, the four aircraft then flying had logged a total of some 350 hr of flying time. The only significant problem that arose during the test programme was the occurrence of a low-frequency vibration in the tailplane, accompanied by a lateral vibration in the rear fuselage. This was found to be due to a breakaway in the airflow over the top of the fuselage caused mainly by the relatively steep slope downwards behind the flight deck. Investigation showed that this airflow was extremely sensitive to excrescences on the forward part of the fuselage, and that the correct positioning of the radio aerials, and even of the windscreen wiper, was critical. The matter was aggravated because the truncated fuselage did not have the damping effect normally provided by the tailplane, and also because the smoothly flowing air from the underside of the fuselage swept upwards to meet the turbulent air from the top and deflected it up towards the tailplane. The eventual cure was the fitting of a row of vortex generators on the top of the flight-deck blister, together with a breaker strip on the underside of the fuselage to deflect the upward flow of air. All the airworthiness tests and formalities were completed by September 1960, and both British and United States certificates of airworthiness were granted in December of that year. As finally certificated, the Argosy Series 100 had an all-up weight of 88,000 lb, a payload of 28,000 lb and a range in still air, with maximum payload and no reserves, of 750 miles.

In August 1960 the Argosy was flown by a British European Airways

An impression of the Argosy flight deck as built into the mock-up.

The Argosy Series 100, G-AOZZ, on test before delivery to BEA in December 1961.

pilot who found it easy and pleasant to handle with light and responsive controls. He was particularly impressed by the spaciousness of the flight deck, the arrangement of which had been the subject of consultation with the technical committee of the British Air Line Pilots' Association. In asymmetric flight, with the critical No.4 engine shut down, the propeller feathered, and with the flaps at take-off position, there was still plenty of rudder control in hand at 90 mph, at which speed the stall-warning stick-shaker came into operation. This pilot found the noise level in the flight deck to be rather excessive and, due to the unusually high position

Although shown in the livery of Riddle Airlines at the 1959 Farnborough Air Show, G-APRN was, in fact, destined for BEA.

occupied by the crew, his first landing was not as smooth as he would have wished. Landing the Argosy from the elevated position above the cargo hold was evidently something that required getting used to: it was not this pilot, but another, who is said to have described the experience as being like landing a cottage from the bedroom window. An American test pilot who flew the Argosy also found it presented no problems, having excellent flight characteristics with a gentle nose drop at the stall preceded by a mild aileron snatch. With the flaps in the landing position and the undercarriage down, the aircraft stalled level, but in the clean condition there was a tendency for either wing to drop; there was also a mild pre-stall buffet.

The Argosy G-APRN, now in the colours of BEA, was delivered to that airline in November 1961.

The Argosy's first public appearance was at the Paris Air Show in June 1959, when G-APRN was put on display at Le Bourget; this was followed by another public showing at the SBAC Exhibition at Farnborough in the following September when both G-APRN and G-APVH were exhibited. Shortly afterwards, G-APRN set out on its first two overseas sales and demonstration tours during which it visited Copenhagen, Stockholm and Oslo between 6 and 10 October, followed by visits to Paris, Zürich and Rotterdam between 14 and 17 October, 1959. For these demonstrations the aircraft was arranged as a combined passenger and freight carrier, and it was flown on the tours with four tons of freight, including a spare Dart engine, and 24 passenger seats in the rear cabin. At this time the price of the Argosy was being quoted as £460,000.

At the Paris Air Show in 1959, the Argosy had appeared in the livery of the first customer, Riddle Airlines of Miami, who signed an order for four aircraft in February 1959. Riddle Airlines was, at that time, the fifth largest all-freight operator in the United States, with a fleet of some 32 aircraft. The Argosy was chosen by them for use in connection with an operation known as 'Logair'; this involved the running of a regular service

The first customer for the Argosy was Riddle Airlines Inc, of Miami, which took delivery of N6507R in August 1961.

to carry bulky freight for the US Logistic Command between USAF bases within the United States. The first aircraft to be delivered to Riddle Airlines was registered N6501R. It was fitted with extra fuel tanks and was flown to Miami, leaving Prestwick on 12 December, 1960. Meanwhile, the original order had been increased to a total of seven aircraft, all of which were delivered by August 1961. In operation on the Logair routes, the Argosy fleet was scheduled to fly more than 12,000 miles each day with a utilization of up to 13 hr a day for each aircraft. It had been hoped that Riddle Airlines would also use their Argosies on other US domestic routes, so that the advantages of the aircraft could become apparent to their competitors, a number of whom were, at that time, discussing possible deals with Armstrong Whitworth: in the end the Argosies were confined to the Logair routes and no new American customers were obtained. Unfortunately, the Logair contract with Riddle Airlines came to an end in June 1962, and the Argosies were returned to Armstrong Whitworth. Subsequently two other operators, Capitol Airlines, Inc, and Zantop Air Transport, were jointly granted a new Logair contract; the former airline took over five of the ex-Riddle Argosies and the latter chartered the remaining two from Calhoun Equipment and Servicing, Ltd, who had meantime become the owners of the aircraft. Eventually, all seven of the Argosies in America became the property of Calhoun Equipment who, in turn, leased them to Zantop Air Transport which, by now, was the sole Logair contractor. To confuse the picture still further, Calhoun Equipment changed its name, in 1968, to Universal Airlines. While operating with Zantop Air Transport, one of the Argosies, then registered as N601Z, was wrecked in the course of making a forced landing on a public highway.

Towards the end of the 1960s, Universal Airlines withdrew its Argosies from the Logair operation, and the aircraft were cocooned until, in 1970, four of them were sold and returned to Great Britain where the wing spars of three of them, having reached the limit of their fatigue life, were renewed. The new owner was Sagittair Ltd, a freight carrier which, in 1970, started a scheduled service linking Heathrow Airport with the East Midlands Airport and the industrial centre of Lille in France.

At the end of the 1960s, BEA decided to enter the air freight business in earnest and, in April 1961, placed an order for the three remaining Series 100 Argosies. The first of these, G-APRN, was delivered to the corporation on 6 November, 1961, with the other two, G-APRM and G-AOZZ, following on 29 November and 21 December respectively; regular services started in December 1961 with two aircraft on the routes and one based at Stansted Airport for crew training. The pilots of BEA found the Argosy very easy to fly, and the training programme, which occupied nine hours flying, was, therefore, concerned mainly with emergency procedures. Within two months of starting operations, the BEA Argosies were flying four times a week to Milan, twice a week to Paris and Jersey, five times a week to Manchester, three times a week to Glasgow and six times a week to Copenhagen, Düsseldorf and Frankfurt. During this introductory period there were the inevitable teething troubles, concerned principally with the hydraulic and electrical systems; nevertheless, working on a round-the-clock basis, the aircraft succeeded in attaining an impressive rate of

A telling publicity picture illustrating the ease with which the Argosy could be loaded and unloaded.

utilization which, in the end, exceeded that of any other aircraft in the BEA fleet. From an operating point of view, BEA's main problems arose from the Argosy's lack of speed and its restricted climb performance. The comparatively low speed, besides having an adverse effect on the operating costs, resulted in the aircraft being unduly affected by headwinds, and this made realistic scheduling difficult. The poor climb performance was particularly apparent on the Milan–London sector, where a combination of hot weather and downdraughts from the mountains could make it difficult and, indeed, sometimes impossible for the Argosies to attain the safety height of 16,000 ft for crossing the Alps.

Another aspect of loading the Argosy. The protective lining of the cabin was a modification introduced for BEA. (*Rolls-Royce Ltd*)

When first introduced by BEA, the Argosy was about the right size for the corporation's requirements, but in spite of this and the high utilization achieved BEA were unable to make a profit with the aircraft. As business built up the payload capacity of the Argosy became a limiting factor, and BEA started negotiations for the purchase of the improved version then being built at Bitteswell. This new venture, on which work had started in 1962, was known as the Argosy Series 200 and was intended to bring about an all-round improvement in the aircraft's commercial capability, the first requirement for which was the raising of the all-up weight. This necessitated redesigning the wing, the Shackleton structure having by now reached the limits of its development potential. The new wing emerged with the same aerodynamic geometry, but with a more modern type of fail-safe

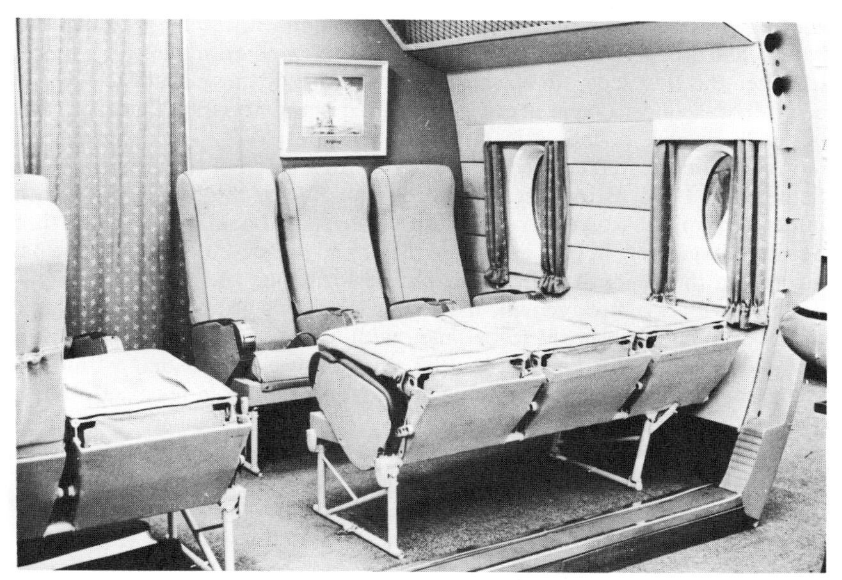

All the civil Argosies were normally employed as freighters, but this exhibition mock-up illustrates the type of passenger furnishing visualized by the designers.

structure employing a box spar; this produced a wing that was not only stronger, but was also some 400 lb lighter than the previous design. Another important feature of the Series 200 resulted from a modification to the doors which made it possible for the standard 9-ft wide freight pallet to be loaded straight into the hold without manoeuvring. A proposal to fit the Dart 10 engine of 3,060 hp was abandoned on the score of expense, but other changes included a revised main landing gear with larger brakes, bigger propellers measuring 12 ft in diameter, integral wing tanks in place of bag tanks, and a revised flight deck arranged for two-crew operation. While the first Series 200 was under construction, a decision was made to fit up-rated Dart 7 Mk.532/1 engines giving some 12 per cent more power, and with this alteration the designation of the type was changed to Series 220. As it finally emerged, the Argosy Series 220 had a gross weight of 93,000 lb, an increase of 5,000 over the Series 100 but with no increase in the empty weight.

The first Series 220, G-ASKZ, made its maiden flight on 11 March, 1964, with Eric Franklin at the controls and, to the surprise of all concerned, it exhibited stalling and low-speed problems: this was disappointing because there had been no change in the aerodynamic configuration of the aircraft as compared with the Series 100, which had proved quite satisfactory in these respects. Eventually, the alteration in the stall characteristics was traced to the different flexing pattern of the new wing structure, and a cure was effected by fitting leading-edge wedges inboard of the inner engines and a large wing fence extending around both the leading and trailing edges to cure the aileron snatch. In addition, some elevator buffet, which had occurred on the early test flights, was eliminated by linking together the two separate elevators. As a result of these changes, the new aircraft was said to have acquired handling characteristics that were even better than those of the Series 100.

As before, the makers decided to lay down a batch of ten aircraft and, in September 1964, BEA placed an order for five of the Series 220 on the understanding that Armstrong Whitworth took back the original three Series 100 aircraft in part exchange. BEA had decided to purchase the new aircraft in the belief that the improved performance and payload capacity, coupled with an improvement in the corporation's ground-handling facilities, would enable a profit to be made with a fleet of five aircraft, of which one would normally be on stand-by duty. It was hoped that within two years each aircraft would be achieving a utilization of at least 3,000 hrs a year with a 65 per cent load factor.

In September 1964, BEA signed a contract for five Series 220 Argosy aircraft. On the left Sir Arnold Hall, then vice-chairman and managing director of the Hawker Siddeley Group, with Anthony Milward (later Sir Anthony), chairman of BEA.

The first aircraft for BEA, G-ASXL (designated the Series 222 to indicate equipment to BEA standard) was delivered in January 1965; the fifth, and last, of the order, G-ASXP, reached the corporation in the middle of the following June. Apart from the superior performance, BEA pilots noticed that the aircraft was generally similar to the Series 100 in its main handling characteristics, with improvements in the stalling behaviour and in the effectiveness of the stall warning. The increase in power had not adversely affected the asymmetric handling of the aircraft, and the climb on three engines was better. In addition, the reduction of the maximum flap angle (from 40 deg to 34 deg) had improved the approach behaviour. The

The first Argosy Series 222, the 220 as modified to BEA requirements, made its maiden flight on 17 December, 1964.

introduction of the new aircraft into BEA service was followed by an increase in the frequency of some of the existing cargo services and with the opening up of new routes to Stockholm, Amsterdam and Brussels. With the improved carrying capacity now available backed by a better ground organization, it was hoped that a profitable Argosy operation would, at last, be possible; but it was not to be. The Argosies continued to show a loss in the corporation's books right up to the time that they were finally withdrawn from service, with the last flight taking place on 30 April, 1970, when G-ASXM flew a return service to Jersey. In the same month BEA announced that the four surviving Argosy aircraft had been sold to Midwest Airlines, a subsidiary of Transair Ltd, of Winnipeg, in Canada, who planned to use them to fly heavy equipment to the oil fields in the Arctic islands of Canada's Northwest Territories. In BEA, the Argosies were replaced by some of the corporation's Vickers Vanguards converted for freight operation; these aircraft were faster and cost less to operate, but they took longer to load and unload and were not able to accommodate some of the more bulky items, such as Rolls-Royce cars and heavy machinery which had been routine consignments in the previous aircraft.

One of four Argosy Series 222 aircraft purchased by Transair Ltd, of Winnipeg, from BEA. The aircraft CF-TAZ takes-off from Resolute Bay in the Canadian Northwest Territories.

In 1971 the Argosy G-APRN was acquired by Sagittair Ltd, a British freight operator.

The three Argosy Series 100s had operated with BEA from the end of 1961 onwards without serious incident, but the Series 222s were not so fortunate. The second aircraft to be delivered, G-ASXL, was lost in an accident in Italy on 4 July, 1965. Flying in turbulent cloud, the aircraft was following the ILS beam into Milan airport but, due to the wrong identification of a navigation beacon, it flew into the ground on a hill top some thirty miles distant from the airport. The aircraft was totally destroyed but the crew escaped unhurt. This aircraft was replaced in November 1966 by a new Argosy, G-ATTC, ordered from the makers (who by then had lost their identity and had become an integral part of Hawker Siddeley Aviation Ltd). On 4 December, 1967, another BEA Argosy, G-ASXP, was destroyed in an accident during a training flight at Stansted Airport. On this occasion the starboard outer engine was cut to simulate an engine failure just after take-off. Due, it is believed, to the propeller of this engine going into ground fine pitch, the aircraft became uncontrollable, cartwheeled on the starboard wing, crashed and caught fire. The crew escaped through a hole in the damaged fuselage; no replacement aircraft was ordered in this case. The final incident, which only narrowly escaped being a disaster, occurred over France on 17 February, 1968. While *en route* from Milan, the starboard outer engine of G-ATTC suffered a reduction-gear failure; the propeller came off and, in doing so, wrecked the adjacent No.3 engine. In addition, one of the flying propeller blades severely damaged the side of the fuselage. In spite of these daunting circumstances, the captain succeeded in making a safe landing at Le Bourget Airport, a feat of airmanship which earned him a certificate of commendation presented by the corporation.

While the original A.W.650 was being designed and built, several possible variants were considered by Armstrong Whitworth. Although the four-Dart layout was considered to be the best for a civil aircraft, it was recognized that there would be some economic advantages in a twin-engined version using two Rolls-Royce Tyne propeller-turbines. The possibility of a requirement for larger engines had been foreseen early on, and the tail booms of the Argosy had been spaced widely to allow for this contingency. This variant was known as the A.W.651. The layout of the basic aircraft also lent itself to changes in the design of the fuselage, and this led to the proposed A.W.670 short-haul freighter for which a completely new fuselage was designed to fit the standard A.W.650 airframe. With an interior width of 15 ft, the bigger fuselage could have accommodated six cars in two rows side by side, while above the freight compartment was another, narrower, cabin capable of carrying 30 passengers. The principle of fore-and-aft loading was retained but, as the aircraft was intended for short-haul operation only, the fuselage would not have been pressurized and the design of the doors was, consequently, simpler and lighter. Using this same fuselage outline, plans were formulated for the A.W.671, a passenger version known as the Airbus; this could have accommodated about 126 passengers, and calculations made in 1958 showed that this aircraft, with four Dart engines, would have been able to operate over a 200-mile stage at a direct operating cost of less than 2d per seat mile.

In 1969 the Argosy G-APRM was leased to Rolls-Royce Ltd for the transport of Olympus engines and components for the Concorde airliner between Great Britain and France.

None of these variants was ever built, but during 1957 and 1958 interest in a military version of the Argosy was revived and, as a result of discussions between the Air Ministry, the Ministry of Supply and Armstrong Whitworth, a specification was drawn up for a military freighter based on the Argosy Series 100: by accepting this aircraft as a starting point, a big saving in development costs was anticipated. In January 1959 a provisional order was placed for twenty aircraft for use by the RAF, and this was confirmed just before the SBAC Air Show at Farnborough in the following September; later, the order was increased to fifty-six aircraft.

The rear doors designed for the military Argosy C Mk.1 were fitted temporarily to the Argosy G-APRL for full-scale air tests.

Numerous modifications were necessary to meet the RAF's requirements: these included the capability of air-dropping a load of 14,000 lb and provision of a more robust floor suitable for vehicles with an axle load of 8,500 lb, a strengthened wing to allow for an increased all-up weight of 97,000 lb, and more fuel, bringing the total to 4,140 gal. The most important difference between the civil and the military version was that the sideways-opening doors at the rear end of the fuselage were replaced by hydraulically-operated doors hinging upwards and downwards, and capable of being opened in the air. At the same time, the rear portion of the fuselage was given more headroom so that a Saracen armoured car could be accommodated. As a result of these changes, the outline of the rear fuselage was altered and the total length was increased by some $5\frac{1}{2}$ ft. Another major alteration was the deletion of the nose doors, the space gained being used to accommodate catering equipment, a lavatory, a crew-entry hatch, and a prone position for the navigator. Also incorporated in the military Argosy was a large escape hatch in the roof of the cabin, a modification that had originally been built into the first Riddle Airlines aircraft in order to comply with the United States ditching regulations. In addition, the RAF's aircraft carried two inflatable dinghies, stowed in the wing roots, each capable of holding 26 people. The military version of the aircraft was known by the makers as the A.W.660, and by the RAF as the Argosy C Mk.1.

At one time the Argosy was tested as a bomber: for this purpose racks capable of carrying 1,000-lb bombs were fitted externally to the lower sides of the fuselage. A few production aircraft had provision made for these racks, but there is no record of them ever having been used in service. Another trial installation was an air-to-air refuelling probe, but trials disclosed that the difference between the speed of the Argosy and that of the standard RAF tanker was such as to make the operation impracticable. A scheme was also drawn up for using the Argosy itself as a tanker but, as far as is known, this idea was never tested. The Argosy C Mk.1 was fitted

The military Argosy C Mk.1 flew for the first time from Bitteswell on 4 March, 1961. Its number was XN814.

with the Dart R.Da.8 Mk.101 engine which developed 2,470 shp. With these engines the performance of the aircraft was not up to expectations, especially as regards the cruising altitude attainable in hot weather. As a result it was decided to re-equip the fleet with the Mk.102 version of the engine which, with its higher permissible cruising rpm, brought about an improvement of more than 2,000 ft in the cruising altitude in the worst conditions. For hydraulic and electric power on the ground, and for starting the engines, the C Mk.1 was fitted with a Rover 1S/60 gas-turbine auxiliary power unit situated in the port tail boom.

The interior of the Argosy could be adapted to a number of rôles. For paratroop dropping, hammock-type seats for 54 men could be fitted. Alternatively, airline-type seats for 65 passengers could be attached to existing tracks set in the floor. Stores to be air-dropped would normally be packed in containers carrying 2,000 lb, nine of which could be accommodated; another method was to use special platforms, two of which could be carried, each holding 12,000 lb of stores. When used as an ambulance, the aircraft could accommodate up to 48 stretcher cases. The flight deck was designed for two pilots, a navigator and an air engineer; equipment included a Smith's 10A autopilot and UHF, VHF and HF communication radio. For the navigator there was a sextant, Doppler (situated in the

The exit from the Argosy for parachute troops was through side doors in the rear of the fuselage.

starboard tail boom), Decca, Rebecca, ADF, VOR, ILS and weather radar with a scanner fitted in the prominent nose radome. The principal duty envisaged for the C Mk.1 was that of providing air support for ground forces by dropping paratroops and supplies, including light vehicles, guns and armoured scout cars. In order to ensure accurate air dropping the navigator occupied the prone position in the nose from where he gave steering directions to the pilot during the run up to the dropping zone; the navigator was also responsible for giving the green light to the paratroops and for releasing the drogue parachute which pulled the heavy stores out through the rear doors. In order to explore the effects of the new doors on the airflow at full scale, the second Argosy, G-APRL, was temporarily fitted with these doors and air tests were begun on 28 July, 1960; the tests proved quite satisfactory, with the doors both opened and closed, with a minimum of tail buffet up to speeds of 140 kt. By early 1961, after

Another view of the Argosy C Mk.1 XN814 with the rear doors open for dropping heavy loads by parachute.

conclusion of the tests, G-APRL had reverted to its normal condition. The first production Argosy C Mk.1, with the Service number XN814, made its first flight from Bitteswell aerodrome on 4 March, 1961, and all the fifty-six aircraft had been delivered by 1 April, 1964. The contract for the RAF aircraft had been negotiated on a fixed-price basis, and it is a melancholy fact that the deal resulted in a loss to the company, reputed to be in the neighbourhood of £5 million.

After the first batch of RAF instructors had completed a course with Armstrong Whitworth at Bitteswell, a conversion training unit was

The Rolls-Royce Dart propeller-turbines and the undercarriage of the Argosy C Mk.1.

RAF Argosy aircraft on parade at Benson aerodrome in Oxfordshire.

established by the RAF at Benson aerodrome; following this, No.114 Squadron became the first to be equipped with the Argosy, beginning operations with the new aircraft in February 1962. In the following June a second Argosy squadron, No.105, was re-formed at Benson with crews and aircraft hived off from No.114 Squadron: this new squadron then moved to Khormaksar, an aerodrome in the Aden Protectorate, as it was then. November 1962 saw the re-forming of No.267 Squadron, also at Benson, and its equipment with Argosies during the early months of 1963; later, in May, half the crews and aircraft of this squadron were detached to form the nucleus of another re-formed squadron, No.215, which moved to Changi aerodrome, Singapore, in August 1963. During this period the two squadrons at Benson were supplied with aircraft, as required, from a central pool which was maintained and administered by the station's engineering wing.

Towards the end of 1967, when the British commitment in the Middle and Far East began to be reduced, No.215 Squadron in Singapore was disbanded and its crews and aircraft returned to Benson to join Nos.114 and 267 Squadrons, the remainder of the aircraft and crews going to No.70 Squadron then stationed at Akrotiri in Cyprus. Meanwhile, No.105 Squadron had been moved from Aden to Muharraq, Bahrein; later, in February 1968, this squadron was disbanded and the men and machines integrated with Nos.114 and 267 Squadrons. Its place at Muharraq was taken by a detachment flight, formed, in rotation, from the two squadrons at Benson, its purpose being the maintenance of supplies from Bahrein to the Gulf stations of Sharjah, Masirah and Salalah, and to provide support for the British forces in the Gulf and, on occasions, for the Trucial Oman Scouts. The Argosy proved to be well suited to the work in this theatre; the stage lengths averaged 300 to 500 miles which meant that at all times the full payload capacity of the aircraft could be used.

Following the reduction in the number of Argosies required for support and transport duties, some of the aircraft from the disbanded No.105 Squadron were transferred, beginning in February 1968, to No.115 Squadron then stationed at RAF Watton; here they were modified for signals duties, mainly the calibration of radio aids, a task which eventually took them as far afield as Central Africa and Australia. Another result of the run-down of the Argosy squadrons was that the training aircraft attached to No.242 OCU at Thorney Island aerodrome were no longer required and, in April 1969, they were transferred to No.115 Squadron which, by then, had moved from Watton to RAF Cottesmore. The next squadron to go was No.267 which was disbanded in May 1970, with its crews and aircraft joining No.114 Squadron. Later in 1970, No.70 Squadron in Cyprus began to lose its Argosies as it re-equipped with the Lockheed Hercules; however, the Argosy was greatly preferred for carrying passengers, and two were retained at Akrotiri for short-range and VIP transport duties as well as for sea-search and rescue missions. By the middle of 1971 No.114 was the only Argosy squadron remaining in Air Support Command and this was itself disbanded on 8 October, 1971. As the squadrons were eliminated many of the Argosies were sent to RAF Kemble for storage pending a decision about their future use.

The military Argosy had extra headroom at the rear of the freight hold so that a Saracen armoured car could be carried. (*Ministry of Defence*)

During its decade of service with the RAF, the Argosy established for itself a reputation for versatility and reliability; its relatively simple systems and engineering, and the notable reliability of the Dart engine, made it easy to maintain. It also became popular with the aircrews and with passengers, especially those who jumped from it, who much preferred it for this purpose to the aircraft which took its place in Air Support Command. Few problems were encountered during the introductory phase of the Argosy, but in the winter of 1962–63 the fleet was grounded in Europe for a while because of the freezing up of the aileron and throttle controls. This was caused by defects in the sealing of the wing panels which allowed moisture to enter and freeze on the control linkages. A procedure for carrying out a descent with the throttles locked in the cruising position was devised, and the aircraft were then permitted to fly below the freezing level until the trouble was finally overcome by rendering the wing watertight in the appropriate places. Accidents were few: in March 1964 an Argosy on a training flight undershot the runway at Khormaksar and ditched in shallow water just off shore; damage was slight and the aircraft was shipped home and repaired by Armstrong Whitworth at Bitteswell. Another accident during a training flight, involving a three-engined landing, occurred at Benson in June 1970; this resulted in the writing off of the aircraft but without injury to the crew. More serious was a fatal accident in May 1968 when an Argosy of No.267 Squadron hit an obstruction and crashed during a low-level run along the runway at El Adem in Libya.

The uses to which the RAF Argosies were put were many and various: apart from some regular scheduled runs such as, for instance, a thrice-weekly service to Sardinia via stations in Germany, the Argosies of Air Transport Command regularly carried troops and their equipment to places ranging from the north of Norway to Cyprus and the Gulf. Also, in their rôle as passenger aircraft they were frequently used to carry members of the Imperial Defence College on official visits to India and the United States, as well as to countries in Western Europe. The potentialities of air support were well demonstrated when No.114 Squadron, with its Argosies, was called upon to support No.29 Fighter Squadron which had

A typical military load for an RAF Argosy.

Three Argosy aircraft of Transport Command, later to become Support Command, RAF. Reading from the front, XR142, XN856 and XN847. (*Ministry of Defence*)

been sent at short notice to N'dola in Zambia at the time of the Rhodesian crisis in December 1965. Other less urgent duties undertaken by the Argosy squadrons have included dropping the RAF free-fall parachute team, the *Falcons*, at air displays, and supporting the *Red Arrows* aerobatic team at similar events at home and overseas. Finally, routine training flights (during which a payload was invariably carried) regularly extended as far as the Bahamas, the Azores, West Africa, and Ascension Island in the South Atlantic.

The sales record of the Argosy to airlines was disappointing, the more so because, on many occasions, success seemed so close. The aircraft had been designed to the specific requirements of the major airlines but, by the time it was ready, the price had risen by some £200,000. The result was that, after some hesitation, the majority of the potential customers opted for the cheaper, if less satisfactory, alternative of adapting second-hand passenger aircraft for cargo work. Later, when the Argosy itself entered the second-hand category, signs were not lacking that the few surviving civil aircraft and, perhaps, some of the surplus military aircraft, would eventually find useful employment carrying the heavy cargoes for which they were designed.

A.W.650 and 660

Dimensions: Span 115 ft (35·05 m); length 86 ft 9 in (26·44 m); fuselage length (A.W.650) 60 ft 7 in (18·46 m); fuselage length (A.W.660) 64 ft 7 in (19·69 m); height 29 ft 3 in (8·92 m); wing area 1,458 sq ft (135·5 sq m).

	A.W.650 **Argosy Series 100** *Four 2,020 ehp Dart 526*	**A.W.650** **Argosy Series 220** *Four 2,250 ehp Dart 532*	**A.W.660** **Argosy C Mk.1** *Four 2,470 ehp Dart R.Da.8*
Max weight:	88,000 lb (39,916 kg)	93,000 lb (42,184 kg)	97,000 lb (43,999 kg)
Max overload weight:	—	—	105,000 lb (47,627 kg)
Empty weight:	46,000 lb (20,865 kg)	49,000 lb (22,226 kg)	56,000 lb (25,401 kg)
Payload:	28,000 lb (12,701 kg) or 89 passengers	31,000 lb (14,061 kg)	29,000 lb (13,154 kg)
Cruising speed:	280 mph (451 km/hr)	285 mph (459 km/hr)	253 mph (407 km/hr)
Service ceiling:	20,000 ft (6,096 m)	—	23,000 ft (7,010 m)
Fuel capacity:	3,300 Imp gal (15,000 lt)	3,400 Imp gal (15,456 lt)	4,140 Imp. gal (18,820 lt)
Max range, still air:	2,000 miles (3,219 km)	2,100 miles (3,380 km)	3,450 miles (5,552 km)

APPENDIX A

Projects

In common with other British aircraft manufacturers, Armstrong Whitworth of Coventry worked on a large number of design studies which were, in the end, never built; some of these were developed in considerable detail, while others were limited to a preliminary outline. The majority of these proposals were for military aircraft to meet Government specifications, but a number were intended for civil use. No complete list of these Armstrong Whitworth projects has survived, but a list of those known to have had A.W. type numbers is given below, together with details of certain other designs for which no A.W. numbers have been discovered.

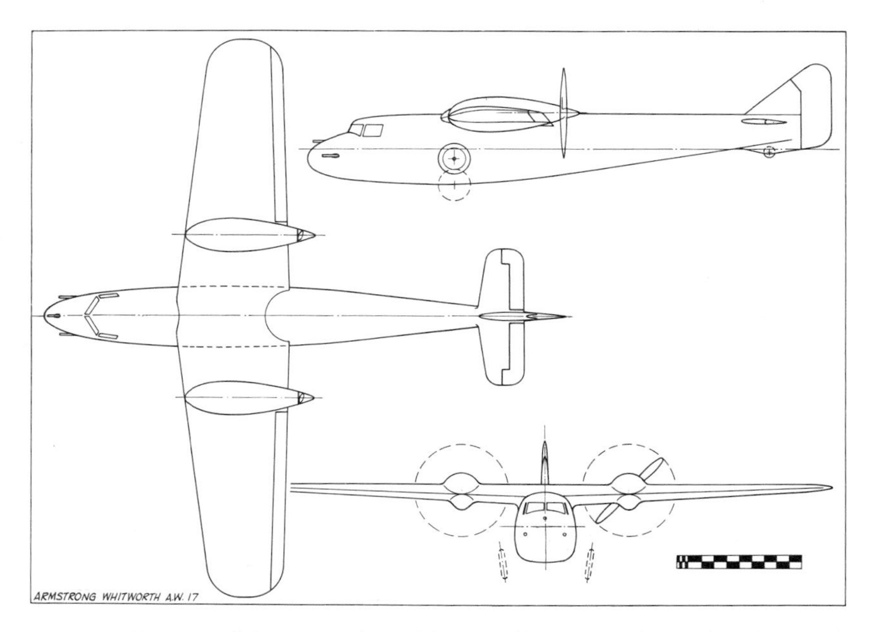

A.W.17 Single-seat fighter monoplane with two Rolls-Royce pusher engines. Span 46 ft (14·02 m); length 42 ft 6 in (12·95 m); height 8 ft 9 in (2·67 m); wing area 320 sq ft (29·73 sq m). Type number subsequently re-allocated to Aries biplane.

A.W.18 Heavy bomber monoplane with four Armstrong Siddeley Panther engines. Span 100 ft (30·48 m); length 77 ft 3 in (23·55 m); all-up weight 25,500 lb (11,567 kg).

A.W.20 Day bomber monoplane with two Rolls-Royce F.XI pusher engines. Span 50 ft (15·24 m); length 44 ft (13·41 m); wing area 375 sq ft (34·84 sq m); all-up weight 8,500 lb (3,856 kg).

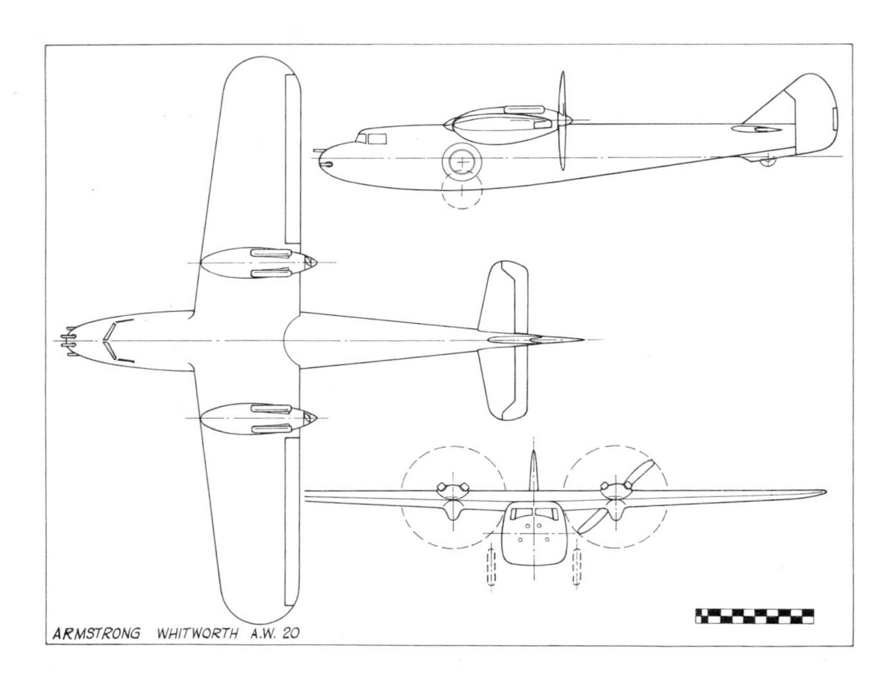
ARMSTRONG WHITWORTH A.W. 20

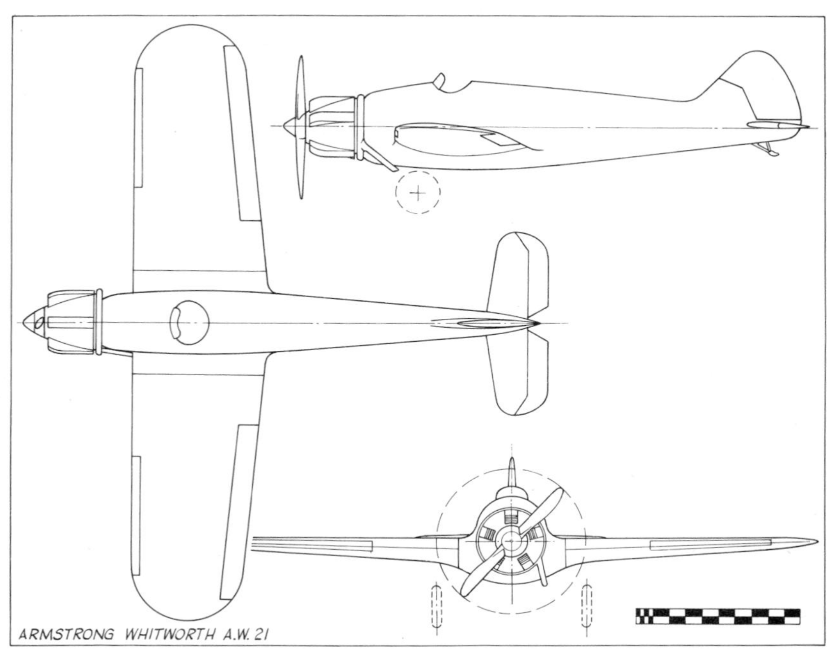
ARMSTRONG WHITWORTH A.W. 21

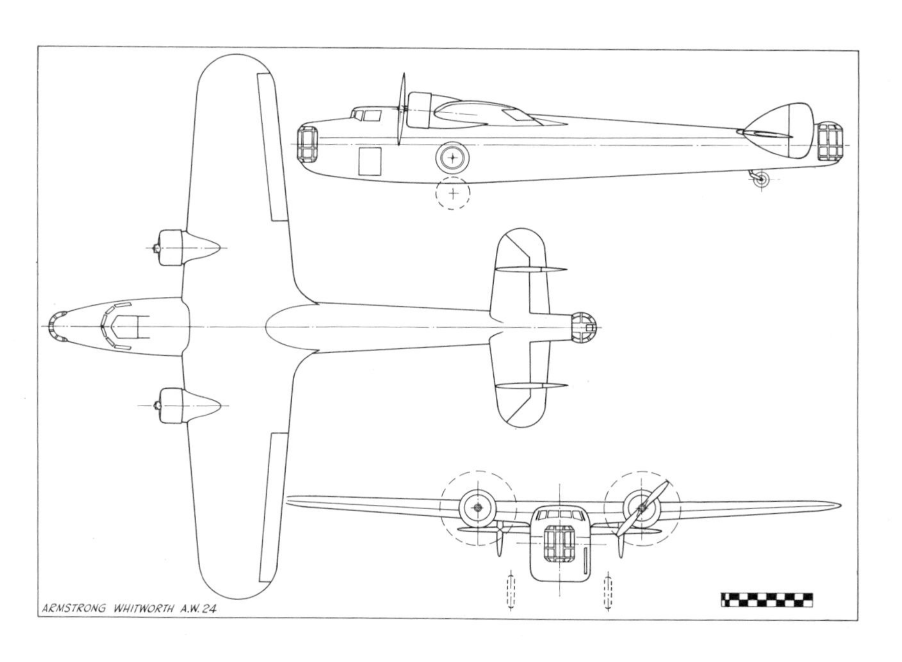
ARMSTRONG WHITWORTH A.W.24

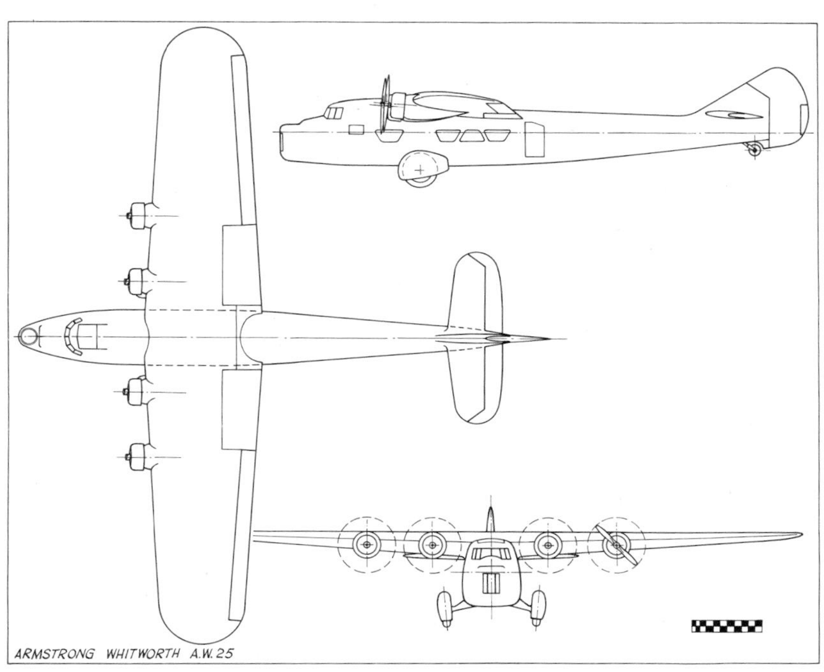
ARMSTRONG WHITWORTH A.W.25

A.W.21 Single-seat day and night fighter monoplane with corrugated wing skin and one Armstrong Siddeley Panther or Hyena engine. Span 37 ft 6 in (11·43 m); length (Hyena engine) 31 ft 5 in (9·58 m).

A.W.22 Fast-climbing monoplane with Armstrong Siddeley Tiger engine. Span 38 ft (11·58 m); all-up weight 3,500 lb (1,588 kg).

A.W.24 Day bomber monoplane with two Armstrong Siddeley Panther engines. Span 62 ft (18·90 m); length 60 ft (18·29 m); wing area 632 sq ft (58·72 sq m); all-up weight 10,660 lb (4,835 kg).

A.W.25 Bomber monoplane based on A.W.XV Atalanta with four Armstrong Siddeley Jaguar engines. Intended for Russia. Span 90 ft (27·43 m); length 75 ft (22·86 m); wing area 1,285 sq ft (119·38 sq m); all-up weight 25,000 lb (11,340 kg). Maximum speed 178 mph (287 km/hr); range 1,240 miles (1,996 km).

A.W.26 Bomber similar to A.W.25 but with Armstrong Siddeley Panther engines and increased performance. Alternative proposal for Russia.

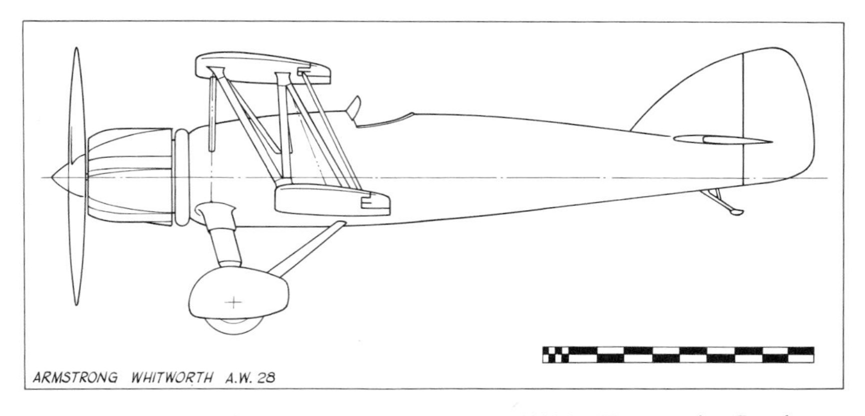
ARMSTRONG WHITWORTH A.W. 28

A.W.28 Single-seat fighter biplane with Armstrong Siddeley Hyena engine. Based on an enlarged A.W.XVI. Length 27 ft 11 in (8·51 m).

A.W.30 Twin-engined bomber monoplane based on A.W.23 Bomber Transport but with more slender fuselage. All-up weight 18,650 lb (8,460 kg). For submission to Belgium and Czechoslovakia.

A.W.31 Single-seat fighter biplane with Armstrong Siddeley Tiger engine. Similar to A.W.XVI but with equal-span wings.

A.W.32 Braced monoplane two-seater with Armstrong Siddeley Tiger engine. Span 45 ft (13·72 m); length 36 ft (10·97 m); wing area 295 sq ft (27·41 sq m); all-up weight 6,000 lb (2,722 kg).

A.W.33 Two-seat fighter monoplane with two Armstrong Siddeley Double Genet Major engines. Designed to specification F.22/33 for a twin-engined turret fighter. Span 48 ft (14·63 m.); length 39 ft (11·89 m); wing area 335 sq ft (31·12 sq m); all-up weight 6,500 lb (2,948 kg). Maximum speed at 13,000 ft (3,962 m) 255 mph (410 km/hr).

A.W.34 Two-seat fighter monoplane with two Armstrong Siddeley Terrier engines designed to specification F.5/33 for a two-seat turret fighter. Similar to A.W.33. Span 47 ft (14·33 m); wing area 350 sq ft (32·52 sq m).

A.W.36 Army co-operation biplane with Armstrong Siddeley Tiger or Panther engine. Based on Atlas II with new body fairing and wheel spats.

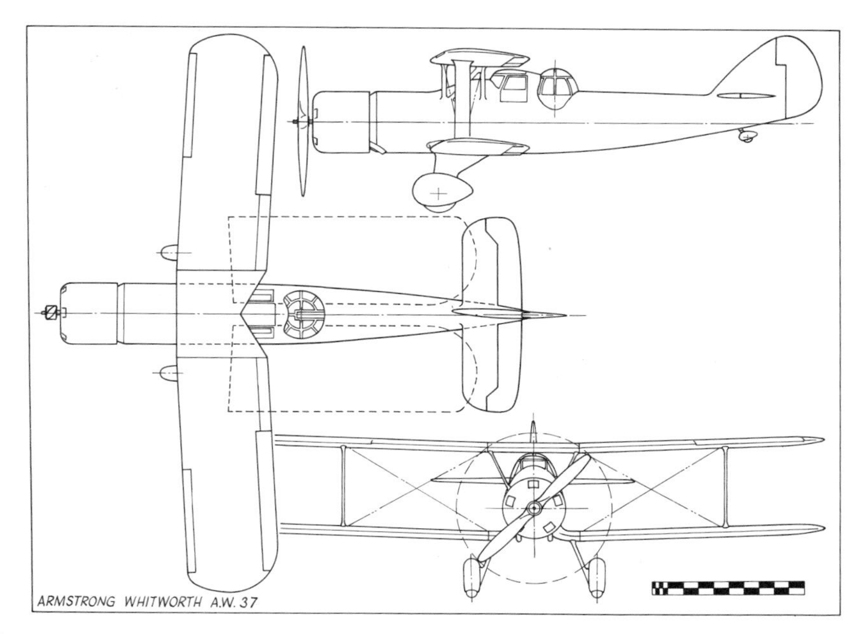

A.W.37 Two-seat general-purpose biplane with Armstrong Siddeley Panther or Hyena engine; folding wings. Span 39 ft (11·89 m); length 34 ft 10 in (10·62 m); wing area 437 sq ft (40·60 sq m).

A.W.40 Monoplane mail carrier with two Armstrong Siddeley Serval engines. Based on A.W.34. Intended for Canada.

A.W.43 Monoplane airliner with four engines to British Airways specification. Span 90 ft (27·43 m); length 72 ft (21·95 m); wing area 966 sq ft (89·75 sq m).

A.W.44 Bomber; modification of A.W.41 Albemarle with four Bristol Hercules engines. Span 84 ft 6 in (25·75 m).

A.W.45 Medium bomber monoplane with two Rolls-Royce Merlin engines.

A.W.48 Heavy bomber monoplane with four engines, designed to specification B.1/39. Armed with two turrets each with four 20-mm cannon. All-up weight 50,000 lb (22,680 kg). Speed 280 mph (451 km/hr); bomb load 10,000 lb (4,536 kg); range 2,500 miles (4,023 km).

A.W.49 Ground-attack fighter monoplane with one Rolls-Royce Merlin X or Napier Sabre IV as a pusher. Twin tail boom layout with laminar-flow wing. Span 48 ft (14·63 m); length 36 ft 2 in (11·02 m); wing area 325 sq ft (30·19 sq m); all-up weight 12,000 lb (5,443 kg). Maximum speed (Sabre engine) 355 mph (571 km/hr) at 3,000 ft (914 m).

A.W.50 Tailless monoplane with four Metropolitan-Vickers F.3 turbojets. Span 120 ft (36·58 m); wing area 2,000 sq ft (185·81 sq m); all-up weight 50,000 lb (22,680 kg).

A.W.51 Tailless glider; scaled-down model of A.W.50. Span 40 ft (12·19 m); wing area 220 sq ft (20·94 sq m).

A.W.53 Torpedo-bomber designed to specification S.6/43. Two Rolls-Royce Merlin 26 engines. Span 60 ft (18·29 m); length 48 ft (14·63 m); wing area 638 sq ft (59·27 sq m); all-up weight 25,000 lb (11,340 kg).

A.W.54 Reconnaissance bomber; two Rolls-Royce Merlin 26 engines; folding wings, tricycle undercarriage and midships gun turret. Designed to specification S.11/43. Span 59 ft (17·98 m); wing area 500 sq ft (46·45 sq m); weight 20,000 lb (9,072 kg). Maximum speed 330 mph (531 km/hr) at 9,500 ft (2,895 m).

A.W.54A Reconnaissance bomber; two Metropolitan-Vickers F.3 turbojets with augmented thrust. A revised design to specification S.11/43 because A.W.54 was not fast enough. Span 55 ft (16·76 m); length 43 ft 6 in (13·26 m); wing area 530 sq ft (49·24 sq m); weight 19,000 lb (8,618 kg). Maximum speed 450 mph (724 km/hr).

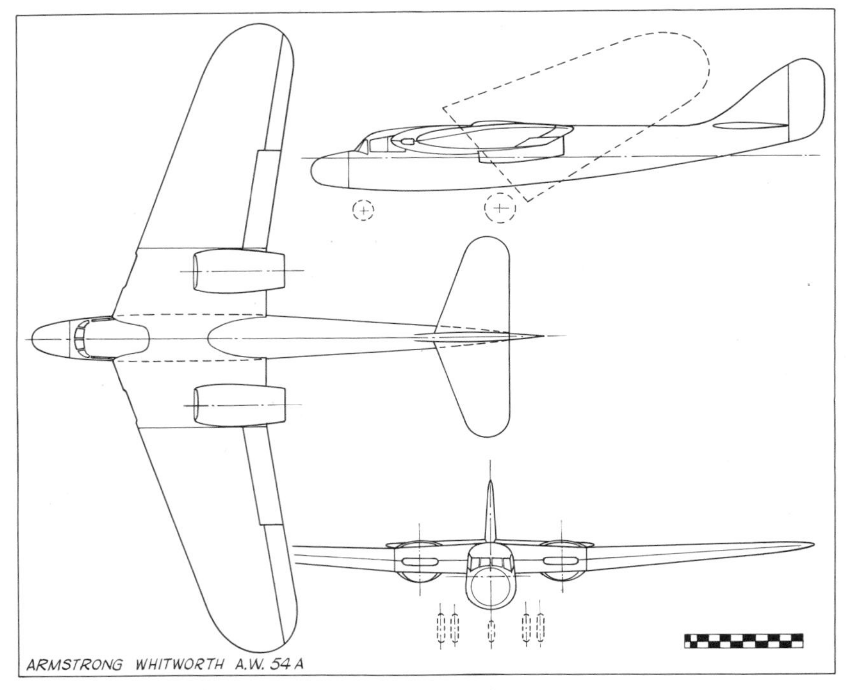

A.W.59 Supersonic fighter with variable-sweep wings.

A.W.65 Medium-range civil transport. Designed to specification OR323. Redesigned and built as A.W.650 Argosy.

A.W.66 Medium-range military transport. Designed to specification OR323. Redesigned and built as A.W.660 Argosy.

A.W.165 Two-seat all-weather fighter; two Armstrong Siddeley Sapphire turbojets, one with jet-pipe below the fuselage, the other exhausting at the rear. Wing swept back 55 deg at leading edge; powered controls with all-moving tailplane. Span 46 ft 9 in (14·25 m); length 80 ft (24·38 m); wing area 730 sq ft (67·82 sq m); all-up weight 31,100 lb (14,106 kg). Maximum speed Mach 1·25 at 40,000 ft (12,192 m); rate of climb 30,700 ft/min (154·3 m/sec); acceleration M = 0·9 to M = 1·2 at 50,000 ft (15,240 m) calculated as 3·7 min.

A.W.166 High-speed research aircraft to specification ER134T. After contract was awarded to the Bristol company, the design was modified into a Mach 2 two-seat fighter with two Armstrong Siddeley Sapphire Sa.10 turbojets with re-heat. Span 39 ft (11·89 m); length 73 ft (22·25 m); height 13 ft (3·96 m) wing area 434 sq ft (40·32 sq m); all-up weight 31,000 lb (14,061 kg).

A.W.167 Transatlantic airliner with rear-mounted engines.

A model of the A.W.168 project, a naval strike aircraft.

A.W.168 Naval strike aircraft to specification M148T/NA39.
A.W.169 Supersonic all-weather fighter to specification OR329.
A.W.170 Preliminary layout for a transport aircraft.
A.W.171 Narrow-delta aircraft type 'A' to specification ER161T.
A.W.172 Narrow-delta aircraft type 'B' to specification ER161T.
A.W.173 Target aircraft.
A.W.174 Airliner with podded engines.
A.W.176 Medium-range VTOL airliner for BEA.
A.W.651 Freighter aircraft; the Argosy with two Rolls-Royce Tyne propeller-turbines.
A.W.670 Short-haul freighter aircraft; the Argosy with a wider fuselage.
A.W.671 Short-haul airbus; the Argosy redesigned to carry 126 passengers.
A.W.680 STOL military transport with propeller-turbines.

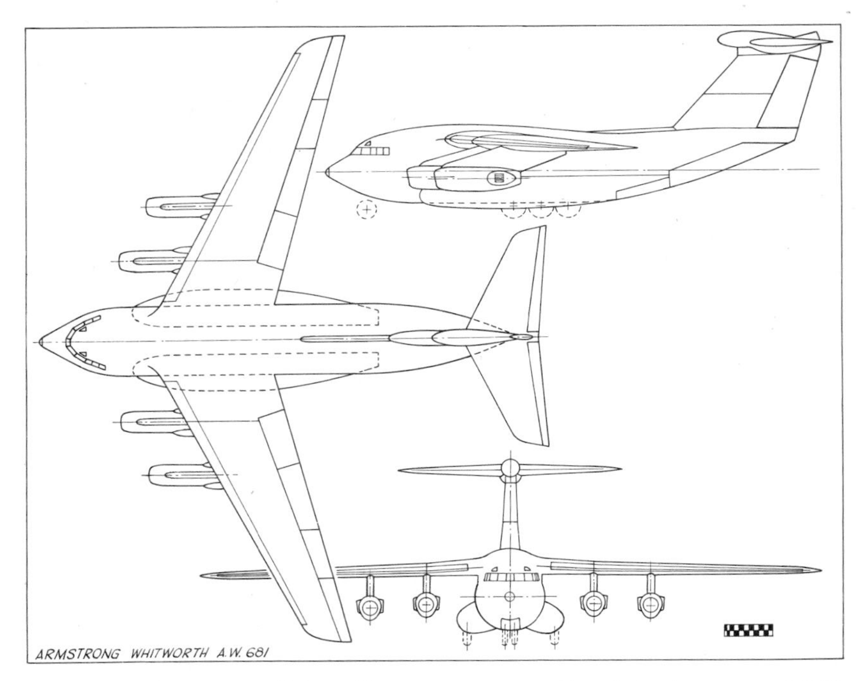

A.W.681 Long-range STOL military transport capable of development to VTOL, designed to specification OR351. Shoulder wing and high tail, upswept fuselage with loading doors and ramp suitable for air dropping supplies. Four Rolls-Royce Medway RB 142 engines with vectored-thrust nozzles. Boundary-layer control with blown leading edges, flaps and ailerons. Span 134 ft (40·84 m); length 104 ft 2 in (31·75 m); height 37 ft 10 in (11·53 m); wing area 2,250 sq ft (209·04 sq m); all-up weight 181,200 lb (82,194 kg); max payload 35,000 lb (15,876 kg); max range 4,800 miles (7,725 km); max cruising speed Mach 0·71 above 25,000 ft (7,620 m). Contract for full design study 3/63, contract to build 9/63, cancelled 2/65.

A.W.682 Civil freighter aircraft.

A.W.690 VTOL development aircraft; conversion of Nord Noratlas transport by the addition of lift engines.

Un-numbered Armstrong Whitworth Projects

Genet Monoplane A scaled-down version of the A.W.XV Atalanta with two Armstrong Siddeley Genet Major engines. Purpose uncertain, but probably intended for the carriage of freight or mail. Span 64 ft (19·51 m); length 50 ft 6 in (15·39 m); wing area 655 sq ft (60·85 sq m).

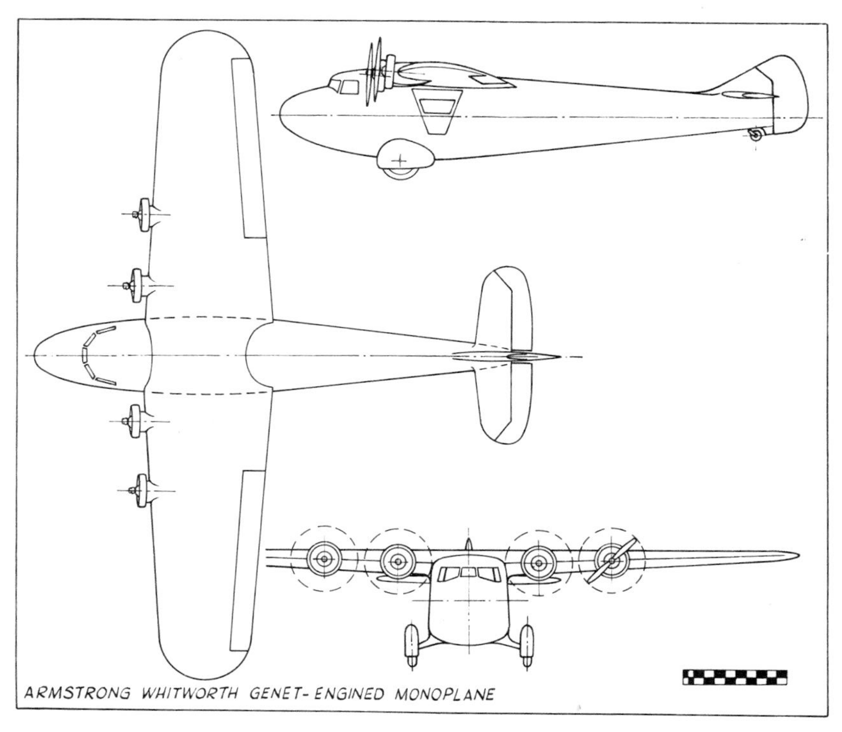

ARMSTRONG WHITWORTH GENET-ENGINED MONOPLANE

F.9/35 Two-seat fighter with two Armstrong Siddeley Terrier engines; a development of the A.W.34 project. Span 39 ft (11·89 m); length 37 ft 3 in (11·35 m); wing area 259 sq ft (24·06 sq m).

Multi-engined transports During discussions with Imperial Airways about their requirements, Armstrong Whitworth drew up alternative proposals for low-wing monoplanes with two, three and four engines. From these designs was developed the A.W.27 Ensign. Twin-engined aircraft: 16 passengers; span 85 ft 0 in (25·91 m); length 73 ft 2 in (22·33 m). Three-engined aircraft: 24 passengers; span 103 ft (31·39 m); length 90 ft 0 in (27·43 m). Four-engined aircraft: 33 passengers; span 116 ft 6 in (35·51 m); length 98 ft 9 in (30·10 m).

Heavy Bomber Four-engined bomber to specification B.12/36. Designed to take Rolls-Royce Merlin, Rolls-Royce Vulture or Armstrong Siddeley Deerhound engines. War load, 2,000 lb (907 kg) of bombs or 24 troops. Span 98 ft (29·87 m); length 90 ft (27·43 m). Maximum speed: (Merlin) 313 mph (504 km/hr); (Vulture) 370 mph (595 km/hr); (Deerhound) 350 mph (563 km/hr).

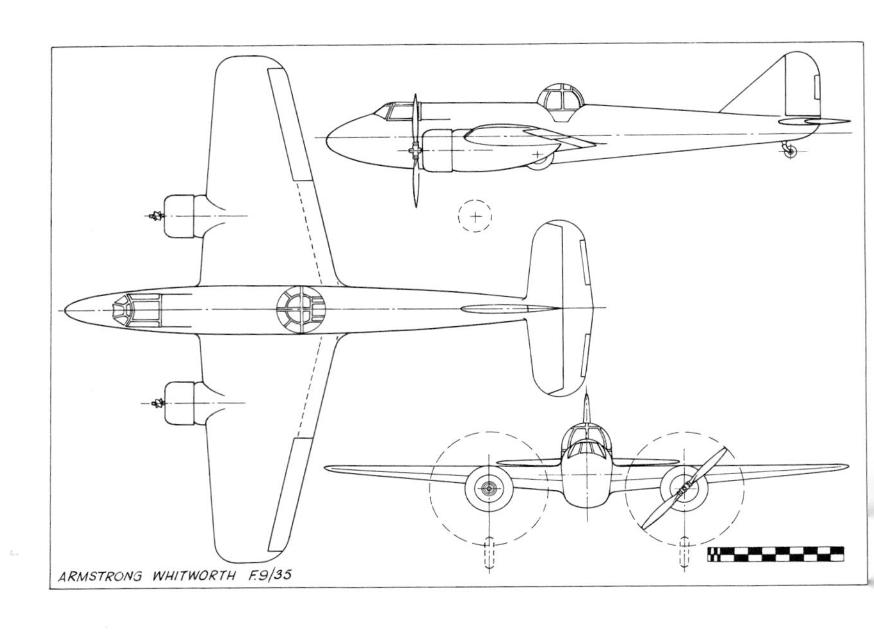
ARMSTRONG WHITWORTH F.9/35

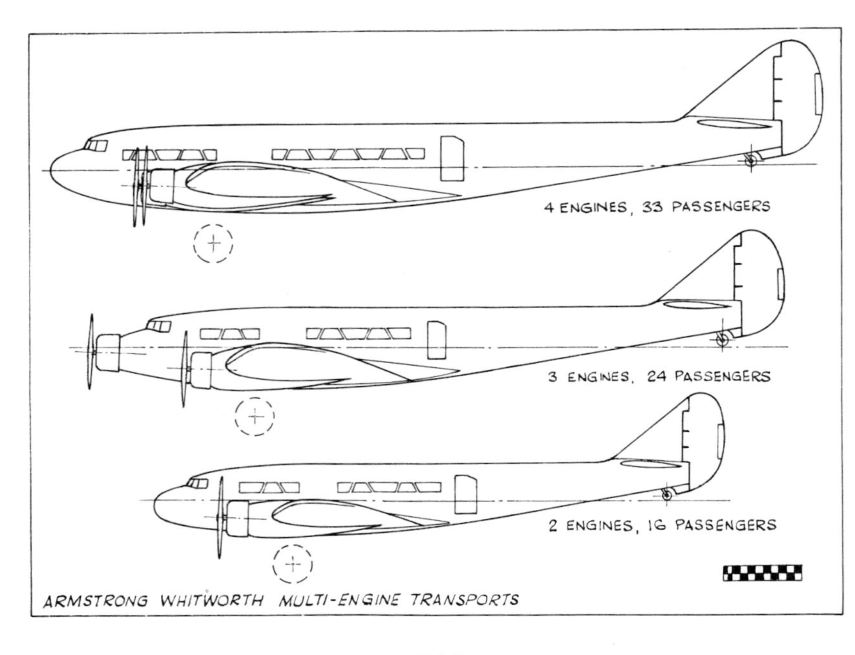
4 ENGINES, 33 PASSENGERS
3 ENGINES, 24 PASSENGERS
2 ENGINES, 16 PASSENGERS
ARMSTRONG WHITWORTH MULTI-ENGINE TRANSPORTS

Day and Night Fighter Two-seat monoplane with two Rolls-Royce Merlin pusher engines designed to specification F.11/37. Four-gun turret placed above and behind the pilot; nosewheel undercarriage. Span 43 ft (13·11 m); length 43 ft 3 in (13·18 m).

Heavy Bomber High-speed, long-range bomber; larger version of the Whitley with four Bristol Centaurus III engines. Span 135 ft (41·15 m); wing area 2,013 sq ft (187·02 sq m); all-up weight (overload) 103,000 lb (46,720 kg). Maximum speed at 18,000 ft (5,486 m) 302 mph (486 km/hr).

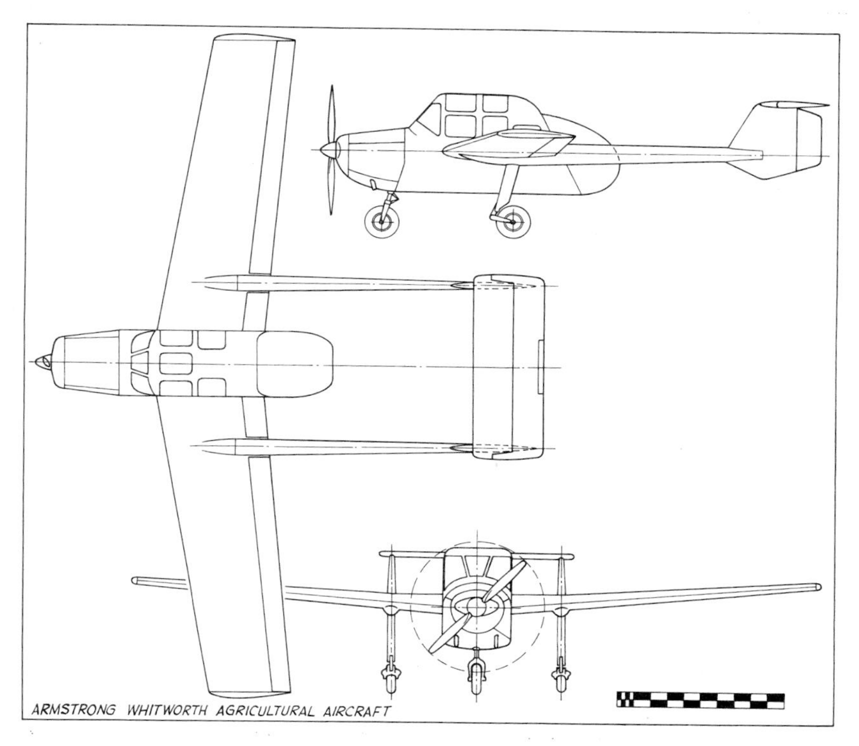

Agricultural Aircraft Agricultural and general-purpose aircraft with one Lycoming pusher engine; design drawn up in 1957. Twin-boom layout; convertible for freight or four passengers; payload 1,600 lb (726 kg); crop-dusting speed 80 mph (129 km/hr). Detachable full-span leading-edge slats for crop spraying duties. Span 40 ft 10 in (12·45 m); length 29 ft 10 in (9·07 m); wing area 230 sq ft (21·37 sq m); all-up weight 4,000 lb (1,814 kg).

Car Ferry Short-range car ferry, designed in 1958, with two Rolls-Royce Dart propeller-turbines. Accommodation for four medium-sized cars and 21 passengers or up to 72 passengers. Span 92 ft (28·04 m); length 75 ft (22·86 m); height 26 ft (7·93 m); wing area 1,027 sq ft (95·41 sq m); all-up weight 39,360 lb (17,853 kg).

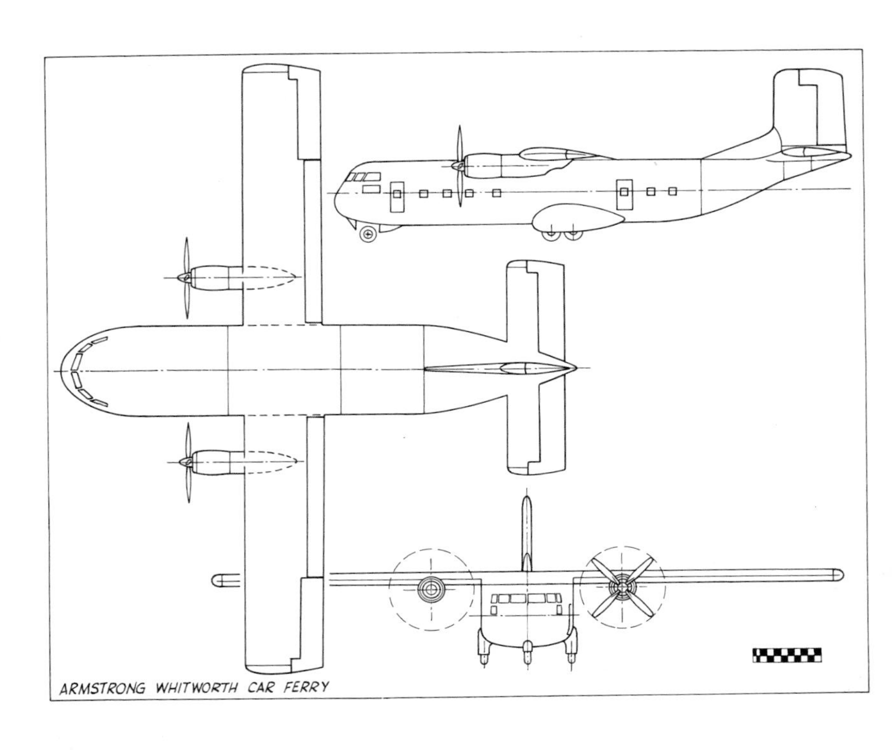
ARMSTRONG WHITWORTH CAR FERRY

APPENDIX B

Other Organizations' Aeroplanes

Between the years 1914 and 1959, Sir W. G. Armstrong Whitworth Aircraft Ltd and its forbears built, between them, some 5,500 aeroplanes to other people's designs. These aircraft types have all been dealt with in considerable detail elsewhere, and in this chapter only enough information is included to remind readers of the types' salient points and to recount the facts that relate to Armstrong Whitworth's part in their production.

The first to enter the sub-contract business was the Sir W. G. Armstrong Whitworth and Co Ltd, of Newcastle, which built between 300 and 350 such aircraft (the exact number is uncertain); in 1917, at the request of the War Office, the Siddeley Deasy Motor Car Co Ltd embarked on the building of aeroplanes and, by the war's end, had completed 1,127 machines to Government design. Finally, came Sir W. G. Armstrong Whitworth Aircraft Ltd, which, from 1933 onwards, produced a total of 4,033 aeroplanes to Hawker, Avro and Gloster designs. The sub-contracting undertaken by Armstrong Whitworth of Coventry grew naturally from the amalgamation with the Avro Company in 1928 and with the Hawker company in 1935, and it was logical that the resources of the combine should be used to the best advantage at times of heavy demand. Furthermore, in later years, Armstrong Whitworth gained a reputation for high-quality workmanship and—notably—for punctual delivery; as a result, the company was called upon to undertake a major share of the sub-contract work within the group until, in the end, such aircraft represented nearly sixty-five per cent of the company's total output.

The aircraft types, and the numbers involved, were as follows: Armstrong Whitworth, Newcastle: B.E.2a (8), B.E.2b (25), B.E.2c (50*), Bristol Fighter (250). Siddeley Deasy: R.E.7 (100), R.E.8 (1,027). Armstrong Whitworth, Coventry: Hart (456), Lancaster (1,328), Lincoln (281), Meteor 4 (45), Meteor 8 (430), Meteor NF (592), Sea Hawk (490), Hunter (278), Javelin (133).

The B.E.2a, B.E.2b and B.E.2c

The first aeroplanes to be built by Armstrong Whitworth for the Government were eight B.E.2as which had been ordered in 1913. The B.E. series originated at the Army Aircraft Factory at Farnborough (renamed the Royal Aircraft Factory in 1912) and the first aircraft of the type, the B.E.1 which appeared in 1911, was the result of collaboration between two of the Farnborough designers, F. M. Green and Geoffrey de Havilland. The B.E.1 was very advanced for its time, both structurally and aerodynamically, and it did much to establish the fashion for the tractor biplane which was to persist for so many years.

* Estimated

A B.E.2a aircraft photographed in the Gosforth factory.

The B.E.2a, powered by a 70 hp air-cooled Renault engine, appeared towards the end of 1912 and was basically similar to the preceding B.E.1 and B.E.2 aircraft. The structure was of wood, fabric covered, with unstaggered two-bay biplane wings. The tailplane was semicircular with divided elevators, and the rudder had no fixed fin; lateral control was by wing warping. The undercarriage had two long skids to protect the propeller.

While the first eight B.E.2as were still under construction in 1913, Armstrong Whitworth received a further order from the War Office, this time for twenty-five B.E.2b aircraft. The B.E.2b was a further refinement of the type with a redesigned fuselage and other improvements, including, in later versions, the substitution of ailerons for wing warping.

After the outbreak of war in 1914, the B.E.2a and the B.E.2b soon gave place to the better-known B.E.2c, which was built in large numbers by numerous contractors, including Armstrong Whitworth. The B.E.2c, which was designed to have automatic stability, according to the ideas of T. E. Busk, had a fuselage similar to that of the B.E.2b, but the

The B.E.2b, the second Royal Aircraft Factory type to be built at Gosforth. (*Imperial War Museum Q57578*)

The last B.E. variant to be built at Gosforth was the B.E.2c. (*Imperial War Museum Q33852*)

wings were of new design, being heavily staggered and with ailerons on all four planes; the new tailplane was rectangular and a vertical fin was added to the rudder. Early examples of the B.E.2c had the 70 hp Renault engine and the characteristic undercarriage skids, but later production models were powered by the 90 hp RAF 1a engine and had a simplified V-type chassis. The B.E.2c gave good service as a reconnaissance aircraft in the opening stages of the war, but it was quickly outclassed and soon became an easy victim of enemy fighters.

Armstrong Whitworth built eight B.E.2as and twenty-five BE2bs but it has not been possible to trace the Service numbers of these aircraft. The total number of B.E.2cs built by Armstrong Whitworth is uncertain, but two batches built at Gosforth, amounting to 50 aircraft, carried the serial numbers 1780 to 1800 and 2001 to 2029.

	B.E.2a	**B.E.2c**
Span:	**35 ft 0 in (10·67 m)**	**37 ft 0 in (11·28 m)**
Length:	**29 ft 7 in (9·02 m)**	**27 ft 3 in (8·31 m)**
Wing area:	**352 sq ft (32·70 sq m)**	**371 sq ft (34·47 sq m)**
All-up weight:	**1,600 lb (726 kg)**	**2,142 lb (972 kg)**

The R.E.7

It was in 1917 that the Siddeley Deasy Motor Car Company in Coventry received its first contract to build aeroplanes, the order being for one hundred R.E.7 biplanes. The R.E. series of aircraft was developed by the Royal Aircraft Factory at Farnborough to fill the need for an aircraft to work in co-operation with the army, the initials R.E. standing for reconnaissance experimental. Some measure of automatic stability was considered to be an essential requirement for this particular duty, and T. E. Busk, at the Factory, had spent much of his short career developing this characteristic in the early B.E. and R.E. aircraft.

The R.E.7, No.2400, one of 100 built by The Siddeley Deasy Motor Car Co. (*Imperial War Museum Q76551*)

The R.E.7, which appeared in 1915, was a large biplane with two-bay wings and with the top plane extensions braced by outward-sloping struts. A variety of engines were fitted to the R.E.7, but most production aircraft had either the 160 hp Beardmore or the 150 hp RAF 4a. This latter engine was already being built by Siddeley Deasy in Coventry and, logically, was the powerplant selected for the R.E.7s built by the company. Structurally, the R.E.7 was of interest by reason of the fact that steel tubing was used in fabricating the forward part of the fuselage; otherwise the method of construction was conventional except for the undercarriage, an elaborate affair with oleo shock-absorbers and a small wheel projecting in front of the propeller instead of the more usual skid.

Because of its large wing area, the R.E.7 was a good weight lifter and it was, in consequence, used principally as a bomber carrying the big 336-lb bomb designed by the Royal Aircraft Factory. During its brief operational career, the R.E.7 dropped a number of these bombs with good effect during 1916.

The R.E.7s built by Siddeley Deasy carried the serial numbers 2348 to 2447. The first to be built, 2348, was initially fitted with the RAF 4a engine, but this was later replaced by the 160 hp Beardmore; at the same time the aircraft was experimentally modified into a three-seater.

Span upper:	57 ft 0 in (17·37 m)
Span lower:	42 ft 0 in (12·80 m)
Length:	31 ft 11 in (9·73 m)
Height:	12 ft 7 in (3·84 m)
Wing area:	548 sq ft (50·91 sq m)
All-up weight:	3,450 lb (1,565 kg)

The R.E.8

The R.E.8, which followed the R.E.7 on the production line at the Siddeley Deasy Coventry factory, although designed for reconnaissance duties, bore little resemblance to any of the R.E. series of aircraft that had gone before. Unfortunately for those who had to fly in it, the R.E.8 perpetuated the philosophy that a reconnaissance aeroplane should be inherently stable, and it therefore lacked the manoeuvrability which would have improved its defensive capabilities; it did, however, have the crew correctly placed, with the pilot in front of the observer, who could thus use his gun to protect the aircraft from stern attacks.

The R.E.8 gained a bad reputation from the start: its performance was not up to expectations and it seemed to have a dangerous tendency to spin; furthermore, when it appeared on the Western Front during 1917 it suffered heavy losses from enemy fighters. It was, nevertheless, produced in large numbers, more than 4,000 being built by numerous contractors, and it remained in front-line service until the end of the war, giving invaluable support to the army both in France and in the Middle East by artillery spotting, photography and bombing.

Siddeley Deasy built more than a thousand R.E.8 aircraft; E254 was one of them.

The R.E.8 was conventional both in design and construction and was built of wood with fabric covering. The heavily-staggered, single-bay biplane wings were of unequal span, with the extension wings braced by wires. The engine was the 150 hp RAF 4a. Ailerons were fitted to all four wings and the tail surfaces were conventional with a rather small vertical fin. Later production models had a larger fin with a consequent improvement in the aircraft's spinning characteristics.

The Siddeley Deasy Motor Car Co, having already proved its capabilities with the R.E.7, was an obvious choice as contractor for the R.E.8, particularly as the RAF 4a engine was being built in the company's Parkside factory. Siddeley Deasy received its first order, for one hundred R.E.8s, towards the end of 1916, and this was followed by eight repeat orders, the total output by Siddeley Deasy amounting to 1,027 aircraft, with the production rate rising eventually to about twenty machines a week.

The R.E.8s built by Siddeley Deasy were numbered as follows:

A3405–3504, A3681–3830, B6451–6624, B6628–6630,* B7681–7730, E1–300, E1151–1250, F1553–1602 and F3246–3345

Span upper:	42 ft 8 in (13·00 m)
Span lower:	32 ft 8 in (9·96 m)
Length:	27 ft 10 in (8·48 m)
Height:	10 ft 10 in (3·30 m)
Wing area:	377·5 sq ft (35·02 sq m)
All-up weight:	2,870 lb (1,302 kg)

* These three aircraft were included in the contract for conversion to R.T.1s, but were probably completed as R.E.8s.

In 1918 the Bristol Fighter took the place of the F.K.8 in the Gosforth factory. (*Vickers Ltd*)

The Bristol F2B Fighter

By the year 1918, the F.K.8, which had been Armstrong Whitworth's main preoccupation in Newcastle since the autumn of 1916, was becoming obsolete and, in the spring of that year, production of this aircraft ceased and its place was taken by the Bristol Fighter, 250 of which had been ordered in February 1918.

The Bristol F2B Fighter, first produced in the autumn of 1916, was one of the outstanding aircraft of the First World War. Designed as a fighter-reconnaissance aircraft, the Bristol Fighter, with its high performance, combined the best characteristics of the fast, manoeuvrable, single-seat fighter with the fire power of the two-seater, and it proved itself to be a formidable opponent in the battles on the Western Front from the middle of 1917 onwards.

The engine of the standard Bristol Fighter was the Rolls-Royce Falcon, but production of this engine could not keep pace with the demand, and other powerplants had, perforce, to be used, with some inevitable loss of performance. One of the alternative engines was the 200 hp eight-cylinder water-cooled Sunbeam Arab, and it was this version that was ordered from Armstrong Whitworth. But the Arab engine was, itself, a disappointment: it suffered from severe vibration problems and, at some stage during the production run at Gosforth, the Siddeley Puma engine was substituted. This change-over probably occurred after the Armistice, by which time some sixty per cent of the order had been completed. The Bristol Fighter continued in production at Gosforth after the end of the war, but it cannot be confirmed whether or not all the 250 aircraft ordered, which were allotted the serial numbers E1901 to E2150, had been completed when, according to the company records, the contract was cancelled in September 1919.

Span:	39 ft 3 in (11·96 m)
Length:	24 ft 10 in (7·57 m)
Height:	9 ft 5 in (2·87 m)
Wing area:	405·6 sq ft (37·63 sq m)
All-up weight:	2,800 lb (1,270 kg)

The Hawker Hart

The Hawker Hart, first flown in the summer of 1928, brought about something of a revolution in the RAF: the merits of the closely-cowled water-cooled engine (first demonstrated in England by the Fairey Fox of 1925) were fully exploited by Sydney Camm, the Hawker designer, and resulted in the Hart, a two-seat day bomber that was faster than the RAF's current single-seat fighters. It was a shapely single-bay biplane of steel construction, fabric covered. The wings were of unequal span with a slight sweepback on the top wing. With the then new Rolls-Royce Kestrel engine, the Hart had a top speed of 184 mph at 5,000 ft.

Hart production included a version for service in India, a communications aircraft, and a dual-control trainer, but other duties, including fighting and army co-operation, were performed by numerous variants of the basic design, namely the Demon, the Audax, the Hardy, the Hind and the Hector. This last, powered by the Napier Dagger engine, entered service in 1937 and survived to go into action against the Germans in the spring of 1940. The Hart was undoubtedly the most versatile biplane ever employed by the RAF, and it and its derivatives were built in larger numbers than was any other British aircraft between the two wars.

The Hawker Hart, of which more than 450 were built by Armstrong Whitworth. (*Cyril Peckham*)

So great was the demand for the Hart that it was widely sub-contracted, and the Armstrong Whitworth company was among those chosen for the task. The first contract placed with Armstrong Whitworth was for twenty-four bombers ordered in 1932, but subsequent orders for further day bombers, trainers and communication aircraft, brought the total up to 456 by the time production in Coventry ceased in 1937. The Hawker Harts built by Armstrong Whitworth were numbered as follows:

K3031–3054 (Day bombers), K3855–3904 (Day bombers and communication aircraft), K3955–3972 (Day bombers), K4297–4298 (Communication aircraft), K4437–4495 (Day bombers), K4886–5052 and K6415–6550 (Trainers)

Hawker Hart Trainer

Span:	37 ft 4 in (11·38 m)
Length:	29 ft 4 in (8·94 m)
Height:	10 ft 5 in (3·18 m)
Wing area:	349·5 sq ft (32·47 sq m)
All-up weight:	4,150 lb (1,882 kg)

The Avro Lancaster Mk.II, with Bristol Hercules engines, was built by Armstrong Whitworth as an insurance against a shortage of Rolls-Royce Merlins.

The Avro Lancaster

The best of the British heavy bombers to take part in the 1939–1945 war, the Avro Lancaster, was produced almost by accident: the twin-engined Manchester bomber which preceded the Lancaster went into action in the autumn of 1940, but had to be withdrawn from service in the summer of 1942 after its Rolls-Royce Vulture engines had proved unacceptably unreliable. By adopting drastic—and somewhat unofficial—methods, the Avro company quickly redesigned the aircraft to take four Rolls-Royce Merlin engines in place of the two Vultures. In this configuration, known originally as the Manchester III but later renamed Lancaster, the aircraft proved to have an outstanding performance and was put into large-scale production by Avro and by a number of sub-contractors in Great Britain and in Canada; more than 7,300 were built. The Lancaster was the only bomber capable of carrying the 22,000-lb 'Grand Slam' bomb, and, among its many notable exploits, it will always be remembered for the raid in May 1943 when the Möhne and Eder dams were breached.

Armstrong Whitworth received their first contract for the Lancaster in 1941, and the first aircraft came off the line in 1943 during which year 96 of the four-engined bombers (in addition to the last 277 Whitleys) were delivered. To guard against a shortage of Merlin engines, the Lancaster Mk.II, with Bristol Hercules radial engines was ordered from Armstrong Whitworth, but when in fact no shortage of Merlins occurred, production of the Mk.II was cut back and replaced on the Coventry production line by the Mk.III, to which was fitted the Packard-built Merlin. Also produced by Armstrong Whitworth, at a later stage, was the Lancaster Mk.IB (FE), designed for operation against the Japanese. Armstrong Whitworth produced a total of 1,328 Lancasters, with production rising to a peak in 1945, during which year 645 aircraft were delivered.

The Lancasters built by Armstrong Whitworth bore the following serial numbers:

B Mk.I

LL740–758, 771–813, 826–867, 880–923, 935–977; LM 100–142, 156–192, 205–243, 257–296; NF906–939, 952–999; NG113–149, 162–206, 218–259, 263–308, 321–367, 379–421, 434–469, 482–503; RF120–161, 175–197; TW647–671, 858–873, 878–911; SW296–316.

B Mk.II

DS601–635, 647–692, 704–741, 757–797, 813–852; LL617–653, 666–704, 716–739.

B Mk.III

RF199–216, 229–273, 286–326; SW283–295.

Avro Lancaster B Mk.III

Span:	102 ft 0 in (31·09 m)
Length:	69 ft 4 in (21·13m)
Height:	20 ft 6 in (6·25 m)
Wing area:	1,297 sq ft (120·49 sq m)
All-up weight:	50,000 lb (22,680 kg)
All-up weight (with 22,000-lb bomb):	72,000 lb (32,659 kg)

The Avro Lincoln

The Avro Lincoln bomber, which in 1945 overlapped with the Avro Lancaster on the Armstrong Whitworth production line, was the last piston-engined aircraft to serve with RAF Bomber Command. Designed as a replacement for the Lancaster, the Lincoln, which first flew in June 1944, went into service just too late to play a part in the Far East war for which it had been primarily intended. Subsequently, it formed the mainstay of Britain's bomber force until it was withdrawn from front-line service at the end of December 1955, giving place to the Canberra jet bomber.

The Lincoln was based on the successful Lancaster formula but was larger all round and had more powerful Rolls-Royce Merlin engines. It had a range of more than 3,500 miles and retained the good handling qualities that had made the Lancaster so popular with pilots. The Lincoln was used to equip twenty squadrons of the RAF and, in later years, served as a flying test-bed for many gas-turbines, including the Rolls-Royce Derwent.

During 1945 Armstrong Whitworth built 24 Lincolns but, with the end of the war, the massive orders that had been contemplated were cut back: during 1946, 131 Lincolns were completed at Baginton at a reduced tempo, and by March 1951, when production ceased, 281 aircraft had been delivered to the RAF by Armstrong Whitworth. In addition to the

This Avro Lincoln was one of 281 built at Coventry.

RAF aircraft, a further eighteen were laid down by the company for the Argentine Air Force, but there is some evidence that these aircraft may have been handed over to the Avro company for completion.

The serial numbers of the Avro Lincolns built by Armstrong Whitworth were as follows: RF329–370, 383–427, 440–485, 498–539, 553–577; SX923–958, 970–993; WD122–133, 141–149.

Span: 120 ft 0 in (36·58 m)
Length: 78 ft 4 in (23·87 m)
Height: 17 ft 4 in (5·28 m)
Wing area: 1,421 sq ft (132·01 sq m)
All-up weight: 82,000 lb (37,195 kg)

A mixed formation of Gloster Meteor 4 and 8 aircraft, both of which types were built by Armstrong Whitworth. (*Courtesy D. James*)

The Gloster Meteor Mk.4 and Mk.8

In 1946 Armstrong Whitworth started making Meteor components for the Gloster Aircraft Co; three years later, in January 1949, the company was asked by Glosters to supply 45 complete Meteor 4s under sub-contract.

The Gloster Meteor, Britain's first operational jet aircraft, made its first flight on 5 March, 1943, and it went into action in the spring of 1945, just before the end of the war in Europe. The Mk.4 was powered by two Rolls-Royce Derwent 5 turbojets, and it soon made its mark on history by twice breaking the world's speed record, first at 606 mph in November 1945, and then at 616 mph in September 1946.

The first Armstrong Whitworth built Meteor 4 flew in 1949, and the last aircraft of this type was delivered from Baginton in April 1950. Of the forty-five Mk.4s completed by Armstrong Whitworth, seven were diverted to the Egyptian Air Force. The Meteor 8, which followed the Mk.4 in the Baginton factory, was ordered direct from Armstrong Whitworth by the Ministry of Supply. It had been developed by Glosters from the Mk.4 and included numerous modifications designed to improve its high-speed handling qualities, including a new tailplane without a ventral fin, and a more streamlined cockpit canopy. Other changes were a longer fuselage, additional tankage and an ejector seat. The engines were up-rated Derwent 8s.

The first twenty-two Meteor 8s to be built by Armstrong Whitworth were delivered during 1950; in the following year 172 were completed with production reaching a peak at 201 aircraft in 1952. The final 35 aircraft, making up a total of 430 Meteor 8s, were delivered in 1953.

The Meteor 4s built by Armstrong Whitworth carried the Service numbers VZ386–429,

The Armstrong Siddeley Sapphire powered Gloster Meteor 8.

and VZ436; of these, VZ420–426 were sold to Egypt. Among the 430 Meteor 8s constructed by Armstrong Whitworth were VZ518–532, 540–569; WF638–662; WK707–756 and 906–935.*

	Meteor 4	**Meteor 8**
Span:	37 ft 2 in (11·33 m)	37 ft 2 in (11·33 m)
Length:	41 ft 0 in (12·50 m)	44 ft 7 in (13·59 m)
Height:	13 ft 0 in (3·96 m)	13 ft 0 in (3·96 m)
Wing area:	350 sq ft (32·52 sq m)	350 sq ft (32·52 sq m)
All-up weight:	14,550 lb (6,600 kg)	15,7C0 lb (7,122 kg)

The Prone-Pilot Meteor

The last Meteor 8 to come off the Armstrong Whitworth assembly line, WK935, was modified for an experiment, initiated on behalf of the RAF Institute of Aviation Medicine, in order to evaluate the practicability of the 'prone-pilot' theory. The idea was that a pilot lying on his stomach would not suffer a blackout during tight turns because, in this position, the 'g' forces would not cause the blood to drain from the head, as is the case with a pilot sitting upright.

The alteration involved the addition of some eight feet to the aircraft in the form of a tapering nose, in which the pilot lay prone on a padded bed, inclined slightly head upwards with his knees partially bent. His elbows were supported by armrests with the forearms free to operate the controls, while his feet were held on the rudder bar by raised edges on the pedals. The controls were duplicated in the normal cockpit and a safety pilot was always carried during the tests. The problem of how the prone pilot should bale out in an emergency was overcome by arranging for the bed, and its supporting floor, to hinge downward so that the pilot would slide off feet first underneath the aircraft. Wind-tunnel

* WK935 converted for 'prone-pilot' experiment.

The experimental prone-pilot Meteor was adapted from the Mk.8 by Armstrong Whitworth.

tests on a model at Baginton had indicated that this method would enable the pilot to fall well clear of the aircraft at speeds up to at least 500 mph.

The one and only 'prone-pilot' Meteor first flew from Baginton in February 1954 and it was, incidentally, the last of the Armstrong Whitworth 'first flights' to be made from that aerodrome. By the end of 1955 the experiments were completed, and it had been shown that there was no particular difficulty in operating the controls and no tendency to black out. On the other hand, initially at any rate, the pilot suffered some discomfort from the action of 'g' forces operating in unaccustomed directions; in addition, pilots also found it difficult to look sideways and, more particularly, backwards. The final view taken was that the disadvantages of the system outweighed the advantages; this conclusion being influenced, no doubt, by the successful development of the anti-'g' flying suit, which enabled the same, or better, results to be obtained with the pilot sitting in the normal position.

Span:	37 ft 2 in (11·33 m)
Length:	52 ft 5 in (15·98 m)

The Meteor Night Fighter

During the production run of the Meteor Mk.4 and Mk.8, Armstrong Whitworth were given the task of developing a night-fighter version of the aircraft, a job which involved a considerable amount of design work to adapt the Meteor to carry a crew of two and the necessary radar equipment. The first of the series, known as the Meteor NF.11, closely resembled the Mk.7 trainer; it had an extended nose to accommodate the AI radar, the Mk.7-type cockpit with the sideways-opening canopy, the tailplane of the Mk.8 and the long-span wings of the Mk.3. As the nose section was occupied by the radar equipment, the four 20-mm cannon were mounted in pairs in the wings outboard of the engine nacelles. Provision was made for the carriage of long-range fuel tanks fitted either beneath the fuselage, under the wings or on the wingtips. The engines were Rolls-Royce Derwent 8s.

The next development of the basic Meteor night fighter undertaken by Armstrong

The development of the Meteor NF.11 was the responsibility of Armstrong Whitworth.

Whitworth was the NF.12, which first flew on 21 April, 1953, and which had a lengthened nose to house a later type of radar imported from America. The NF.13, a tropicalized version for operation in the Middle East, first flew on 23 December, 1952, and this was followed by the NF.14, which flew on 23 October, 1953, and which had a one-piece, Perspex, sliding canopy designed by Armstrong Whitworth. The final version developed in Coventry was the TT Mk.20, a target-towing aircraft built for the British Government and some NATO countries. Production of the Mk.20 was confined to conversions of existing NF.11s, made between December 1957 and February 1965.

Altogether, 592 Meteor night fighters were built at Baginton with serial numbers as follows:

Meteor NF.11: WD585–634, 640–689, 696–745, 751–800; WM143–192, 221–270, 292–295, 296–307 (twelve aircraft for France), 368–371 (four aircraft for France), 372–374, 375–383 (nine aircraft for France), 384–403 (twenty aircraft for Denmark, serialled 501–520).

A longer nose, housing more advanced radar, characterized the Meteor NF.12.

Meteor NF.12: WS590–639, 658–700, 715–721.
Meteor NF.13: WM308–342, 363–367.
Meteor NF.14: WS722–760, 774–812, 827–848.
The overseas distribution of the Meteor NF.13 was as follows:

Syria		*Egypt*		*Israel*		*France*	
RAF serial	Syrian serial	RAF serial	Egyptian serial	RAF serial	Israeli serial	RAF serial	French serial
WM330	473	WM325	1427	WM309	4FXND	WM364	NF-F 364
WM332	471	WM326	1428	WM312	4FXNC	WM365	NF-F 365
WM333	476	WM328	1429	WM320	4FXNE		
WM336	472	WM338	1430	WM334	4FXNB		
WM337	474	WM340	1431	WM335	4FXNF		
WM341	475	WM342	1432	WM366	4FXNA		

The following Meteor NF.11s were among those converted by Armstrong Whitworth to Meteor TT Mk.20s for the RAF between December 1957 and February 1965:

WD610, WD612, WD641, WD649, WD652, WD657, WD706, WD711, WD767, WD780, WD785, WM 147, WM151, WM160, WM242, WM255 and WM292.

In addition, the following Danish NF.11s were similarly converted by Armstrong Whitworth:

504 (ex-WM387), 508 (ex-WM391), 512 (ex-WM395), 517 (ex-WM400), 518 (ex-WM401) and 519 (ex-WM402).

Meteor Night Fighter

Span:	43 ft 0 in (13·11 m)
Length (NF.11 and 13):	48 ft 6 in (14·78 m)
Length (NF.12):	49 ft 11 in (15·22 m)
Height:	13 ft 11 in (4·24 m)
Wing area:	374 sq ft (34·75 sq m)

A Coventry-built Hawker Sea Hawk, XE456.

The Hawker Sea Hawk

The first Hawker jet fighter to go into production, the Sea Hawk, resulted from the P.1040 fighter which had been turned down by the RAF but accepted by the Royal Navy for development into a carrier-borne interceptor fighter according to specification N.7/46. The first production Sea Hawk emerged from Hawker's factory in November 1951, but by this time the Hawker company had become committed to a large and urgent order for the Hunter and, after 35 Sea Hawks had been built by the parent company, it was decided that both the development and the construction of the Sea Hawk should be undertaken by Armstrong Whitworth.

The Sea Hawk single-seat fighter was powered by a Rolls-Royce Nene turbojet with a novel bifurcated jet-pipe exhausting through the fuselage sides just aft of the wings. The straight, tapered wings were designed to fold upwards, butterfly fashion, and the fixed armament consisted of four 20-mm cannon under the nose. Provision was also made for the carriage of rocket projectiles, 500-lb bombs and under-wing drop tanks.

The first order for Sea Hawks received by Armstrong Whitworth came in May 1951 direct from the Ministry of Supply, and was for 100 aircraft, soon to be increased to a total of 185 aircraft, and this was followed in 1952 by an order for 116 aircraft, placed on a sub-contract by the Hawker company; a further order from the Ministry of Supply for 99 aircraft brought the total ordered from Armstrong Whitworth for the Royal Navy to 400. Subsequently, 22 Sea Hawks were built at Coventry for the Netherlands and another 68 for Germany. Altogether, Armstrong Whitworth built 490 Sea Hawks in addition to the 35 built in the first place by the Hawker company. India also acquired a number of Sea Hawks which are believed to have been ex-Royal Navy Mk.3 aircraft modified to Mk.6 standard. The Armstrong Whitworth works record shows that fourteen Sea Hawks were thus modified for India at Coventry.

The first Sea Hawk to be completed by Armstrong Whitworth, WF162, flew on 18 December, 1952, and a further sixteen aircraft were delivered during 1953. The first batch of sixty aircraft produced were F Mk.1s; the next batch consisted of forty F Mk.2s, which had power-boosted aileron controls. The first flight of the Mk.2 took place on 24 February, 1954, and that of the Mk.3 on 13 March, 1954, the latter aircraft having a strengthened wing structure to take additional external stores. The Sea Hawk Mk.4, a ground-attack version, flew on 26 August, 1954, but the Mk.5 was never built as such, the fifty or so examples all being Mk.3 aircraft modified by being fitted with a more powerful Nene engine. Similarly, the first Mk.6s consisted of Mk.4s modified with the more powerful engine; in this case, however, a batch of eighty-seven Mk.6s was built from scratch by Armstrong Whitworth. The Mk.6 was powered by the Nene Mk.105 and joined the Fleet Air Arm in 1956, some remaining in front-line service until 1960.

The Sea Hawks built by Armstrong Whitworth were numbered as follows:

Mk.1: WF162–166, 178–192, 196–235.

Mk.2: WF240–279.

Mk.3: WF280–289, 293–303; WM906–945, 960–999; WN105–119.

Mk.4: WV792–807, 824–871, 902–922; XE327–338.

Mk.6: XE339–344, 362–411, 435–463, 489–490.

For Holland, Mk.50: 6-50–6-71.

For Germany, Mk.100: VA220–236; VB120–136. Mk.101: RB240–256, 360–376.

Span:	39 ft 0 in (11·89 m)
Length (Mk.6):	39 ft 8 in (12·09 m)
Wing area:	278 sq ft (25·83 sq m)

The Hawker Hunter

The outstanding success of the Hawker Hunter resulted in large orders, spread over some ten years or more, for the RAF and the air forces of ten other nations; in all, more than 2,000 Hunters were built. At the peak production time Armstrong Whitworth were called upon to assist and, during the years 1954 to 1957, was responsible for producing 278 aircraft to Ministry of Supply contract and as sub-contractors to the Hawker company.

The Hawker P.1067 Hunter made its first flight on 20 July, 1951, powered by a Rolls-Royce Avon turbojet. It had swept wings with a moderate loading and fully-powered controls. The fixed armament of production aircraft consisted of four 30-mm Aden guns mounted in a removable pack situated underneath the nose. The first Hunters joined the RAF in the summer of 1954, and from then on they gradually took over duty from the Meteor 8s of RAF Fighter Command. In the course of its career, the Hunter was adapted for other rôles, including ground attack and fighter-reconnaissance duties; a two-seat

Hawker Hunter production started at Coventry in March 1954.

version was built for training purposes, and this was adapted also for deck-landing training by the Royal Navy. All versions of the Hunter had Avons, except the F Mk.2 and F Mk.5, which had Armstrong Siddeley Sapphires. On 7 September, 1953, the prototype Hunter, WB188, fitted with a special Avon engine with re-heat, established a new world's speed record of 727·6 mph.

Armstrong Whitworth received their first order from the Ministry of Supply in March 1951, and the first batch to be completed consisted of F Mk.2s with Sapphire engines. Production of the Mk.2 was limited to 45 aircraft; one of these, WN905, crashed during flight trials and, as a result, the original contract requirement for 150 aircraft was reduced to 149. The balance of the contract, from the 46th aircraft onwards, consisted of Mk.5 aircraft, a version of the Mk.2 with more internal fuel and under-wing pylons for external tanks and stores. The second contract received by Armstrong Whitworth from the Ministry of Supply was for one hundred F Mk.6 aircraft, a developed version with a more powerful type of Avon engine. The first Mk.6 built by Armstrong Whitworth flew from Baginton on 25 May, 1955; when this order had been completed the Hawker company ordered a further twenty-eight Mk.6 aircraft from Armstrong Whitworth on a sub-contract basis.

The Service numbers of the Hunters built by Armstrong Whitworth were as follows:

Hunter F Mk.2: WN888–921, 943–953.

F Mk.5: WN954–992; WP101–150, 179–194.

F Mk.6: XE581–583, 609–614; XF373–389, 414–463, 495–527; XG150–168.

Span:	33 ft 8 in (10·26 m)
Length:	45 ft 11 in (13·99 m)
Height:	13 ft 2 in (4·01 m)
Wing area:	340 sq ft (31·59 sq m)
All-up weight (F Mk.6):	17,750 lb (8,050 kg)

Gloster Javelin

The last of the aircraft to be built under sub-contract by Armstrong Whitworth was the Gloster Javelin twin-engined all-weather fighter, of which 133 were built in Coventry during the two years from 1956 into 1958.

The Gloster Javelin F(AW)Mk.1 was the first delta-wing aircraft to go into service with the RAF and was the first British aircraft to be designed from the start as an all-weather fighter. The prototype Javelin made its first flight on 26 November, 1951, and the first production aircraft flew in July 1954. The development of the Javelin, with its novel delta wing, encountered a number of difficulties, not least of which was the occurrence of a super stall which led to a fatal accident during the maker's tests in June 1953. The Javelin first entered service with the RAF in December 1955.

The trans-sonic Javelin was powered by two Armstrong Siddeley Sapphire turbojets mounted side by side; the crew of two were seated in tandem. In all, nine versions were produced, including a dual-control trainer. Early marks were armed with four 30-mm Aden guns, but later versions had two Aden guns and four de Havilland Firestreak air-to-air missiles. From the Mk.4 onwards, all models had an all-moving tailplane.

The first Javelins built by Armstrong Whitworth, F(AW)Mk.4s, came off the assembly line in 1956, and 32 of these aircraft were completed when the production was switched to the F(AW)Mk.5, which had a redesigned wing with increased internal fuel capacity. Coventry-built Mk.5s numbered 44, and these were followed by the F(AW)Mk.7, of which 57 were produced. The Mk.7 was the first of the series to carry the Firestreak

The Gloster Javelin was the last aircraft to be built under sub-contract by Armstrong Whitworth. Production ceased in 1958.

weapon; it also had more powerful Sapphires. Most of the Mk.7 aircraft built by Armstrong Whitworth were modified to F(AW)Mk.9 standard, many of them before delivery. The modifications entailed the fitting of re-heat Sapphire engines and making provision for in-flight refuelling.

The Javelins produced by Armstrong Whitworth carried the following serial numbers:

Javelin F(AW)Mk.4: XA720–737, 749–762.

F(AW)Mk.5: XA662–667, 688–719; XH687–692.

F(AW)Mk.7: XH785–795, 833–849, 871–899.

Span:	52 ft 0 in (15·86 m)
Length:	56 ft 3 in (17·15 m)
Height:	16 ft 0 in (4·88 m)

APPENDIX C

Production Details of Armstrong Whitworth Aircraft

The production information set out below includes aeroplanes designed by Sir W. G. Armstrong Whitworth Aircraft Ltd, of Whitley Abbey, Coventry, and its parent companies, Sir W. G. Armstrong Whitworth and Co Ltd, of Newcastle upon Tyne and Gosforth, and The Siddeley Deasy Motor Car Co of Parkside, Coventry. Accûrate totals for many of the types are not easily arrived at because of the destruction of records and also because of the somewhat haphazard method of allocating type and constructor's numbers, coupled with the maker's habit of occasionally allotting new constructor's numbers to aircraft being modified.

Sir W. G. Armstrong Whitworth & Co. Ltd

F.K.1 One aircraft only, built at Gosforth as a private venture; no serial number allotted.

F.K.3 In the official records and statistics of the time, the F.K.3 and the F.K.8 were referred to indiscriminately as 'A.W. biplanes'; it is, therefore now difficult to arrive at accurate production figures for either type. The following list of available serial numbers, totalling 500 aircraft, probably represents a near approximation of the number of F.K.3s built.

Built by Armstrong Whitworth at Gosforth: Contract No.94/A/103, placed about 9/15: 5328–5334, 5504–5553, 5614, 6186–6227; 100 aircraft. Contract No.87/A/496, placed about 11/16: A8091–8140; 50 aircraft.

Built by Hewlett & Blondeau Ltd, Luton: Contract No.87/A/475, dated 19/6/16: A1461–1510; 50 aircraft. Contract No.AS/130731/1, dated 3/8/17: B9501–9800; 300 aircraft.

Individual Aircraft: 5332 tested at Upavon, 8/15; 5519 with a 105 hp RAF 1b engine, tested at Upavon 6/16; 5528, with a 120 hp Beardmore engine tested at Upavon in the spring of 1916; 5552, a standard production aircraft with a 90 hp RAF 1a engine, tested at Upavon, 5/16; A9972 erected from spares by No.58 Squadron at Cramlington; B9518 became G-EABZ, C of A 14/5/19, cancelled 5/20, operated by E. D. C. Herne at Porthcawl; B9603 became G-EALK, C of A 16/9/19, cancelled 9/9/20, owned by L. G. Lowe; B9612 became G-EAEU, C of A 10/7/19, crashed 12/19, operated by Kingsbury Aviation Co Ltd; B9629 became G-EABY, C of A 14/5/19, cancelled 5/20, operated by E. D. C. Herne at Porthcawl.

F.K.8 As with the F.K.3, the total number of F.K.8 biplanes built is uncertain because of a lack of differentiation between types in official documents. The following list of available serial numbers, totalling 1,652 aircraft (including the prototype), probably represents a near approximation of the numbers of F.K.8s built.
Built by Armstrong Whitworth at Gosforth: Prototype aircraft with 160 hp Beardmore engine, A411 (c/n 630). Contract No.87/A/508, dated 1/8/16: A2683–2732, 9980–9999; B201–330, 5751–5801; 251 aircraft. Contract No.AS13163, dated 24/4/17 and 2/11/17: B3301–3400, B5802–5850; C8401–8651; 400 aircraft. Contract No.35a/1088/C921, dated 27/5/18: F4221–4270; 50 aircraft.
Built by Angus Sanderson & Co, Newcastle upon Tyne: Contract No.AS3390, dated 1917: C3507–3706; 200 aircraft. Contract No.AS17566, dated 19/12/17: D5001–5200; 200 aircraft. Contract No.35a/1089/C922, dated 27/5/18: F3442–3491; 50 aircraft. Contract No.35a/1710/C1819, dated 5/7/18: F7347–7546; 200 aircraft. Contract No. 35a/2255/C2569, dated 19/8/18: H4425–4724; 300 aircraft of which the first 188 are known to have been delivered.
Individual Aircraft: A2696 fitted with 150 hp Lorraine-Dietrich engine; B201 fitted with Bristol Fighter undercarriage and tested by No.35 Squadron in France, 6/17; B214 and B215 fitted with 150 hp RAF 4a engine; B233 fitted with experimental exhaust system by No.10 Squadron in France, 7/17; B4120, 4145, 4165, 4166, 4167, 4177, 4198, 4200 rebuilt by No.2 (Northern) Aircraft Repair Depot; D5150 became G-EAET, C of A 15/6/19, cancelled 8/19 by A.I.D., operated by the London and Provincial Aviation Co; F7348 became G-EATO, C of A 15/7/20, scrapped in 1922, owner R. E. Duke; F7484 became G-EALW, C of A 13/7/20, crashed 9/20, operated by Air Ltd; H4473 became G-EAIC, C of A 7/8/19, cancelled 6/20, owned by T. Neville Stack; H4561 became G-AUCF, operated by Queensland and Northern Territory Aerial Services Ltd, crashed 25/2/23; F4231 became G-AUDE, operated by Queensland and Northern Territory Aerial Services Ltd, damaged in forced landing 13/9/23; H4573 became G-EAVT, C of A 3/11/20, owned by Handley Page Ltd, believed exported; H4585 became G-EAVQ, C of A 20/10/20, owned by Handley Page Ltd, believed exported; H4600 became G-EATP, no record of C of A, owned by Major Tryggve Gran; H4612 became G-EAJS, C of A 10/9/19, sold to Sweden 11/19.
The Triplanes Considerable doubt exists about the correct designation of the two types of Armstrong Whitworth triplanes, but all the evidence is against the F.K.12 appellation previously accepted. The most likely numbering would appear to be F.K.5 and F.K.6.
F.K.5 One aircraft only; built as a private venture; no known serial number.
F.K.6 Contract No.87/A/328, dated 23/3/16 called for four aircraft numbered 7838–7841; only 7838 was built.
The Quadruplanes The first Armstrong Whitworth quadruplane was probably designated F.K.9, although the use of this number lacks positive confirmation; certainly, the much revised production version was called the F.K.10.
Built by Armstrong Whitworth at Gosforth: Contract No.87/A/1252, dated 25/11/16: A5212–5213, probably the prototypes of the F.K.9 and F.K.10 respectively. Two aircraft. Contract No.CP100565/16, date uncertain, N514; one F.K.10 aircraft.
Built by Angus Sanderson & Co, Newcastle upon Tyne: Contract No.87/A/1457 dated 30/12/16, amended to 3/8/17: B3996–4000: five F.K.10 aircraft. Another 50 aircraft, A8950–8999, were ordered under this contract, but the order was later cancelled and the numbers re-allocated.
Built by the Phoenix Dynamo Manufacturing Co Ltd: Contract No.CP135178/16, date uncertain; N511–512 (N513 was cancelled). Two F.K.10 aircraft.
Individual Aircraft: N511 and N514 were at Manston at times during the first half of

1917. Both were written off there in August 1917 and were listed by the Admiralty in March 1918 as no longer in commission.
F.M.4 Armadillo Built at Gosforth; official licence No.18 dated 7/1/18 for two aircraft, X19 and X20. Only X19 completed.
Ara Built at Gosforth; contract No.35a/1221/C1134 dated 5/6/18: F4971–4973. F4973 was abandoned before completion. Two aircraft.

The Siddeley Deasy Motor Car Co Ltd

R.T.1 Built at Parkside; contract No.AS7903 for six aircraft: B6625–6630; only three built, B6625–6627, all taken from the existing R.E.8 production.
Individual Aircraft: B6625 and B6627 fitted with 200 hp Hispano-Suiza engines; B6626 fitted with 150 hp RAF 4a engine.
S.R.2 Siskin Built at Parkside; initial order for six aircraft, C4541–4546; only three completed, C4541–4543. Later, C4541 was fitted with a Jaguar engine.
Sinaia Built at Parkside; Original order believed to be for four aircraft but serial numbers allotted for two, J6858–6859, of which only J6858 was completed. Erected and test flown at Farnborough.

Sir W. G. Armstrong Whitworth Aircraft Ltd

Awana Contract No.306069/20: J6897–6898 (c/ns 13–14). J6897 was initially incorrectly numbered J6860.
Wolf Contract No.195547/21: J6921–6923 (c/ns 15–17). Civil aircraft: G-EBHI (c/n 18), first flight 16/2/23, C of A 4/9/23, cancelled 1931; G-EBHJ (c/n 28), first flight 16/8/23, C of A 10/12/23, cancelled 1931; G-AAIY (c/n 428), C of A 16/8/29, cancelled 1931.
Siskin II Civil aircraft; G-EBEU (c/n 10), C of A 11/7/23, flown both as two-seater and single-seater; G-EBHY (c/n 11), C of A 25/6/24, single-seater.
Siskin III Prototype J6583 (c/n 12); contract No.342619/22: J6981–6983 (c/ns 19–21); contract No.369339/22: J6998–7003 (c/ns 22–27); contract No. 439840/23: J7145–7181 (c/ns 29–65); contract No.530519: J7549–7554 (c/ns 133–138); contract No.576184/25: J7758–7764 (c/ns 147–153), J7820–7822 (c/ns 157–159). Civil aircraft: G-EBJQ (c/n 66), no record of C of A; G-EBJS (c/n 67), no record of C of A. (These two aircraft may have been J6981 and J6982 temporarily registered as civil aircraft.)
Individual Aircraft J7001 converted to Siskin IIIA; J7148 fitted with experimental enclosed cowling; J7161 fitted with supercharged Jaguar IV engine; J7758–7759 transferred to RCAF, J7758 crashed 6/27.
Siskin IIIDC Two-Seater Contract No.823022/28: J9190–9236 (c/ns 299–345); for the RCAF: 307–308 (c/ns 398–399); for Esthonia: c/ns 604–605. Civil aircraft: G-ABHT (c/n 651), C of A 16/5/31, written off 8/6/31; G-ABHU (c/n 652), C of A 30/5/31.
Individual Aircraft The following RAF Siskin IIIs were subsequently converted by Armstrong Whitworth to Siskin IIIDCs: J7000, 7002–7003, 7146, 7149–7150, 7152–7154, 7156–7158, 7160, 7162, 7164–7165, 7167, 7170, 7173, 7180–7181, 7549, 7552, 7554, 7760–7764, 7820–7821. Converted to Siskin IIIAs: J7176–7179.
Siskin IIIA Prototype (c/n 160), no serial number recorded; probably converted Siskin III J7001. Contract No. 625304/25: J8048–8060 (c/ns 161–173); Contract No.709171/26: J8381–8404 (c/ns 174–197); contract No. 751234/27: J8623–8631

A Siskin IIIA of No.41 Squadron, RAF, competing in the race for the Sassoon Cup, May 1927. (*Flight International 4621*)

(c/ns 198–206), J8632–8633 (c/ns 281–282); J8634–8659 (c/ns 209–234); J8660–8661 (c/ns 283–284); J8662–8672 (c/ns 237–247); contract No.783693/27 for RCAF: c/ns 207–208, 235–236, 395–397, 699; of these, 207 became RCAF 21 then 303, 208 became RCAF 20 then 302, 235 became RCAF 22 then 304, 397 became RCAF 59 then 305, and 699 became RCAF 210 then 309; no traceable RCAF numbers for c/ns 236, 395–396; RCAF 303 temporarily carried the civil registration G-CYZE.

Built by other manufacturers Blackburn Aircraft: contract No.772529/27: J8864–8905; Bristol Aeroplane Co: contract number unknown: J9897–9911, 8822–8863, 9304–9330; Gloster Aircraft Co: J8933–8974, 9331–9352, 9912–9921; Vickers (Aviation) Ltd.: contract No.855124/28: J9353–9379; contract No.937776/29: J9872–9896.

The RCAF Siskin No.20, taken in August 1929. (*Canadian Forces No.HC3069*)

Summary of **Siskin III** *Variants:*

Siskin III: RAF 64	64
Siskin IIIDC: RAF 47. RCAF 2 AST 2, Esthonia 2	53
Siskin IIIA: A.W. built: RAF 88, RCAF 8	96
Blackburn built: RAF	42
Bristol built	84
Gloster built	74
Vickers built	52
Total	465

Individual Aircraft J8390 used for catapult trials aboard HMS *Repulse* in the summer of 1929; J8627 converted to Siskin IIIB standard; J8428 employed for tests at Farnborough from 1927. This aircraft is something of a mystery because it does not fit into any known production batch; a possibility is that it was the prototype Siskin IIIA which was initially flown without a serial number.

Siskin IV One aircraft only, G-EBLL (c/n 143), no record of C of A, flew in 1925 King's Cup air race.

Siskin V Two civil aircraft only, G-EBLN (c/n 97), C of A 30/7/25, and G-EBLQ (c/n 102), C of A 30/7/25. Constructor's numbers 68 to 132 were allotted to a Roumanian contract, later cancelled. Aircraft confirmed built with Roumanian serials were: Nos. 1, 2, 4, 10, 13, 14, 15, 28, 29 and 33; all Roumanian aircraft were scrapped except two civil aircraft mentioned above and one aircraft, c/n 73, which was tested to destruction at Farnborough.

Ape Contract No.437548/23: J7753–7755 (c/ns 144–146).

Argosy Air Ministry contract No.497579/24: G-EBLF *City of Glasgow* (c/n 154), C of A 9/26, withdrawn 1934; G-EBLO *City of Birmingham* (c/n 155), C of A 30/6/26, written off in Africa 16/6/31; G-EBOZ *City of Wellington* later *City of Arundel* (c/n 156), C of A 23/4/27, withdrawn 10/34. Ordered by Imperial Airways: G-AACH *City of Edinburgh* (c/n 362), C of A 19/5/29, crashed at Croydon, 22/4/31; G-AACI *City of Liverpool* (c/n 363), C of A 3/6/29, crashed in Belgium 28/3/33; G-AACJ *City of Manchester* (c/n 364), C of A 6/7/29, sold to British Airways 1936; G-AAEJ *City of Coventry* (c/n 400), C of A 21/8/29, withdrawn 1935.

Atlas Prototype aircraft G-EBLK (c/n 139), first flight 10/5/25 not confirmed, to RAF as J8675 under contract No.735668/26 with new wings and the new constructor's number 278.

RAF Army Co-operation Aircraft Contract No.750052/27: J8777–8801, 9039–9050 (c/ns 248–258, 297–298, 261–272, 285–296); contract No.837619/28: J9516–9564 (c/ns 401–425, 429–452); contract No.933799/29: J9951–9999, K1000–1037, 1113–1114 (c/ns 461–509, 510, 537–575); contract No.35536/30: K1507–1602 (c/ns 606–615, 641–650, 656–695, 700–719, 723–738).

RAF Trainer Aircraft Contract No.837620/28: J9435–9477 (c/ns 347–359, 365–394); contract No.972069/29: K1172–1197 (c/ns 511–536); contract No.34471/30: K1454–1506 (c/ns 576–603, 616–640); contract No.103834/31: K2514–2566 (c/ns 745–764, 774–783, 787–796, 805–817).

RCAF Army Co-operation Aircraft Ordered under Air Ministry contract No.783694/27 then allotted to RCAF: c/ns 259–260, first registered as G-CYZA and G-CYZB, then RCAF serials 17 and 16, then 402 and 401; c/ns 279–280, RCAF serials 18 and 19,

The RCAF Atlas No. 409 (*Canadian Forces No.RE13718*)

then 403 and 404; ordered under Canadian contract: c/n 427, RCAF serial 112, then 405; transferred to RCAF from RAF during 1934: J9564, 9951, K1529, 1531, 1540, 1545, 1550, 1556, 1561 and 1566 became RCAF 406–415.

RCAF Trainer Aircraft Constructor's No. 426, RCAF serial 111.
Other Atlas Exports To Greece; c/ns 360–361, crated for transport; to Japan: constructor's No. 453.
Civil Atlas Trainers G-ABDY (c/n believed to be 140), C of A 25/9/30; G-ABHV–G-ABHX (c/ns 653–655) and G-ABOO (c/n 739) for Air Service Training Ltd.
Atlas II G-ACAI (c/n 830), converted from Atlas I G-EBYF (c/n 346); G-ABIV (c/n 696), C of A 12/10/31, used for Tiger engine development.
G-ABKE (c/n 697), used for Panther engine 100-hour test. For China: constructor's Nos. 768–773, temporarily registered G-ABRU–G-ABRZ; constructor's Nos. 799–804 and 821–822, delivery of all fourteen aircraft not confirmed.
Individual Atlas Aircraft J8799 tested as a seaplane; J9951 sold to Egypt in 1939; J9998 flown as a seaplane and used as a practice aircraft by the 1931 Schneider Trophy team; No.402 remained on strength in the RCAF until 5/42.
Summary of Atlas Production

Prototype aircraft						1
RAF	Army Co-operation:	271	Trainers	175	Total	446
RCAF	„ „	15	„	1	„	16*
Greece	„ „	2	„	—	„	2
Japan	„ „	1	„	—	„	1
Civil	„ „	—	„	5	„	5
Atlas IIs for China						14
Atlas IIs civil						3
					Total	478

Ajax Prototype aircraft G-EBLM (c/n 141), C of A 23/1/26, to RAF as J9128; G-EBNI (c/n 142), C of A 8/2/26, to RAF as J9129; contract No.743656/27: J8802–8803 (c/ns 273–274), 'day bombers'.

* Ten aircraft out of this total were transferred from the RAF.

With the narrow-chord wings, the Starling Mk.II was classed as an interceptor fighter. (*Courtesy P. Jarrett*)

A.W.14 Starling

Starling I One aircraft, J8027 (c/n 277), built under contract No.576942/25, appeared at 1929 Olympia Aero Show as G-AAHC.

Starling II J8028 (c/n 455); A 1 (c/n 459); A 2 (c/n 460). Number built uncertain, see page 175.

A.W.XV Atalanta Built for Imperial Airways.

G-ABPI (c/n 740), first flight 6/6/32, C of A 15/8/32, *Atalanta*, later *Arethusa*, to Indian Trans-Continental Airways Ltd 8/33, as VT-AEF, to Indian Air Force as DG453 until struck off strength 6/44.

G-ABTG (c/n 785), C of A 12/9/32, *Amalthea*, crashed at Kisumu 27/7/38.

G-ABTH (c/n 741), C of A 27/9/32, *Andromeda*, dismantled in Egypt after damage to wing in 6/39.

G-ABTI (c/n 742), C of A 2/1/33, *Atalanta*, to Indian Air Force as DG451, destroyed by fire in a landing accident 22/8/42.

G-ABTJ (c/n 743), C of A 18/1/33, *Artemis*, to Indian Air Force as DG452 until struck off strength 6/44.

G-ABTK (c/n 744), C of A 18/3/33, *Athena*, destroyed by fire on the ground at New Delhi 29/9/36.

G-ABTL (c/n 784), C of A 4/4/33, *Astraea*, to Indian Air Force as DG450, withdrawn 9/42, cannibalized and struck off strength 11/43.

G-ABTM (c/n 786), C of A 20/4/33, *Aurora*, to Indian Trans-Continental Airways Ltd as VT-AEG, to Indian Air Force as DG454, force-landed in a swamp near Calcutta 4/42, written off and burnt on site.

The A.W.XV *Andromeda* at Moshi, with Kilimanjaro in the background.

A.W.XVI Prototype S1591 (c/n 698), designed to specification N.21/26; second prototype A 2, then G-ABKF (c/n 722), C of A 31/12/31; G-ACCD (c/n 828), C of A 28/6/33; four aircraft delivered to China: G-ABRH, G-ABRI, G-ABRJ (c/ns 765–767), C's of A 19/12/31, and G-ABZL (c/n 823), C of A 16/1/33.
Individual Aircraft G-ABKF on tour with Sir Alan Cobham in Africa 1932, subsequently used as test-bed for experimental Hyena engine; G-ACCD converted to A.W.35 Scimitar.
A.W.17 Aries One aircraft only, contract No.725892/26, J9037 (c/n 454), first flight 3/5/30 not confirmed.
A.W.19 One aircraft only built as a private venture to specification G.4/31, c/n 923, A 3 then K5606, used for Tiger engine development.
A.W.23 One aircraft only, c/n 1251, K3585, designed to specification C.26/31, first flight 4/6/35. Subsequently to Flight Refuelling Ltd as G-AFRX, C of A 30/8/39, destroyed by enemy action at Ford aerodrome 18/8/40.

Egeria coming in to land at Khartoum; the runway was constructed during the war. (*Imperial War Museum CH14755*)

A.W.27 Ensign Built for Imperial Airways and BOAC.
G-ADSR *Ensign* (c/n 1156), first flight 24/1/38, C of A 29/6/38, delivered 5/10/38, withdrawn at Cairo 9/44 and dismantled 1/45.
G-ADSS *Egeria* (c/n 1157), first flight 26/5/38, C of A 18/11/38, delivered 17/11/38, broken up at Hamble 13/4/47. Intended transfer to Indian Trans-Continental Airways, as VT-AJE *Ellora*, prevented by outbreak of war.
G-ADST *Elsinore* (c/n 1158), first flight 7/11/38, C of A 14/11/38, delivered 11/11/38, broken up at Hamble 28/3/47.
G-ADSU *Euterpe* (c/n 1159), first flight 12/11/38, C of A 2/12/38, delivered 24/11/38, withdrawn at Cairo 2/45 and dismantled 1946. Intended transfer to Indian Trans-Continental Airways, as VT-AJF *Everest*, prevented by outbreak of war.
G-ADSV *Explorer* (c/n 1160), first flight 24/11/38, C of A 2/12/38, delivered 24/11/38, broken up at Hamble 23/3/47.
G-ADSW *Eddystone* (c/n 1161), first flight 11/12/38, C of A 8/5/39, delivered 15/6/39, broken up at Hamble 21/4/47.
G-ADSX *Ettrick* (c/n 1162), first flight 27/2/39, C of A 12/6/39, delivered 7/6/39, damaged in an air raid and abandoned at Le Bourget 1/6/40, subsequently repaired and used by the Germans with Daimler-Benz engines.

G-ADSY *Empyrean* (c/n 1163), first flight 19/6/39, C of A 23/6/39, delivered 21/6/39, broken up at Hamble 26/3/47.

G-ADSZ *Elysian* (c/n 1164), first flight 25/6/39, C of A 30/6/39, delivered 29/6/39, destroyed by enemy action on Merville aerodrome 23/5/40.

G-ADTA *Euryalus* (c/n 1165), first flight 19/8/39, C of A 23/8/39, delivered 19/8/39, damaged by enemy action 23/5/40 and cannibalized in 1941. Intended transfer to Indian Trans-Continental Airways, as VT-AJG *Ernakulam*, prevented by outbreak of war.

G-ADTB *Echo* (c/n 1166), first flight 30/8/39, C of A 19/9/39, delivered 31/8/39, broken up at Hamble 20/3/47.

G-ADTC *Endymion* (c/n 1167), first flight 5/10/39, C of A 9/10/39, delivered 7/10/39, destroyed in an air raid on Whitchurch aerodrome 24/11/40. Intended transfer to Indian Trans-Continental Airways, as VT-AJH *Etah*, prevented by outbreak of war.

G-AFZU *Everest* (previously allocated G-ADTE) (c/n 1821), first flight 20/6/41, C of A 26/6/41, delivered 24/6/41, broken up at Hamble 16/4/47.

G-AFZV *Enterprise* (previously allocated G-ADTD), (c/n 1822), first flight 28/10/41, C of A 1/11/41, delivered 30/10/41, force-landed in desert near Dakar, repaired by French and registered F-AFZV and, later, F-BAHD. Eventually taken over by Germany.

A.W.29 One aircraft only, c/n 1168, K4299, first flight 6/12/36, designed to specification P.27/32.

A.W.35 Scimitar Prototype G-ACCD (c/n 828), first flight 25/6/34, converted from A.W.XVI and retaining same registration marks, c/n and C of A; G-ADBL (c/n 460*); four aircraft for Norway, c/ns 985–988.

Individual Aircraft G-ADBL preserved at Whitley until about 1958.

A.W.38 Whitley

Whitley Mk.I Two prototypes K4586–4587 built to specification B.3/34, c/ns 1169–1170, first flight, K4586, 17/3/36. First production order to contract No.421118/35: K7183–7216 (c/ns 1171–1204).

Whitley Mk.II Contract No.421118/35: K7217–7262 (c/ns 1205–1250).

Whitley Mk.III Contract No.522438/36: K8936–9015 (c/ns 1389–1468).

Whitley Mk.IV Contract No.522438/36: K9016–9048 (c/ns 1469–1501).

Whitley Mk.IVA Contract No.522438/36: K9049–9055 (c/ns 1502–1508).

Whitley Mk.V Contract No.75147/38: N1345–1394, 1405–1444, 1459–1508, 1521–1528; P4930–4974, 4980–5029, 5040–5065, 5070–5112. Contract No.38599/39: T4130–4179, 4200–4239, 4260–4299, 4320–4339. Contract No.106962/40: Z6461–6510, 6552–6586, 6624–6673, 6720–6764, 6793–6842, 6862–6881, 6931–6959, 6970–6980, 9119, 9125–9134, 9140–9168, 9188–9189, 9200–9232, 9274–9323, 9361–9363, 9384–9390, 9419–9443, 9461–9490, 9510–9515; AD665–714; BD189–238, 252–296, 346–395, 411–422, 435–445, 493–512, 530–560, 626–639, 659–674; EB283–313, 337–367, 384–391, 402–410; LA763–793, 818–856, 868–899, 914–951; c/ns 1509–1820, 1823–2976.

Whitley Mk.VII Contract No.106962/40: Z6960–6969, 9120–9124, 9135–9139, 9190–9199, 9364–9383, 9516–9529; BD423–434, 561–574, 620–625, 675–693; EB282, 327–336, 392–401; LA794–798, 813–817; c/ns 2977–3122.

Whitley Mk.V Freighter Converted from Mk.V bombers for BOAC. G-AGCF–G-AGCH ex BD360–362, C's of A 5/5/42; G-AGCI–G-AGCK ex BD382–384, C's of A G-AGCI 8/6/42, G-AGCJ and G-AGCK 21/5/42; G-AGDU ex Z9208, C of A 18/7/42; G-AGDV ex Z9216, no C of A; G-AGDW ex Z6660, no C of A; G-AGDX–

* This constructor's number is suspect; it was first given to an A.W.XIV said to have been converted to an A.W.XVI.

G-AGDZ ex BD385–387, C's of A 22/5/42; G-AGEA ex BD388, C of A 26/5/42; G-AGEB–G-AGEC ex BD389–390, C's of A 8/5/42.
Individual Whitley Aircraft Mk.II K7243 used for development of Deerhound engine from 1/39 until crashed 3/40; Mk.III K8966 stationed at Baginton for Tiger engine development; Mk.Vs N1348, N1386, Z9390, BD530 and LA893 were used by RAE for glider towing experiments; G-AGCI crashed at Gibraltar 29/9/42, all other BOAC Whitleys were handed back to the RAF during 1942–1943; Mk.V LA951 used by the makers as a general test vehicle and as a tug for the A.W.52G glider. This was the last Whitley to remain airworthy; it was withdrawn and broken up in March 1949.
Summary of Whitley Production Prototypes two; Mk.I, 34; Mk.II, 46; Mk.III, 80; Mk.IV, 33; Mk.IVA, seven; Mk.V, 1,466; Mk.VII, 146. Total 1,814.

The prototype Albemarle S.T.Mk.I.

A.W.41 Albemarle Two prototypes P1360–1361 built at Hamble to specification B.18/38. Production aircraft assembled by A. W. Hawksley Ltd. Mk.I, P1362–1401; V1598–1599. Mk.IV, V1760; S.T. (Special Transport) Mk.I Series I, P1479, 1500–1510; S.T.Mk.I Series II, P1554–1569, 1590–1609, 1630–1659; S.T.Mk.II, V1601–1647, 1694–1723, 1738–1759; S.T.Mk.V, V1761–1787, 1809–1828, 1841–1842; S.T.Mk.VI, V1843–1885, 1917–1941, 1962–2011, 2025–2039; G.T. (Glider Tug) Mk.I, P1402–1409; 1430–1478, P1511–1529; 1550–1553; G.T.Mk.II, V1600; G.T.Mk.VI Series I, V2040–2054, 2067–2068; G.T.Mk.VI Series II, LV482–501, 532–577, 590–623.
Summary of Albemarle Production Prototypes two; Mk.I, 42; Mk.IV, one; S.T.Mk.I Series I, 12; S.T.Mk.I Series II, 66; S.T.Mk.II, 99; S.T.Mk.V, 49; S.T.Mk.VI, 133; G.T.Mk.I, 80; G.T.Mk.II, one; G.T.Mk.VI Series I, 17; G.T.Mk.VI Series II, 100. Total 602.
A.W.52G One aircraft only, RG324, tailless glider linear scale model for A.W.52, first flight 2/3/45 towed by Whitley Mk.V LA951.
A.W.52 Two experimental tailless jet aircraft built to specification E.9/44. TS363, first flight 13/11/47, crashed 30/5/49; TS368, first flight 1/9/48, scrapped at Farnborough 6/54.

The Apollo coming in to land with one engine shut down. Note the large Fowler flaps. (*Royal Aircraft Establishment 84572*)

A.W.55 Apollo Two aircraft only. VX220/G-AIYN (c/n 3137), first flight 10/4/49, to the Aeroplane and Armament Experimental Establishment, Boscombe Down aerodrome 24/9/52, to Armstrong Whitworth for structural tests 12/54; VX224/G-AMCH (c/n 3138), first flight 12/12/52, to Empire Test Pilots' School, Farnborough aerodrome 3/54, to Royal Aircraft Establishment 12/54 for structural tests, civil marks not used.

A.W.650 Argosy

Series 100 No prototype, first production batch, 10 aircraft.

G-AOZZ (c/n 6651), first flight 8/1/59, to BEA 21/12/61, returned to makers 28/6/65, to Universal Airlines 12/68 as N896U, to Sagittair Ltd 10/71 as G-AOZZ.

G-APRL (c/n 6652), first flight 16/3/59, to Riddle Airlines Inc 24/8/61 as N6507R, to Capitol Airlines Inc 10/62, to Zantop Air Transport 30/6/64 as N602Z, to Universal Airlines Inc 1/67 as N890U. New wing spars fitted at Bitteswell 8/69.

G-APRM (c/n 6653), first flight 24/4/59, to BEA 29/11/61, returned to makers 17/7/66, to Rolls-Royce Ltd 6/69.

G-APRN (c/n 6654), first flight 13/5/59, to BEA 11/61, returned to makers 3/5/65, to Universal Airlines 1/69 as N897U, to Sagittair 9/71.

The Argosy G-APVH on its way to the Farnborough Air Show in 1959.

G-APVH (c/n 6655), first flight 20/7/59, to Riddle Airlines 22/6/61 as N6504R, to Capitol Airlines 1/7/62, to Zantop Air Transport 1/7/64, to Universal Airlines 1/67 as N891U.
G-APWW (c/n 6656), first flight 21/9/59, to Riddle Airlines 24/1/61 as N6503R, to Capitol Airlines 1/7/62, to Zantop Air Transport 1/7/65, to Universal Airlines 1/67 as N892U. New wing spars fitted at Bitteswell 9/69, to Sagittair 1/72.
N6501R (c/n 6659), first flight 19/11/60, to Riddle Airlines 11/12/60, to Capitol Airlines 1/6/62, to Zantop Air Transport 20/3/63 as N601Z, crashed 14/10/65.
N6502R (c/n 6660), first flight 16/12/60, to Riddle Airlines 5/1/61, to Capitol Airlines 1/7/62, to Zantop Air Transport 1/9/65, to Universal Airlines 1/67 as N895U. New wing spars fitted at Bitteswell 10/69.
N6505R (c/n 6657), first flight 20/2/61, to Riddle Airlines 11/6/61, to Capitol Airlines 1/7/62, to Zantop Air Transport 3/63 as N600Z, to Universal Airlines 1/67 as N893U, to Sagittair as G-AZHN.
N6506R (c/n 6658), first flight 26/6/61, to Riddle Airlines 17/7/61, to Capitol Airlines 1/7/62, to Zantop Air Transport 1/9/65, to Universal Airlines 1/67 as N894U.
Series 200
G-ASKZ (c/n 6799), first flight 11/3/64, cannibalized for spares 9/67.
Series 222 Modified to B.E.A. requirements.
G-ASXL (c/n 6800), first flight 17/12/64, to BEA 28/1/65, crashed in Italy 4/7/65.
G-ASXM (c/n 6801), first flight 10/2/65, to BEA 2/3/65, to Transair Ltd 6/70 as CF-TAG, to Aer Turas Independent Airlines as EI-AVJ *The Consortium*.
G-ASXN (c/n 6802), first flight 10/3/65, to BEA 26/3/65, to Transair 8/70 as CF-TAJ.
G-ASXO (c/n 6803), first flight 12/4/65, to BEA 28/4/65, to Transair 3/70 as CF-TAX.
G-ASXP (c/n 6804), first flight 27/5/65, to BEA 16/6/65, crashed at Stansted 4/12/67.
G-ATTC (c/n 6805), first flight 30/10/66 to BEA 21/11/66, to Transair 4/70 as CF-TAZ.
A.W.660 Argosy C Mk.1 Ordered 1/59, first production batch XN814–821, 847–858 (c/ns 6743–6762); second batch XP408–413, 437–450, (c/ns 6763–6782); third batch XR105–109, 133–143 (c/ns 6783–6798).
Individual Aircraft XN814 first flight 4/3/61; XP413 ditched in shallow water at Khormaksar, Aden, 23/3/64 salvaged and repaired: XP441 crashed at Benson 10/70; XR143 last C Mk.1 delivered to the RAF 1/4/64.

Index

(Page numbers for illustrations are in italics)